IN THE VISION C

Experience in Continuation of
IN QUEST OF GOD

by Swami Ramdas

About this design: In the center of a radiant circle, in Sanskrit, is the syllable, "**OM**,"
said to be the seed word from which the manifest Universe is born.
The words on the banner underneath, also in Sanskrit, are the Ram Mantra:
OM SRI RAM JAI RAM JAI JAI RAM

Ruhaniat Press ❖ Sufi Ruhaniat International
San Francisco California USA ❖ www.RuhaniatPress.com

RUHANIAT
PRESS

Ruhaniat Press, an imprint from Sufi Ruhaniat International, brings forward important publications that add to the wealth of spiritual wisdom inspiring seekers toward inner and outer love, harmony, and beauty. Contact us at ruhaniatpress@ruhaniat.org or 1-800-332-4494.

Ruhaniat Press
Sufi Ruhaniat International
410 Precita Avenue
San Francisco CA 94110
www.RuhaniatPress.com

Content design by Farrunnissa Rosa and Wahhab
Cover design by Professor Nuria Sabato and Farrunnissa Rosa

Anandashram
PO Anandashrama, Kanhangad, Kerala, India 671531
Phone: 0467-2203036
Email: anandashram@gmail.com
www.anandashram.org

ISBN 978-0-9973999-3-6
eISBN 978-0-9973999-4-3
Library of Congress Control Number: 2017942209

First Edition, San Francisco California USA

RUHANIAT
PRESS

BELOVED PAPA SWAMI RAMDAS

In the Vision of God

Table of Contents

Foreword

Throughout human history it is rare that someone so fully awakens that they both are limitlessly free, and live life to the fullest in human form. Swami Ramdas is just such a being. Through his autobiography, the transmission of his awakening, his joy, and his wisdom, and the guidance of how to live in the world move right off the page into our heart.

After receiving the initiation of *Om Sri Ram Jai Ram Jai Jai Ram* from his father, Swami Ramdas, then known as Vittal Rao, renounced the worldly life in 1922 and wandered as a mendicant *sadhu* all over India and the Himalayas in various states of God-intoxication, with heart as his only refuge and with Ramnam—Om Sri Ram Jai Ram Jai Jai Ram—ever on his tongue.

After his awakening, he wanted to test the mettle of his realization. In the Vision of God is his first-hand account of those ten years of pilgrimage, which joyfully captures his path of complete surrender to the Will of God in a most inspiring way.

Swami Ramdas's being, guidance, and teachings are especially close to our Sufi Ruhaniat International lineage because he was a guide to our teacher, Hazrat Murshid SAM (Samuel L. Lewis, Sufi Ahmed Murad Chisti).

In the 1950s, Murshid SAM reported a recurring vision with the face of a saint accompanied by poetry, "In one year's time, by land or sea, I will come to thee." In 1954, in keeping with the vision, Papa (Swami) Ramdas and Mother Krishna Bai came to San Francisco on their World Tour and Murshid SAM found his "Hindu" Guru.

Papa Ramdas has been one of the most important guides in my life. I find his autobiography amongst my very favorite books in the English language, so I am delighted we can keep this important work in publication.

OM SRI RAM JAI RAM JAI JAI RAM!

Pir Shabda Kahn
Sufi Ruhaniat International
7-Dec 2017

"Remember, God brought me to Papa. I needed an element of *Bhakti* for my own development. I feel personally attached to Anandashram, and believe I shall so feel till the end of my days." – Murshid SAM

Preamble

by Swami Ramdas

By the command of the almighty Lord, Ramdas, His child, undertakes the task of continuing the story of his experiences from the time and place where he broke off at the end of his first book "In Quest of God". The narrative of "In Quest of God" extends over to one year's life after the great change came upon him. The purpose of the present book is to draw further the thread of the same narrative, and it contains an account of his later experiences in the course of nine years that have elapsed. Before proceeding with the story it would be necessary for him to place before the reader a brief summary—mainly concerning his spiritual struggle and evolution during the first year—so that it might bring out in a proper perspective the later experiences chronicled in this book.

It was in the year 1921, in Mangalore, that the all-merciful Lord of the universe first fired Ramdas's bosom with a keen longing to realise Him. From that time his life was undergoing a marvelous change. His one overwhelming passion and aim of life was to live for God and God alone. God's powerful Name was indelibly stamped on his tongue. Now it was that he was becoming conscious of a divine influence working silently but irresistibly in him gradually dominating and possessing him. He felt an awakening within the very core of his being. With steady steps and unflagging zeal he now entered upon a path of rigorous self-discipline. The trials and hardships of the path did not daunt him. Repeated appeals, persuasions and remonstrances could not make him swerve an inch from this path. He was calm, earnest and determined. As time passed in prayer, fasting and repetition of God's Name, the consciousness of divine possession and guidance assumed such a predominance that at last the divine voice within him drove him forth from Mangalore into the wide world.

What was his condition at this momentous hour? He was a dazed and helpless creature caught in the grip of an all-powerful Being. He did not know what he was doing. He was under the full control of an almighty Power without any offer of resistance on his part—just as a baby in the hands of its mother. Verily, it was God alone who held him—a God who is at once his divine mother and master, so real, loving, kind and good. Blessed indeed is the day when God made Ramdas entirely His own. O mother and master divine, all glory to Thee! How tenderly He nursed and guided His newborn offspring during his first year's itinerant life all over India forms the theme of "In Quest of God".

During that period what was his mental state, manner of life and outlook upon the world? His mind was merged in a unique stillness of peace; his life was one of unreserved self-surrender; and, as regards the world, in a sense it was not there for him, that is, he was dead as it were to the world. He was travelling from place to place like an automaton as if in a dream, indifferent to—nay, unconscious of—his body and environments. All through it, God to whom he had surrendered up his life was mysteriously influencing his movements and controlling and taking care of him in every way. It was really an entire dedication on one side and a watchful, benevolent protection on the other.

He experienced that he was living and moving in a new world in which he felt that there was none other than himself and his great master—Ram, his all in all. In this wonderful vision of inexpressible ecstasy and peace he struggled to dwell always. This exalted consciousness, possessing as it did the characteristic of perfect vacancy or emptiness, was filled with an ineffable rapture of peace, silence and repose. The dual throng, pleasure and pain, good and evil, cold and heat, etc. relating to the physical body affected him not, for his mind was not there to take note of these sensations; it would always be in tune with the infinite spirit of stillness and peace. There were occasions when under certain conditions he would be dragged down with a jerk as it were to the sense of the old world and its associations, but he would be instantly pulled up by that silent and watchful spirit within.

In those days Ramdas's haunts were caves, jungles, ruins, riversides, grave-yards, hills and cremation grounds. It appeared that these places exerted on him a strange fascination. Instinctively he avoided the din and bustle of the city life and was unconsciously led away from it to dreadful solitudes. The sense of fear had vanished from him entirely—danger and death had lost their terrors for him. A feeling of perfect assurance, security and protection was ever with him. The powerful Ram-*mantram* never left his lips. He was uttering like a machine. It has been revealed in "In Quest of God" how miraculously he was more than once saved from terrible situations—to mould, transform and manipulate him as He willed—a wax lump in His dexterous hands.

Some friends of Northern India who had met him during his first year's wandering life declared that they observed him as having been possessed by extreme dispassion. He was indifferent alike to his body and to the external world and was found absorbed solely in *Ramsmaran* or God-remembrance. He was also discovered to be like a child, passive, docile and obedient. He was bathed, clothed and fed and led in all things. In fact, he had neither attraction nor repulsion for the world. His attitude towards it was simply inexpressible, for he felt, in fact, nothing to interest him in the world, and curiosity he had none. It was simply a wonderful state. Even intellect and emotion seemed to have ceased to function. Truly, God by His power had eradicated from his heart the false, self-asserting ego, and was working Himself in its place—the one great power who causes both the internal and external movements in this world of phenomena.

At this period Ramdas scarcely talked. He was perfectly fearless. Love and hate, like and dislike, conveyed no meaning for him. In brief, he could be likened to a dry leaf tossed at random as the wind of divine will listed. It was thus that he was guided back by God to Mangalore after a year's absence.

In the Vision of God

CHAPTER 1: PANCH PANDAV CAVE

(i) Unity of Religions

Panch Pandav Cave is on the Kadri hill at a distance of two miles from Mangalore town. Of the six caves on this hill the one occupied by Ramdas was the largest. It is so situated that at dawn the sun's rays pierced straight through the darkness inside the cave flooding it with their golden effulgence. He remained in this cave for nearly three months. He was then clad in a coarse *khaddar* cloth, and used for *asan* and bed a bare deerskin. A tiny earthen dish with cotton wick and coconut oil served the purpose of a lamp. Added to these, a copper water pot comprised his equipment in that solitary retreat. His diet consisted of milk and plantains twice a day.

During the day he had a stream of visitors from the town and other parts of the district. They would take unfeigned delight in listening to the story of his travels and experiences in the course of a year's absence. The visitors were drawn from all castes and creeds. Hindus, Christians and Muhammadans, all alike, vied with each other in granting him the joy of their company. Itinerant *sadhus* and *sannyasins* would also bless him with their visits.

He discoursed with the Hindus upon the one supreme Brahman as the sole cause of creation, preservation and destruction. This great Reality has incarnated in India and other parts of the world in different ages to subdue evil and establish the rule of love and righteousness. Rama, Krishna, Buddha, the great *rishis*, *mahatmas*, and saints point to the one goal as the highest aim of life; viz., liberation and union with God. Human life is solely intended for attaining this blessed state. The supreme Lord is seated in the hearts of all beings and creatures. He is absolute existence, consciousness and bliss—Satchidananda. You can realise Him through one-pointed devotion and complete self-surrender. The initial step on the path to this goal is purity and control of mind which is acquired through concentration. An easy method for concentration is constant repetition of the divine Name and performance of all actions as a sacrifice to the Lord. You may call God by any name— Rama, Krishna, Shiva, or any other name you hold dear. The Name Himself is Brahman. The reiteration of the Name coupled with the meditation on the attributes of God purifies the mind. Prayers, hymns, and fasting are necessary aids. You must develop the divine qualities of compassion, peace and forgiveness. God reveals Himself in that heart in which these ennobling virtues reside. Now the divine light shining within you dissolves the ego-sense, and your identity with the Godhead is realised. This experience grants you the knowledge of immortality. Thereafter, you dwell in a divine consciousness and your vision becomes universalised, bringing you supreme peace and ecstasy. Now it is that you behold the whole universe as the very expression of God whom you have discovered within you. Now God is everywhere for you, in everybody and everything. This transcendent vision unlocks the infinite fountain of love in your heart—a love that fills and embraces the entire cosmos. All distinctions now disappear in the equality of this vision. This supreme state of beatitude bestows on you liberation and immortal joy. Believe that incarnations or divine teachers like Jesus Christ, Muhammad, Zoroaster, and others are also manifestations of the same great Truth. Verily all the different religions are so many paths that lead mankind to the one universal God.

To the Muhammadans, Ramdas would speak of Allah, Muhammad. Allah means the almighty. Islam signifies the way to peace. God is indeed all power and peace. Prophet Muhammad established Islam among the warring and ignorant tribes of Arabia so as to awaken in them the spirit of peace, love and brotherhood. He taught the way to reach Allah—the almighty. How to obtain

Him? He says, "Surrender your will to Allah's will. Have full faith in His omnipotence and understand that everything happens by His will." Self-surrender is the path pointed out by Muhammad. He emphasised that surrender comes only through perfect self-control by prayer and fasting. He enjoins upon his followers to say *Namaz* or prayers at least five times a day. This communion would keep them in continued recollection of God, forming a strong basis for a life of purity and peace. Conditions for this attainment are: practice of love, compassion and kindness to all fellow-beings. He held that they should exercise toleration towards other faiths which also take the aspiring souls towards God. His dictum is really this: there should be no compulsion in religion. He laid specific stress upon charity, sincerity, honesty and fellow-feeling. He preached that unity born of self-sacrifice and mutual love makes you recognize the oneness and omnipotence of God. To realise unity amongst mankind is to dwell in the one God—in the mansion of eternal power and peace, and to earn everlasting life.

To the Christians, Ramdas would say: To have faith in Christ means to accept him as your ideal. Your sole aim should be to attain the Christ-ideal and to live up to his pure and selfless life. Let the thought of Christ-ideal possess your very soul and inspire your life and its activities. Christ is an embodiment of divine love. He defines God as love, and this truth he has come to prove in his life. What is the nature of the love he enunciates? It is a mingled perfume of meekness, purity and mercy. Blessed is he who is filled with the fragrance of love, because he will then be a true and accepted child of God—love of God has become manifest in him. He exhorts: Love one another and God dwelleth in you. It is this supreme love that converts you into the image of God. This supreme love enables you to enter into the kingdom of eternal happiness. The kingdom of heaven is nothing but a blissful consciousness which is born of everlasting life. He reveals the secret of this kingdom when he says: "The kingdom of heaven is within you." The Father and the Son are one. Identification with the Son is identification with the Father. Father is eternal peace manifest as the Son the infinite love. So your life should be ruled by Christ, that is love. Then he leads you to the realm of the Father, the absolute peace. Do not think that Christ is the only way to salvation. Great souls have been, long before Christ, holding aloft the torch of divine knowledge for the illumination of the world. Christ held humility as the highest virtue; love and sympathy for all alike as the criterion of conduct; and resignation to the will of God as the means for the attainment of the kingdom of heaven or everlasting life and peace.

Ramdas does not belong to any particular creed. He firmly believes that all creeds, faiths and religions are different paths which ultimately converge to the same goal. The very sight of a Muhammadan reminds him of Muhammad; of a Christian, Jesus Christ; of a Hindu, Rama, Krishna or Shiva; and of a Buddhist, Buddha; of a Parsi, Zoroaster. All the great teachers of the world are from one God—the first eternal cause of all existence. Whether it be in the Gita or the Bible or the Koran or the Zend Avesta, we find the same note insistently ringing; viz., self-surrender is the supreme way to liberation or salvation.

(ii) Service of God

Reverting to the mode of life Ramdas was leading in the cave, he would rise at about three o'clock early morning and run down directly to the water tanks for bath. Though the path to the tanks was rough and risky, he would not forego his morning dip even in the darkest night. After bath he would sit in *asan* for meditation till day-break. For some days his meditation consisted of only the mental repetition of Ram *mantram*. Then the *mantram* having stopped automatically, he beheld a small circular light before his mental vision. This yielded him thrills of delight. This experience having continued for some days, he felt a dazzling light like lightning, flashing before his eyes, which ultimately permeated and absorbed him. Now an inexpressible transport of bliss filled every pore of his physical frame. When this state was coming on, he would at the outset become oblivious of his hands and feet and then gradually his entire body. Lost in this trance-state he would sit for two to three hours. Still a subtle awareness of external objects was maintained in this state.

Some friends would pay him visits early in the morning when he was absorbed in the trance, and he had at the time a hazy recognition of their presence. He could hear sounds of talk, if any, mere sounds without sense or meaning for him. Whenever he fell into the trance he would feel its grip so firmly that he could not easily shake it off. At the longest it would not last more than three hours. After returning to body-consciousness he would be engaged in singing to himself some hymns glorifying God, and also in the loud recitation of the *mantram*. In fact, except when conversing, reading or writing, he used to utter the *mantram* ceaselessly throughout the day.

The trance experience brought about another change; viz., sleep thereafter became a state of half-wakefulness or awareness during which he was filled with pure ecstasy. Sometimes, at dead of night, a friend would pay him a surprise visit. Although Ramdas was in the trance-state, he could know the friend's approach even when he was yet a furlong from the cave. It was during this time that Ramdas, as willed by the Lord, devoted two hours past midnight to the work of writing the book "In Quest of God". The last days in the cave also saw the trance condition encroaching upon the hours of the day while no visitors were present. The utterance of the *mantram* would stop of itself and he would transcend the body-consciousness. Here a unique experience is worthy of note. One morning he was standing inside the cave gazing on the golden orb of the rising sun, and he felt the trance stealing over him and very soon he was entirely absorbed in it. Some time passed and he came back to the body-idea. A casual downward glance disclosed to his view a serpent coiled round his right leg. Its forked tongue was briskly licking his big toe. Ramdas was not affected by the sight. In the same motionless posture he watched the loving attention of the serpent. A minute or two thus passed and the reptile slowly unwound itself and crept out of the cave. He recollects to have addressed it thus: "O beloved Ram, why are thou in such a hurry to go?" The Lord's *lila* is really wonderful. All forms are His and He plays in various ways. The serpent friend conceived such a great love for Ramdas that it would come to see him every morning consecutively for three days after which it stopped away for good.

In accordance with a distinct command from the Lord within, he observed a vow of silence for seven days. Despite the pressure of friends he could not break it before the fixed time. For, he felt he was quite helpless in the matter. Surely, God had complete mastery over His servant.

Ramdas had noted a batch of lepers underneath the banyan trees in the Mangalore *maidan*. One of the lepers, whose disease was in an advanced state, was conveyed every day in a hand-cart by a small stout lad for alms from door to door. The face of this leper was so much disfigured by the fell disease that his features were quite indistinguishable. His whole face was one big sore—red and dripping with pus. His eyelids, nose and lips had all been eaten by the disease.

As commissioned by the Lord, Ramdas undertook to feed these lepers at noon. The kind visitors to the cave condescended to offer food for them. On collecting food from three houses a day, he would go to the *maidan* reaching at about one o'clock in the afternoon and feed them. The leper who had the worst attack came in for service first. His toes and fingers also having fallen a prey to leprosy, he could with great difficulty raise the food to his mouth.

While he was engaged in eating, Ramdas would be busy in driving away the flies that were settling on his face which at other times he covered with a piece of cloth. Ramdas had also to rub off gently the stream of pus coursing down his cheeks into his mouth. The remaining food would then be distributed to the boy and other lepers. The Lord put him to this service for about two months. All the time, far from feeling any weariness or repugnance, he performed the task in a spirit of enthusiasm surcharged with an objectless ecstasy. A few days before he bid adieu to the cave, the feeding work was suddenly stopped by the command of the Lord. O Lord, Thou feedest all Thy creatures in Thy own inscrutable ways, Ramdas is but an instrument in Thy omnipotent hands.

Soon after the feeding of the lepers had ended, a Malayali, that is, a native of Malabar, came to stay with Ramdas in the cave for a few days. He was so emaciated that he was only skin and bones. Ramdas thanked God for his having given him another opportunity to serve Him in the form of this skeleton-bodied Malayali. Ramdas scarcely found this friend in a talkative mood. The only expression that was now and again issuing from his lips in a weak voice was "Krishna, *sharan*, *sharan*". Ramdas would both at noon and in the evening run down to the city and by begging collect food to feed this welcome guest. O Lord, Thy manifestations are most marvelous. The lepers and the Malayali that he served are Thyself in those forms. The entire universe is Thy Self-revelation in which Thou art manifest in a variety of masks. Thou art the one absolute Truth, birthless and deathless; pure Satchidananda, eternal existence, knowledge and bliss.

Amongst the daily visitors mention has also to be made of a goat and a cow. Both would appear at the cave regularly for their share of plantains. The goat played with Ramdas with great familiarity. He would dance on his seat and sometimes climb on his shoulders. The cow on the other hand would quietly come to the entrance and with outstretched neck receive a plantain and then walk away.

(iii) Young Aspirants

The kind mother—Ramdas's wife in his old life—was laid up with fever for some days owing to the strain of the journey by steamboat while accompanying him from Hubli to Mangalore. He was visiting her once in every two or three days until she recovered.

During one of the visits, the reputed saint of Puttur, Krishnarao, was in the house. He came to where Ramdas sat beside the ailing mother. At the sight of him, Ramdas prostrated at his feet. He sat down.

"Was it necessary that you should have entirely renounced the householder's life and taken up the *diksha* of *sannyas*?" he asked.

"Ram willed it so. Ramdas could not help it." Ramdas replied.

"Your Ram must then be wonderful. May I know where He is?" he questioned.

"He is residing in the hearts of us all, because He is all-pervading." Ramdas rejoined.

"I cannot see Him. How can we know that it is His will that guides us?" he asked again.

"He is invisible to the ordinary eye, but can be seen through a purified vision," Ramdas said. "Only when you see Him, you realise that it is His will that directs your actions. Freedom from attachment and complete surrender to Him are the conditions of this supreme vision."

"I cannot fully understand what you say," Krishnarao persisted. "I believe that worldly life need not be abandoned in order to realise God."

"True," Ramdas replied. "Ramdas still belongs to the world, not in a partial sense but in totality. His Beloved is not only in particular persons but is discovered to be residing, in all His power and glory, in all beings, creatures and things."

Here the conversation ended, and Ramdas left the house and returned to the cave.

One day at about five o' clock in the evening, a Saraswat lad of 14 years of age, who was an occasional visitor to the cave, dropped in. He was in tears. With an outburst of anguish he exclaimed: "Rama, I will in future always dwell with you. I am not going to give you up. I desire to dedicate my life to Ram Nam."

"Ram," Ramdas advised him, "you cannot remain here. Your parents will be anxious about you. Go back to them."

"I have nothing to do with parents, house and the world. You are my all in all," the lad said, "I will go on repeating the holy Name in your society."

"You can do the same in your house," Ramdas suggested. "It is not necessary that you should stop with him for uttering the Name."

"No," he said, "I cannot take the Name in our house. I am forced to go to school for which I have conceived a disgust."

"Where is the harm in attending school?" Ramdas asked.

"Oh! I have had enough of it. I fell into the society of certain boys who always indulged in unchaste talks, and my mind got terribly distracted. I will never again step into a school."

"In that case," Ramdas replied, "you may not attend school but remain pure by practicing devotion at home. You are too young to take the proposed step without consulting your parents. Be guided by them. They mean always well. Only do not give up taking the holy name. Trust Him whose Name you are uttering. Avoid the company of boys who defile your mind."

"Don't ask me to go back. My father, mother, teacher and all are yourself." Saying thus the boy entered the interior of the cave and, taking his position in a dark nook, went on with *Ram-Japa*. Ramdas going up to him told him again to return to the city as it was growing dark. For some time he stood firm and would not yield, but at last agreed to go back to his parents. The night having come on, it was now quite dark. So Ramdas offered to escort him to his house which lay in the precincts of a temple in the city.

While descending the hill with the lad Ramdas met a friend with a lantern coming to invite him for a *kirtan* party in the house of his master. Ramdas handing the boy to his charge asked the friend to take him to his house. Ramdas proceeded to attend the *kirtan* party.

A few days later, another young man, a Kanarese brahman just out of his teens, walked in at dusk and proposed to throw in his lot with Ramdas. Here again the school life had driven him from home, relations and friends. This young man was thoroughly stubborn and refused to return to his friends in spite of Ramdas's utmost efforts. He remained for the night. He would disappear for the day, wandering aimlessly on the extensive tract of the Kadri hill and regain the cave in the night. He did not care for food. Ramdas would share with him what little food he was getting which consisted of but a small quantity of milk and a few plantains. For about a week the young man continued to live a life of an apathetic recluse. For the last night of his stay he stopped away, but turned up early the following morning, his clothes soiled with the brown stains of the earth. He said that he spent the night in the open on the hill, lying down on bare ground.

At noon a party of four men arrived at the cave. These were the young man's friends. His parents lived in a village, and he was in Mangalore for his studies. His friends asked him to go with them but he refused point-blank to do so. Then they appealed to Ramdas to advise him. Ramdas assured them that he had used all his powers of persuasion to induce him to return to his house but he had failed. However, he called the young man by his side and resting his hand on his shoulders said: "Ram, don't cause any further sorrow and pain to your parents. Do please go back." Strange as it would appear, the young man now obeyed and left with the friends who had come in search of him.

(iv) The True Vision: Samadarshan

For two years from the time of the significant change which had come over him, Ramdas had been prepared to enter into the very depths of his being for the realisation of the immutable, calm and eternal spirit of God. Here he had to transcend name, form, thought and will—every feeling of the heart and faculty of the mind. The world had then appeared to him as a dim shadow—a dreamy nothing. The vision then was mainly internal. It was only for the glory of the Atman in His pristine purity, peace and joy as an all-pervading, immanent, static, immortal and glowing spirit.

In the earlier stages this vision was occasionally lost, pulling him down to the old life of diversity with its turmoil of like and dislike, joy and grief. But he would be drawn in again into the silence and calmness of the sprit. A stage was soon reached when this dwelling in the spirit became a permanent and unvarying experience with no more falling off from it, and then a still exalted state came on; his hitherto inner vision projected outwards. First a glimpse of this new vision dazzled him off and on. This was the working of divine love. He would feel as though his very soul had expanded like the blossoming of a flower and, by a flash as it were, enveloped the whole universe embracing all in a subtle halo of love and light. This experience granted him a bliss infinitely greater than he had in the previous state. Now it was that Ramdas began to cry out "Ram is all, it is He as everybody and everything." This condition was for some months coming on and vanishing. When it wore away, he would instinctively run to solitude. When it was present, he freely mixed in the world preaching the glory of divine love and bliss. With this externalised vision started Ramdas's mission. Its fullness and magnificence was revealed to him during his stay in the Kadri cave, and here the experience became more sustained and continuous. The vision of God shone in his eyes and he would see none but Him in all objects. Now wave after wave of joy rose in him. He realised that he had attained to a consciousness, full of splendour, power and bliss.

Ramdas gave up the cave and set forth once again on a wandering life. He gave a touch of the inexpressible bliss he was enjoying to all who came in contact with him. Vast crowds thronged around him wherever he went. Divine love thrilled his entire being at the sight of big multitudes. In a state of perfect ecstasy he delivered himself out in accents of love and joy.

CHAPTER 2: KOLLUR AND KASARAGOD

(i) Real Contentment

H. Umanathrao, a pure and selfless soul with his devoted wife, came down from Kundapur, a small town to the north of South Kanara, to take Ramdas over to his place. Ramdas left Kadri cave. The object of Umanathrao was to get him the *darshan* of a venerable saint staying at the famous temple of Mukambika of Kollur. The same evening they reached Kundapur. They travelled by motor-bus. The kind friend provided him with a separate room, the upstairs of a house facing his own.

Ramdas passed happily a period of about a month and a half in Umanathrao's delectable company. Umanathrao was a true philosopher. He lived a life of selfless service. He was simple and unassuming by nature. He held a British university degree in medicine. In a spirit of renunciation he had given up Government employment and had taken up private practice. He was greatly loved by all the people of Kundapur for his ready medical aid at all hours. He was kind and sympathetic towards all alike: rich and poor, old and young, high and low. He would not take any fee for his services from the poor and even from the rich he would not accept any remuneration when he was not in need of money. He was entirely free from anger, guile and malice. He was extremely charitable. He would often speak of the world as only a play of God, and that the best way to live in it was to witness the game dispassionately. The light of divine love ever illumined his heart. When occasions arose, he would do the meanest service for the relief of his fellow-men. He also possessed a keen sense of humour and was remarkably witty. He was indeed a pure, godly and noble soul.

A month passed, and Ramdas reminded Umanathrao of the proposed trip to Kollur. Arrangements were at once made to start. Ramdas, Umanathrao and another friend, crossing a river by boat, came to the road leading to Kollur which lay through a dense forest. Here they boarded a bullock-cart. The path was narrow and rugged—cut through a vast extensive jungle spreading all along the way to Kollur. The jungle was infested with wild beasts. Kollur was reached without anything of importance having occurred on the way.

Kollur is a small village on a plateau bounded on three sides by tall mountains called Kotashadri hills. A dense forest of giant trees growing on these lofty and towering hills lent a peculiar majesty and fascination to the place. In the centre of the village is situated the shrine of Mukambika—the Mother of the universe. Umanathrao led Ramdas directly to the part of the outer building of the temple where the saint was lodging. Ramdas bowed down before the holy saint. He appeared to be over 70 years old. His eyes were large and greenish in tint and their expression was distant and listless but mingled with a gleam of tenderness and cheer. He owned a flowing grey beard that lent sanctity and light of wisdom to his full and beaming face. He was seen squatting on the floor, wearing only a *kaupin*. Having enquired after the welfare of the visitors he straightaway launched into religious talks.

He recounted a good many stories from Bhagawat and other sources. He discoursed eloquently upon *bhakti* or love of God. In the enthusiasm of the talks his body would convulse with spiritual rapture. At intervals he would shut his eyes and sit silent for a minute or two, his face lit up by strange, spiritual glow. He referred to his body as a monkey prone to all sort of tricks.

"Look here," he would say pointing to his body, "this monkey is often up to his tricks. The limbs get so cramped with rheumatism that they refuse to move about freely," and he would add with a chuckle, "the monkey is always full of *chesta*."

His legs were so weak that he could hardly walk without help. He lived alone and still was always cheerful and contented. His strictures upon worldly life were sharp and severe. The saint would keep the party engaged with his lofty discourses till late in the night. He would never get tired of talking about God and His glories. Whenever he was alone, he was observed to be busy writing down in pencil the name "Ram" with which he had filled up many note-books. Altogether, the stay with the saint lasted only three days. On the second day they were joined by a young but blind *sadhu* led in and attended on by an elderly widowed lady. The *sadhu* appeared to be about 20 or 22 years old. Owing to two cataract spots on the pupils he had become stone-blind. Dr. Umanathrao went up to him and examining his eyes gave him to understand that a simple operation would restore his sight, and that he was prepared to do that much for him. The *sadhu* turned round and said: "Kind Sir, I would have nothing of what you say. I am perfectly contented with the lot God has bestowed on me. What do I care for the external and perishable sight when the internal has opened? The former is a snare, and God through His infinite mercy has deprived me of it so that my inner vision may all the more be pure and glorious. I am happy and cheerful in the contemplation of the divine Lord who dwells in the hearts of all. May He always keep me in tune with Him."

As he spoke thus, his eyes, the light of which had gone out, were filled with tears and his face shone with a wonderful lustre.

The three days glided away most blissfully in the society of these saints. Before leaving the village the party visited the shrine of Mukambika. They returned to Kundapur. Stopping with Umanathrao for a fortnight more Ramdas left for Mangalore. On the way he halted for two days at Udupi where he met K. Anandrao, a pure soul living a retired life engaged in austerities. Ramdas enjoyed his most delightful company. Anandrao read out to him selected quotations from various philosophical works he had studied. In fact he poured into Ramdas the very essence of the highest truths. He was all love and kindness. In this connection, Ramdas cannot help mentioning the remarkable love and regard with which he was uniformly treated by all, including the members of the family to which he belonged in his past life.

Ramdas, during his stay at Udipi, took a stroll with a friend to a distant water-spring where he bathed. On return they paid a visit to the celebrated temple of Sri Krishna founded by Sri Madhavacharya, the great religious reformer of southern India.

(ii) The Power of God's Name

Stopping at Udipi for a couple of days Ramdas proceeded to Mangalore, where too he had to stay only for a short time. P. Anandrao, an elder brother of his former life, eagerly wished to take him to Kasaragod—a town to the south of Mangalore where he lived. At Ramdas's request he arranged to procure for his occupation a small room in a newly built *dharmashala* in the midst of three temples. In the vicinity of the temples were two tanks in which he would have the morning bath. Anandrao was very kind and loving. He was keen on Ramdas's comforts. The little room was fully equipped with the simple necessities of Ramdas's life. They consisted of a soft mat with a deer skin spread upon it, two ochre-coloured *khaddar* pieces, a couple of mats for visitors, a hurricane lantern, a country leaf umbrella, one copper water pot and some religious books. A piece of cardboard was also nailed to the wall above his seat with the divine Ram *mantram* written in bold Kanarese characters thereon. Ramdas gives these details since a strange event that happened has a close bearing upon them. His diet was milk, fruits and plain boiled rice.

During the first few days, crowds of visitors gathered round the rest-house to see him; of these, school-boys formed the majority. Many earnest devotees of God also visited him. In the nights he was often taken out to attend *kirtan* parties where the popular devotional songs of the great Indian saints were sung. These songs contained the essence of the sublime Hindu philosophy. They treated of devotion, knowledge and renunciation. Their direct mode of appeal elevated the mind and filled it with divine fervour. Among the hymns the most popular were those of Kabir and Tukaram. Indeed their poems were rare gems of spiritual thought in which were blended perfect rhythm, lofty idealism and pure emotion.

In the afternoon Ramdas was engaged in reading the English translation of Tulsidas Ramayana and rendering it in the vernacular for the benefit of the devotees who thronged the small room. They were imbibing with avidity the spiritual nectar provided by Tulsidas in his immortal work.

One day a young man, weighed down by despondency and despair, came to Ramdas. He recounted the tale of his woe. Ramdas advised him to repeat the Ram mantram and assured him that all would be well. The friend would thereafter visit Ramdas every day, and he was found immersed in the *japa* of Ram-Nam. A few days passed and he came to Ramdas with a cheerful face and told him that the impending calamity that threatened him had passed off without scathing him in the least. All victory to the powerful Name! The Name of the Lord has undoubtedly the power of dispelling ignorance, pain and misery. So saints all over the world are never tired of glorifying the Name.

One early morning two old visitors who had retired from active life came to see Ramdas. They started a cosy little chat over their domestic worries.

"The thatching season has come." one was saying to the other. "I have been on the lookout for grass bundles for the purpose but could not procure any, as grass-vendors could be rarely seen. I am much worried."

"That is nothing," cried the other. "My trouble is worse. Our front-gate needs repair. Stray buffaloes get free access to my garden and lay waste every blessed thing I have planted. I called in carpenters for mending the gate but they slipped out of my hands like eels. I can hardly sleep in peace at night."

So on and so forth ad infinitum. Ramdas listened for a time to their frank exchange of confidences regarding their private troubles. He felt he was one too many on the spot and realised that they would better enjoy themselves without the presence of a third party who had no interest in their discourse. So he quietly glided out of the room and made his way with rapid strides to the top of a hill outside the town. Rambling for an hour he retraced his steps to his little room. But where were the birds? They had flown away. However, they dropped in again the same evening and beseeched him to forgive them for their indiscretion in discussing their private worries in his presence, at his retreat.

With all the sweetness that Ramdas could command he said: "The room in which Ramdas lives is open to all, for, people who are beset with worldly troubles may freely resort to it and gain peace and calmness through the remembrance of God. On the other hand, if they come to the room with a bundle of their cares and opening it spread its contents, they are simply denying themselves the much needed solace which the room would otherwise yield.

In one voice they agreed with what Ramdas said, and promised not to commit the blunder again.

(iii) God Assumes All Forms

Another extraordinary experience worth narrating in some detail befell Ramdas. About ten o'clock in the night on a rainy day, a strange looking individual entered his room. Besides his being clothed in rags, his hair was dishevelled. He had with him a small bundle suspended on a rough palm stick. He looked as if he were demented. He came in and took his seat near Ramdas.

"May I rest here tonight?" he asked in a queer sing-song manner. Ramdas said that he was quite welcome.

He sat on the mat and opened his bundle which contained a bizarre assortment of small bits of cloth in varied colours. Taking out the rags he scattered them on the ground. Then glancing at Ramdas he laughed a merry laugh.

Ramdas thought to himself: "O Lord, Thou cometh in wonderful disguises." After a while the strange visitor gathered up the scraps remade the bundle. Next approaching Ramdas he chanted the burden of a popular Kanarese song, the purport of which was: "Thou art the ever pure, all-merciful and mysterious Govinda." He sang forth this verse in his own peculiarly passionate and impressive style. He spoke in the Kanarese tongue. Suddenly, stopping his music, he directly looked at Ramdas's face and said: "You see, my clothes are old and worn out. Would you not part with one you are using for me?" pointing to the cloth worn by Ramdas.

Ramdas at once divesting himself of the cloth handed it over to him. The visitor carefully folded it and laid it beside him.

In an imperious voice he spoke next: "Now let us sleep. Reduce the light. Mind you, don't put it out." Obediently Ramdas carried out his bidding. He laid himself down pretending to sleep, and Ramdas followed suit. Five minutes had not elapsed when he sprang into a sitting posture calling on Ramdas to do the same. Ramdas yielded. The light was made brighter.

"I have yet to demand something more." he said.

"Everything in this room," Ramdas replied, "is Ram's property, and since you are He you have a right to it. You may freely ask and take."

Meanwhile, Ramdas had covered himself with the other spare cloth.

"I need also the cloth you have just put on," and he stretched forth his hand. Without a word Ramdas surrendered up the second cloth.

Some minutes passed and he said: "I have need for a water pot. If you have no objection, you may give the one over there," pointing to the vessel in the corner of the room. Emptying the pot of its water, Ramdas passed it on to him. As desired by him, Ramdas made up the things into a bundle. Then he called for the mat, the deer skin, the lantern, the umbrella, the spare *langoti*, one after the other, at almost regular intervals.

Ramdas felt that God was out to test him if he had any sense of possession still left. His dedicated life did not admit of any attachment to things of the world. Whenever he gave away the things to this strange friend, he did so in a spirit of delightful spontaneity. With a rising emotion he addressed the visitor: "O Lord, Thy tests are wonderful. Everything is Thine and Thine alone." At this, the visitor broke out into his usual offhand laughter. He demanded also a few religious books which were in the room. All articles were tied up in a cloth and formed a pretty big bundle.

Later he said with a note of warning in his voice: "Look here, you have given me many valuable articles. It is possible, when I am gone with them, you might regret your folly. What say you?"

"No, not at all," quickly responded Ramdas, "since you are taking away your own things. Ramdas has no cause for regret."

"Now, then," he broke out, "give me that board on the wall." It also went to swell the bundle.

The room was now almost empty. Being monsoon it began to rain heavily. The night had advanced and it was about 3 a.m. Ramdas had nothing on except a *kaupin*.

"One thing more," he still cried. "I may also require the pair of spectacles you have on." The pair of spectacles was duly handed over to him, examining which he remarked that it would fit him.

"Yet one thing more," he said.

"You may demand anything" replied Ramdas. "Ramdas has dedicated his entire life to thee."

"Pass me the *kaupin* you are wearing." he asked calmly.

It was beyond any doubt now that God Himself was here for a crucial test. Ramdas with perfect nonchalance born of complete self-surrender loosened the *kaupin* from his otherwise naked body to offer it to him. But before Ramdas had removed it outright, the strange friend stopped him with his hand saying: "No, no, you may retain it, I need it not." He then eagerly asked, "Can you follow me?"

Ramdas lost no time in replying: "By all means."

"Not now, some other time," he said and prepared to start. It was now raining in torrents. In one hand he held the lantern and in the other the umbrella, and the palm pole flung across his shoulder with the bundle suspended on it, at his back.

Standing on the landing steps he flashed a parting shot. "What do you think of me? I am not mad. I am not." he said with great emphasis.

"You are He, you are He," gasped out Ramdas, his throat fully choked with emotion.

The friend descended the steps and walked away.

Ramdas returned to the room and the moment he sat down on the floor, he was lost in a deep trance. It was broad daylight when he recovered from the trance. He beheld quite a crowd swarming at his door, of whom Anandrao was one. The news had been conveyed to them by the servant who was bringing for Ramdas his morning milk and fruit. They assumed that a thief must have decamped with all the missing articles from the room. They inquired of him how it had all happened.

Ramdas only replied: "The Lord Ram provides through one form and takes away through another."

This brief and enigmatic explanation did not, of course, satisfy them. So he had to give out a detailed account of the incident of the previous night. All listened to the story with breathless interest. One of them suggested that the rogue should be hunted down and captured.

"For what fault of his?" asked Ramdas, "He has taken only his own things. There is no law on earth," added he, "that can punish him for it. He is not a rogue. He is the Lord Himself."

An irrepressible smile lit up the faces of all who heard him. They seemed to have understood him and quietly dispersed. Before noon the same day, Anandrao, all kindness and love as he was, furnished the room afresh, so that it looked again as if nothing had been removed from it. A few days later, the new water-pot had to be substituted by another, the second one having gone into the possession of an itinerant *sannyasini* who was badly in need of one.

Anandrao sought to replace the pair of spectacles but Ramdas declined saying: "The Lord has deprived Ramdas of spectacles because he may not need them in future. His will be done."

Ever since then Ramdas has been doing without spectacles, as his sight has been completely restored.

One evening, while Ramdas was reading the treatise on Raja Yoga by Swami Vivekananda, a desire arose in his heart to practice *pranayama*. No sooner did this thought flit across his mind than a young *raja-yogi* stepped into the room and sat beside him. Ramdas at once saw that the Lord had sent the *yogi* to instruct him in this great science.

That very night the *raja-yogi* initiated Ramdas into the mysteries of *raja vidya* or royal science as he called it. Thence forth Ramdas was mostly occupied in the practice of *asana* and *pranayama*. As the practice went on, he experienced a dead stillness and peace overtaking him. Accordingly, the incentive to reading and talk vanished. He became composed and silent. This change was marked and remarked upon by the daily visitors. Hunger, hitherto dormant, was aroused, and he had to take larger quantities of food than usual—the rule of *satwic* diet being broken. Under the strain of incessant practice of *pranayama*, he felt great physical weakness. A craving for solitude now seized him, so that he might undergo the new experiences in an undisturbed place. He proposed the change to Anandrao who immediately arranged to shift him to a place about two miles from Kasaragod.

CHAPTER 3: KUDLU – KADRI HILL

(i) Pranayama

Kudlu is a countryside two miles to the north of Kasaragod. Ramdas was lodged in a tiled house of three rooms on the slope of a valley, above which was an extensive uninhabited plateau, green with verdure and shrubs. At the foot of the house was a shallow excavation, from one side of which was flowing down a narrow jet of pure sparkling water, supplied by a hidden spring. Majestic silence reigned over the valley. It was a fit abode for undisturbed meditation. God willed that Ramdas should live in such a place.

In right earnest Ramdas stared the practice of *pranayama*. For long hours he would sit up for the exercise. He became in regard to food highly eccentric. The supplies came from Anandrao who was visiting him every morning to look after his needs. His pure love made him bear with remarkable patience Ramdas's innumerable freaks and fancies in the matter of diet. He changed his diet from day to day from one thing to another, and at last, went for some days on mere water-fast. Then he would again revert to the usual means.

These experiments in diet coupled with incessant practice of *pranayama* reduced his body and gradually weakened it. The mind lapsed into a state of perfect listlessness and torpor. It seemed to have descended into the very depths of inexpressible stillness and silence. On and on the practice continued. The utterance of the *mantram* stopped entirely. All the hours of the day and night were devoted, almost without break, for control of breath. At times due to over-exhaustion he would drop down an emaciated and limp figure. The *raja-yogi* who initiated him came on a visit. He watched the keen struggle through which he was passing and encouraged him on. He advised Ramdas to feed the body properly. One thing, however, became evident to Ramdas—this exercise was dealing a death-blow to memory, reason and the subtler emotions of the heart. The mind became blank and arid—inactivity and silence was the result.

It was the will of the Lord that Ramdas should also gain this experience of *pranayama*—a mode of mind-control prescribed by the great sage Patanjali. This discipline forms a part of *ashtanga yoga* as taught by the sage. It is incumbent on the aspirant that he should follow all the eight rules of the yoga together, of which *asan* and *pranayama* are two. *Brahmacharya* or continence is held to be absolutely necessary, as also a watchful guidance from an experienced teacher of yoga. The path is not meant for all people. Householders, engaged in affairs of life, will do well to avoid it. For, failure in observance of the rules of this yoga is likely to cause derangement of the brain and other diseases. For the householder the most suitable discipline for concentration of mind is repetition of the divine Name and devotional music, in other words, the path of *bhakti* or devotion. The practice of *pranayama* continued unabated for a month, and then Ramdas gave it up. The usual repetition of the *mantram* became once more an automatic function of the tongue. Activity returned, and he took long walks on the meadow both in the morning and evening. He wandered aimlessly. The extensive view of the green vegetation all around absorbed him. He witnessed his own loneliness—his mind resting on the bosom of the motionless spirit of tranquility. The world about him looked like a vast glistening canvas on which pictures of variegated tints were laid by a master artist—the green earth below and the blue expanse above were bathed in the bright glory of the sun.

In the course of his rambles he was accosted by a Muslim: "Why do you come near our habitation? Our children get frightened on seeing you. Will it not be better for you to adhere to your solitary retreat?"

Ramdas heard and passed on.

On another occasion he unconsciously directed his steps towards the seaside which lay about a mile and a half from the retreat. He had to pass through a small village peopled by Muslims. When he was walking along one of the streets, a number of Muslim boys clustered round him and stopped his progress. They began to pat on his head, pull his ears and nose, make faces at and dance round him. All the while, some Muslim mothers were observing the scene from a distance. Thinking that the boys were harassing Ramdas, they rushed forward and drove them away.

He continued his stroll to the seashore. He sat on the sands looking on the giant waves rolling noisily and lashing against the rocks on the shore. He remained for a time in a state of complete abstraction as his eyes swept on the limitless azure sheet of water before him. Then he retraced his steps to his abode.

(ii) The Battle of Elements

In this blissful and undisturbed retreat, insects and birds freely gave Ramdas the joy of their society. They would unhesitatingly enter the rooms and play about fearlessly. They seemed to have instinctively understood that he was their friend. Surely, for Ramdas they were manifestations of the great Truth that he adored and loved. He would share his eatables with them.

At this place, as inspired by Lord, he composed some poems, prayers and essays. These have already been published in the book At the Feet of God.

The season being monsoon the nights were attended with heavy showers. One memorable night the rainfall was unusually violent. There were deafening peals of thunder preceded by flashes of lightning. Rain and storm raged in all their fury. A mass of rushing water was dashing against the sides of the house. Every thunder-crash shook the building to its very foundation. The maddened wind was whistling through the shutterless windows beating torrential showers of rain into the room. In the midst of this warfare of the elemental gods, Ramdas was seated unmoved in the room, in a state of perfect exaltation, watching the progress of terrific scene. Every situation of dread and danger only hardened the fibre of his being. The terrors of the storm did not affect him. The Truth—God within him—spoke out: "I am in the storm, the wind and the rain. I am in the thunder and the lightning. I am the active creator, the merciful protector and ruthless destroyer. I am all in all. I am all."

The storm still raged on. Ramdas heard a sudden thud on the floor about two yards from where he sat. He turned in the direction from which the sound came and discovered a big wild cat, black as jet, standing with a fixed gaze at him. It had jumped down from the top of the wall. Its lustrous eyes gleamed in the dim corner of the room. Ramdas at once stood up and taking the lantern walked towards it. It was about twice the size of an ordinary cat—tall, gaunt and ferocious. It did not await Ramdas's approach. It leapt on the nearest window sill and, wriggling out through the iron bars, disappeared into the rain and darkness outside. Till morning Ramdas enjoyed the glorious battle of the elements.

One evening a devotee from Kasaragod came to fetch him. It was arranged to perform a *nagar bhajan*. He, in the company of a saint belonging to the Sri Krishna Chaitanya cult of Bengal and other devotees, danced to the music of *nama sankirtan* in the street procession. Ever since this event he was frequently coming to the town. On one occasion he had the *darshan* of Swami Shivananda, the preceptor of the *raja yogi* who initiated him into *pranayama*.

After his return to Kasaragod, Ramdas had a three days' water-fast during which he stopped with an old devout mother in the town. The fast broken, he proceeded again to Mangalore and stopped for some time on the Kadri hill.

(iii) Enter Ramcharandas

Ramdas reached Mangalore by an evening train and directly made his way to the Kadri hill. He came to a *dharmashala*, situated close to the famous seven tanks. The rest-house was in charge of a young boy by name Madhav. The boy welcomed him with unfeigned delight. He offered Ramdas a deer skin on which he took his seat on a raised platform. Madhav was a well-built and healthy lad. He conceived a great and abiding love and regard for Ramdas. His perfect trust enabled him to lay before Ramdas the story of his life. He narrated: He lost his mother when he was still a little child, and was thus thrown adrift into the world. He passed under the care of his relations from place to place. So, his higher education was neglected. His elder brother had disappeared many years ago and his whereabouts were unknown. His father, a petty clerk in some office, was touring with his officer in the district. He was without a home. The boy had a religious turn of mind from his childhood. He frequented *kirtan* parties and sought the society of *sadhus*. His inherent craving for freedom and peace was thus intensified. He prayed to God to grant him a situation in which he could spend all his time in devotion.

Ramdas found that the boy's nature was pure and lovable. He was put in charge of the rest-house by a merchant of the city who provided him with his bare needs. His time was his own which he spent in meditation. He was indeed an earnest seeker after Truth. He was simple and guileless. Ramdas felt a strange attraction for him at the very first sight. He questioned Ramdas how he could control the restless mind. Ramdas gave him the Ram *mantram* and, thereafter, the *mantram* was always on his lips.

On Ramdas's expressing to him his desire to remain in a perfectly solitary place, Madhav suggested the cave just a few yards above the *dharmashala* on the hill. This cave had been newly rebuilt by raising mud walls at its entrance. Ramdas leaving his seat asked the boy to lead him to the cave. The cave was a narrow and low hole just sufficient for one person to lie down. The mud walls were still undried and the floor was damp. It had a small doorway with shutters. Ramdas entered the cave and told Madhav that he had decided to spend in it the night and some days more. Madhav spread the deer skin on the floor of the cave, and then returned to the rest-house.

Madhav was all kindness to him. He served him in every possible way, but there was something weighing on his mind, and he looked worried. Ramdas found out that he had a debt of a few rupees. God arranged for it and set him free.

Ramdas's stay in the cave was marked with many periods of fasting. But for his extreme physical weakness during the fasts, he was perfectly at ease and cheerful. It must be noted here that whenever God inspired him to undertake a fast he experienced great elation, similar to what a hungry man would feel when he was provided with a sumptuous feast.

In all, he remained in the cave for a month and a half. He received visits from many devotees of the city. He also went occasionally to the city in the evenings to attend *kirtan* parties. Once he was invited to a marriage function. A girl in the house was bed-ridden on account of serious illness. Ramdas saw her and prayed to the girl's father to entertain the poor of the town with a dinner in the name of God and for the sake of the ailing girl. Generous-hearted man as he was, he agreed to the suggestion. He said that he had already resolved to do so. The feeding of the poor came about in due course, but Ramdas was not in Mangalore for the occasion, as he had left the place earlier. A year later he learnt that the suffering girl had recovered soon after the feeding of the poor. Trust in God is always rewarded.

Meanwhile, Madhav had developed a great attachment for Ramdas. One day Ramdas told him that the Lord willed that His child, that is Ramdas, should take once more to a wandering life. Now the boy appealed, in a piteous voice, that he might also be permitted to go with him. He added that it would be utter misery for him to live separated from Ramdas. At this Ramdas warned him: "Well, Ram, the path which Ramdas follows is a hard one. For him danger and death have no terror. You must know that he is a reckless, wild and fearless wanderer. He deliberately courts suffering because he has discovered joy in it. Your case is different. So be advised. Do not seek to accompany him."

Madhav would not yield to persuasion. He was very obstinate. He assured Ramdas that he was prepared to go through any trial in his company, but would never give him up. Ramdas had to acquiesce.

Ramdas decided to start on foot on a long travel to the north, via Gokarn – an important place of pilgrimage on the west coast of India—and informed Madhav about it. Madhav got things ready for the journey. He equipped himself with some cooking utensils and foodstuffs which he shoved into a scrip prepared for the purpose. At this stage he made a request to Ramdas. He desired to change his name, and wanted Ramdas to suggest a new one. Ramdas gave him the name Ramcharandas which he adopted from that time forward. So Ramdas will refer to him henceforth as Ramcharandas.

CHAPTER 4: TOWARDS GOKARN – GOKARN

(i) Institution—A Bondage

On a moonlit night at about three o'clock in the morning, Ramdas and Ramcharandas left Mangalore. Ramdas walked at a brisk pace with Ramcharandas close at his heels. They passed through many villages, and at midday made a halt in the vicinity of a few thatched huts underneath a grove of coconut trees. There was a well close by. Ramcharandas prepared some *khichdi*. After finishing meals they rested for about two hours in the cool shade of the trees. Then they prosecuted their journey. In the evening they arrived at a *mofussil* town, Moolky, where Ramcharandas escorted Ramdas to the house of one of his relations. They lodged for the night with the friends who were very hospitable. Ramcharandas's aunt, who was there, dissuaded him from going with Ramdas. They presented to him in lurid colours the discomforts and difficulties of a *sadhu's* life, but they could not induce him to change his mind.

Next day at dawn the *sadhus* proceeded on their travel and reached Udipi where they put up for the night with Srinivasrao, Ramdas's younger brother in the former life. Leaving Udipi the next morning they came to Kalyanpur at midday where they were welcomed with great joy by a *bhakta*. They proceeded onward. From early dawn to 11 a.m. and then from 3 p.m. until dark they tramped on day after day. At Kundapur they halted at the dispensary of Rama Bhatji, a friend of H. Umanathrao, who had shuffled off his mortal coil a few months before their visit.

Crossing the Gangolly by ferry, they came at noon to a hamlet called Kirimanjeshwar. Here they stopped near a Shiva temple. On the bank of a large tank, in which they bathed, they refreshed themselves with food cooked by the ever willing Ramcharandas. The scenery of the place was charming. The place was close to the sea. The roar of the rolling waves could be heard at a short distance. The land was covered with an extensive forest bounded by hills. Tradition has it that the spot was sanctified in ancient days by the austerities of Agastya Muni. So, that part of the village bears the name of Agastyamuni Ashram. The *pujaris* of the temple declared that the water of the tank possessed wonderful virtues. The water was indeed pure and sweet in spite of the washing and bathing for which it was used by the villagers. Ramdas was greatly captivated by the singular fascination of this place. After resting for sometime they started again.

They passed through Byndoor and Bhatkal and reached Shirali. Here Ramcharandas proposed to visit the famous Saraswat Chitrapur *math*. It was God's will that Ramdas should only wait in the jungle outside the *math* buildings while Ramcharandas entered the *math*. After a while he returned with *bhiksha*.

Chitrapur *math* is a religious institution belonging to the enterprising and intelligent Saraswat community in which Ramdas had his old birth. The religious head or *guru* of the community has his headquarters in Chitrapur. The present head of the *math* is a young man of great purity, character and spirit. Ramdas had the good fortune of having his *darshan* in the Kasaragod Ashram. His *guru* was conservative in his methods of control over the community, but he was a great *tapaswi*. His successor, the present Swami, possesses a broad outlook and has relaxed the stringent rules of the previous regime.

No institution can justify its existence if it does not keep abreast of the changing times. Evolution is the law of life and change is its keynote. While stagnation means deterioration and misery, progress denotes freedom and happiness. The former stands for discord and chaos and the latter for harmony and peace. Religion points to the vision of God—the supreme liberation and bliss born of the immortal. This vision is not circumscribed by tradition and doctrine because it transcends all limitations. The rules of life should be so set and adjusted that they might admit of being outgrown when the keen hunger of the soul seeks utter freedom in God. If this truth is ignored, life becomes a complex tangle in which the soul is caught enchained and helpless—hopelessly struggling to be free from the net of its own making.

The seed must have a ground so prepared that it might break through the soil and spring out into growth. Also favourable conditions have to be provided for the plant to evolve into a big tree, then into flowers, and lastly fruits. It must not be forgotten that fruit is the consummation of the seed. So an institution is the garden where every facility for the cultivation of the soul might ultimately transcend the institution for the higher, true and complete vision of life—just as the tree outgrows its fence and spreads its branches freely in the air, or as the pupil outgrows the school life for that of the world. Else an institution becomes at once an organised bondage and an incubus that warp and crush the healthy evolution of life to its destined goal of freedom and joy.

Ramcharandas and Ramdas marched onward. Talk between them was scarce. Ramdas exhorted the boy to keep on uttering the Ram *mantram*. After some halts on the way they at last reached Gokarn.

(ii) *Guru* and *Chela*

Gokarn is a place of pilgrimage because of its noted shrine of Mahadev. It is on the seacoast—the temple being about a furlong from the seashore. The structure of the temple is extensive and of ancient model. The most important annual festival of the temple is Shivaratri. Ramdas had arrived there about a fortnight prior to this day of celebration. Pilgrims from various parts of the country were now pouring in for this great occasion.

Ramcharandas and Ramdas reached here at midday. They were invited for dinner at the house of a prominent merchant of the place where they were treated with great kindness and love. Then they went to the temple of Mahadev and saw a crowd of pilgrims at the entrance in the outer yard. Pilgrim *sadhus* were scrambling for place on either side of the main door of the temple. For, here it was that they received the greatest attention from the pilgrims who came with offerings.

"Swamiji, let us also settle down here—there is still room for us," suggested Ramcharandas.

"Ram," replied Ramdas, "What if we pitch upon a retired and secluded spot? That seems to be the right thing."

"No, Swamiji," interrupted Ramcharandas, "this is the best place for us, since we have the double advantage of being near the *murti* of Mahadev and also having the society of the *sadhus*."

His reasons proved unassailable and Ramdas submitted. A portion of the ground was immediately cleared of its pebbles and loose earth by him, and some spare cloths were spread on it to signify that the place had been booked and marked. Night came on. They took their seats on the coveted piece of ground. Ramcharandas felt proud of their enviable position since it lay only second in the line to the right-hand side of the main entrance. The first position was occupied by two *sadhus*—one elderly and the other young. Before dark both the sides of the doorway, up to the extremity of the wall, were filled by *sadhus*. Of the *sadhus* to their left, the elder was the *guru* and the younger the *chela*.

"Ramgiri—prepare the *chilam*," said the *guru* in a gruff and authoritative voice to his *chela*.

"All right, Maharaj-ji," replied the *chela* meekly.

The *chela* released a satchel from his shoulder and extracted from it two small pouches—a *chilam* or earthen pipe, a coil of coir rope and a match box. From one of the pouches he took out a compressed lump of green leaves—*ganja*, and placing it tenderly upon his left palm, soaked it freely with water from his *lota*. After removing the seeds and squeezing the water out, he opened the other pouch and inserting his fingers, took out a goodly pinch of dry yellow tobacco. Then he mixed the tobacco with the rinsed *ganja* on his palm.

Now pressing the mixture into a bit of a cake he laid it on his thigh. Next he cut out a small length of the coir rope and making it into a ring, set fire to it. While it was burning he filled the *chilam* with the mixture of *ganja* and tobacco. The coir ring—burnt into red live cinder—he swiftly carried with his fingers to the mouth of the *chilam*. "Maharaj-ji," he called out to his *guru* who was now deeply engaged in a talk with another *sadhu*, who had come from the other side, seeing the active preparation for a *ganja* smoke. The *chela* offered the *chilam* to his *guru*.

With eyes red with anger the *guru* growled at his *chela*: "Idiot, where is my *safi*?" (i.e., the small piece of cloth used at the smoking end of the *chilam*). "How dare you offer me the *chilam* without it?—you fool."

The *chela*—like a scared animal—searched for the rag while, all the time, his *guru* was fuming with rage. However, he got the thing and no sooner had he wetted it than the *guru* snatched it away from him and rolled it on the nether end of the *chilam*. But before taking it to his lips, in a loud and shrill voice, he chanted out the usual invocation to Shankar, the Lord of Kailas: "Bom—Bom—Mahadev—Kailaspati—Bholanath—Shanker, etc." He then lifted the pipe to his mouth and took a prolonged pull at it, giving vent, at the same time, to a sharp hissing noise. Lowering the pipe he let out the smoke from his upturned mouth, as if it were the funnel of a railway engine belching out a cloud of smoke.

The *chilam* was now handed to the guest, the other *sadhu*, who was awaiting his turn with the eyes of a hawk. While he was manipulating the *chilam* the *guruji* by way of digression said: "Ramgiri is a perfect ass," referring to his *chela*. "He is a stupid and useless fellow. He was worse but has improved somewhat since he fell into my company."

These words of the *guru* seemed to have entered like iron into the soul of the *chela*. They must have rankled and boiled his interior. He flushed red and his tightly compressed lips showed that he was trying to suppress his feelings. His turn of *chilam* came. He took it out of the guest-*sadhu* and having his own safi, for the *guru* would always consider it below his dignity to allow the *chela* to use his safi, commenced smoking. Again it was *guruji's* turn and it was handed to him. A few minutes passed. The *ganja* had started its work on the brain of the smokers. While its intoxication lulled the mind of the *guru*, it raised the spirit of revolt in the *chela*. His long pent-up wrath—a flame nourished by the constant insults and ill-treatment of his *guru* burst in all its fury. With a look of withering scorn and contemptuous smile at his *guru*, he broke out: "I have had enough of you, you beast. For twelve long years have I borne the insults you heaped on me—you were cruel and heartless. You treated me worse than a dog. All along I was meek, submissive and obedient. I served you sincerely to the best of my ability. I thought at first I could, by serving you, understand the ways of devotion and knowledge. I craved for a life of freedom based upon the vision of God. I have now found out that you are merely an adventurer, vile and despicable, ignorant and conceited, but too late. For, the vice of *ganja* smoking you taught me has enslaved me and bound me to your hateful person. I struggled hard many a time to break away from you but in vain. I am inextricably caught in the clutches of this fell vice—and you, wretch, have brought about this ruin for your selfish ends. The intoxication of this soul-destroying drug has weakened my will, destroyed my memory and distorted my reasoning faculty. I began to babble incoherently like a maniac under its influence. I knew I was going down and down into a bottomless pit of perdition—dragged down by your pitiless hands. 'O God,' I used to cry out often, 'save me, save me.' In spite of my unchanged condition, I trusted Him. I was sure He would help me out. The day has come. I give you up for good. God has at last called me away. All praise to Thee, O Lord."

Now his eyes were wet with tears, he was trembling like a leaf in the wind. He stood up, made straight for the outer entrance and passing out vanished into the darkness.

This scene was intently watched by all the *sadhus*. Ramdas turned to Ramcharandas and asked: "What do you think of it, Ram?"

"I did not bargain for this disturbance," he replied.

"Whereas Ramdas enjoyed it all—it was a play worth witnessing. However, what do you say to a move tomorrow?"

"Why not, by all means," quickly rejoined Ramcharandas.

Meanwhile a quarrel was in progress between the guest *sadhu*—who has sneaked away when Ramgiri was growing hot in his denunciation of his *guru*, and another *sadhu*, his neighbour, who appeared to have encroached upon his room during his short absence. They created quite a racket. The night was spent in pandemonium.

Ramdas and Ramcharandas abandoned the place next morning and came out of the temple. Having finished their midday meal at another devotee's house, who was also kind and hospitable, they wended their way to the beach-side. They discovered on the beach a vast enclosure and some buildings in it. On enquiry they learnt that it was a brahmachari ashram. Ramdas wished to pay a visit to the ashram and both of them entered the main gate, and going up to an open outhouse, took their seat on a low bench inside. Shortly after this, two young men clad in ochre-coloured robes put in an appearance and advancing towards the visitors saluted them.

Ramdas felt very happy to see them, because they looked so fresh and healthy—the light of *brahmacharya* beaming on their face. Ramdas expressed these feelings to them and inquired after their *guru*. One of them replied that their *guru* was away from Gokarn, collecting funds for the upkeep of the ashram.

He said: "We have a *goshala* which keeps us engaged in attending on the cows. We have also to work in the garden, as we are growing our own vegetables."

At the speaker's hint, the other brahmachari left them and returned after a few minutes with two aluminium cups full of buttermilk.

"Kindly accept this drink. It is prepared out of the milk of our ashram cows," they pleaded.

Ramdas and Ramcharandas with great delight drank the beverage which tasted like nectar. Then bidding the young men adieu, they left the ashram.

(iii) Fine Joke Indeed!

It was by now about four o'clock in the afternoon and they were on the sands facing the roaring sea. As Ramdas looked round, his eyes rested on the hill close by projecting into the sea.

Turning to Ramcharandas he said: "Ram, let us go up that hill and see if we can find a place to spend the night. From the top of the hill we can also have a fine view of the sea and land."

Ramcharandas agreeing, they walked in the direction of the hill. They had to wade through the waves on the shore—the waters were not deep. They reached the landing and climbed up a slope, and came upon a small reservoir of water, the supply of which was kept constant by a never failing spring. They drank at the spout the cool and sweet water and proceeded further up. Here was a small temple of a *Devi*. They were told by the *pujari* that the spring and the tank went by the name Ramatirtha. They proceeded past the spring higher still, Ramdas leading the way. A few yards further progress brought them on the top of the hill which was a vast undulating plateau. At a distance of about a furlong from where they stood, they descried on the highest level an oblong solid structure of stone. Ramdas silently tramped on towards it, closely followed by Ramcharandas.

When they reached the structure they found that it was cut out of one solid mass of rock—the roof was a low dome formed of the same rock as its thick walls. They entered the rock chamber. It was cubical in dimensions, the floor area being about ten feet square. The interior of the dome resembled a hollow cup. Entrance was from two narrow arched passages sufficiently high, directly facing each in the opposite walls.

"Ram," explained Ramdas to Ramcharandas, "we shall occupy this place for the nights during our stay in Gokarn."

Ramcharandas looked round and the prospect did not appeal to him, for a cold breeze was blowing over the spot from the direction of the sea.

"Cold will be extreme here in the night," he remarked.

"We are out to bear sufferings in the name of God," put in Ramdas, "at least that is the secret of Ramdas's life. Let us cheerfully face the situation in which God has chosen to place us."

He kept silent which meant half consent. After a time he suggested: "Swamiji, to provide against the cold let us at least have a fire. There is a little way off down on the slope—a grove of trees. We can collect from beneath them a sufficient quantity of dry twigs to serve our purpose for the night."

Ramdas consenting, both set out in the direction of the trees and collected in their cloths a pretty large quantity of twigs, and returned to the rock chamber.

Presently the sun was setting in the far horizon illuminating the hill and all the space around it with its golden effulgence. Ramdas stood still facing the sea. It was a gorgeous sight. A silent prayer went up from him to the throne of the almighty Lord of such lavish grandeur and beauty that it merged him in His blissful omnipresence. Night gradually threw her dark mantle over land and sea. He turned to the rock chamber. The breeze had now developed into a gale. Ramcharandas was engaged in making fire. On peeping into the chamber, Ramdas saw that the impatient boy had struck about half a dozen matches to light the dry twigs, and he had failed. The strong breeze which blew into the chamber would not permit of a fire. Even the twigs were swept away by the wind. The cold had also increased. Ramcharandas was not to be easily foiled. He struck match after match fighting at the same time to keep the twigs in their place, but all to no avail. He threw the empty match-box down in utter disgust, and turning to Ramdas, with a face completely devoid of cheer, cried vehemently: "Swamiji, no fire for the night!"

The gale had now developed into a hurricane. Even the cloth on the body could not be retained; the wind was icy cold. They sought refuge in one of the corners of the chamber. Even there the wind blew with all its force.

"Nice mess we are in," grumbled Ramcharandas, struggling to keep the coverlet tight on his body.

The humour of the situation struck Ramdas more than anything else, and he could not resist a hearty laugh.

"It is God's will, Ram. He means always well," consoled Ramdas.

The night was pitch-dark and escape from the place was out of the question. Ramcharandas drawing deep breaths crept towards Ramdas and, in the posture of a rabbit at feed, stuck close to him.

"Ram, what is the fun?" Ramdas asked.

"Fine joke, indeed!" he growled. "Rather than spend the nights here, also tomorrow and the subsequent days of our sojourn in Gokarn, we had better show a clean pair of heels to Gokarn as soon as the day breaks."

At this Ramdas rolled on the floor with uncontrollable laughter, and Ramcharandas had this time the good humour to join in the merriment.

"Tomorrow's question be for tomorrow," said Ramdas. "Now about the present. Keep on repeating Ram *mantram*. Since there is no fear of sleep encroaching upon the *japa*, let us fill the hours with the Lord's remembrance."

Although the lips were shivering with cold, the *japa* went on at an incredibly brisk rate. After all, every circumstance in which God places us has its own advantages, if we would only see. Morning dawned. As the first streaks of light from the rising sun dispelled the gloom of darkness, a voice filtered out from within the coverlet of Ramcharandas. He had fully enveloped himself with the cloth clutching at its corners with a dogged pertinacity.

"Swamiji, what does Ram want us to do next? If I may suggest...."

Ramdas anticipating what he was driving at, said: "Yes, Ram, we shall leave Gokarn and proceed still further north. Let us start."

At these words Ramcharandas well-nigh bounded from the corner in which he had cooped himself. Shouldering his arm bag and, taking up the water vessel or *lota*, he was ready in an instant to set out. They descended and came upon the main road. A ten-mile walk brought them to a spring and tank in the midst of a jungle. Here they made a halt and, with the provisions Ramcharandas carried, he prepared some *rotis* and *dal*. A bath at the cool spring and the simple fare refreshed them. They rested on the grass under the shade of trees till the rigour of the hot sun abated.

CHAPTER 5: GOA FRONTIER – SUPA

(i) Orange Robe Counts for a Badge of Thieves

Onward they went until they reached Karwar where they stopped at a *dharmashala*. Next morning they resumed their journey. About four o'clock in the evening they sighted a river which they had to cross. Here they witnessed a wondrous spectacle. Thousands of men, women and children had assembled on both the banks of the river and still larger numbers were streaming to the spot from opposite directions. On enquiry they learnt that in mid-river were half a dozen crafts floating, and a famous *sadhu* by name, Satchidanand, was in one of them, and the large crowds of people had come for his *darshan*.

Each pilgrim carried with him or her a coconut, perfumed pastilles or agarbatties and some camphor, as offerings to the *sadhu*. The devotion of these simple country-folk was indeed marvelous. Truly, faith strikes its deep roots more easily in the unsophisticated minds of villagers than in those of the so-called civilised people of the cities.

The river was duly crossed, and Ramdas and Ramcharandas reached in the evening a village where they stopped for the night in the temple of a goddess. Here they had come near the Goa province—a Portuguese territory, the frontier lying few miles off. Next day by noon they arrived at the frontier. When they were about to pass the gate, their progress was rudely arrested by a huge dog which stood on the path, barking ominously at them. From a hut, a few yards to the right a man called out: "You cannot pass unless you give an account of yourselves here come here, both of you."

Accordingly, they went up to the hut. The man, a Roman Catholic, was the gate-keeper. He explained, on seeing their clothing dyed in *gerrua*, that the goo government had issued a circular that no *sadhus* should be permitted to enter their territory.

"Why are they so hard with *sadhus*?" queried Ramcharandas.

"*Sadhus*! Fine fellows they are!" said the gate-keeper with a spice of sarcasm. "Recently a rich man's house was robbed by a wandering *sadhu* in Goa and the police are still after him. Hence the order for their exclusion. So you had better retrace your steps as you came."

"Brother, do you think," Ramcharandas asked, "that we belong to that type of *sadhus*?" and added: "We assure you we mean no ill to anybody."

"Mine is not to judge who is a true and who is a false *sadhu*. I am here only to obey orders. You cannot pass," he replied firmly.

Ramcharandas utilized to the full all his powers of eloquence and persuasion but in vain. For, he was looking forward most eagerly to a visit to the *Kula Devi* temple of Goa—the original temple which commanded allegiance from all Saraswats of Southern and Western India. After repeated appeals, the gate-keeper said: "I can allow you to go in on one condition and it is that you should change your clothes; i.e., give up the coloured ones for plain white, and pass off as ordinary travellers and not as *sadhus*."

Ramdas was all along watching the scene. Now Ramcharandas turned to him with a questioning look.

"Ram," said Ramdas, "it appears to be God's will that we should not step into the Goa territory. As regards changing the cloth, Ramdas for one, is not for it. He would prefer to go back rather than do anything against the will of God dwelling in his heart. Surely, it is His pleasure that we should turn back."

They left the place and before dark regained the village from which they had started, and spent the night in a small room of a rest-house. Ramcharandas was sorely disappointed. Next morning they went to the bazaar, where a kind shop-keeper, a Catholic, suggested that they might travel to the North, via Kadra, to which place they could go by a ferry-boat. The shop-keeper fed them with some biscuits and bread. Then going to the river-side they leapt into a large boat bound for Kadra. A fee of one anna each had to be paid which charge Ramcharandas met from the few annas he owned.

The boat moved on slowly with many a halt on the way because it was carrying also some cargo. However, at dusk they reached Kadra. As night advanced severe cold set in. Having found no room in the local rest-house, they sought shelter on the open verandah of the village headman's office, which stood directly facing the river. A cold breeze had by now begun to blow from the river. Here again the night was spent in a manner similar to the one in the rock chamber on the Ramatirtha hill.

Early at daybreak they started. Now they had to traverse a path along the gradual ascent of a hill through a dense jungle. Some travellers, who carried long sticks with a spear at one end coming from the opposite direction, warned them against wild bears. When the Lord's Name was on their lips where was fear? As usual Ramdas walked at a brisk pace with Ramcharandas close behind him.

At noon they reached a small village where a halt was made. After bath they ate a few boiled potatoes and, resting for an hour, started again. The jungle extended still further. They now travelled on level ground and legged on. At sunset they reached the village—Coomarwadi. That day from daybreak to sunset they had covered 36 miles—the distance from Kadra to Coomarwadi.

(ii) The Mother Cow

At Coomarwadi they found shelter in a spacious rest-house. Quite a crowd of villagers collected in the house to see the *sadhus* whose visit to that place was a source of great delight to them. They were extremely kind and hospitable—especially a school master who arranged for their milk etc., and also a fire in their room to keep off cold. Stout logs of dry wood were kept burning all through the night. The cold was intense. The same friend procured for them besides milk, boiled roots *kandamool*. The edible roots were very delicious. He said that the long tract of forest land from Kadra to Londa railway station, measuring some 70 miles, went by the name Dandakaranya. Sri Ramchandra on his way to Lanka had passed through this land. The place was *tapobhumi*. The Sadhu Satchidanand, whom they passed by beyond Karwar, had attained illumination in the forests close to their village.

A small ashram was being built at the back of the village over the *samadhi* of a saint from the funds collected by this *sadhu*. The schoolmaster friend promised to escort them to the holy place the ensuing day.

In the morning, as decided on the previous night, the kind schoolmaster took them to the ashram which lay only a short distance from the village. The ashram was in course of construction.

Nearby, there ran a small stream of water in which they had their bath. After finishing their dinner at the schoolmaster's, they returned to the *dharmashala*. This friend also presented Ramcharandas with some money which he accepted. Hundreds of visitors from the village poured on them their pure and simple love.

Next day they proposed to leave the place. Fifteen miles from Coomarwadi lay a village named Supa. Their next halt was fixed to be at Supa. The schoolmaster sent a friend in advance to inform the residents of Supa of their visit. At about five o' clock in the evening they reached Supa. They met hundreds of people on the outskirts of the village waiting to welcome the *sadhus*. They were duly escorted in procession to a Maruti temple on the bank of the Supa river. In the front room of this temple they were lodged. Arrangements were also made here to burn fuel to keep the room warm. On account of the continuous rush of visitors, Ramdas had to keep awake and sit up day and night. So he confined himself to milk diet only.

The following day was Shivaratri. There was a *murti* of Shiva in the middle of the river on a raised platform. Access to it was possible only by boat. The *patel* or village headman attended to the needs of the *sadhus*. He took them for the *darshan* of the *murti* on the river, and also to the noted temple of Sri Ramchandra. When they returned to their seat in the temple of Maruti, they beheld hundreds of people awaiting their arrival with offerings.

Thereafter commenced a regular flow of visitors. Both for the *darshan* of the *sadhus* and celebration of Shivaratri, thousands of people from the neighbouring hamlets had poured into Supa. The visitors continued to come throughout the night. When Ramdas expressed his wish to depart on the following day, the kindhearted *patel* pressed him to stay a day longer, and he yielded. On the last day of their stay, a limping elderly lady followed by her husband came to the temple with a cup of fresh milk. The time was morning. The couple sat beside Ramdas and made him drink the milk. The husband, an overseer's clerk, then told the story of the milk.

He said: "Maharaj, one day, about a year ago, we found at our door a cow which was reduced almost to a skeleton. She was so weak and emaciated from starvation that she was hardly able to walk. She dragged herself along with great effort. Seeing her pitiable condition my wife suggested that we might give her shelter and tend her, to which I agreed. The cow appeared to have been disowned and left at large. My wife took her inside the house and got her a place in our bedroom. She fed and nursed her with great care and love. The cow grew stronger day by day. We treated her as one of us. She could freely go about in the house. She was named Krishnabai. Her resting place in our room was kept scrupulously clean."

"Now we were occupying a rented house. Maharaj, we are poor but we know those who are poor and honest are very near to God. So we are happy. It happened that the owner of the house in which we lived came to know that we had given lodging to a cow inside the house. He protested against this and gave us notice that unless the cow was kept in a separate hut we should vacate his house. My wife felt this very much but would not part company with the cow. She could not even bear the idea of a separate shed for her. She appealed to me to look for another house. Kind Providence, without much effort, provided us with another house—the owner of which did not object to our having the cow inside the house."

"From about six months we have been living in the new house. Meanwhile, the cow, as though to reward us for our services, has presented us with a she-calf—to which she gave birth only yesterday. The milk we have brought for you is Krishnabai's first yield. We consider we have offered it to God Himself."

What wealth of love and devotion!

(iii) Love's Triumph

As the day advanced the rush of visitors increased. Presents flowed in, in abundance. The offering of coconuts swelled into a big pile. There was quite a shower of grapes, dates and sugar candy which Ramdas distributed freely amongst the innumerable village children. Ramcharandas heartily joined in this task. Now people thickly thronged the room, the doorway and outside.

At about ten o' clock in the forenoon two Muhammadan policemen came to the temple. They wedged their way through the crowd and, roughly brushing aside the people at the entrance, got into the room occupied by Ramdas and Ramcharandas. Their grisly beard and rolling eyes signified their stern mission. Stamping their boots on the ground they glared at the *sadhus*. One of them, taking out a note-book and pencil from his pockets spoke in a loud and commanding voice: "Are these the *sadhus*? Well, give me your address. Quick, we are in a hurry." Addressing Ramcharandas, "Here, come along—which is your native place?"

Ramcharandas was perplexed and turned to Ramdas for a hint. "Ram, don't hesitate," said Ramdas. "Give your name and tell him that you are a native of Mangalore."

His name and address were duly noted down by the policeman. Now he turned his gaze at Ramdas. "Your name!" he shouted.

"Ramdas," Ramdas replied.

"Native place?" cried he.

"The whole universe," rejoined Ramdas.

At this reply he stiffened and, working up his eyes into a ferocious stare, blurted out: "Beware, none of your jokes with me. Don't you see who I am? Which is your native place?" he repeated.

"The whole universe," Ramdas replied again.

Ramdas was cool and all smiles. The reiteration thoroughly roused the policeman. Stamping his right foot down with great force he growled: "None of your fooling with me! If you don't reply sensibly I will have you arrested and put into custody. Do you understand?"

Ramdas answered: "If you are so kind as to take this servant he would thank you indeed. It matters little where he thinks of God—a prison is as good a place as any other," and with a cheerful smile he added, "O God, Thy *lila* is wonderful. It is Thou alone who hast come in this form. The mother sometimes, when she wants to subdue the obstinate will of her child, puts on a frightening mask and pretends to be a hobgoblin. So long as the child is unaware of the fact that it is the mother who is behind the mask, it yields to fear, but when it knows that it is the mother who personates the frightful thing, instead of being moved by the sight, it pulls down the mask and reveals to itself her real identity. So it is with Thee. Thou art He—the Beloved of Ramdas. Thou mayest assume any disguise but he can see Thee through it. He is not afraid of Thee. He replies in the words which Thou Thyself hast taught him."

The policeman listened to him patiently. Ramdas was calm and cheerful as ever. A sudden change came upon the policeman. The ferocious look vanished from his eyes giving place to one of resignation. His hot and flushed face resumed its calmness and colour.

"Maharaj," he addressed Ramdas with eyes lowered and hands folded, "a thousand pardons for my folly. Without knowing you I harassed and abused you in strong language. The thing that disarmed me was your face which remained ever smiling, during all the time I was rating and insulting you. I behaved like a brute. Pardon, pardon I seek."

Then silently pocketing his note-book he proposed to depart with his companion. Ramdas then offered them each a piece of coconut and some dates as *prasad* which they received in all humility and left the place. Love triumphed over hate and harshness!

He subsequently learnt the cause of the policeman's rough behaviour. It appeared that two Hindu policemen had been sent before by the Police Station Officer for obtaining the addresses of these *sadhus*, but at the crowded entrance of the temple some visitors had persuaded them not to annoy the *sadhus*, assuring them that they were not ordinary *sadhus*, and so to demand their addresses would be an insult to them. So being Hindus these policemen desisted and returned without the information which they had been asked to procure. At this the Station Officer's ire was roused, and he deputed two Muslim policemen to carry out his orders. Hence their overbearing attitude.

The kind *patel* presented Ramdas with a long cloak of thick cotton cloth, as a protection against cold.

CHAPTER 6: ON THE WAY – NARSOBAWADI

(i) Muslim Friends

Next day the *sadhus* started from Supa. After visiting Castle Rock, via Londa, they came to Belgaum by train. From Belgaum they travelled on foot. They reached the town named Shahapur. Here the skill of Ramcharandas in cookery failed him. He served Ramdas with half-boiled vegetables with which he had a stiff fight before they could be driven down the throat. After a night's halt they proceeded onwards. While passing through this fertile country they came upon sugar-cane fields. The farmers were so kind as to invite these itinerants and offer them the cool drinks of sugar-cane juice and *jaggery*.

As they journeyed forward they had to traverse vast tracts of hilly land. Here a word has to be said about the condition of their feet. The incessant travel from day to day on hard and rocky ground had worn out their soles so much that there were on them blisters, sores and deep cults. Unmindful of this Ramdas was walking as usual at a rapid pace, but Ramcharandas grumbled and limped behind him. At noon they reached a town in the heart of an extensive and elevated plateau. For miles around the place there was hardly any human inhabitation.

On entering the town they procured sadavrat or alms of food-stuffs from the temples of the place. They fixed upon a small room of a rest-house on the road-side for preparing meals. While Ramcharandas was busy cooking, Ramdas, whom he would never allow to help in any way, sat in the open verandah. Presently a Muhammadan merchant came and took his seat on the edge of the verandah facing Ramdas. The Muslim friend broke into a lively talk, in the course of which he drew out many particulars about these wanderers. He was touched at the sight of the torn and lacerated feet of both. Love welled up in his tender heart.

He said: "It is my great wish that you should have your meal prepared out of my food supplies."

He took Ramcharandas to the bazaar, and returned with a rupee worth of first-class rice, possessing a natural sweet odour, *dal* and *ghee*. When the dinner was getting ready, the friend further said: "I have a mind to spend on you five rupees. The balance of rupees three and odd shall be utilized for your tickets on the motor bus that runs from here to Kolhapur. The bus starts in an hour's time. Your feet are so bad that I would you should go at least these thirty miles by bus."

God is indeed all love and compassion. The kind Muslim saw them safely seated in the bus and left them.

At five in the evening they reached Kolhapur railway station. On alighting from the bus, Ramdas enquired of the bus driver, who was again a Muslim, as to what was the railway fare from Kolhapur to Sheroi station the nearest halting place on the way to Narsobawadi. His reply indicated that for each the railway fare would be about a rupee. Now Ramdas made out that Ramcharandas possessed only a rupee and some small change. Of course, Ramdas was prepared to travel on foot if the funds on hand did not permit of travelling by railway. The bus driver was closely watching them. When he discovered that they did not possess sufficient money for two tickets, he slipped into Ramcharandas's hand a rupee saying: "Now it is all right for both. You may go by train."

Where did this spontaneous flow of help come from? Surely from the heart of a feeling and loving God!

It was quite dark when they reached Sheroi station. Narsobawadi was about nine miles from the railway station. After groping about in the dark for a place of rest they came to a Maruti temple in which they spent the night. Early morning next day they started and reached Narsobawadi before noon.

(ii) Sense of Possession—An Obstacle

Narsobawadi is one of the most important shrines in Maharashtra. It is situated on the banks of the river Krishna. On the bank on a higher level stands the temple of Dattatreya, the great avadhuta whose life and teachings speak of the loftiest spiritual realisation. He is verily an avatar of God. The *sadhus*, washing their clothes in the river, bathed in its cool running waters. Next they visited the temple wherein they had the *darshan* of Dattatreya's image of white marble, dressed and decked with diadem and ornaments. They sat for some time on the outer platform.

It is a custom here that the *sadhus* and poor devotees usually obtain their food by *madhukari*; i.e., by collecting doles of cooked food from four or more houses. At midday, along with others, Ramdas and his young companion also started for *madhukari*. They visited four houses and collected in all eight balls of rice and some *dal*. They came with the meal to a clean spot under the shade of a large spreading tree. The rice and *dal* were mixed in an aluminium plate which Ramcharandas carried with him. Often when alone, these *sadhus* would eat together from the same plate. So they started eating. Scarcely had they taken two or three mouthfuls when a huge kite from above swooped down and carried away in its talons two big lumps of mixed rice from the plate.

"This is very fine!" cried Ramdas. "How kind of the kite to join us in this precious feast!" They went on with the meal and finished it.

A little incident having a peculiar significance of its own deserves to be noted here. When the *sadhus* were jointly collecting the doles of *madhukari* from door to door, a critical devotee who was also one of the mendicants remarked: "Ah! there go the *guru* and his *chela*—a funny pair," pointing to Ramdas and Ramcharandas.

Ramdas lost no time in assuring him that they were not *guru* and *chela* but they were Ram and His servant—Ramdas being the servant and the other Ram.

Soon after meals the *sadhus* left Narsobawadi and travelled via Sangli and Miraj towards Pandharpur. Their feet were getting from bad to worse. Still they tramped on breaking journey only for the nights. Thorny trees and bushes are the characteristic features of this part of Maharashtra. The avenue trees on the road-side were full of thorns, bunches of which dropped on the way. In addition to the laceration and swelling of the feet sharp thorns now found their lodging in them. Ramcharandas cried out with pain whenever a thorn pricked him. Every time Ramdas would prescribe only one remedy and that was ceaseless remembrance of God by repetition of His divine Name which meant forgetfulness of the body and its pains. As they walked on Ramdas dilated upon the subject of complete dependence on God.

"Ram, you are carrying a bag containing cooking utensils and provisions. Now for cooking meals you have to go abegging for fuel, grains, etc. Ours is a life of freedom which should not be hampered by these encumbrances. God feeds birds of the air and beasts of the field. Would He not feed us also who have put ourselves entirely in His hands? Ours is to fill our mind with His remembrance, and have no care for anything else. So Ramdas suggests that the bag be given up and begging for food be also stopped. Then you will know how wonderfully God looks after us."

"What shall we do with the scrip and the things in it?" asked Ramcharandas.

"Wait, God will show the way," replied Ramdas.

Shortly after this talk they reached at noon a small grass hut on the road-side, occupied by a *sadhu*. Here they halted to slake their thirst from a neighbouring well. The *sadhu*, owing to an attack of some eye disease, was short of sight. He was very hospitable and kind. He begged that they might stop with him for the midday meal. They agreed. With the help of Ramcharandas the old *sadhu* prepared meals. It was now discovered that the *sadhu* had only earthen pots for cooking. The meal being ready the simple and devout *sadhu* first fed his guests, after actually worshipping them in the orthodox style. Then he dined upon the remnants of the food left by them. After some rest they prepared to start.

Ramdas turned to Ramcharandas and said: "Ram, God has not been slow in creating an opportunity for parting with the bag and utensils. He wills that we should hand over the bag to the *sadhu* here. The *sadhu* is in need of metal vessels. So leave the articles with him and also any money you possess."

Ramcharandas is a pure soul. He cheerfully resigned the bag to the *sadhu*. There yet remained with him a small bag which contained a black deerskin meant for Ramdas's use, which he would not give away, and a brass *lota* with a cup which he carried in his hand. As for Ramdas, in addition to the cloth with which he covered himself, the long coat presented at Supa lay across his shoulder.

The sun was still hot. They continued their journey. Going over a mile they took shelter for a while under a neem tree. Ramcharandas released the bag from his shoulder and laid it on the grassy ground. The *lota* was still in his hand. Ramdas spread the cloak on the ground and sat on it. Now Ramdas went on expatiating on the qualities of self-surrender.

"The sense of possession is a great obstacle to the realisation of God," he started. "The idea of 'I' and 'mine' must disappear entirely before the aspirant can find absolute freedom and peace in union with God. Verily, everything belongs to the Lord who dwells in the hearts of all creatures and things. Attachment to any external object narrows our vision, creates the ego and gives rise to the false notion that we are separate from God; i.e., from the universal life and spirit. So to reach the goal—eternal freedom and bliss—we ought to surrender up the ego, and behold all life and forms as the manifestation of the one underlying and in-dwelling Truth who is universal and eternal."

Ramcharandas listened to what Ramdas said with great concentration, and Ramdas was completely lost in the essential truth of what he was expounding. Then they got up and walked on. When they had travelled about a mile and a half it was discovered that Ramcharandas was not carrying the smaller bag.

"Ram, what became of your other bag?" asked Ramdas.

He looked surprised and retorted: "What became of your coat, Swamiji?"

The fact was both had forgotten to take the things from the place where they had rested beneath the tree.

"Wait here, Swamiji," exclaimed Ramcharandas, "it is not a long run from here. I shall return to the spot and fetch the things."

"None of it, Ram," replied Ramdas. "God thought that even those articles were unnecessary for us; so He has freed us from their possession. Then, why go in for them again?"

How unerring are the ways of the Lord! It was clear that the Lord wanted them to be all for Himself. His grace descends on His devotees for dispelling the shadow of I-ness—the root of all ignorance, in order that we may realise our perfect union with Him.

(iii) How God Feeds!

The *sadhus* proceeded until they reached a village where they stopped in the temple of Maruti. Their rule usually was to be satisfied with one meal a day. During the nights, Ramcharandas would take only light eatables when available. Almost every village in Maharashtra—for that matter in India—contains a temple and a rest-house near the temple. During this travel they invariably spent their nights either in a temple or a rest house. They started on their journey always in the early hours of the morning. At noon, next day, they were approaching a village where they would have to make their midday halt.

"Remember, Ram," hinted Ramdas, "that we are not to beg for our food. Leave the question entirely to the Lord. Let us simply go to a temple and remain in it engaged in the repetition of His Name."

Reaching the village they entered a temple of Vithal and took their seats in the verandah. Time was close upon 12 noon. A visitor to the temple, seeing the *sadhus*, asked: "Why are you sitting here idly? It is time for the midday meal. Go to the brahman locality where you can beg for your meals."

Ramdas did not reply, and Ramcharandas was also silent. The man walked away. Half an hour passed. Ramcharandas exhibited by his looks that he was growing skeptic. About ten minutes later another man came and put them the question: "Have you had your midday meal?"

Ramdas replied in the negative.

"How do you manage to have one?" was his next query.

"The Lord sees to it," was Ramdas's quiet reply. The words seemed to have gone home.

"The Lord you speak of bids me take you to my house for meals, but there is one difficulty. I belong to the tailor caste. I don't know if you are willing to take food at my hands," he said.

"You are the Lord Himself in the eyes of the *sadhus*, so there can be no objection," rejoined Ramdas.

"I am coming presently," he said, and disappeared only to return soon with a water vessel and a rope. He took the *sadhus* to a well, and gave them a bath. Then he led them to his house which was situated a few yards from the temple. They were welcomed by the tailor's wife and children with immense joy and kindness. With great love, the family served both with a sumptuous meal. They left the house and returning to the temple took rest for some time. Then they started again.

On the way Ramdas queried Ramcharandas: "Don't you believe, it was God Himself who fed us with such love?"

Ramcharandas was not in a mood to talk and kept silent. The day passed. Another day came. At midday they found themselves in another village. Here again they stopped in the local Vithoba temple. The sun had passed the meridian. Time flew swiftly and it was nearing one o'clock. There was no sign of food. Ramcharandas was getting impatient and restless. "Swamiji, Vithoba is very slow this time. I am afraid He has forgotten us altogether."

"Give up all thought of food, Ram. Simply remember Him. Let us submit to His will," exhorted Ramdas.

Waiting for some time more—seeing nothing forthcoming—Ramcharandas said that he would prefer to have a nap, and lay himself down. But while hunger was keenly gnawing at his stomach, where was sleep for him? He was now and again lifting the cloth from over his eyes and peeping in the direction of the street. Every moment he looked for the coming of food. It might have been two o'clock when Ramcharandas jumped into a sitting posture and cried out: "Swamiji, Swamiji, after all, Vithoba is coming. Behold, there He is in the street running to us!"

Yes, a dark-skinned man was hastening towards the temple. Coming directly to the *sadhus* he enquired if they had meals (as though he did not know it!). On receiving a negative answer, he left them and returned in a few minutes with two plates of food. Placing the plates before the *sadhus* he urged them to eat. Urging, of course, was unnecessary. They commenced to eat forthwith. Just then, a *kirtan* party of about ten also entered the temple. They brought with them cymbals, *mridang*, and *veena*. They sang choice hymns of Tukaram and danced as the meal progressed. What did all this show? God was not satisfied in giving them merely food for the body but had also arranged for a spiritual treat. Such are the gracious ways of the Lord!

In the Vision of God

CHAPTER 7: PANDHARPUR – SHETPHAL

(i) Dependence on God Is Liberation

Eventually they reached Pandharpur, the famous shrine of the deity, Vithoba. This was Ramdas's second visit to Pandharpur. They entered the city when it was quite dark. They wandered in the streets in search of a *dharmashala*. At last they met an old woman—a simple, pious soul.

"Mother, will you please point out the way to a *dharmashala*?" Ramdas asked her.

"By all means, mother," she replied. "Follow me, mother, I will lead you to it."

Both the *sadhus* followed closely at her heels. She went on speaking: "My mother Rukmini is so great, so merciful. She has assumed all forms. Everywhere I behold her. She is the man, bird, beast, stone, trees, stars, sun, moon. Oh! My mother has become all. How glorious She is! She is ever kind, kind."

This was the vision of the old mother. She saw her divine Mother manifested everywhere. They arrived at the entrance of the temple of Rukmini. Here the old mother prostrated on the floor, facing the main door and lay on the ground in a state of ecstasy for about five minutes. Then rising up she turned to Ramdas, and said: "Now, mother, come along, let us proceed."

After passing through many streets and by-lanes they at last came to a *dharmashala* in which they settled down for the night. Ramcharandas must have felt very hungry. He said he would go out into the city and get some food to satisfy his hunger. Soon he left and returned after about two hours. Early next morning they directed their steps to the Chandrabhaga river. Here Ramcharandas came out with an unexpected request.

"Swamiji! I want you to initiate me formally into *sannyas*. I would have my head shaved and clothes dyed in ochre before having ablutions in the sacred river."

Ramdas was taken by surprise at this strange proposition and replied: "Ram, your proposal is simply astounding. Understand, *sannyas* is not a thing which another can impose on you or initiate you into. *Sannyas* does not mean shaving the head and donning orange robes. It signifies a state of internal renunciation of attachment to the transitory objects of the world. Mere change of appearance and dress is hypocrisy, if in mind and heart you have not given yourself over to the Lord. If you feel a real mental recoil from the objects of senses and have an experience of ecstasy in the remembrance of the Lord who dwells in you and everywhere in the world, by all means make any change you like in clothing and appearance, provided you are sure that by such a change you are helped in your spiritual growth, and get fixed in your faith and conviction. Do not forget that the goal is the vision of God. Now your question is to be decided by yourself. Another cannot solve it for you. Ramdas can only lay bare his own experiences before you. He is wearing orange robes because the cloth is reminding him every time he looks at it, that he has consecrated his life in its entirety to the Lord. He belongs to none but Him who is infinite love and bliss. So consult the voice of God within you and act."

Ramcharandas heard in silence and did not thereafter press the point. They finished ablution in the river and sat for a time on the sands.

"Swamiji," suggested Ramcharandas, "we should not leave this place for at least four or five days. The plight of our feet is simply deplorable. They are quite unfit just now for further exertion."

In reply Ramdas had to speak at some length on a subject on which for some time past Ram was inspiring him to enlighten Ramcharandas: "Don't misunderstand Ramdas, take it, in the first place, that he is your best well-wisher. You have been exceedingly kind and good to him from the time of your contact with him. You have also suffered a great deal. Ramdas had warned you that to throw your lot with him would prove a painful affair. However, it is well you shared with him the discomforts and trials of the long journey from Mangalore to Pandharpur. Experience is a great teacher. Now you want Ramdas to remain here for some days so that the sores of their feet may be healed, while the voice within him bids him start from here before this very evening, and he has to obey the voice. Ramdas is not dragging you into another course of suffering when it is evident that you are not prepared for it. Moreover a travel by yourself will do you much good. Independent life will grant you increased faith in God. His constant remembrance will imbue you with a consciousness of strength and security. You will thus grow perfectly fearless in your complete dependence upon Him. Give up your slavish adherence to Ramdas. Roam about by yourself. God dwells within you. Be aware of His fellowship always."

Ramcharandas's attachment and love for Ramdas had reached such a degree that separation from Ramdas meant for him not an ordinary wrench, with the result that Ramdas's advice fell flat on him.

"Swamiji," he remonstrated, "I cannot bear to think of a severance from you. I simply cannot leave you."

His attitude was firm and unyielding. Time passed. Ramdas lapsed into a listless mood. The sun had risen high. Ramcharandas broke the silence.

"Swamiji, shall we go to any one of the *annakshetra*s? It is nearing time."

(ii) Why This Lamentation?

Both moved towards the city. Passing through the streets they came to the noted *annakshetra* where Ramdas had occasion to dine during his last visit to Pandharpur. The *kshetra* used to feed with rich meals six *sadhus* every day. When they reached the place Ramdas found seven *sadhus* waiting at the entrance of the *kshetra*. The manager of the house was to select six out of the waiting *sadhus*. Ramdas felt an inclination to leave the place, as he did not wish to stand in competition with others, in the matter of selection. He had done so on a former occasion at another *kshetra* of this city. But there was Ramcharandas who would, of course, refuse to take meals without him. However, he stayed.

At the usual time the manager turned up with a note-book to take down the names of the *sadhus* he would select for dinner he picked out six *sadhus* including Ramdas and Ramcharandas. The rest of the *sadhus* departed except one who appealed to the manager to take him also. The manager told him that he could not do so as the rule was only for feeding six. He also added that he had his chance only the previous day. Ramdas made out that the attraction for the *sadhu* was the luxurious food, served in this particular *kshetra*. When the *sadhu* saw that he pleaded in vain, he requested Ramdas to speak for him. Ramdas with folded hands prayed to the manager: "Ramji, do take him also. In a feeding house an extra man can be accommodated."

With a few sharp words the manager cut short his advocacy as much as to say: "Mind your own business."

The lucky (?) six were asked to enter the house. Ramdas walked in along with others, dazed and depressed. The extra *sadhu* was left behind.

Meals were served for six. The thought of the *sadhu* outside troubled him. The meal progressed. He could hardly eat anything. It was a dinner of sweet balls and cakes. After finishing the meal he came out and what did he behold? The extra *sadhu* was still sitting on the door-step. At the sight of him Ramdas felt as though an ice-cold douche of water were suddenly poured over him. His hair stood on end and a deep aching was felt at the heart as if from a stab. Calling Ramcharandas quickly to his side, Ramdas asked him if he had any eatables with him.

"Yes," he replied, "I have about half a seer of fried gram, tied up in my cloth."

"At once hand over the gram to the *sadhu* and also any money you possess."

He was given the gram and also a few annas, but Ramdas's heartache did not heal.

"Ram, God wills that Ramdas should leave this place immediately," Ramdas said.

He walked away from the spot at a running pace, Ramcharandas at his heels. His heart shook with an uncontrollable emotion. Tears began to flow down his cheeks in a regular stream and he wept and wept like a child. Ramcharandas looked at him with a questioning glance. Ramdas ran on until he reached the railway lines. Here he slowed down, but the weeping continued. In his intense grief he gave vent to the following words: "O Lord! Why didst Thou make him do this? Why didst Thou prompt him to eat a meal in the *kshetra* while a hungry man was going without one outside? Thou didst direct him to do a most ignoble and cruel thing." Then the rising tears overwhelmed him and he cried bitterly. Again: "O Lord! Why didst Thou not advise him in time, either to surrender his turn in favour of the extra *sadhu* or, at least, later on, to hand over the served leaf to the *sadhu*, and to move away from the place? Thou art, O Lord, his sole guide in all matters. Now what hast Thou made of him?—an utterly selfish fellow. How cruel of him to have behaved like this!" and he wept and wept.

"Swamiji," broke in Ramcharandas, "your grief is quite unreasonable, judging from your attainment and your attitude towards life. You have been all along hammering into me the truth that everything happens by God's will, and He means always well. So the way in which He made you act in this case cannot but be for good. Then why this lamentation?"

"You are perfectly right, Ram," Ramdas answered. "God does everything for the best. It was He alone who induced him to act as he did. Again, it is He who is making him feel contrition for it and complain and cry as he does."

Ramcharandas became silent. Ramdas was now walking recklessly on the loose gravel by the side of the railway sleepers. He might have covered about three miles when a wail from behind arrested his attention and progress. He looked back. Ramcharandas was discovered sitting a few yards in the rear on a sleeper.

"Swamiji, my feet are paining horribly. I cannot walk. The pointed stones are playing havoc with me."

Ramdas leapt on the smooth footpath down on one side and called Ramcharandas to follow him. They walked on at a slow pace.

"Ram," Ramdas said, "Don't you see at a short distance ahead a small railway station? Go up to it and board any train running towards Kurduwadi. Ramdas goes on his way alone. Why?—he is not alone; he has Ram in the form of the sorrow that had beset him to keep communion with. He will nourish it and enjoy its company. Go, be brave, God is with you. Make for the North. See places and gather experience. But one thing, do not forget the Lord's Name. Taking His name gives you the consciousness that He is ever with you."

While Ramdas was thus instructing him, a train was sighted at a distance, coming towards them from Pandharpur.

"Here the train is approaching. Run up to the station without any delay and reach it in time to catch the train," directed Ramdas.

Now Ram's will did prevail, forced by necessity. Most reluctantly Ramcharandas took final leave of Ramdas and moved towards the station with as much speed as he could summon under the circumstances.

(iii) God Makes Amends

Ramdas saw Ramcharandas get into the train. Now he wandered aimlessly. Often he burst into tears at the thought of the dinner. The grief dulled his brains into a state of apathy. He found solace only when he withdrew within himself and entered into the silent depth of his being. During the night he stopped in the rest-house of a small way-side hamlet. One of the villagers offered him some eatables which he did not accept. He was not in a mood to eat anything.

In this manner he roamed on for two days, without food, from village to village. He did not care for food nor would he touch any when it was placed before him. He was now feeling a sort of searedness at heart. His feet were swollen due to thorn-pricks and blisters. In this condition, on the third day, he arrived at a village named Shetphal. He went into a temple of Maruti and laid down his tired body on the hard stony floor and, covering it with his only cloth, rested. The time was midday. He had hardly taken half an hour's rest when he heard the footsteps of somebody entering the temple. He had screened his head with the cloth. The visitor having performed his *puja* of Maruti for about five minutes approached Ramdas and asked: "Who is that?"

Ramdas remained silent. Then he pulled off the cloth from Ramdas's face and questioned: "Why are you lying down here like this? Have you eaten anything for the day?"

Ramdas simply replied: "It is the will of Ram that he should not eat," and was covering himself again when the stranger caught Ramdas by the arm and drew him up into a standing posture. He was a tall and strong man. Then he almost dragged Ramdas forcibly with him saying: "Ram's will is that you should take meals in my house. Come along. I will not allow you to starve."

Ramdas had to submit. The kind friend's house consisted of a long narrow room facing the street, the front portion of which was used for a shop of sundries and the back as residence. He led Ramdas directly into the interior where a young girl was busy preparing meals.

"Child," he said to his daughter—such she was, "serve this *sadhu* first. Cook for him some soft *rotis*, for he is without any teeth."

Spreading a gunny bag on the floor he made Ramdas sit down on it.

He said: "Maharaj, I am a poor petty shop-keeper" and pointing to the girl, "this is my only daughter, I have no wife. The girl is unmarried. So you will have no objection to eat from her hands."

It was evident from his words that there is a certain class of *sadhus* who are opposed to eating food prepared by married women. However, Ramdas neither belonged to that class nor did he favour the views held by them on this point.

Now the food was ready. The kind shop-keeper mixed in a brass plate two *rotis* with a quantity of *dal* curry converting the whole into a soft mixture. Then he fed Ramdas with his own hands, just as a mother would feed her child.

"Lord, art Thou making amends for what Thou madest him do in the *annakshetra* of Pandharpur," thought Ramdas. What love! What kindness!

Taking leave of the shop-keeper Ramdas rambled on and, after passing many a village, came to Anjangaum. Here in the street a man directed him to the house of the Kulkarni—a village officer.

Ramdas entered an old-fashioned square block of buildings and took his seat on one of the verandahs. He saw two men sleeping on the opposite side, their bodies concealed beneath white sheets. There was none other visible outside on the verandah. The time was about ten o'clock in the morning. As was his wont, he was humming to himself the Ram *mantram*. The sound of the divine Name seemed to have roused one of the sleepers from his slumber. Rubbing his eyes he sat up awakening the other also. The latter went inside while the former looked at Ramdas and asked him what he wanted.

"Ram has directed His servant here for *bhiksha*," Ramdas replied.

These words seemed to have produced an electric effect on the questioner. He invited Ramdas to a seat on a mat. Now Ramdas went on talking in a spontaneous flow about the glories of God and the power of His Name. Soon after, they were joined by the other friend. The first one was the Kulkarni, the master of the house, Madhavrao by name, and the second was his family priest Govind Joshi, a resident of Upalai, a village about three miles from Anjangaum. At the first sight, both of them fell in love with Ramdas. Madhavrao was overflowing with kindness. He drew Ramdas's leg towards him and fell to rubbing the soles.

"The feet are not only worn out and swollen, but also a number of thorns have stuck in," he remarked.

Joshi and Madhavarao worked briskly on Ramdas's soles with two needles, and pulled out all the thorns. The friends observed the deep cuts and also that the skin at place had worn out so much as to reveal the flesh.

Madhavrao procured some *ghee* and filling the dents with it, also smeared it all over the soles. Then he took Ramdas for a bath. He applied oil all over his body. Ramdas had no bath for several days and exposure to the heat of the sun during the day and to the cold in the night, and starvation into the bargain, had turned the skin dry, dirty and coarse. With all tenderness Madhavrao washed the body with hot water and soap. While the bath was in progress Ramdas reminded him of Sri Krishna and Sudama.

With all love the Lord had tended and nursed the emaciated body of His devotee!

Bath over; he was fed with a simple and wholesome meal. The day and part of the night passed in talks on devotion and lives of the saints. The ensuing day Govind Joshi proposing to take Ramdas to his village, Upalai, left Anjangaum with him, and reached the village before dark.

Govind Joshi was a poor old man. When Ramdas entered his hut, for such it was, he was welcomed by Joshi's wife, as if she was awaiting his arrival. As he sat down she began to massage his legs and talk to him so familiarly that she appeared to have known him for years. A simple, childlike, splendid soul she was!

He remained in Upalai for a couple of days. The villagers came to see him in hundreds. Joshi and his wife, who had also a son, treated him with great hospitality. Indeed, hospitality is the pride and glory of Hindu households. He gave the devout couple the names Atrimuni and Anasuya, and their son Datta, and their house Atri ashram.

From Upalai he went to Angar to which place he was invited by Balwantrao, the Kulkarni of the village. Here again he received kindness and love from all alike. With the aid of an escort he next proceeded to Mohol, where he lodged with Janardan Pant, a schoolmaster and a great devotee. He was pure-hearted, and was also a sincere seeker of Truth. Here Ramdas met another schoolmaster, Babooji, a devout soul, who arranged for his journey to Sholapur by motor-bus.

With Babooji he arrived at Sholapur, and put up in the local Panduranga temple. He stopped here for a day and left for Bijapur.

CHAPTER 8: HUBLI

(i) The Heart of the Mother

Ramdas once again started alone on foot. He walked on and on through fields, meadows and woodlands. About a week's *satsang* with the village devotees has assuaged his grief brought on by the incident at *annakshetra* at Pandharpur. The Lord had brought it about in his own mysterious way. He is truly the great healer of our sorrows. As he journeyed on, he came upon an elevated land, covered with a wild growth of shrubs. When he was passing through it a wish to smoke crossed his mind. He smoked tobacco sometimes but did not carry any with him. Where was the possibility of having a smoke in the midst of a jungle, a solitary place far away from the hunts of men? But, for the Lord nothing is impossible.

Suddenly, a man from behind the bushes came on towards him. Looking at him, the first thing Ramdas noticed was a *bidi*—a country leaf-cigarette—poised on his ear. The man quietly removed the *bidi* from the place on his ear and offered it to Ramdas. He would not touch Ramdas. He dropped the *bidi* into his hands. Then, taking out from his pockets two smooth black stones and a bit of cotton wool, and striking the stones one against the other, he produced a spark that set fire to the piece of cotton. He handed the burning cotton to Ramdas on a leaf. Ramdas lit the *bidi* and began smoking. All this was the work of a few seconds. So far, Ramdas had no talk with him. They walked on the same road, but he maintained a certain distance.

Ramdas broke the silence with the question: "Why do you, brother, shrink away from Ramdas and walk so far apart?"

"O master," he replied, "I am a pariah by caste. How can I go very near you or touch your sacred person?"

No sooner did Ramdas hear this, than he rushed towards the pariah and, throwing his arms round his shoulders, embraced him.

"You are not an untouchable. You are Lord Vithoba Himself. Are you not the same *dhed* who ran to the rescue of Damaji Pant, the noted saint of Mangalvedha?"

He laughed knowingly and recapitulated the incident.

"Now, master, where are you going?" he asked.

"Don't know where," was Ramdas's reply.

He said: "Two miles from here, there is a tiny village on the banks of the river Bhima. Do proceed to that village. It has only one shop. You go and stand before the shop, and the Lord will attend to all your needs. I can escort you as far as the outskirts of the village. My way lies in a different direction."

Ramdas acquiesced. There was no further talk. He was merged in a blissful abstraction. The village loomed in view. He made straight for it. He was now only about fifty yards from the village-huts when he turned back to look for his strange companion. The so-called pariah had disappeared.

The sun had risen right overhead. As advised by him, Ramdas stopped before the only shop of the village. An unusually stout woman was attending to the customers with the help of a young man. The mother saw Ramdas. Suddenly her maternal heart went out for her child, the lone wanderer. Brushing aside the customers, who had crowded in front of her shop, she beckoned him with both hands to draw near.

"Son, son," she said to the young man by her, "first give this *sadhu* something to eat."

Soon, in the outstretched cloth of Ramdas rained a pretty large quantity of parched rice, *jaggery*, dates, etc. The stout mother jumped down from her seat in the shop and called for a blanket. With the blanket she stepped as quickly as her heavy body could permit to the verandah of Mahadev temple on the other side of the road, opposite to her shop. Spreading the blanket on the floor, she invited him to take his seat. He was duly installed on the blanket. She got also a *lota* of drinking water for him.

The mother squatted opposite to him and tenderly urged him to eat. But this time a number of small boys had gathered round him. He distributed the major portion of the eatables among the children and partaking himself of some of them drank the water.

"Sadhuji," the mother then said, "the river Bhima is nearby. Have your ablutions in the river and then return. I shall either take you home or fetch the meal over here."

He got up and traced his steps to the river where he washed his clothes and had a bath. Returning he found the mother waiting for him.

"Come along, sadhuji." she said, "I am taking you home." He followed her. The sun was very hot and the ground was burning. He had nothing either to cover his head or to protect his feet. About half-way the mother realised the situation. Her soft heart felt the pangs of remorse.

"What a heartless creature I am!" she cried, I ought not to have taken you out in this hot sun. I could have brought meals for you in the temple. You have no sandals on your feet. The ground is hot like a frying pan. Fool, fool that I am!"

The mother had, of course, leather sandals on her feet. Hence her remorse was all the more poignant.

"Never mind, mother," he assured her, "your child is accustomed to the heat."

"Come on, let us walk quickly. We have only a short distance to cover," she said.

Her unwieldy body swayed to and fro as she hastened on. They arrived at the door of her cottage, but to her great dismay it was locked, for her daughter-in-law had gone to the neighbouring house closing the doors. She had the key. Her return would surely take some time, and Ramdas meanwhile had no place to stand but in the sun.

The mother called out "Lakshmi! Lakshmi!" Drawing deep breaths she spoke: "What shall I do? You have to stand barefooted on the burning sand!"

She found a way out. She lifted up Ramdas bodily from behind—he was a feather-weight to her—and held him standing on the lower crosspiece of the door-frame, and bawled out for her Lakshmi who at last came running. She could not resist giving a bit of her mind to the daughter-in-law, and a goodly slice it was!

Inside the house, he sat on a plank offered by the mother. At her bidding the girl Lakshmi placed before him a plate of food which consisted of two thick *rotis* and *dal* curry. He started eating.

He found the *rotis* stiff and unyielding to the fingers. However, he attempted to crush and mix them with the *dal*. They would not submit to the process. He put some pieces of *roti* with *dal* into the mouth and tried to swallow them. Of course, it must be noted that he had at that time hardly three or four teeth in his mouth. So mastication was out of the question. He swallowed the *rotis* piece after piece until a big-sized one got stuck up into the throat. Suffocation ensued. He tried to push down the bit or throw it out by a cough. The mother watched the struggle and light dawned on her.

She exclaimed: "Cursed be my wits! Lakshmi, are you also so blind? The *sadhu* has no teeth, and you have served him with cold and stiff *rotis*. How can he eat them? Now look! his throat is choked. Good Lord! Lakshmi, you are perfectly heartless. You have not offered him even water to drink. Quick, quick, give him some water. See, his face has turned red; he is gasping for breath!"

Immediately a tumbler of water was placed in his hands and he drank. The piece of *roti* was washed down the throat. Now the mother pounced upon the plate of food and, while taking it away, said: "This is going to do you no good." "Lakshmi," she told the girl, "prepare at once fresh *rotis*. Make them soft. Look to it at once."

While Lakshmi was busy, the mother milked the she-buffalo, standing in the square-yard in the centre of the building. In a few minutes she heated the milk. Lakshmi's trained hands made soft *rotis*. The mother crushed two of them in the hot milk in a plate. The softened meal was then placed before him.

"Sadhuji," the mother then appealed, "you must forgive me. I am after all a foolish and useless woman; forgive me. The food is now all right; please do justice to it."

After dinner the mother accompanied him back to the temple, and taking leave of him returned to her home. Such was the heart of the mother. He directly started on his journey and walked until sunset when he reached a way-side village.

(ii) Is There God?

Thus from village to village he travelled on. Again the plight of his feet grew worse due to incessant walking. He was now nearing Bijapur. On leaving a village in the afternoon, he had covered a distance of about three miles. It might be past three o'clock when he met some men coming from the opposite direction. They stopped him and enquired whither he was going. He, of course, told them that he wanted to reach Bijapur. One of them warned him that he would not reach Bijapur before dark, as he had to traverse yet twenty miles, and there was not a single village on the way where he could halt. In darkness he might lose himself and be caught in a jungle. He suggested that Ramdas might start early next morning. Meanwhile he might give them the pleasure of his company for the night.

Ram takes care of His child at every place!

He retraced his steps with these kind friends and spent the night in their village. Early next morning, long before dawn, he started again and covered about ten miles by forenoon. Here he found on his left a big area of cultivated fields. In the middle of the farm was a well from which water was being drawn by pikotah for irrigating the fields. A farmer and four bullocks were at work. Ramdas went to the well to quench his thirst and did so by descending into the well. When he came up, the driver of the bullocks beckoned Ramdas to go to him. He made Ramdas sit beside him in the cool shade of a large tree near the brink of the well. Ramdas smoked a few puffs from his *chilam* of tobacco.

"Now, I have a question to ask you," he said. "Are you sure, sadhuji, that there is a God? For my part I have strong doubts about His existence."

Ramdas replied: "God is there for them who have faith, and not for them who have not."

"Listen then to my tale," he continued, "my occupation as you see is agriculture. I have a family consisting of my wife, three grown-up daughters, a son and his wife. The green fields around this well are of our cultivation. All the members of the family are toiling in the fields from morn till night. These four bullocks also work for long hours for irrigating the fields. We are all actively at our tasks throughout the year. With all this you will be surprised to learn we are not having sufficient to procure bare creature comforts." Pointing to his daughters who had by now assembled near Ramdas, he added with a bitter tone: "Look, maharaj, at the clothing of my girls. They are in rags. You say there is God. If there is one, He must be very cruel; if cruel He is not God."

"For Ramdas," Ramdas replied, "God is not a mere matter of faith or speculation. He is a certainty. In spite of what you say of your conditions, Ramdas can assure you that God is, and He is all kindness and love. We are not to judge His existence by the material comforts we obtain in life or by the absence of such comforts. The trials and sufferings we undergo are necessary for our spiritual growth. For the sake of God, princes have renounced kingdoms and have taken to the beggar's bowl and rags. Life is misery for him who knows no contentment, however affluent he may be in circumstances. A poor man content in his cottage is far happier than a monarch discontented in his palace. Contentment is a gift of God which we get through faith and submission to Him. God never means us harm. Our want of belief in His benevolence is the source of our misery. You may say yours are hard facts that sternly face you. They are nothing when you assign them the right value, and thus understand the true purpose of life. Verily, God is not for him who frets and fumes. Brother, do not give way to despair. Submit to His will and all will be well."

He heard Ramdas in silence while his eyes were filled with tears. Ramdas left him and proceeded on his journey.

Ramdas's mind set to work: whence is the misery of the agriculturist? No doubt, one suffers by one's own actions or karma. How did karma in this case work through external causes? The middleman and the moneylender were certainly the ostensible causes of the poor man's ruin. The heartless exploitation by the tradesman on the one hand and the greediness of the moneylender on the other must have crushed him down. The ceremonies and festivals, over which large sums of money are wasted, should have driven him into the clutches of the latter. Added to these, there are the caprices of the weather and seasons and, to top it all, heavy taxation.

At midday he arrived at a village where, under a grove of trees, there was a tank in which he had his bath, and then his *bhiksha* in the neighbouring village. Resting for an hour in the cool shade of the grove he continued his journey. Bijapur now lay only at a distance of six miles which he made up by five o'clock in the evening,

He went to the house of Shankarlal Oza, the kind merchant-friend whose hospitable roof had sheltered him, when he had visited Bijapur on the previous occasion. At his pressure Ramdas stayed with him for two days. He and his ailing wife proved by their kind attention that they were the very embodiments of love. Shankarlal noticed the condition of Ramdas's feet. They were so much swollen that they appeared to be stricken with elephantiasis. He spoke with great concern about this matter in the presence of his friends who, touched by his reference, raised a contribution for his railway fare to Hubli. Ramdas had told him that he was to go to Hubli.

(iii) You Are in the Upper Story, Eh!

On the third day he left by the evening train. After purchasing the ticket Shankarlal found a balance of eight annas left from the amount subscribed by the friends. He urged Ramdas to accept the money and, in spite of his protest, he slipped it into the pocket of a long coat Ramdas was then wearing, as also the ticket.

Night passed, the day dawned. The eight anna change was jingling in his pocket. He did not know what to do with it. Till then he was not in the habit of carrying money, because he needed none. The Lord looked after him in all matters without giving him occasion to handle moneys. When the train stopped at a station, a blind beggar got into the compartment. Here was a way out of the situation, thought Ramdas, and handed the beggar a two-anna bit, reserving the balance for any beggars who might come along at subsequent stations. Station after station passed and yet no sight of a beggar.

At about ten o' clock, the train steamed into the Hubli station. Alighting, Ramdas came to the road. What to do with the money? The question was insistently forcing itself on his mind. Ram bid him to go straight to Ubhayakar's house and in the afternoon to Sri Siddharudh *math*. He walked as far as the gate of Ubhayakar's house but no, he could not enter the gate with money in his pocket. He wanted to dispose of it but there was no way. However, he turned and retraced his steps towards the station, and half-way stopped on the road. "O! what to do with the money?" No beggar was anywhere visible. He thought of flinging the coins into the ditch on the side of the road but again no, Ram wanted him to hand over the money to somebody. Where was that somebody? What a problem! O Lord!

The matter may have only an ordinary significance for the reader, but for Ramdas it was a momentous and crucial question. Once again he wended his way to Ubhayakar's. When he was nearing the house he discovered a sweeper, just emerging from the compound of the municipal office: "Here is Ram, come to the rescue", muttered Ramdas. Ramdas passed the loose coins to him which he accepted with great joy. A weight seemed to have been lifted off his heart. Now he entered Ubhayakar's house.

Subbarao Ubhayakar—a saintly soul—gave him a glad welcome. All the members of his household were overflowing in their kindness to him. The old saint showed him the Krishna temple, built through his effort and initiative. The *murti* of Sri Krishna—of marble, pure and white as snow—is a charming figure, indeed a beautiful work of art.

Returning home the saint asked Ramdas: "Where do you wish to go next from Hubli?"

"Bangalore," was the reply.

"Well, our people are leaving the day after tomorrow for Bangalore. You may accompany them," he suggested. Ramdas agreed.

In the afternoon he visited the famous *math* of Sri Siddharudh Swami. This was his second visit to the *math*. Sri Siddharudh was the same great personality that drew thousands to his feet.

Ramarao—son of Shivarao Chandragiri who has since assumed *sannyas*, attended on Ramdas with all love, a noble son of worthy parents.

Ramdas stayed at the *math* for two days. In the nights he took shelter in the veranda of the *samadhi* temple. On the second night, a little after dark, a devotee of the *math* came to him.

"Would you like to have something to eat?" he asked.

Now Ramdas was in no mood to eat, nor was he in the realms of duality.

"To whom are you putting the question?" was Ramdas's counter-stroke.

"To you, of course," he replied pointing his finger at Ramdas.

"Is there such a thing as you and I when all is one?" Ramdas rejoined. "Is not all that is visible like the snake in the rope, like the son of a barren woman, like the horns of a hare, like a flower....."

"You are in the upper story, eh!" he remarked as he took to his heels and disappeared from view.

Next day Ramdas returned to Ubhayakar's house and left Hubli by the midday train in the company of the ladies of the house. These mothers looked after him very tenderly on the way. They reached Bangalore early morning the following day.

CHAPTER 9: AGASTYASHRAM – MANGALORE – ERNAKULAM

(i) Ten Days' Fast

With Ramdas the kind mothers motored to their house, a fine little bungalow. He remained for half an hour in the house. Ram bid him slip away from the place. He rapidly legged it towards Malleswaram. His idea was to go to Bhawanishankarrao whom he had occasion to meet at Kundapur, the previous year. Ramdas reached Malleswaram, an extension of the Bangalore City, studded with hundreds of newly built, neat houses. Now which was Bhawanishankarrao's house? He had never visited the place before. Ram must guide him, and He did.

After passing through a network of side-streets he came unconsciously to the very street in which Bhavanishankarrao lived. Again a few yards from his house on the road, he met Bhavanishankarrao's father who guided him to the house. Bhavanishankarrao and other inmates of the house hailed him with unfeigned joy.

Here he met again Sitabai—now the widowed wife of the late Dr. Umanathrao at Kundapur. Over a year ago Umanathrao had shuffled off his mortal coil. Sitabai's devotion and renunciation were remarkable. In the house there was regular devotional music in the evenings, and reading of Ramayan in the afternoons. Bhavanishankarrao and his sister Sitabai took prominent part in them. Now Ramdas's diet had changed to milk and fruit. He stopped with these kind and devout people for four days. He felt a distinct call from Kirimanjeshwar, beyond Kundapur, which also goes by the name of Agastyamuni Ashram.

On the fifth day by the night train, Ramdas started from Bangalore and arrived at Kasaragod the next evening. Here he availed himself of the *darshan* of his *Gurudev* and other devotees of the place. Stopping here only for a day he proceeded to Mangalore. His goal was Kirimanjeshwar and he must reach it at the earliest possible time. He had come to know that he was to undergo at that place a long fast. After passing through Mangalore where he paid a flying visit to Mother Rukmabai, he proceeded straight to Udipi and thence hurried on to Kundapur. Here he was put up at Ram Bhatji's dispensary. The following day he crossed the ferry and reached Kirimanjeshwar.

Directly on arrival at Kirimanjeshwar, he had a dip in the tank opposite to the temple. Drinking some water he rambled till evening in the extensive woods, in the midst of which he discovered a tiny temple of a goddess. The temple consisted of an inner, dark, narrow chamber where a stone image of the *Devi* was installed, an airy and neat front room, with a smooth and shining floor, and an outer verandah. For ingress there was only one low door. He decided to occupy the front room of the temple. His possessions were only one coverlet and two *kaupins*.

His mode of life here was something like this: three baths—morning, noon and evening—in the tank, and water drink also at the same time from it. The tank lay about fifty yards from the *Devi*'s temple. Nights were spent in the front room of the temple and days in the woods. The inner shrine was lit for some hours in the night with an earthen coconut oil lamp. Every evening a mother of the neighbourhood would attend to this. She must have been lighting the wick at an earlier hour in the evening, for he saw the light on return to the temple after dark. One day she happened to be late and he was already in the front room. She came as usual and entered, but at the sight of the figure of Ramdas, dimly visible in the darkness of the room, she cried out with raised hands in terror and ran away frightened. Thereafter, she stopped away entirely and the lamp remained unlit.

Sometimes of an evening, Ramdas would take a walk to the seashore. He found there a huge rock jutting out into the sea. Getting a perch upon it he would watch the giant waves, lashing against the sides of the rocks. The sea-crabs would be playing about him and white seagulls flew overhead. The long belt of sand glistened in the sun. At the close of the day he would meet with a most imposing sight when the sun was setting. The gradual descent of the flaming orb into the bosom of the blue sea charmed his sight. Here, despite the loud roar of the waves, he experienced a calmness that passes expression.

Day after day went by in silence, water-fast and baths in the tank. Some villagers hearing of his fast attempted to break it by making him drink milk and eat fruits. But he was indifferent alike to the offerings and the offerers. One day, in his aimless rambles, he approached the bazaar where most of the shops were owned by Muslims.

"Who is that man?" a passer-by enquired of a merchant pointing at Ramdas. The merchant replied, his forefinger touching his temples, "He is a half-crack."

Ramdas heard the remark and going up to them corrected the merchant's words: "No, brother, not merely a half-crack; why not say a full-crack which is the truth?"

He was taken aback at this sudden and strange confession. Ramdas passed on.

Now, what was the effect of the fast on Ramdas? After the third day he began to feel physical weakness. Again three days more, his power of locomotion diminished considerably. He could not walk to the tank at a stretch. He had to sit down at several stages on the way. There was also a marked emaciation of the body. Eight days later, he could only crawl on all fours for his bath and drink. He used to lie flat on his back on the smooth floor of the room. While trying to rise he would feel as though the back was glued to the floor. He was awake all the night and day. There was no sleep for him. Except extreme physical weakness he had no pains in the body. The mind was filled with perfect peace. Remembrance of God had become a settled and continuous function of the mind. When sitting quiet or lying down, he was often totally unconscious of the body.

On the ninth day, the village *munsif* of the place, a Saraswat, visited him at the *Devi*'s temple with presents of milk and plantains. Ramdas gave him to understand that he had no command from God to eat. He had no idea as to when the fast would be broken. However, he assured the friend that when he did so he would first take food in his house. The day for it was not far off. The fast ended two days later. Ramdas trudged on to his house which was over a mile from the temple. He had to take long rests on the way.

The kind friend, so also his faithful wife, considered it a happy privilege to feed Ramdas. After the meal, taking permission of the kind host, he left for Kundapur in a motor-bus, the friend having secured for him a seat in it. He reached Kundapur by evening.

(ii) Well-Baked Brick!

In Kundapur, Ramdas as usual occupied the upstairs of Ram Bhatji's dispensary. The medical friend treated him with utmost regard and love. He preferred to live on milk diet. Here he met Ramcharan, a well-educated Northern India *sannyasi*, who was taking keen interest in the social amelioration of the masses. The *sannyasi* conceived an unusual affection for Ramdas and got attached to his person.

Ramdas's stay in Kundapur was during the mango season. The friends who visited him gorged him, as it were, with mangos of the season. He was also made to drink large quantities of milk. The result was, he got an attack of diarrhea accompanied by fever. The fever completely took hold of him.

His body had already weakened owing to the ten days' fast. Instead of feeling discomfort, during the fever, he passed through an experience of indescribable ecstasy. Even when the fever was at its heights, he danced through sheer joy.

Ram Bhatji growing anxious proposed to treat him with medicine. Ramdas did not like that the fever should be driven out in that manner. He had accepted the fever as a welcome guest, and in its company he was having a blissful time. "Why should you," Ramdas replied, "think of ejecting it? Let it take leave of Ramdas at its own sweet will." Ramdas would have nothing to do with his medicine. The fever raged on for two days. On the night of the second day, he expressed to Ram Bhatji his desire to leave Kundapur on the next day.

"No, Ramdas," he remonstrated, "I cannot allow you to start until the fever has abated."

Meanwhile Ramdas had received an invitation from Sanjivarao of Ernakulam asking him to go over to him at once. He tried to persuade Ram Bhatji to yield to his plan but he was adamant.

"Well, can you permit him to start in case Ram frees him from fever by tomorrow morning?" Ramdas tempted him.

Ram Bhatji snapped. "By all means," he replied at once. He felt Ramdas's pulse; the temperature was at its height. He left him and went down. His anxiety drove him up again at about four in the morning to see how Ramdas fared. The friend examined him only to find that the fever had entirely left him. His thermometer indicated normal temperature. He was glad but was also surprised and puzzled, and at last submitted: "God's ways are wonderful!"

"You have to keep your word, Ram," Ramdas said. "You should arrange to send him off by the earlier motor-bus to Mangalore."

"All right," he said lowly.

At eight a.m. Ramdas was sitting in the bus, running towards Mangalore. The *sannyasi*, Ramcharan, accompanied him. He passed Udipi and reached Mangalore in the evening. They stopped at Sitaramrao's for a couple of days.

During this time, Ramdas and Ramcharan had an invitation for dinner at the house of M. Ramrao, father of Mother Rukmabai, who was then living with him. Ramcharan was unaware of the old relationship. They went and were treated with loving hospitality both by the mother and her father. When departing, the mother asked when she would have the next occasion to see Ramdas. He simply replied, "Ram's will." At this, her eyes were filled with tears. All the time Ramcharan was observing the scene, and a member of the house meanwhile apprised him of Ramdas's relationship with mother, in his former life. Ramdas and Ramcharan left the house and while on the road, Ramcharan, shooting a curious look at him, remarked in a humorous vein: "You are not an ordinary *sadhu*. You are a well-baked and hardened brick."

What he meant by the observation was significant!

The stay in Mangalore being over, he caught the mail train to Ernakulam.

(iii) All Credit Is to the Lord

Sanjivrao, a brother of Ramdas by past life, was at the station to receive him. He was lodged in a small room in Sanjivrao's house. His diet consisted of milk and fruit. He stopped in Ernakulam for about two months.

Here he got, through Sanjivrao, books from the public library, and became a voracious reader. He perused over fifty volumes of religious literature. Amongst them he read the bulky volumes of Max Muller's translations of the upanishads, bhashya of Shankaracharya, etc. Every day some prominent *vakils* and officers paid him visits. The outstanding event of his stay at this place was the feeding of the poor. It came about in the following way.

One day, when the friends had, as usual, gathered in his room, he threw a suggestion that they might join together in providing the poor people with a meal. They instantly took up the idea and raised amongst themselves the necessary funds to feed about a thousand people. Amongst the contributors special mention has to be made of a generous soul, who wishes to remain unknown, who bore the major share in this charitable service. He is so simple and unassuming that he performs all acts of benevolence without anybody's knowledge. Truly he has been able to realise the saying: "The left hand does not know what the right hand gives."

The ensuing Sunday was fixed for the function. V. Iyer, a *vakil*, undertook to manage the affair. It was monsoon time and the rainfall was heavy and continuous. The compound of the local Registrar's office was decided upon, as the place for cooking and distribution of food. By beat of tom-tom, the public were informed of the approaching event. By Saturday night, all things were got ready and the preparation of meals commenced. The meal was to be a plain one. The sky was dark with heavy clouds and rain was pouring in torrents. In the night V. Iyer came to Ramdas and complained: "Swami, there is no sign of abatement of the rain. If it also continues tomorrow the feeding would be impossible."

When a thousand had to be fed, of course, it could not be done except in the open air.

"Don't be anxious, Ram. Leave the matter to God," Ramdas assured him.

The preparations were ready by daybreak but the heavy rain continued. In the early morning V. Iyer again visited Ramdas—this time with a look of despondency.

"What shall we do?" he exclaimed.

"We do nothing," remarked Ramdas. "The Lord does everything. It was through His will that we arranged the whole matter. It is for him to see that it is carried out successfully."

The hour had been proclaimed as eleven o'clock in the morning. Nine o'clock struck. It was raining as heavily as ever. Half past nine, quarter to ten and the rains still persisted. Now the strange thing happened. The clouds slowly dispersed. The rain stopped and the sun shone out. Within half an hour in the cloudless sky appeared the bright sun as though he belonged to summer. Exactly at eleven o'clock the food distribution commenced. Ramdas was escorted to the spot to witness the function. The sight of the vast crowd, inside and outside the compound and on the road, thrilled his heart. The feeding went on uninterrupted by noise or confusion. The almighty Lord ate through thousands of mouths.

One of the friends counted the number of people fed and found them to be nearly three thousand. Food intended for a thousand sufficed for thrice the number. Having eaten their fill many people had also carried the food to their homes.

If there is one country in the world, where beggary and starvation have taken hold of vast masses of the population, it is India. The remedy lies in the eradication of ignorance and selfishness from the minds and hearts of the exploiters, within and without. The case of the exploiter is in fact harder than that of the exploited. For, he sows a karma which will bring dire retribution on himself. An inner realisation of equality, based upon a purified vision and awakening of the spirit of sacrifice through love and compassion, can alone bring peace, harmony and happiness into the world.

All classes of the needy and poor were fed including the so-called untouchables. By three o'clock the serving of meals ended; all were satisfied to the last man. When the compound was free from crowds, quite an army of crows descended to the ground and cleared off the scattered remnants of rice. Indeed, in the economy of nature, crows play the part of scavengers. So the compound was, as it were, swept clean. The wondrous thing was that at four o'clock the clouds gathered again in the sky, and it began to rain in right earnest. Ramdas returned to his room. The feeding of over three thousand poor people, from food prepared for one-third of the number and the cessation of the rain for six hours, during the time of food distribution, were really glorious works of God.

He recollects that some people who witnessed and took part in the function lauded Ramdas for its success. He unceremoniously stopped them with the remark: "All the credit is only to the Lord. Don't make much of the servant for what the Master has done."

CHAPTER 10: KALADY – KASARAGOD – IN THE STEAMBOAT

(i) Birthplace of Sri Shankaracharya

One evening Ramdas was unusually inebriated with ecstasy. In the presence of some friends, of whom V. Iyer was one, he talked with great fervour on the universal aspect of God. Iyer was eagerly listening.

"The whole universe is permeated through and through with God," said Ramdas. "The visible and invisible worlds are all He—as manifest and unmanifest. There is nothing and none but He. All, all is He. Such is the truth. Where then is the idea of 'I' and 'you' – 'mine' and 'yours'. All are He and His."

In this strain Ramdas spoke on. The words flowed out of him in an irresistible stream. Ramdas saw that a blissful light had filled the room and the people sitting in it were like faint shadows. The compelling words and the atmosphere produced a marvelous effect on Iyer. His face was aglow with a strange lustre; his eyes became moist.

"I have, then, no relations and no home; where shall I go to?" he cried out with a touch of deep pathos and anxiety. He trembled and swayed on one side. The other friends at once held him and led him out of the room and made him lie down on a bench. He fell into a trance-like sleep for half an hour, after which he returned to outer consciousness. Now, coming to Ramdas, he said: "Swami, I am going home."

"So you have recovered the ego which you had lost for a while," Ramdas observed with a smile. He nodded in the affirmative and left.

Sanjivrao and the other friends proposed to take Ramdas on a visit to Kalady—the birthplace of the renowned Shankaracharya situated at a place, a few stations from Ernakulam. A party of about a dozen people consisting of the friends and their families started. They reached the small village in due time. They directed their steps to a garden on the bank of the Alwaye river where stood two temples—one of Sharada and the other of Mahadev. In front of the temples there was a raised plastered pedestal—rectangular in shape—signifying the spot where the remains of Shankaracharya's mother had been interred.

The surrounding scenery was most fascinating. It possessed all the beauty, simplicity and calmness of the countryside. Around the shrine, groves of jack-fruit and mango displaying exuberant verdure, and the tall coconut trees shooting up from their midst to a great height and nodding their crested tops in the breeze, yielded shade and coolness, and cast a bewitching spell on that sacred spot.

An aged brahman—an old resident of the place—recounted to the party the ancient episodes and legends relating to the place, and also told them of the visits of eminent personages to the shrine. He said that he had the unique privilege of serving Swami Vivekananda when he came to Kalady, during his itinerant life.

The well-known incident in Shankaracharya's life which determined his adoption of *sannyas*, when he was still a boy, took place on the bank of the river Alwaye. The boy Shankara was insisting upon his mother to permit him to live a life of utter dedication to God, instead of the ordinary life of a householder, immersed in the worldly cares and desires. The mother would not agree.

One day, when the mother had taken the boy as usual for a bath in the Alwaye river and he was knee-deep in water, a crocodile suddenly caught his leg and began to drag him away into the deep waters.

"Mother, mother," he called out, "a crocodile has caught hold of my leg and is dragging me down into the depths of the stream. I will presently sink and be devoured by it. There is only one way to save me and that is, if you would consent to my adoption of *sannyas*, the crocodile will set me free."

The situation alarmed the fond mother. In an instant she saw she would rather prefer her only son alive, though a *sannyasi*, than he be a prey to death in the guise of the crocodile.

"All right, my so, I agree," she answered desperately.

The crocodile disappeared leaving the boy to come up free and safe. The mother kept her word and Shankara became one of the greatest philosophers the world had ever produced.

The party had their ablutions in the sacred river and, after *darshan* of the deities in the temples, returned to their rooms in the *dharmashala* where dinner was cooked by the mothers to the accompaniment of devotional songs. Altogether, it proved to be a most blissful trip. By evening the party reached back Ernakulam.

During his stay at Sanjivrao's, he and his wife and children treated Ramdas with all love and kindness.

(ii) Untouchability—A Tar Stain

Ramdas now felt a call from Kasaragod and wrote to Anandrao about it requesting him, at the same time, to arrange for an abode in a solitary place for his stay. In due course he arrived at Kasaragod and was put up in a thatched hut on the Pilikunji Hill.

Here he lived on goat's milk and plantains. The *raja yogi* again came to him and together they danced in the nights to the chant of Ram *mantram*. Later on, a new *sannyasi* from Buntwal also joined them. In the evenings, with other friends from the town, he would also dance in ecstasy to the music of God's Name in the front yard of the hut.

Ram willed that a dinner should also be given to the poor of Kasaragod. In this instance Ramdas worked actively for collection of funds. He visited the most prominent men of Kasaragod for contributions and also accepted small sums from the poorer classes. On request Anandrao managed the affair. The hillock of Ramgiri was selected for the feeding, and a Saturday was fixed for the purpose.

Due preparations were made, and by midday nearly a thousand people assembled at the appointed place. The principal classes represented were cobblers, pariahs and fishermen. Although these classes were looked upon as untouchables by the higher castes, even as among themselves they had distinctions. They sat down for meals in three different lines. The meals were served. Ramdas felt that he should also join them in the dinner. So he took his seat in the line of the pariahs. The *raja yogi* and the new *sannyasi*, seating themselves in front of Ramdas, ate with him from the common leaf. Whilst eating thus the precious gift of the gods, he experienced inexpressible joy.

For Ramdas there was no distinction of any kind. The idea of superiority and inferiority on any ground is born of utter ignorance. Wars, strife, and misery in the world are all there because of these inequalities. While the inner spirit of all life and manifestation is one, where is room for caste, class, creed, race and colour distinctions? The darkest blot on the purity and beauty of the universal life is "untouchability." It is like a tar stain on a white canvas. Harmony, peace and freedom can be attained only by the realisation of the inner unity of all life, and equality in all its outer expression.

Ramdas's Gurudev who lived with his son Anandrao, one day came to the hut on the hill with great difficulty. The infirmities of age had told upon his otherwise strong constitution. He brought with him a tender coconut and some sweet home-made bread. Ramdas was continuing to live merely on milk and fruit. Gurudev insisted on his eating the bread. Ramdas begged of him to be excused. Being touched, and tears welling up in his eyes, Gurudev urged him again to eat the bread, but he was firm and would not have it. He however drank the water of the tender coconut. Soon after, Gurudev returned home. During this incident there were in the hut about half a dozen visitors. Now one of them, affected by disappointment felt by Gurudev, said with a touch of reproach in his voice: "You say he is your Gurudev and still you refused to eat the bread offered by him with such love; how do you explain this?"

"It is He within and without;" Ramdas replied with a smile, "from without He says, 'Eat'; from within He again says, 'Don't eat.' Ramdas always obeys the voice within."

"Why should He speak externally in a manner different from your inner prompting?" interrogated the friend again.

"That is His wonderful *lila*," Ramdas answered.

The friend did not press the matter further.

One day Ramcharandas came suddenly, as if he dropped from the clouds. He carried with him a well-tanned tigerskin and a *yoga-danda*. He said that, after wandering over some parts of Northern India, he felt a keen longing to see Ramdas again; so he was here.

"Swamiji, I have brought this tigerskin for you all the way from Jhansi where a devotee presented it to me. Pray accept it," said Ramcharandas.

"Ramdas does not need it, Ram," replied Ramdas, "since he goes about with only one cloth. You may keep it for yourself."

"It is intended for you and you must have it," he urged. "I shall carry it for you. I shall follow you wherever you go. I am not going to leave you this time," he added with emphasis.

"What is that wooden cross for?" asked Ramdas.

"It is for *dhyan*. It is great help for sitting erect during meditation," he explained.

"As you are young and energetic, you should not depend upon this contrivance. It is an unnecessary encumbrance. Give it up," Ramdas suggested.

But Ramcharandas argued at great length in favour of it and showed his aversion to renounce it. However, he sought to stick to Ramdas again. At this time, Gurudev fell seriously ill and, at the juncture, Ramdas received a letter form Madhavrao of Anjangaum, inviting him to attend a religious festival to be shortly performed in his house. It was a nine days' festival. The letter was soon followed by a telegram, stating that the presence of Ramdas at the function was indispensable. He felt the urge from within but hesitated owing to the serious nature of Gurudev's illness. Now he placed the matter before Gurudev himself, begging him to decide.

"Would you leave your Gurudev in this condition?" he questioned.

Ramdas could no longer resist. He abandoned the idea of responding to the call from Anjangaum. Madhavrao was informed accordingly by wire. In reply he again telegraphed that Ramdas should not fail him. This time he left the question entirely to Ram, remained calm and waited. Ram has always His own ways!

The following day, when he went to see Gurudev, he found him not only feeling much better but also strong enough to move about. Ramdas asked him if he would approve of his leaving for Sholapur District. He willingly gave his consent.

Lord! Thy ways are indeed mysterious!

(iii) Goa Policeman—Smitten

Before starting, Ramdas made Ramcharandas understand that no purpose would be served by his accompanying him. But he was stubborn, as ever.

Ramdas reached Mangalore in the evening, of course, followed by Ramcharandas. It was decided to start by steamboat leaving Mangalore the next day for Bombay. From Kasaragod arrangement had already been made for Ramdas's boat ticket. He advised Ramcharandas to stay on the Kadri hill and devote his time to meditation and communion with God. But Ramcharandas would not submit to the advice. He left Ramdas in the night with the object of collecting the amount necessary for his boat-fare. At Sitaramrao's where he had halted, Ramdas's aunt by the former life, coming to know the situation regarding Ramcharandas, paid twenty rupees for his boat-fare. She pressed this amount on Ramdas, asking him to hand it over to Ramcharandas who, she fully believed, would meet him at Mangalore Port. The mother was a kind, pure and noble soul.

Next day, he looked for Ramcharandas at the harbour but could not find him. He got into a steam-launch and crossing the river reached the boat, and went aboard. What was the first thing that met his gaze as he stepped on to the deck? Our ubiquitous friend Ramcharandas was quietly sitting in a corner on a bench with his tell-tale tigerskin. Ramdas went and sat beside him. The *yoga-danda* had disappeared.

"Swamiji, I came by an earlier launch," he said smiling.

Ramdas then handed to him the money presented by the kind mother.

The boat sailed and reached the port of Marmagoa the next morning. There was a halt of about two hours at this port. Meanwhile, some Goa policemen entered the ship for inspection. One of these, while passing through the deck, cast a casual glance at Ramdas. Ramdas was a deck or third-class passenger on the boat. The sight of Ramdas seemed to have produced an extraordinary effect on him. He stopped and, leaning against the railing opposite Ramdas, began to gaze intently on him. The policeman could hardly take his eyes off Ramdas who was also watching his strange behaviour. About half an hour later he came to Ramdas.

"Follow me, both of you," he said.

They obeyed. He escorted them directly to a Hindu restaurant in the harbour, ordered tea and eatables for both, while he sat on the bench in front observing them. He paid the charges of the tiffin and they followed him back to the deck. Except for the first few words that he spoke, he was perfectly reticent. Thereafter, again until the steamer whistle sounded announcing departure from the port, the policeman was quietly looking at Ramdas from his position by the railing. He was somewhat disturbed when he had to leave the boat. With many a backward glance he finally jumped down on the dock. The steamboat left the port.

Intimation had been sent from Mangalore about the date of Ramdas's arrival in Bombay. In Bombay he found himself in the blessed home of Sanjivrao—blessed because both Sanjivrao and his wife were embodiments of love. They simply deluged him in their overflowing love. Many neighbours in the *chawl* and others from outside came to see him and engaged him in talks on the greatness of God and His Name. Evenings were spent in devotional music. Throughout his stay at Sanjivrao's he enjoyed pure ecstasy.

Time to leave Bombay at last came. He started with Ramcharandas by the night train and reached Angar station in the afternoon next day. At the station he was greeted and embraced with exceeding joy by Govind Joshi who was waiting with milk for him. After partaking of the milk they proceeded on foot to Anjangaum. Before sunset they reached the outskirts of the village where in advance hundreds of the village people were eagerly looking forward to his arrival. He was taken in procession to the house of Madhavrao who welcomed him with rapturous delight.

CHAPTER 11: ANJANGAUM – ANGAR

(i) An Honest Rebel

Ramdas had a unique experience during the visit to the Sholapur District. The reader may remember that Ramdas had visited Anjangaum once before a year previously and had been the recipient of great kindness and hospitality at the hands of the devotee, Madhavrao Kulkarni. The celebration in his house was of navavidha *bhakti*, that is, nine kinds of devotion. The devotee who is a high-class brahman had engaged the services of over a dozen brahmans to perform the various functions of the sacred festival. Besides Ramcharandas, Ramdas was later joined by Bhavanishankerrao of Bangalore.

Ramdas arrived at Madhavrao's house only two or three days before the close of the festival which had a run, as usual, for nine days. Since his arrival, Madhavrao's house had a rush of visitors to see Ramdas. Now the attention of most of the inmates of the house and the people of the village was diverted from the religious ceremony towards him. The brahmans did not at all like the turn of events. They remonstrated with Madhavrao against the undue prominence paid to a wandering *sadhu*. Poor Madhavrao was in a sore fix! His love and regard for Ramdas would not diminish in spite of the repeated onslaughts of the brahmans against his fidelity to Ramdas.

The inevitable last straw was not lacking in the present case. The situation was growing every moment more and more tense. At the request of Madhavrao and other guests, Ramdas was made to distribute *prasad*. The brahmans demurred to accept it from the hands of Ramdas. However, some of them most reluctantly received it from him, and there was an honest rebel. His name was also Ramdas, hereafter referred to as 'brahman Ramdas." He stood up and defiantly spoke out: "I refuse to debase myself by taking *prasad* from his hands," pointing towards Ramdas.

This outburst stunned Madhavrao and the whole congregation, as though a bomb had suddenly exploded in their midst. Ramdas only smiled and told Madhavrao not to mind the brahman's words and there was no harm done. The other brahmans, discovering in brahman Ramdas an intrepid leader, thenceforth gathered round him and raised a united standard of revolt.

Madhavrao was thoroughly frightened. He feared that the celebration which went on so far smoothly would be upset. He understood Ramdas perfectly. He took care to see that Ramdas was not brought into contact with them, so that there might be no room for discontent or disruption. While previously at dinner Ramdas and the brahmans were sitting in one line, Madhavrao now divided up the ranks and so arranged matters that no invidious distinctions were palpably noticed. However, the celebration terminated without further unpleasantness, although the brahmans maintained the tenseness of the situation to the end. Ramdas was all the time an amused witness of the whole game. The matter, however, did not stop here.

Ramdas had meanwhile received an invitation from a neighbouring village. The brahman Ramdas who came to know of it proceeded to the village in advance and warned the devotee, who would have Ramdas at his place, not to take him there. He told the devotee and others that Ramdas was an impostor in the garb of a *sadhu* and, for all that they knew, he might be an outcast and was not therefore worthy of being associated with the brahmans of their status. Fine things about Ramdas indeed!

But the devotee Balwantrao of Angar—Angar being the name of the neighbouring village—would not be prejudiced. He had on the last occasion come in touch with Ramdas and had been all kindness and love. He ran down to Anjangaum and took over Ramdas to Angar. Nearly fifty villagers from Anjangaum followed him including Madhavrao and many members of his household. Divine love was fully at work in the hearts of these simple and pure country-folk. It was a walk of about three miles. Ramdas and party duly reached Angar.

The brahman Ramdas was there. He came and sat near Ramdas. His looks were full of contempt and his manner cold and overbearing. There was now quite a crowd around Ramdas. The brahman asked Ramdas a question: "What is *panchikarana*?"

Ramdas replied that he was not learned and his knowledge of such matters was very little. At this he laughed derisively and then raising his voice told the assembled people that they were veritable fools to have come to pay homage to an impostor whose only qualification was his colossal ignorance. The hearers did not relish this pointed attack and hung their heads down. As for Ramdas, he broadened his usual smile and remained perfectly calm and quiet. Hundreds of visitors streamed into Balwantrao's house, and afforded Ramdas the happiness of their company. Their love for him was marvelous. The brahman chafed and burned with the fire of jealousy. The day passed. Next day there was a big feast. The brahman openly refused to join it.

In the evening he proposed to perform a *harikatha*. On such occasions Ramdas was made to sit in a prominent place, and the performance would take place in front of him in the midst of a vast multitude. So also did it happen this time. The brahman Ramdas, who brought about the situation to serve his purpose, indirectly levelled at Ramdas a most spirited diatribe. After dilating at length upon the qualities of a hypocritical *sadhu*, he concluded the *katha* with this peroration: "Vagabonds and frauds are abroad, pretending to be *sannyasins* and *sadhus*. Beware of them! Only dull-headed people run after them, make much of them and eventually fall an easy prey to their wiles and machinations."

Ramdas was not any the worse for a fresh baptism of abuse. God so willed it and he submitted, his equanimity undisturbed.

(ii) A Wonderful Transformation

Two days later, there was another dinner arranged by a pious merchant of the place. In those days Ramdas was mostly on milk-diet and would take a little food once in two or three days, along with the devotees at their dinner party. On this occasion also the brahman Ramdas had been invited. But he failed to turn up at the appointed time. All the guests waited for his arrival. He was, however, not to be seen. The merchant started to fetch him and after a search found him, but could only persuade him to attend the feast after a great deal of entreaty. At last he came. His face was charred; his looks were haggard and eyes sunk in their sockets. It was evident that envy was fast consuming him. On seeing him come, Ramdas felt really glad and asked the merchant to serve him first.

"No, no," he shouted, "I am not going to take any meals today. I have vowed to fast."

Ramdas begged of him to take at least some sweets. He pondered for a while and to the infinite delight of Ramdas and all, consented to have sweets. Accordingly, some sweet balls or *ladoos* were placed before him. Ramdas requested all the guests not to start eating until the brahman had commenced to eat. He had about three or four *ladoos*. All hail, a God of love, Thou hast at last triumphed!

It was observed that the brahman did not feel quite at ease. The kindness and love offered in return for harshness and hate on his part almost overpowered him. He left the scene suddenly. That evening at four, a *harikatha* function was arranged by a devotee to be performed at his house by an old *haridas* of the village. Of course Ramdas attended it with Ramcharandas and Bhavanishankerrao. Now the last two would not, in the ordinary course, remain in the town after five in the evening, but would run up to the neighbouring hillocks and spend the nights together in meditation and repetition of Ramnam. When *kirtan* was still going on they left the place at the usual time and disappeared on the hills.

A mysterious event now took place. Some devotees of Anjangaum (the last village visited by Ramdas) who were away when he was there, but who had seen him at the time of his visit over a year before, were hastening to Angar with the object of meeting him. On their way they happened to pass the hill on which Ramcharandas and Bhavanishankerrao were sitting. Strangely enough, they beheld, as they approached the hill, three men sitting in a line, Ramdas in the middle and the other two, one on each side. They were not surprised. They thought that he in company with the two friends must have gone to the hills for an evening spell. They did not like to disturb the trio, since they discovered them in a state of meditation.

They proceeded straight to Angar hoping to meet Ramdas on his return at nightfall. As they entered the village, they heard the sound of cymbals at the *kirtan* party, and led by the sound they came to it. But what was their astonishment to see Ramdas sitting in the assembly attending to the *kirtan*, while they had clearly seen him on the hillock which they had passed a little while ago! He was on the hills and at the same time at the *kirtan* party too! They were bewildered. They related the matter to the brahman Ramdas who formed one of the assembly at the performance. This miraculous incident produced no small effect on the brahman.

At about eight o'clock that night he met Ramdas at a milk party. His attitude towards Ramdas had, in the meantime, entirely changed. He fell at Ramdas's feet and wept bitterly. He condemned himself in scathing terms and begged piteously to be forgiven. Ramdas asked him what the matter was. It was then that Ramdas heard from his lips the whole story of the double personality. While Ramdas listened his hairs stood on end, his eyes were filled with tears, and his entire frame thrilled with indescribable ecstasy. He only muttered: "It is all Ram's glory. His ways are inscrutable." From the ensuing day, until Ramdas left Angar, this brahman participated heartily in all the festivities and closely associated himself with Ramdas. He evinced a marked love, kindness and regard for Ramdas. What a wonderful transformation! Certainly, there is no more potent force than divine love!

CHAPTER 12: UPALAI – PANDHARPUR – IN THE TRAIN

(i) The Devil Exorcised

From Angar, Ramdas went to Upalai with Ramcharandas and Bhavanishankerrao and many others and was put up in Govind Joshi's house as on the previous occasion. Here again he observed a water fast for three days. Vast crowds of people gathered around him. Govind Joshi's wife was greatly disturbed over the fast. Her motherly heart ached for him. She made several attempts to persuade him to take at least some milk during the fast but he would not take it. Govind Josh in his overflowing love presented Ramdas with a red woollen shawl and a cap of the same material, for the time was winter and the cold was severe. The red shawl he gave away to Ramcharandas. On the fourth day the people of the whole village arranged for a feast in Vithoba's temple. People of all castes joined in the dinner.

On the morning of the day fixed for the feast, Maruti, a boy who was famous for his mastery of the Gita and for his wonderful intellectual powers in expounding it, requested Ramdas to pay a short visit to his house. Ramdas agreed and in the company of about fifty devotees went to his house. Along with others Ramdas took his seat on the open verandah. Now a woman of the house was brought out and made to sit in the yard below, in front of him.

"This woman," Maruti said, "is possessed by a devil; please have pity on her."

Ramdas looked at her. Her long loose hair was hanging down over her shoulders and arms in a state of disorder, her face was unusually red; her eyes wide open and revolving in a weird manner. When his eyes met hers she suddenly gave vent to a shrill shriek and began to tear at her hair. Now he asked the assembled devotees to sing the Name of God in chorus. The measured cadence of the sound saturated and thrilled the air. At this the woman became wild and furious and, standing up, uttered scream after scream. After the lapse of a quarter of an hour the singing was stopped and the woman squatted down. Maruti had adorned Ramdas with a flower garland. Taking it out and going to the woman, as inspired by Ram, he threw the garland around her neck, and leaving the place returned to Joshi's house.

In the evening, after the feast, Janardan Pant, who had met Ramdas at Angar, performed a *harikatha* in front of the temple, a large crowd having collected to listen to him. When the performance was in progress, Ramdas observed an old man pushing through the crowd, carrying in his arms the woman who was supposed to have been possessed by the devil. He took his seat with the woman in the temple at the back of Ramdas. The *harikatha* lasted for two hours and he retired to the small room which he occupied in Joshi's house. Here came the old man with the woman. She prostrated before Ramdas and sat beside him. He saw a great change in her appearance. A settled calmness was on her face. Her eyes were lowered and there was a look of resignation in them. Her lips were moving automatically as it were, and a low sound was heard to be issuing from them. Ramdas listened and found her repeating in a low tone "Ram, Ram, Sitaram," the names sung in a chorus in her presence in the morning. The old man who accompanied her spoke: "Maharaj, soon after you left us this woman who is a relation of mine fled from the house, and ran like a galloping horse, myself and another pursuing her. We had a hard race. For two miles she ran and then she stopped. However, we overtook her, gasping and exhausted. She cried out in a loud voice: "Oh! I cannot stay there any longer. I am unable to bear the presence of that saint (meaning Ramdas). I am going away."

Then it appears the old man asked her: "Are you sure, you are leaving for good? Say that on oath."

Then she said: "Mahadev, Hanuman, Rama are my witness. I am going, I am gone." So saying she collapsed and fell down unconscious, and the old man with the help of others had to convey her home. From this time she had become her old self again, but she was still weak.

For Ramdas devils are none other than the evil passions that range in the human breast. They take possession of persons and dominate over them. The only way to drive them out is to awaken in their mind and heart the purity, light and glory of the indwelling Truth. As at the appearance of light, darkness vanishes, so in the presence of the pure spirit of God, the evils of the mind disappear, softening the heart with love and joy.

Some of the devotees desired that Ramdas should meet them again in Pandharpur on the Kartik Ekadashi fair, an important annual festival of that shrine, where they would all assemble for the occasion. So Ramdas and others including Janardan Pant started from Upalai, and on the way halted at Shetphal where they stopped for the night. *Bhajan* and *kirtan* were performed by the villagers during the night. Ramdas had also the opportunity of again seeing and embracing the shop-keeper who had fed him forcibly during the last visit.

(ii) God Is Love—In Our Heart

The party arrived at Pandharpur on the day previous to Ekadashi. Ramdas proposed to occupy the sands of the river Chandrabhaga, and accordingly they settled down on the bank, a few yards from the river. The night was cold. Chill breezes were blowing towards them from the river. The night was spent in wakefulness. Next day, the day of the festival, one by one, the several devotees whom he had met in their villages, began to pour in. Here he came in touch with a new devotee by name Prem Singh, a Rajput. He was fascinated with Ramdas and closely stuck to him. Ramdas observed fast on this day, taking only a small quantity of milk.

As the day advanced, the crowd of pilgrims on the banks increased rapidly. Nearly a *lakh* of people studded both the sides of the river. The vast crowd was divided into groups and some of them had tents pitched on the sands. From various camps hundreds of lights gleamed in the dark. The name of 'Vithal'—the deity of Pandharpur temple—rang forth from thousands of throats, while dancing and singing also commenced in many camps. Large crowds squatted round the central figure of a saint performing *harikatha*, preaching to the masses the value of devotion. This kind of preaching to the accompaniment of music started at several centres.

He attended one of these performances. He listened for about half an hour to the discourse of Dada Maharaj, a saint from Satara and famous in Maharashtra. Of what he said, one thing struck Ramdas as pre-eminently true; viz., "It is not that we have to love God but to realise in our hearts God who is love."

When Ramdas had returned to his seat, one of the devotees coming to him said: "Maharaj, throughout the day there was a huge rush at the entrance of the temple for the *darshan* of Vithoba. So access to the temple was difficult. Now, it being midnight, the way to the inner sanctum of the temple is clear. If you wish I can take you for the *darshan* of Vithoba."

"Ram," Ramdas replied, "Ramdas is witnessing already in front of him Vithoba in thousands of forms. Can't you see Him squatting, standing, walking, dancing and singing in these multitudinous human forms? Do you think Vithoba is only seated in the stone image within the temple? Recognize the truth that He is seated in the shrine of your own heart and in the hearts of all beings and creatures. Verily, He is in all. He is all."

The devotee dropped the suggestion. The night passed. The following day, the whole party of devotees—about fifty in number—had an invitation for dinner from Dhondo Pant, a brahman resident of Pandharpur. After dinner six of the party including Ramdas started on foot for Mohol. A devotee of Mohol led the party and took them to his house.

A small incident relating to Ramcharandas's penchant for *japa-mala* may be cited here. Before starting from Pandharpur he came to Ramdas and handing him a rosary of white *tulsi* beads said: "Swamiji, I would have a *mala* in future because I wish to keep an account of the *japa*. Do turn it once on your fingers and give it to me."

"Ram, *japa-mala* is unnecessary for you. You are expected to repeat the divine *mantram* at all times and in all places," Ramdas replied.

"No, Swamiji, I feel the need of a *mala*," he persisted.

"All right, as Ram wills" said Ramdas and while revolving the *mala* between his fingers, it snapped with a sharp sound. The other friends sitting close by exclaimed, turning to Ramcharandas: "Right, Swamiji told you not to have a *mala*, so it snapped."

"Why not?" put in Ramcharandas doggedly. "I shall buy a new one and of a stronger make," and he disappeared for some time and turned up with a new *mala* of black shining beads.

"Now, Swamiji, you may hold it in your hand for a few minutes and then return it to me," which Ramdas did and he got back the *mala* this time in sound condition.

Thereafter, he would ostentatiously handle the *mala* and move the beads on his fingers. On the way to Mohol he would approach Ramdas frequently and say: "Swamiji, I have done five thousand *japa* today," to which Ramdas replied with a laugh: "Ram, as you progress in the task of turning the *mala*, your ego seems to be assuming vaster proportions while the object of the *japa* is to diminish it; you are a wonderful Ram!"

(iii) The Supreme Purpose of Life

At night, on the ensuing day, Ramdas attended the *harikatha* of Janardan Pant at his house in the same village. On the third day devotees from Angar, Anjangaum and Upalai took part in the feast provided by Babooji. The same evening Ramdas, Ramcharandas and Bhavanishankerrao left Mohol for Bangalore by train. At the station Ramcharandas did accept a present of rupees eight from Janardan Pant, although Ramdas advised him not to. Some friends including Janardan Pant and Prem Singh followed them as far as Sholapur station where they had to detrain and catch the Bombay Mail. The train arrived but it was overcrowded. There was no room in the third-class carriages. Wherever they sought entrance into the carriage, they were repulsed by the passengers. Observing their struggle two policemen came to the rescue. They rushed forward and opening the door of a carriage provided sitting accommodation for the trio. The policemen were full of love and kindness. Why this?—because God is in all.

The train started. It might have just passed out of the station when a stout Irani (Persian) who was occupying an upper berth, jumped down and requested Ramdas to climb up and have his berth, upon which a thick quilt had been spread so that one could lie on it comfortably. Ramdas declined his kind offer and said that he preferred to remain where he was.

"May I be permitted to sit by your side for a few minutes?" he asked Ramdas.

"By all means," answered Ramdas, and made room for him. He wedged himself between Ramdas and Ramcharandas.

"Do advise me," he urged, "as to how I can remove the illusions of the mind and free it from the turmoil to which it is always subjected, and realise God. I am simply caught up in the attachment to wife, house, money and property."

"You have diagnosed," Ramdas replied, "the disease aright and also have a clear understanding of the remedy for it. Know in the first place that the God you seek is within yourself. He is the life and soul of the universe and to attain Him is the supreme purpose of life. Evil and sorrow are due to your belief that you are separate from this universal Truth. The ego has set up this wall of separation. Have a strong and intense longing to realise Him, that is, to know that your life is one with the life of the universe. Then surrender up the ego by constant identification with Him through prayer, meditation and performance of all action without desiring their fruit. As you progress on this path, which is the path of devotion, knowledge and self-surrender, your attachment to the unrealities of life will slacken, and the illusions of the mind will be dispelled. Now your heart will be filled with divine love, and your vision purified and equalised, and your actions will become the spontaneous outflow of your immortal being, yielding you the experience of true joy and peace. This is the culmination of human endeavour and fulfilment of the purpose of life."

"Oh, how clearly and impressively you present the Truth," exclaimed the Irani. "I wish I could have more of your society. Pray, come to Secunderabad which is my place and stay with me at least for a day. My wife and relations will be so happy to see you."

Ramdas could not accept his invitation as his next destination had already been fixed to be Bangalore.

CHAPTER 13: BANGALORE – BOMBAY

(i) A *Sadhu* Magician

In due time, the party reached Bangalore and for the first day stopped at Bhavanishankerrao's house at Malleswaram. Ramdas requested Bhavanishankerrao to arrange for him a separate dwelling place for their stay. A vacant house in the locality near the railway lines, well-known as a haunted house, was pitched upon as his future abode, for the time he remained in Bangalore.

Ramdas and Ramcharandas shifted to the house. It was a straggling and irregular pile of buildings with a decidedly desolate look about it. They selected a spacious room in it for their occupation.

Bhavanishankerrao provided Ramdas with a mat and two blankets. The season was cold. Ramcharandas also settled down beside Ramdas to his left. Ramcharandas had the tiger-skin always with him. In the wanderings through the villages of Sholapur he had not failed to offer Ramdas the full use of it. Wherever he rested or slept, it was on the skin. Here, as well, he laid the skin on the blanket, spread out on the floor for Ramdas. He was wearing flashily the red, woollen shawl about his body and a *japa-mala* was seen running on his fingers. His deep love for Ramdas revealed itself in the unstinted and joyous service he rendered to him. He tenderly looked after Ramdas in every way.

The news of Ramdas's arrival spread, and visitors from the suburbs and the city came to see him in large numbers. For bath and midday meal he had to go to Bhavanishankerrao's house where he was bathed with particular love and care by Sadashivrao, brother of Bhavanishankerrao. When he was soaping the body briskly Ramdas would remark: "Take care, Ram, if you exert undue pressure whilst rubbing this clay pot (meaning the body) it might break to pieces." And he would laugh.

Very often Ramdas was served with meals first. One day in preparing the *dal* curry, the mother of the house had forgotten to add salt. He took meals without noting the omission. They found it out when they tasted the curry only at their meals. They asked him how it was that he did not call for salt when he was eating the tasteless stuff.

"He never felt anything wrong with the taste," Ramdas replied. "In fact his mind was not there to discriminate taste." Among the visitors were poet Chattopadhyaya and his talented wife, Kamaladevi. They brought with them many of their friends among whom were a senior wrangler and his devout mother. The poet courted Ramdas's society frequently and for long hours. Being a votary of the goddess of emotion and beauty, he was by nature affectionate and loving. Ramdas enjoyed his company immensely.

One evening in the course of a talk with Ramcharandas, Ramdas discoursed upon attachment and the sense of possession: "Attachment to things is the source of fear and anxiety—the destroyer of peace. The sense of possession is responsible for the restless nature of the mind and so it refuses to be concentrated upon the absolute Truth of your being. Give up, therefore, attachment to the objects you have with you. 'Possess things but do not be possessed by them.' Whenever you accept presents take it that the Lord Himself gives you the things, and the moment an occasion comes when you have to part with them, give them away, with as much delight as when you received them. Understand that you are returning them only to Him who gave them to you. In the same light consider every gain and loss. The Lord gives and the Lord takes away."

At noon, the next day, Ramcharandas said: "Swamiji, I wish to buy some religious books in Kanarese, and I intend going to the city for the purpose."

"All right, Ram," Ramdas agreed, "but return soon and see that you do not stay away for the night."

He knew that Ramcharandas owned some money, of which he had made Bhavanishankerrao's mother the custodian. He went to the city which lay about two miles from Malleswaram. On his way back from the city, while nearing Malleswaram, Ramcharandas came across two *sadhus* on the main road. They told him that they had nothing to eat from morning, and would feel obliged if he could help them with a four-anna bit. Although the amount that he had taken to the city was all spent, he had still money in reserve with Bhavanishankerrao's mother. So he promised the *sadhus* that he would meet their demand if they followed him.

"In the first place," he suggested to the *sadhus*, "you would do well to have the *darshan* of a *mahatma* residing in this neighbourhood. I will get you his *darshan*, and then shall look to it that you are paid the money promised." The *sadhus* agreeing he came direct to Ramdas with them at his heels. He ran to him in advance announcing: "Swamiji, I have brought two *sadhus* for your *darshan*," and rubbed his hands with glee.

"Very good, Ram," Ramdas replied.

The *sadhus* entered the room. Ramdas requested them to be seated on the blanket occupied by him. It appeared from their respective ages that one was the *guru* and the other his *chela*. The older one was a man of middle age, dark, stout and well-built. He advanced and sat down close to Ramdas on the rug while the younger man sat on the floor at a respectable distance. Ramcharandas occupied his own seat.

A closer scrutiny of the *sadhu* seated beside Ramdas disclosed further particulars of him. He had a short and thick black beard and a dense mass of well-combed hair on his head, clipped to the shoulder on which it rested in curls. His face was of a manly cut, having strong and rough features. He wore a tight, short, half-arm jacket. His body was solid and muscular. Around his neck was a thick red string with a single *rudraksha* in the centre. From this neck chord was hanging down a tiny bottle, suspended by a string. His wrists were bangled with iron wire rings. He spoke with a peculiar intonation from which it was evident that he was a native of Tamil country.

(ii) Wonderful *Lila*

Act I

Now the *sadhu* beckoning Ramcharandas to his side said: "Get me a dry blade of straw!"

Ramcharandas went out and fetched a straw he wanted. Taking it from him the *sadhu* broke it into small pieces with his fingers and asked Ramcharandas to open his mouth. Ramcharandas obeyed, and the *sadhu* threw the pieces of straw into his wide opened mouth. But the strange thing that happened was that they turned immediately into cloves.

"Now let me have some loose earth," he next asked.

Ramcharandas immediately got him some. Taking a handful of the earth he again called on Ramcharandas to open his mouth which he did. The sand was shoved into his mouth, and

Ramcharandas was cheerfully exhibiting a lump of sugar in it. But his cheerfulness was not to last long, as the ensuing events would presently show.

The magical performance over, the *sadhu* turning to Ramdas said: "You appear to be greatly emaciated. Look at me. How strong and healthy I am! I would you were also like me. I can make you stout and vigorous. What do you say?"

"Maharaj," Ramdas replied with folded palms, "Ramdas is perfectly satisfied with his present physical condition. God has made him what he is, and he does not desire anything else."

"No, no," he put in, "you must grow stout, no good to remain as you are." Saying thus he removed the tiny bottle hanging on his neck and poured out of it a small quantity of ashes on his right palm and cried in a voice of command: "Well, open your mouth."

Ramdas had to yield. The ash instantly found a place inside his mouth.

"Swallow it," was the next fiat. Ramdas swallowed.

"This ash has the charm and power of converting you into a robust figure," he assured and replaced the bottle. Now for the second act of the drama.

Act II

The cold being severe Ramdas was made to wear the woollen cap and had his body covered with a blanket. The *sadhu* demanded the cap. Ramdas removing it from his head handed it over to him. When he tried to put it on he discovered that it was too small for his head and would not fit in, the size of his head being much larger than Ramdas's. He returned the cap exclaiming: "This won't do."

Now he called for the *kambal* that covered Ramdas. Promptly it was put in his hands. On examining he found that it was not only coarse and thick but also unwieldy in size. He threw it back. Then the *sadhu's* eyes rested on the tiger-skin, his fingers feeling its smoothness. Now a glance at Ramcharandas showed an anxious look on his face.

"This is a very nice skin." the *sadhu* remarked and, tugging at it, said, "Let me examine it properly."

Ramdas got up and allowed him to draw it towards him. A smile of approval flitted across his face.

"Here," he called his *chela*, "take it; you may fling it across your shoulders; it is so light and soft."

Ramcharandas's face was now quite a study. It was deadly pale. Then the *sadhu's* eyes turned round to Ramcharandas. He did not care to notice the pallor and despair on his visage. The *sadhu's* next object of attraction was Ramcharandas's red and lustrous shawl on which he gazed with steady and intent stare. Ramcharandas was not slow to understand. He knew what was coming. He thought it fit to surrender up the shawl before the *sadhu* asked for it. Instantly unwinding it off his body, Ramcharandas, like a good obedient boy, placed the shawl in front of the *sadhu*.

The *sadhu* appreciated Ramcharandas's power of insight. The shawl met the good fortune of gracing the other shoulder of the *sadhu's* chela. The distraction of the moment had made Ramcharandas drop down the *japa-mala* of shining black beads near his *asan*, and it became the *sadhu's* next object of interest. It must be said here to the *sadhu's* credit that he was a man of taste, nay, he was a consummate artist.

Without ceremony—there was none necessary—the *sadhu* took the *japa-mala* from the floor and spread it out with both hands. A moment more, and it was round his neck, hanging gracefully on his broad chest. With a wide grin he looked at himself self-complacently and felt happy.

Now the third and crowning act of the drama.

Act III

Ramcharandas had promised the *sadhu* four annas. It was time to call for it. Being reminded by him of it Ramcharandas said: "Maharaj, the money is in the keeping of a mother who lives about a furlong from here. I have to obtain it from her."

"No fear," replied the *sadhu* encouragingly; "you may go and fetch it. I can afford to wait here until you return. I don't at all mind the trouble. Do go at once, my boy."

Ramcharandas started and went, only to return within ten minutes indeed, he must have run fast to and fro—clutching in his hand a small meshed pouch of twine which contained all his wealth.

Sitting in front of the *sadhu*, Ramcharandas opened the purse and turning it upside down rolled out the contents, producing a jingling sound. One after the other the coins dropped down on the floor – four silver rupees and a four-anna coin. Ramcharandas was about to pick up the four-anna bit for presenting it to the *sadhu* when the *sadhu's* right hand shot out and his large open palm grabbed the coins, and collecting all of them in his grasp, he transferred them coolly into his pocket. All this was the work of a few seconds. Now Ramcharandas jerked his head up and was gazing at the ceiling with the empty pouch in his hand.

"Ram, why are you so unkind as to withhold the bag? Don't you see that he has greater need of it than yourself?'

These words of Ramdas caused him to lower his upturned head. The last vestige of cheer which he had when the sugar lump was in his mouth had completely vanished from his face. He resigned the bag to the *sadhu* who, refilling it with the coins, tenderly slipped it into his pocket.

The *sadhu* having played his part rose to depart, and without the usual formality of leave-taking he walked out with his *chela* and disappeared.

All the time Ramdas had been with great difficulty suppressing the laugh that was seeking an outlet. Now it burst out with all its pent-up force.

(iii) Feast in the Company of *Rishis*

When Ramdas continued laughing for some minutes, Ramcharandas remained sullen and thoughtful, but later, he also joined in the laugh. He could not help it.

"Swamiji," he exclaimed, "I did not mind so much about the *sadhu's* appropriation of other things, even the money, but, when he took the tiger-skin, to tell you the truth, Swamiji, I could not help feeling an acute shooting pain in the interior of my stomach. I can well understand now," he added with a curious smile, "that you are at the bottom of the whole affair. You seem to be so simple, quiet and innocent. This is all your *lila*. Only last night you warned me against attachment and the sense of possession, and today you have enacted this play, in order to teach me a lesson. This is all undoubtedly your own work."

"Ram," said Ramdas, "you are a marvel. Do you forget that it was you who brought here the wandering *sadhus*, with the apparent object of showing to them Ramdas, while your real intention must have been to present them with all the articles they have taken away from here? They have after all come by their own. So there need be no thought of any loss. Remember, the Lord gives and the Lord takes away."

Shortly after this, on the suggestion of Ramdas, Ramcharandas left for Northern India.

Ramdas received many invitations from the visitors for dinner. He stipulated a condition for accepting the invitations which was that, along with him, a dozen *sadhus* should be fed. Dinners followed one after the other. The one at the senior wrangler Kuppuswami Iyengar's house was attended by the poet Chattopadhyaya and his wife. It was a jolly occasion. An assortment of twelve *sadhus* was a picturesque sight. Each *sadhu* belonged to a separate sect and denomination. There was the tilakdhari, the jatadhari, the clean-shaven and orange-robed *sannyasi*, the *yoga-danda*, the Udasi, the Dashanami, the Brijvasi, the Ramanandi, etc. The meal was served in a spacious hall of the house. The poet and Ramdas sat in the line of *sadhus* for dinner.

The poet, elated by the uniqueness of the situation, remarked: "Ramdas, I feel as if I am transported back to the days of ancient India—to the age of the *rishis*. Am I not really dining in the company of those distant ancestors?"

Indeed, the experience was unparalleled. The *sadhus* dispersed after meals and Ramdas, remaining with the friends for some time, also returned to his retreat.

Some days later, he again started the practice of *pranayama*. Now Bhavanishankerrao also joined him. Throughout the day and night Ramdas went on vigorously with the practice. Once again he was seized with an insatiable hunger. He had to run to Bhavanishankerrao's house twice or thrice a day for food. Once, one afternoon, he found himself in their kitchen, with a voracious appetite, where a mother of the house was preparing rice cakes. He begged for the cakes. The mother was very kind. At first he was served with two cakes which disappeared in a trice and he looked for more. As she served he ate on until he must have devoured about fourteen cakes, in addition to four cups of coffee and half a dozen plantains. Then somewhat satisfied he left the place, and returning to his retreat sat up in *asan* for *pranayama*. In ten minutes the fire of hunger was ablaze again. He jumped out and made for Bhavanishankerrao's house once more, with as much speed as his legs could carry him. Then again he gorged himself with a lot of eatables. Ramdas told them that the gluttonous demon Bakasura must have taken his seat in his stomach! After some time the *pranayama* stopped and the normal appetite was restored.

Ramdas's sojourn in Bangalore was for over two months. He was now feeling a call from Jhansi. The friends of Jhansi whom he had met during his last visit to that city had expressed through repeated letters their keen desire to see Ramdas. He left Bangalore for Kasaragod. Bhavanishankerrao and the members of his household gave him a send-off at the railway station. Their love was indeed illimitable.

In due time Ramdas reached Kasaragod. He once again met the friends of the place and also Ramcharan *sannyasi* who were all eagerly awaiting his return. After the *darshan* of Gurudev he proceeded to Mangalore in the company of Ramcharan.

During his three days' stay in Mangalore he visited the house of a devotee at Pentland Peth where he was treated with great kindness and love. Ramcharan was with him and both had also walks on the Kadri Hill, the scene of Ramdas's *sadhanas* in the previous years.

(iv) Owns Not a Single Copper

From Mangalore, after three days' stay, Ramdas sailed for Bombay. The passengers on the boat looked after Ramdas with great tenderness and care. He reached Bombay docks. No notice of his arrival was given in advance to Sanjivrao of Bombay. Ramdas ran from street to street through the brilliantly lit city, as the boat had arrived in the evening. The policemen at the junction of the roads guided him. He made his way to Gamdevi where Sanjivrao resided. Sanjivrao and his wife were quite taken by surprise but were delighted to welcome him. It appeared they were speaking of him only a few seconds before he suddenly dawned upon them. He stopped in Bombay for about five days.

Mother Rukmabai with her girl Ramabai was at this time staying in Kurla, a suburb of Bombay, in her sister's house. The girl was then about thirteen years of age. Ramdas had an invitation from this house and accordingly he visited it. Rukmabai and her daughter came and sat in front of him.

"Well," the mother said, "what about the marriage of this girl who is growing up?"—a question thrust right into Ramdas's face. "I have not a single pie with me," she continued, "and she has to be married."

"While you own up that you have not a pie he, in his turn, must confess that he too does not possess a single copper!" Ramdas replied with a spice of humour, and laughed.

The answer nettled her a great deal and she placed before him a lurid picture of his dereliction of duty and lack of responsibility. He listened to her with a cool indifference and said: "Why do you worry over the matter? God's will is supreme. All things happen as He wills and at the time determined by Him."

"How can you say so? Do you mean to say then that human effort has no value?" she retorted.

"Human effort," he replied, "is necessary only to learn that human effort as such is useless, and God's will alone is the real power that controls and brings about all events. When you realise this truth, human effort ceases and divine will starts its work in you, and then you do all things in the freedom of the soul, liberated from care, fear and sorrow. This is the real life to be attained. So leave all things to the Lord by complete surrender to Him."

The mother did not seem to be impressed with this philosophy. The talk on the subject came to an end. Next day he returned to Sanjivrao's in the evening.

From Bombay he sailed by steamboat to Veraval. On the boat he found himself in the company of Muhammadans who were very kind to him. There was also a brahman lad on the boat in charge of a tea shop. He took a great liking for Ramdas and provided him with eatables. The other passengers were also very kind.

CHAPTER 14: JUNAGAD – LIMBDI

(i) Saints Are Like Children

Next morning the boat reached Veraval port. Alighting, Ramdas entered the city. Veraval is an important trading harbour. He directed his steps straight to the railway station. On the way he was invited by milk vendors who gave him cups of milk which refreshed him. At the station he met a *sannyasi* in whose company he travelled in the train. Reaching Junagad at ten in the night, Ramdas walked up to the *akhada* of *sannyasis* of which Kashigirji was the mahant. Ramdas had the privilege of living for three weeks in this Ashram when he last visited Junagad. Kashigirji received Ramdas with great delight. Next day he met Maganlal at his residence. Maganlal also was over-flowed with joy at the sight of him. It must be remembered that when he was in Junagad on the previous occasion Maganlal and Kantilal were extremely devoted to him and had treated him with love and care.

It was decided that he should stay in a garden belonging to Kashgirji's ashram at a distance of half a mile from the town. In the garden was a small open thatched hut occupied by two *sadhus*. He joined them. One of them was a man with a long beard and the other, Atmanand by name, was a clean-shaven *sannyasi*.

Atmanand was a man of bulky proportions. He was quiet and calm by nature. One of his characteristics was his spontaneous laugh every five or ten minutes, apparently for no reason. He was indifferent alike to the cleanliness of his body or his clothes. He would be found sitting for hours at one place in silence and with vacant looks, the world having seemingly no existence for him.

The other *sadhu* with the beard was an active old man. He was busy the whole day doing some work or other. He possessed a cheerful and pleasant temperament, except when his only son would come from the city to tease him and pick up a quarrel with him. They used to fight like cocks in a hand-to-hand scuffle. At the bottom of the frequent quarrels, Ramdas could clearly see, there was a strong mutual attachment, for the matter, all strife and violence in the world can be traced to the same source.

Both the *sadhus* were kind and hospitable to him. The time was winter and hence the cold was severe. They had a fireplace in the middle of the floor of the shed. The *sadhus* slept around the fire at right angles to one another. By joining them at bedtime, Ramdas formed another angle. Maganlal would come to him in this garden every day and take him home for the midday meal. The bearded old man cooked *rotis* in the shed for himself and Atmanand. Very often they had to be satisfied with only dry *rotis*, salt, and chillies for dinner. One early morning Atmanand must have felt unusually hungry. He asked the old *sadhu* if there was any remnant from the *rotis* of the previous night. In response the old man placed before Atmanand a napkin containing some fragments of *rotis* which resembled thick pieces of white leather. Rolling up his sleeves Atmanand fell to. Piece after piece of the stiff dry bread found its way into his capacious mouth. He possessed strong teeth with which he munched them. As he went on with the meal, to humour his palate that craved for fine and delicious food, he was uttering at every mouthful of the dry and tasteless stuff: "*Ladoo—ladoo—ladoo; poori—poori—poori; jilabi—jilabi—jilabi; barfi—barfi—barfi.*"

The same afternoon, he complained of stomach ache. Evidently, the dry bread had put his digestive apparatus out of order. "I am going to the doctor," he said and left the garden. He turned up in the evening quite fit and cheerful.

"Maharaj, did you get medicine from the doctor?" inquired the old *sadhu*.

"I did," he replied, with a bland smile. "The doctor gave me four pills; I swallowed them all. They were as big as cricket balls, *ladoos*, you know! The doctor prescribed *ladoos* as the best remedy. Now I am all right; indeed, wonderful pills!" and he laughed.

Once, Maganlal took Ramdas on a visit to a famous saint of Junagad, Vyasji. He was an old man, aged about seventy, and was lean and short in stature. The remarkable thing about him was that his wrinkled skin had a golden lustre. Ramdas spent an hour in his delectable company, for he found the saint simple and pure like a child. He evinced marked love for Ramdas. He put Ramdas two hackneyed questions: "How is one to control the restless mind?"

"By constant repetition of God's Name," Ramdas replied, "and surrender of all actions to Him."

"Where does this practice lead to?" was the next question.

"It leads to the vision of God everywhere which means immortality and bliss."

He was pleased with the answers and fondly embraced Ramdas.

Again, on another occasion, Maganlal escorted him to the distant Muchkund ashram on the way to Girnar Hill in which Ramdas had resided during his previous visit to Junagad. The ashram was now occupied by a *sannyasini*, popularly known as Mataji.

She was a young lady, dressed in ochre-coloured robes, living alone in the ashram. There was a pure lustre on her calm features. The sound of 'Shivoham' was constantly issuing from her lips. She expressed great joy on beholding Ramdas. She lived an austere and holy life. O! Mataji, all glory to thee! After a short stay in the ashram, Ramdas and Maganlal retraced their steps to the city.

Kantilal and his father had their home in Limbdi, a state in Kathiawar. Hearing of his arrival at Junagad, Kantilal came down to take Ramdas to his place. In due course he left Junagad for Limbdi with Kantilal and Maganlal.

(ii) Sugarcandy Mothers

Limbdi is a small state ruled by a Rajput prince who is designated as Thakore Saheb. The ruling prince is Sir Daulat Singh—a broad-minded and generous-hearted man. He is greatly loved by his subjects and has proved himself to be a true guardian of their interests and welfare.

In Limbdi, Ramdas was lodged in Kantilal's house, situated in a by-lane. Coming to know of his arrival, hundreds of people of Limbdi rushed into Kantilal's house to see him. All grades of people streamed in. Officers of the state, merchants and doctors paid him daily visits. Then again men and women of middle and poor classes also came in vast numbers. Every caste, creed and sect was represented, of which the brahman and the Jain communities formed the majority. A large part of the population of the state belonged to the latter class. He received the visitors in a spacious carpeted apartment on the second floor of the building, while for the night he retired to a small room on the third floor.

Before the crowded audience, Ramdas poured himself out in the language of love and joy on the charm and power of God's Name, and on the blessedness of God-realisation. The visitors listened to his discourses with rapt attention. Here he chose to live on milk diet. The news spread, and hundreds of mothers came with *lotas* full of milk from early morning till afternoon. The quantity of milk they brought was so much that he could well-nigh have bathed in it. He had to take a sip—very often a drop through the finger tip—from every milk pot so as to satisfy the kind donors.

Kantilal's house thus became a scene of liveliness and bustle all through the day and till late in the night. Kantilal then made this observation: "Swamiji, you have converted our humble home into a veritable temple."

Being apprised of his arrival, the Thakore Saheb sent one of his officers to invite Ramdas to his palace. About eleven o'clock in the morning, he was taken in a carriage to his princely residence. Kantilal and Maganlal accompanied him. He was received by the prince in a small, well-furnished room. He sat down in an *asan* on the carpet, and the others in the room also squatted on the floor. Beside the prince was seated an English lady. Ramdas talked freely, narrating the experiences he had gained in the course of his travels. He spoke with the familiarity of a child when it recounts its doing to the fondly listening mother. Indeed, there was such a mother among the auditors. She was the English lady, Miss Elizabeth Sharpe, to whom he would refer in future as "Mother Elizabeth", and to the Thakore Saheb as "Raja Ram." Raja Ram was also highly delighted at the frank and simple talks of Ramdas in which he would be so deeply absorbed as to lose all account of time. At half-past twelve, Raja Ram would start glancing at his wrist-watch and exclaim: "Oh! it is past twelve. I have to be in my state office by one." Then the meeting would break up, and Ramdas with the young friends would return to Kantilal's.

For a fortnight he remained in Limbdi, and every day he had to visit the palace where he would spend an hour or two in the society of Raja Ram and Mother Elizabeth, both of whom would come to fetch him in their motor-car. He discoursed upon divine love and eternal happiness, presenting instances in his rambles in which how the former had prevailed. They listened and were lost in a state of sweet oblivion. The pure love in the heart of Mother Elizabeth induced her one day to take Ramdas to her neat little bungalow, in the midst of a beautiful garden. She called her abode, Shri Krishna Nivas. She was so loving and kind.

In the afternoons, the room in which Ramdas received visitors would be filled by ladies. Of these, two mothers who were very old did not fail to come every day. Inspite of their decrepitude they would climb up the stairs on all fours and directly totter towards him and push into his mouth large pieces of sugarcandy. Hence they went by the name sugarcandy mothers. They would softly rub their palms on his cheeks and gazing on him with a fond smile, say: "O! my beloved."

One evening, in response to an invitation of the old Rani Saheb—the widowed Rani of the late Thakore Saheb—he visited the *zenana*, or that part of the palace which was reserved for the ladies of the prince's household. The retired Dewan of Limbdi, a quiet and pious old man, escorted him to the place. The Rani Saheb, of course, observed *purdah*. She sat behind a perforated screen.

In a small front room, he was made to sit on a raised *asan*. The ladies behind the screen could see the people in the outer room but not vice versa. A brahman *puranic* was also there. It appeared that the devout old mother was utilizing her afternoon hours in listening to the readings of scriptures. She desired that Ramdas should speak. He expressed himself in Hindi. He dilated at length on the hollowness of life, if it was not devoted to the attainment of divine knowledge and universal love.

His words flowed in a spontaneous current for nearly half an hour. At the close of his talk, there followed a dead silence for about five minutes. Then the voice of the Rani in a clear and measured modulation filtered through the metallic screen: "Look at his magnificent *vairagya*! How I wish I were a man instead of a woman, hopelessly caught in a golden cage! If I were a man I could have a life like his—free and blissful."

The words were addressed to the Dewan Saheb. In her tone there was a marked tinge of anguish. Having taken some milk and fruit kindly proffered by the Rani Saheb, Ramdas took leave of her and returned to his rooms.

(iii) From the Maze of Illusion into the Maze of God!

Ramdas paid a visit to a *sannyasi* ashram where he was kindly received by the resident *sannyasis*. At their request he spoke a few words on God-realisation which he always held forth as the only purpose of life.

Again he had an occasion to call on the Jain *sadhus* in their chief ashram in Limbdi. Jainism is considered as old as the Vedas. Its teachings, in many respects, resembled those of Buddhism. The creed of non-violence is observed by the Jains in an extreme form. The Jain *sadhus* have a semicircular strip of cloth covering their lips, placed in position by thin ribbons fastened round the nether part of the head. They also carry a soft duster for sweeping the floor before sitting on it, lest they might kill the vermin that may happen to be on it. For similar reasons, they would drink only boiled water and never eat by lamp-light; they finish their evening meal before sunset. Jainism holds absolute purity of life and non-violence as the way, and liberation and peace as the goal.

On spending a delightful half hour with the *sadhus* in this ashram, Ramdas was next taken to another Jain ashram where nearly two hundred Jain ladies had congregated to listen to a discourse by him. He was simply blest with the sight of the kind mothers. He sat on a raised dais and spoke for about three quarters of an hour at a stretch upon purity, love and peace. He was all through filled with an inexpressible rapture. Two prominent and charitable Jain merchants, Ugarchand Shet and Mohanbhai who had conceived a great love for him, had arranged for the visits to the Jain ashrams, and they also entertained Ramdas in their own residences.

During one of his visits to the palace, Raja Ram took Ramdas to his *puja* room where he saw a number of framed silver images of incarnations of God and also pictures of saints. Raja Ram was a devotee of Sri Krishna. He was past sixty but possessed a strong, tall and stout physical frame. His life was controlled by strict discipline. He would rise at three o'clock every morning and spend the hours till daybreak in worship and meditation.

Once he pressed Ramdas to accept a present of a costly silk shawl but Ramdas had to decline the offer, reminding him that the shawl was intended for princes and not for *fakirs*. Ramdas was wearing only one piece of *khadi* cloth. The time was winter, the cold was bitter, and chill breezes were blowing. He was indifferent to the rigours of the season, but the motherly heart of the English lady ached for him. She persuaded Raja Ram to give him some plain, warm clothing.

In fact, Ramdas was content with the simple cloth he had. However, through Raja Ram's and the mother's repeated pressure, he agreed to exchange his *khadi* cloth for a plain, woollen one. The old *khaddar* piece was shared between them—the fents being prized as mementos. Still the mother was not satisfied. Next day she wanted Ramdas to be dressed also in a long, woollen gown. In a short time the gown was ready. It was a heavy thing made of thick tweed on which Raja Ram had set a high value. Ramdas put it on once in their presence and executed a caper or two at which they had a merry laugh. That was the first and last occasion he used the gown.

In the small room, on the third floor, Ramdas remained at nights. Kantilal and Maganlal kept him company. Maganlal possessed a keen sense of humour. He could perfectly imitate the mannerisms of the visitors who came to see Ramdas. He would make Ramdas laugh by his mimicry. Once he wittily remarked: "Swamiji, I have been attentively listening to your teachings but I could not make head or tail of them. It would all seem to me to be only a leap from the *Maya-ghotala* into the *Brahma-ghotala*;" i.e., from the maze of illusion into the maze of God.

Of the visitors that came to see Ramdas from outside the Limbdi state, there were two—Dr. Shukla, a brahman and Chunibhai, a Jain. They hailed from Wadhwan, another Indian state. They expressed a desire to have him with them in their state for some days. He accepted the invitation and proceeded to Wadhwan.

He had also a letter and a money order from Kashirambhai of Surat. The latter had met Ramdas during his visit to Junagad. Now he had settled down in Surat. He asked Ramdas to go over to him for a few days on finishing his tours in Kathiawar.

CHAPTER 15: WADHWAN-SURAT – JHANSI

(i) Ramcharandas Again

Ramdas arrived at Wadhwan city. For the first night he was put up in a vacant hospital building. Maganlal had adhered closely to him and at the time, for him there was none in the world but Ramdas. He followed Ramdas like a shadow, doing every kind of service. On the second day Ramdas was shifted to Chunibhai's house. Here the people of the city started coming to see him. Dr. Shukla, an enthusiastic and earnest seeker after truth, paid him frequent visits. The Dewan of the state, a capable and pious man, also treated Ramdas with great affection. Also some friends from Limbdi came to see him again here. He met a *sadhaka*, Jivaraj, who lived in a small tent outside the city. Suddenly Ramcharandas put in an appearance and proposed again to stick on to him.

Mulshanker, an old brahman from Dhrangadhra, came to take him to his place. Ramdas started. It was decided to go as far as Wadhwan junction by taxi. It was morning. They arrived at the motor-stand. To bid him farewell, quite a crowd followed him. While taxis were available at all times, that day, in spite of their waiting for nearly an hour, no taxi could be had. The friends showed signs of dejection and disappointment. Ramdas all the while was quite cheerful. Eventually there was a return march to the city. Ramdas was seen going back smiling and dancing in the streets.

Turning to the friends he said: "Submission to the Lord's will means no worry and dejection. It is clear, He wills that Ramdas should leave the place by train." There was a noon train. He and the party arrived at the station. Now the question arose if Maganlal should accompany Ramdas any further. He had been away with Ramdas from Junagad for about three weeks. Moreover, Ramcharandas who had now joined him could attend to him. So he asked Maganlal to return to his family, but he shook his head to signify that the advice was no good and he was bent upon escorting him. This was a problem for Ram to solve, but the Lord knows how to carry out His will.

Ramdas declared: "Listen, Ram, if you insist upon following him he will have to take up a water-fast, as long as you are with him. This is Ram's will. What do you say?"

"I shall also do the same," was his calm reply.

"Maganlal," a friend then urged, "you are a fine fellow; you would go with him only to inflict on him a fast; give up the mad idea; better stop away."

He was obdurate for some time but at last yielded. In due time, Ramdas and Ramcharandas arrived at Dhrangadhra with their escort. They were welcomed by a rich merchant who lodged them in the upper storey of a warehouse, facing the main road. Ramdas still continued on milk diet. Here again many people from the city visited him—*sadhus* and householders, men, women and children. He talked to them on his pet subject—devotion to God.

The next morning Maganlal was there in the room, falling at the feet of Ramdas like a felled tree. He seemed to have dropped from the clouds, so unexpected was his appearance. His deep affection for Ramdas had drawn him to the latter again.

"Swamiji, forgive me," he appealed sitting up, "I simply could not resist coming. I am not pressing to go with you any further. When you leave for Surat, I shall turn back to Junagad."

Mulshanker was smitten with love for Ramdas. He was a sweet-natured and meek old soul. He would not be happy if he did not hug Ramdas to his bosom at least half a dozen times a day. He was saying that he had also the blessed opportunity of once embracing Mahatma Gandhi.

Ramdas's stay in Dhrangadhra was short. By an evening train he left for Surat with Ramcharandas. It was here at the station of Dhrangadhra that Ramdas parted with the tweed gown presented by Raja Ram. He forced it on Mulshanker, in fact he threw the robe on his shoulders when the train had just begun to move from the station. Maganlal, parting company with Ramdas, returned to his native place.

(ii) Ramcharandas Turns Dandy

Ramdas reached Rander, a small place in the suburbs of Surat, where the old friend Kashirambhai resided. He and his wife—a noble pair hailed Ramdas with unfeigned delight. They lived a retired life, utilizing most of their time in devotion, *puja* and the reading of scriptures. Sorrow, the great awakener, had completely turned their minds from the unrealities of life towards God, the only Truth. Grown up sons and daughters had passed away before their very eyes, leaving the parents in their old age to the exclusive devotion of God. They overwhelmed Ramdas with their kind ministrations.

One afternoon, Kashirambhai had a special reading of a religious book treating of the seven steps or planes in the spiritual growth of man. The reading over, he faced Ramdas and said: "Shall I tell you to what plane you have reached?" Ramdas did not reply.

"Applying the tests here given," he continued tapping on the book, by his side: "I can declare that you have passed the fifth plane and are approaching the end of the sixth."

Kashirambhai had a humorous disposition. He told a story of two *sadhus* which threw his hearers into fits of laughter:

Once, two *sadhus* came to a town from different directions. One settled down beneath a peepal tree and the other under the shade of a banyan. Hearing of their arrival, a *bania* householder first went to the *sadhu* of the peepal tree and prostrated before him.

"Maharaj," said the devotee, "it appears another *mahatma* has come to our town. Do you know him?"

"Yes," returned the *sadhu* contemptuously, "I know him; he is a buffalo."

Soon after, the devotee arming himself with a bunch of hay visited the *sadhu* of the banyan tree and placing the hay before him, prostrated.

"Well" cried out the *sadhu*, "what do you mean by this? Why this hay?"

"It is an offering, maharaj; deign to feed upon it and bless your devotee," appealed the *bania* with folded palms.

"What! are you mad? Eat hay!" flared up the *sadhu*.

"Maharaj, a *sadhu* below the peepal tree, at the other corner of the town, was good enough to inform me that you were a buffalo. So I thought I could bring you a fitting present," coolly said the devotee.

"How could you believe him? Have you no sense?" asked the *sadhu* reprovingly.

"Maharaj, how could a poor and ignorant man like your slave dare to understand *sadhus*? A *mahatma* alone can know a *mahatma*," returned the devotee.

"Go then and tell him he is an ass," said the *sadhu*.

The *bania* devotee left the place, and directly going to the bazaar, purchased a seer of cotton seeds and making a bundle of it, proceeded to the first *sadhu* of the peepal tree. Untying the bundle he poured out the contents in front of the *sadhu* and prostrated before him.

"How now," asked the *sadhu* with a surprised look, "What is this for? It is cotton seed!"

"Right, maharaj—a stuff so dear to you. Do accept the humble present and making a full meal of it, shower your grace upon your slave," prayed the *bania*.

"Is anything wrong with you? What do you mean, eat cotton seed?" uttered the *sadhu* in consternation.

"Why not? Maharaj, a *sadhu* over there, beneath the banyan tree, told me that you were an ass. An ass has a great partiality for cotton seed."

"You fool," he roared in rage, "don't you see that I am not an ass?"

"How should I know, Maharaj—a poor man like me caught in the meshes of *maya*! It is said: a *mahatma* alone can recognize a *mahatma*," replied the devotee with a sly twitch at the corner of his thin lips.

The *sadhu* was by this time thoroughly roused and, rising to his feet, said in an imperious voice: "Bhaktaraj, take me to the place where the other *mahatma* is. I should like to teach him how to speak of his betters."

They went. It appears there was a terrible fight between the two *mahatmas*, the *bania* devotee witnessing the fun from a distance. The affair ended in the *sadhus* going without food for the whole day!

Rander is situated on the banks of the river Tapti. Ramdas was having his daily bath in the river accompanied by Ramcharandas. In the matter of bath, Ramcharandas exercised absolute control over him. Sometimes he would go to the length of making Ramdas yield to his will by threats, as a mother would do with a contumacious child.

"Swamiji," he would say in a stern voice, "you should not take bath there, come this side."

He would then take Ramdas by the arm and almost drag him into knee-deep water and rub and scrub him as a *syce* would do a horse! There was no doubt that Ramcharandas was doing this out of the great love he bore for Ramdas. In a few days Ramdas found that he had lost all independence of action at the riverside. One day, Ramdas in a humble tone and with joined palms, said to him: "Ram, your treatment of Ramdas reminds him of the attitude of Sri Ramakrishna Paramhamsa's nephew towards him. It is said that he domineered over the childlike saint in a similar way. Eventually, Sri Ramakrishna had to send him away. So Ramdas would also request you to leave him alone and take yourself off."

Ramcharandas grinned and remained silent. He frequented the market place and made friends with many merchants. One day he came to Ramdas and said: "Swamiji, the merchant friends wish to present me with cloth; I could have something for you also. What shall we have?"

"Mendicants as we are, the best suited cloth for us is *khadi* which is coarse and durable and serves all purposes. As for Ramdas, he has already one and does not need any more," Ramdas answered.

His face showed that he did not agree. He went to the market and returned in the evening. What did Ramdas behold? A *sadhu* dressed in tiptop style! He wore a long robe of fine muslin with shining buttons. He flourished in his hand a fashionable and costly umbrella, and white rubber-soled canvas shoes encased his feet. At the sight of this smart figure Ramdas bowed and said: "Ram, you know Ramdas is a humble *fakir*. You are now transformed into a *saheb*. How can a *fakir* have anything in common with a *saheb*?"

Ramcharandas was not a man of words. He smiled away Ramdas's remarks. He would always have his own way.

From the friends of Jhansi, Ramdas received an invitation and railway fare for one passenger. It was evident that he should alone proceed to Jhansi. He broached the subject to Ramcharandas who became rebellious.

"You are always for throwing me up," he spoke passionately.

"It is God's will, Ram, and you have to submit to it," said Ramdas. "Moreover, it behoves you that you should travel alone, gathering experience in your own way. Ramdas would advise you to go to the banks of the Narmada and spend some time in that inspiring atmosphere."

(iii) Krishna, Christ, and Buddha

On the day fixed, Ramdas started from Surat towards the north. Ramcharandas travelled with him for a few stations and then parted company. At Ujjain Ramdas had to break journey. He stopped in a *dharmashala* for the night and the next day set out again. In the train a young Mussalman met him. Sitting by the side of Ramdas he recounted his sorrows. Ramdas spoke to him about surrender to God as the panacea for all ills of life. He wished to know a way to control the restless mind. Ramdas asked him to repeat God's Name.

Arriving at Bhopal, where the train halted for thirty minutes, the Muslim friend provided him with milk and fruits. As Bhopal was his destination, he took leave of Ramdas with God's Name on his lips.

It was midnight when Ramdas reached Jhansi station. Passing the night in the passenger shed, early next morning he made his way to the city which lay two miles from the station. He went direct to Mahadev Prasad's house. At the sight of Ramdas, Mahadev Prasad was convulsed with joy. He fell at Ramdas's feet, kissed them and rising embraced him again and again, tears streaming down his eyes through uncontrollable emotion.

It was over two years before that Ramdas had remained under his hospitable roof for months. With what affection and kindness did he then look after him! His longing to see Ramdas again must have been indeed intense, as it was obvious from the manner in which he received him.

In the evening Ramdas met Ramkinkar—that devoted friend who with such studious care had tended him on his journey to Badrinarayan. He was beside himself with delight on seeing Ramdas. His stay was decided to be in the Ram Mandir in which he had resided on the last occasion. Hence Ramkinkar led him to the temple. The old *pandaji* was there. He came out to welcome Ramdas. His huge frame trembled with emotion and he repeatedly hugged Ramdas to his bosom.

Next day, news reaching the other friends, they came in large numbers. Crowds collected in the temple in the evenings, and Ramdas delivered in English—his knowledge of Hindi being still poor—his message of love and joy. Followers of different prevailing sects and creeds held talks with him, either to clear their doubts or to press their views on him. He appreciated their varied standpoints and reconciled himself to them, because, after all, it was the Lord who has planned this variegated world-play. It was given to him to see and love Him in all.

Ramdas paid a visit to Sipri Bazaar where also he met many friends and returned to the city. Now he expressed a wish to live outside the city. A place was pitched upon named Atkhamba. A small building consisting of a single room and a verandah stood on the far corner of the lake Lakshmitalao. At the edge of the lake there was an eight-pillared minaret, made of red stone, with a beautifully shaped cupola, after the style of Moghul architecture. On account of the eight pillars it came to be called Atkhamba. To sit on the pedestal of this structure, facing the lake, is to view a charming sight—the still waters of the lake reflecting as if in a mirror the surrounding scenery.

A peepal tree spread its extended branches over the building. A stone image of Hanuman, besmeared with red paint, stood below the tree enclosed in an open, rocky chamber. Ramdas dwelt in Atkhamba for more than a month. Crowds also gathered here in the evenings. Ramkinkar kept him company during nights. Mahadev Prasad did not fail a single evening. Sometimes, Ramdas would go out in the mornings for long walks over hills. On one of the hills he came upon a temple in ruins with its image of a goddess, made of white marble, broken to pieces. From the top of this hill one can have an extensive survey of the country all around. He would spend hours here in the refreshing breeze, in calm meditation.

He also paid visits to an old saint in Shyam Chopla. His childlike nature attracted Ramdas to him. He was fond of narrating the account of his wanderings when he was young. He had passed through thrilling experiences. His temple was situated in a jungle far away from the city. Two well-preserved tanks drew many devotees from the city for their daily baths.

Ramdas had the privilege of coming in contact with another saint Nirbhayanandji and his spouse Purnanandji. Both the husband and wife had adopted *sannyas* and were clad in orange robes—a typical pair who had devoted their life to the service of the Lord. They belonged to the well-known Pilikoti ashram of *sannyasis* in Chitrakut. At the time of Ramdas's stay in Jhansi, they lived in a small garden-house removed from the city. Both of them were exceedingly kind to him. Mother Purnanandji was really a pure and lovely soul.

In this connection it must here be placed on record that for Ramdas there is none impure or sinful, although he might mention the particular purity and greatness of the persons he came across. His task is merely to chronicle his experiences with regard to events that befell him and to people who came under his observation. He presents the history from the standpoint of a dispassionate witness of God's *lila*. For, the world is His manifestation in which He expresses Himself in a multitude of forms, assuming various characters. Ramdas looks on all with the same unclouded vision and his love for all is alike, be they saints or sinners. He does not see any difference. It is the Lord who plays all the parts in the world-drama.

An Englishman named Abbot desiring to see Ramdas motored him to his bungalow. Abbot and his aged sister received Ramdas in the verandah. The English mother talked in high admiration of Jesus Christ and his teachings. Ramdas perfectly agreed with her in her laudation of the divine Teacher. But her enthusiasm carried her so far as to speak in contemptuous terms of Sri Krishna, Buddha and others.

"Mother, Ramdas cannot be one with you there," he told her. "He holds Sri Krishna and Buddha in the same high estimation as, if not higher than, Jesus. You are speaking of them as you do, because you have not understood them. Similarly, there are Hindus who speak disparagingly of Christ without knowing him."

The mother combated his view and started attacking it by arguments. But Ramdas remained silent. Abbot did not like the way his sister spoke and tried to pacify her. At last she stopped and Ramdas took leave of them.

Ramkinkar and other friends of Jhansi proposed that Ramdas should be made conversant with Hindi, because many people who came to see him did not understand the English tongue. They felt that they were losing the benefit of his talks. So, one of the friends undertook to coach him up in Hindi. Ramdas was provided with the first Hindi primer and a slate and pencil. He felt that he had just been enrolled in the infant class. He received an hour's instruction from the kind teacher every day. His progress was rapid. In ten days he finished the first primer and in five days more, he passed through the second primer. Then he commenced reading books in easy Hindi, such as Bala Ramayan, life of Samarth Ramdas and Gita Sangraha. He also started indicting letters in Hindi.

Ram-navami, the celebration of the birthday of Sri Ramchandra, was fast approaching and Ramdas bethought him of witnessing the festival in Chitrakut, where they said it was performed on a grand scale. So one day he announced his intention to the Jhansi friends that he was to start by an evening train. Ramkinkar and other friends came to the station to bid him farewell. Ramdas was to travel alone.

CHAPTER 16: CHITRAKUT

(i) A *Bania's* Renunciation

Ramkinkar expressed a wish that Ramdas had a companion to take care of him. Hearing this, a *bania*, who was then on the platform, coming forward said: "I am also proceeding to Chitrakut. I shall be so happy to keep him company and serve him."

Accordingly, side by side, the *bania* and Ramdas took seats in the train. The train steamed out of the station. The *bania* carried a *kambal* and a *lota*. He spread the *kambal* on the bench and making Ramdas lie on it, massaged his feet. While doing this service he opened his mind: "Maharaj, I am disgusted with worldly life. I too would lead the life of a *sadhu*. I have turned my back on a life full of cares and sorrows. Consider me as your disciple and take me under your protection."

"Ramji," Ramdas replied, "there is nothing wrong with the world. It is your mind that is obsessed. So long as your mind is not intensely longing to tear up the veil of illusion that clouds the Truth within you, mere external renunciation is of no avail. It will only be a leap out of the frying pan into the fire. True happiness consists in our right attitude towards life and the world. Now right attitude depends on right vision. The vision comes through the realisation of Truth or God. Do not be deceived. You cannot have liberation and peace by simply turning your back upon the world. Know your mind well. Freedom and joy are within you. Conquest of lust, wrath and greed is the path. Don't cling to Ramdas. He is no *guru*. He can only show you the path. The effort and struggle are your own. Be, therefore, the disciple of Truth."

The *bania's* mind appeared to have been preoccupied. Ramdas's words did not elicit any reply nor did he evince any sign that he had comprehended them. The night passed. Early next morning the train reached the Chitrakut station. Alighting, Ramdas and the *bania* moved towards the hills of Chitrakut which lay about three miles from the station. On the way he had again a conversation with the *bania*.

"Are you doing any *sadhana*, Ramji, for concentration of mind?" Ramdas asked.

"Why not?" he returned, "I am taking God's Name sometimes."

"Sometimes is not good," Ramdas said, "you ought to repeat the Name ceaselessly, and keep up an unbroken flow of remembrance in your thoughts."

"So far as that is concerned I am all right," he cut short.

"Ramji, leave Ramdas alone. You live your own life, because he wanders alone," Ramdas put in.

"No, no" he said with vehemence, "I am not giving you up."

"The path Ramdas walks is beset with pains and dangers. He is fearless and has no dread of death. To follow him would mean for you so much discomfort and misery," suggested Ramdas.

"I too am not afraid of anything. I can adapt myself to any life you choose to live. I am determined to cast my lot with you," he spoke with great emphasis.

Ramdas had no alternative but to submit. So God willed. Now they reached the banks of the river Mandakini in the heart of the town. They came to a bathing ghat where Ramdas took his seat on a low, worn out table. The fit of *vairagya* that had seized the *bania* was at work. He removed his shirt and, calling a passing barber, squatted down on a stone step.

"Shave me clean," he instructed the barber, "I am taking up *sannyas*."

"You mistake me," remonstrated the barber, "I am not prepared to bring down on my head the curses of your wife and children by helping you adopt *sannyas*."

"Brother, why do you mind all that? Do as I ask you," the *bania* pressed coaxingly. "I will give you my shirt and a watch, in addition to the usual shaving charges."

The barber was firm. His fear of the curses outweighed all other considerations. He refused to yield to the temptation. He got up and was about to leave the spot when the *bania* clutched him by the arm and begged: "Shave all the hair on my head and face except the eyebrows and a small tuft on the head. What do you say? You can have no objection now."

At this the barber lowered his leather bag of shaving materials and sat down. He agreed to the compromise. In fifteen minutes the *bania's* face and head, except the tuft in the middle of the latter, were cleared of all hair. He gave away to the barber the shirt and the watch and also some money. Now he turned to Ramdas anticipating a look of approbation from him. Ramdas could only be a cheerful spectator of the performance.

He had now left with him a greasy old cap, which he threw away, two dhotis and a small bag containing some money. On his finger was also a gold ring. One of the dhotis he presented to a beggar. All that he now possessed consisted of one dhoti, a gold ring, some money and a *lota*.

Bath over, he escorted Ramdas to a neighbouring sweetmeat shop where they had a tiffin of purees and milk. Then they sauntered along the bank of the river and came to a place called Phatakshila, where they saw nearly a dozen *sadhus* living in a hut close by the river. Resting for some time beneath a tree they retraced their steps to the town again by noon. The *bania* felt hungry. A recourse again to the sweetmeat shop satisfied the ravenous wolf within.

In the afternoon they went round the famous Kamtanath hill, on which it is said Sri Ramchandra made his abode with Sita for twelve years. In the evening they returned once more to the sweetmeat shop.

For the night Ramdas preferred to settle down beneath a tree and the *bania* slept beside him. The *bania* moved with him like his shadow. He was afraid that Ramdas might give him the slip at any moment. On rising next morning from the grassy bed, the *bania* felt that something was wrong with him.

"We shall go down to Karvi station," he said to Ramdas, "it is only four miles from here, and be back by evening."

It was not for Ramdas now to question why; his was to submit. After a visit to the fascinating tiffin shop they started. On the way, when they were walking through a narrow pass of a hillock, Ramdas had to follow the *bania* closely. Now a hissing noise and a low moan emanated from him. Ramdas jumped on one side and faced him. He was shedding tears.

"What is the matter?" inquired Ramdas.

Wiping away his tears with many a grief-laden hiccup, he said: "I feel so keenly for my wife and children. I ran away from them without their knowledge. They might be remembering me and living in agony over my absence. For myself I don't mind. It is for them my heart goes out." And he burst into tears.

"Ramji, why don't you then return to them?" asked Ramdas.

"You see I have almost burnt my boats. Oh! the barber was right." Now handling fondly the short pigtail on his head he continued. "Yes, the prospect is not after all so bad. I may yet go back to them."

(ii) Failure of the Peace Mission

Thus they arrived at Karvi. The *bania* went directly to the courtyard of a small thatched house near the railway station. Both sat on a bench in the yard, a few steps from the entrance of the house. Two boys were playing in front of it. The *bania* made several signs to the boys who neither recognised nor heeded him. His transformed appearance was the reason for their non-recognition.

Then he called one of the boys and whispered into his ears: "Tell your mother a man wants to see her."

The boy went in. Meanwhile, the *bania* confided to Ramdas the secret of his mission. He had come to his wife's sister's house. He wished to reveal himself to her so that through her he might find a means of reconciliation with his wife. It was evident that he had a quarrel with her which ended in his departure from his house with a threat that he would never darken its doorstep again.

The boy returned and unconcernedly commenced his play with his brother. How could a lady condescend to see a stranger inside her house? Again he drew towards the boy and told him in a low voice: "Tell your mother that her sister Mami's husband has come."

The lad gaped with raised eyebrows at the face of the *bania*, and a smile lit up his chubby face. He again ran into the house and soon reappeared beckoning the *bania* to go in. With a happy face the *bania* now hastened to the house. Ramdas waited. About fifteen minutes—and the *bania* came out. He looked like a whipped dog. His bitter face told of the unpalatable stuff with which he was served by his sister-in-law! She must have given him a big slice of her mind. The burning lashes of her tongue had charred and wrinkled his face!

"Her tongue cuts—like a razor. Bah! a woman's tongue!" he exclaimed knowingly. Then he added: "Maharaj, I have got it now. I am not fitted for a family life. A *sadhu's* life has a charm for me. I will never return to my home, there to face another sister! No, never." The resolution made, he continued: "Maharaj, let us be off from this undesirable place."

It was now past midday. The wolf again sorely troubled the *bania*. He sought a sweetmeat shop and they had a light repast. In spite of his heart having been lacerated with conflicting emotions, his treatment of Ramdas was marked by undiminished respect and kindness. Ramdas could well understand that it was the Lord Himself playing the game. How perfect a player!

When night approached, they sought refuge in a *dharmashala*, but it was so fully crowded that there was no room for them. They came out. The moon was up in the heavens. Its cool and soft rays illumined the retiring world. It flooded the vast railway-yard with its genial effulgence. Ramdas went towards it followed by the *bania*, and crossing the gate they entered the yard. In the yard were scattered large slabs of stones. Ramdas took his seat on one of them, asking the *bania* to occupy another which lay by its side.

"This is a fine place to sleep in for the night," Ramdas remarked.

The *bania* grunted as much as to say that he did not agree with him. He peered suspiciously into the dark spaces below the stones on all sides, but seeing that Ramdas had already laid himself down at full length on his slab, with another long drawn squeak, the *bania* also followed suit. Ramdas gazed on the bright moon above and the limitless blue space all around. He was charmed and absorbed. Suddenly, an unearthly yell issued from the *bania*. Ramdas sat up and looked at him. He was shouting out: "A serpent! a serpent!" He had stood up and was shaking his cloth, the only cloth, with feverish agitation.

"Maharaj, this place is infested with snakes. Let us go away from here," he said.

Ramdas had observed that lizards had made the snug nooks below the stone slabs their home.

"There is no fear, Ramji. They are lizards, not snakes, under the stone. They are harmless," Ramdas assured him.

"Oh!" he cried, "the thing, whatever it is, crawled on my legs. What a horrible sensation I got!"

"Never mind, sleep on; there need be no fear," Ramdas said encouragingly.

Finding Ramdas was in no mood to leave the place, he coiled himself on the stone, covering his body fully from head to foot with the cloth. During the night he started in his sleep twice with a cry of fright; the cries were only the after-effects of the first alarm. The first shriek had terrified the poor lizards so much that they dared not come out of their lairs to touch one who could produce such a soul-racking sound!

The *bania's* peace mission having utterly failed, the next day, they left Karvi again for Chitrakut. Bath in the river over, the favourite tiffin shop entertained them with its purees and milk. The day was hot. They rested for some time in the cool shade of a tree on the river bank. When the sun had descended half way down the heavens, Ramdas proposed that they should go up the hill of Hanumandhara and remain on it for the night.

(iii) *Sadhuism* Is Not a Joke

Ascending over a hundred stone steps uphill, they reached the place called Hanumandhara. Here a big jet of water was pouring down from a height of about fifty feet into a reservoir below, made of brick and mortar. There was also a small rest-house near the waterfall. The place is considered sacred because it is said to have been once occupied by Sri Ramchandra and Sita. From here an extensive view of the surrounding country can be had—vast plains, high hills covered with dense vegetation and the smooth running river, are all presented to the gaze of the spectator. Chitrakut is a land of sages and saints. Hundreds of *sadhus* are still doing penance in their small ashrams called *kutis*, scattered over and around the hills and the riversides.

From where they stood at the waterfall, Ramdas casting a glance upward, saw the mountain rise still higher. He was about to climb up when the *bania* suggested: "Maharaj, there is a neat little rest-house here," pointing to the building, "what if we spend the night there?"

Ramdas without reply, taking to a straggling path, went up, of course, followed by the *bania*. He now came upon a somewhat level piece of ground where stood two huts and an open shed. He entered one of the huts and found in it an image of black stone dressed in female robes, representing Sita. A *sadhu* was sitting near the image in order to collect the pice offered to the goddess by the pilgrims. It appears Sita was using the *mandir* as her kitchen, hence it goes by the name—Sita-Rasuyee.

The other hut was locked up. The *bania* sat inside the open shed to rest his tired limbs. The hill was still higher up by a couple of hundred yards. The whole place was thickly covered with tall wild trees.

"Ramji," Ramdas said to the *bania*, "this place is best suited for *bhajan* and so we shall stop here for the night." He replied that the idea did not appeal to him and that the idea was simply preposterous or something to that effect. The sun had set and darkness was rapidly creeping on the world. The *sadhu* of Sita *mandir* came out and saw Ramdas seated on the root of a tree and the *bania* in the tiny shed.

"How, now," the *sadhu* said, "what are you doing here? Don't you see it is getting dark? Let us go down."

"Ram wills that Ramdas should remain here for the night," answered Ramdas.

"Madness," he muttered, "this jungle is haunted by wild beasts and nobody is permitted to remain here in the open in the nights. The shut-up *kuti* belongs to my *guru* who has gone down to the city for *riddhi-siddhi*. It is his order that none should be here in the night."

"Ramdas obeys the command of Ram who says that he should not move from here," Ramdas rejoined.

"Then, do as you like at your own risk," the *sadhu* retorted. "But one thing," he added, "don't make use of that shed. You, you," turning to the *bania*, "get out of the shed." The *bania* came out.

With a last warning the *sadhu* left the place and went down-hill. About ten yards higher up from the shed, Ramdas saw a flat stone beneath a cluster of trees. Going up, he occupied it. No sooner had the *sadhu* gone out of sight than the *bania* got back to the seat in the shed. Darkness came on.

"Maharaj-ji, please do come to the shed," the *bania* called.

"No, Ramji, this flat stone is large enough to accommodate two persons. So you may also come here," answered Ramdas.

"This is a better place, Maharaj" he urged.

By now it became pitch dark. The *bania* cried out in terror: "O Maharaj, do come, I cannot remain here alone in this dreadful place."

Ramdas abandoning the flat stone went up to him in the shed. With the advent of darkness cold had also set in. The shed, open on all sides, being supported on four bamboo poles, allowed freely the chill breezes to sweep into it. Ramdas sat up while the *bania* lay down to sleep. But where was sleep for him in that fearful place? He was shivering both from dread and cold. At midnight there was a rustling noise among the thickly strewn dry leaves beneath the trees. Hearing the noise, with a sharp cry the *bania* bounded into a sitting posture.

"Maharaj," he whispered, "what is that noise?"

"It is nothing, Ramji," consoled Ramdas, "it may be only mountain rats, sporting about."

"For all that we know, it might be a wild animal or a cobra. I have heard that these jungles are inhabited by large sized cobras," he spoke with deep concern.

"Give up your fears, Ramji, they may be rats," assured Ramdas.

Again an hour later, a similar noise louder and closer was heard. This time the *bania* was thoroughly frightened, and clung to Ramdas as the scared young one of a monkey does its mother.

"What shall we do?" he cried.

"Repeat the Name of Ram," Ramdas suggested, "you need not be afraid of anything when that powerful Name is on your lips. Do repeat it and keep calm."

Thereafter, Ramnam worked on his lips with amazing continuity. Till the appearance of dawn he went on with the *japa*, and no more noises disturbed him. The day-break dispelled his fears. He lay down through utter exhaustion from want of sleep, and directly commenced to snore.

Ramdas got up from the place, and wandering in the jungle, came to the top of the hill. Through the morning mist he beheld the distant landscapes and the faint outlines of the turrets and domes of the temples of Chitrakut. The sight was enchanting and Ramdas stood still for some minutes under its magic spell. He roamed deeper into the forest where he discovered at places dry bones of animals scattered on the ground, the telltale signs of the work of wild beasts.

Remembering the *bania* he hastened to the spot where he had left him. But where was the *bania*? He had vanished. When Ramdas was looking for him, the *sadhu* who had come up inquired: "Whom are you seeking for? The *bania*! When I was coming up I saw him running down as though pursued by a devil." He added with a laugh: "After all he learnt that *sadhuism* is not a joke."

The jungle called Ramdas back again and he rambled freely through it, till about eleven o'clock when he descended the hill and directed his steps towards the river.

CHAPTER 17: CHITRAKUT (*continued*)

(i) The Naked *Mouni*

When bathing in the river, a tall and dark *sadhu* informed Ramdas of a place called Anasuyaji, seven miles from Chitrakut. He had thought of visiting the shrine that day and would be glad to have Ramdas as his companion. Ramdas fell in with his proposal. God always arranges things for him. He took Ramdas to the *sadhu* ashram of Phatakshila where he had dinner in the company of about two dozen *sadhus*.

An incident here is worthy of note. For want of room inside the small ashram, Ramdas had to sit for his meal in the outer veranda. The forests of Chitrakut were teeming with monkeys. The moment a plate containing *rotis*, rice, and *dal* was placed before Ramdas, a stout and powerful monkey coming from behind, with one sudden grab, carried off one *roti* and some rice. At this the *sadhu*, serving food, looking at Ramdas, angrily said: "Why did you allow the monkey to snatch away the *roti*? Dullard!"

"Never mind, Maharaj, he has taken Hanuman's share. Is he not Hanuman?" said Ramdas with a smile.

In response, the *sadhu* intently looked at Ramdas and remained silent.

The meal over, along with the dark *sadhu* and also with two others who made up the party, Ramdas set out for Anasuyaji. They had to pass through an extensive forest of giant trees. When they entered the depths of the forest they could discern footmarks of wild beasts on their track. Presently, they neared a small thatched hut of a *sadhu* who was hewing wood for his night fire. For a few minutes, the party rested beside the ashram and drank the cool water provided by the *sadhu*. He was an old man with a grey beard, bright, hale and cheerful. He spoke of wild beasts as though they were domestic animals.

The party proceeding onwards reached Anasuyaji before sunset. Anasuyaji was an awe-inspiring place. It was a narrow strip of the jungle by the side of the river, having in the background tall, rugged, weird looking crags. Facing the river stood a terraced building in which the resident *sadhus* lived, and at some distance, almost hidden in the dense grove of trees, was the temple of Anasuyaji—the celebrated *pativrata*, wife of the great sage Atrimuni. Here again the image was of black marble, dressed gaudily in feminine robes, after the North Indian fashion.

After slaking their thirst at the river—here the water of the brook was of transparent purity—the party rested beneath a huge tree in front of the terraced house. Night was approaching and along with it also cold. The *sadhus* went in search of firewood to light a fire for the night.

While Ramdas was sitting alone under the tree he heard the clapping of hands from the direction of the terrace. A *sadhu* beckoned to him. Ascending a flight of steps Ramdas reached the terrace and approached the *sadhu* who had called him. The *sadhu* was stark naked. He made signs to Ramdas to sit down on a rough *kambal* which he spread on the floor. Ramdas took the seat and he also sat down. The *sadhu* was a young man but his body was lean and withered by severe austerities. His unkempt hair and beard showed his utter indifference to physical appearance. His looks were distant and dreamy and there was a subtle glow on his brown face. As he expressed himself in signs, it was clear that he was also observing the vow of silence. He had in his hand a short *japa-mala* of *rudraksha* beads which he kept rotating between his fingers.

By signs he made Ramdas understand that he should remain with him for the night. He took Ramdas inside the room which he found in a state of perfect disorder. He prepared a seat for Ramdas beside the fire which burnt in the centre of the room. In silence he spent the night in the *sadhu's* company.

Early next day he asked the *sadhu's* permission to leave the place. He questioned Ramdas by gestures why he did not carry any water-vessel. Ramdas replied it was Ram's will. Out of the debris that lay scattered in his room, he ferreted out a neat little gourd, fashioned into a portable water pot. He placed the gourd before Ramdas and signed that he should take it. He demurred, but the *sadhu* was not to be foiled. His emphatic gesticulations denoted that Ramdas should never go without a water-pot. Ramdas at last submitted and took the gourd and bidding him adieu left the place.

Coming down he joined the dark *sadhu* who was waiting for him. The other *sadhus* had left earlier. Ramdas and the dark *sadhu* proceeded towards Bharat Coop. On the way they came across the huts of cultivators. Here they were entertained by the poor humble villagers with a meal of rice and curds. In the evening they reached Bharat Coop.

Here was a large well with the branches of an ancient and gigantic peepal tree hanging over it. Close by, there were temples of Rama, Sita, Lakshman, Bharat and Hanuman. They settled for the night beneath the tree on the platform around the well. Next morning, after a bath from the well water, they started again. Now the dark *sadhu* parted from him.

Left alone, Ramdas roamed wildly in the jungles for three days, stopping in the nights either in the ruins or under the trees, and subsisting on mowah flowers, picked up from beneath the trees. Mowah is a white flower, shaped like the rose bud with thick juicy petals and is sweet to the taste.

Ramdas had come to Chitrakut a week before the Ramnavami celebrations. There were yet two days more for the festival. As he wandered he again came on the *parikrama* or the path round the Kamtanath hill. On this path, at some distance from each other, were temples, ashrams, and tanks. While going on a round, it was nearing midday, when two devout mothers living in the out-house of a temple invited Ramdas and fed him with great love.

One evening he climbed the hill called Lakshman Tekri. He spent a night there in a solitary spot.

(ii) God Is for Him Who Thirsts for Truth

Along the *parikrama* was a Brahmachari ashram where a dozen young boys were imparted tuition in the Vedic lore and trained to observe the discipline and ritual of the ancient days. In front of the ashram was set up a *yajna kund* where the Brahmacharis assembled every day with their preceptor, and performed *yajna* in accordance with the Vedic rites, accompanied by the incantation of *mantras*. Besides the *yajna kund*, there were also small structures, artistic pieces of Indian architecture facing the ashram. In one of these Ramdas passed a night.

In the course of the rounds of the hill he had come upon a mad-looking *sadhaka*—truly God intoxicated men are in a sense mad—uttering Ramnam aloud ceaselessly, at one time sitting outside the small temples on the *parikrama* and at another walking round.

One night Ramdas took his position on the raised pedestal around the *yajna kund* for his meditation. Here, he was joined by this *sadhaka* who also settled on it beside him. While Ramdas was reciting Ramnam in an undertone, he was as usual taking the Name aloud. Hour after hour passed. They went on with the *japa*. It might have been past three o'clock. Sleep overpowered the *sadhaka*, and he rolled down on his seat and slept.

Half an hour had not passed when he started up with a cry and beheld Ramdas sitting and going on with his *japa*. He became perfectly wild with rage with himself, and spoke with bitterness and deep contrition: "Wretched fool that I am! I allowed sleep to deprive me of *bhajan*. Look, he is still awake. What a control he has on sleep!" referring to Ramdas. "I understand now, it was the food that I ate in the evening that was responsible for this lapse. Oh! I am losing precious time!"

Verily, God is for him who is seized with such a burning thirst for Truth.

Ram-navami celebrations usually continued for nine days. The first day came, and thousands of pilgrims from various parts of India streamed into Chitrakut for *parikrama* or walking round the Kamtanath hill—on which Sri Ramchandra and Sita performed *tapas*—which was considered by the devotees to possess high spiritual merit. So, thick crowds of pilgrims tramped round the sacred hill.

In the course of his walks on this path Ramdas had noted the Pilikoti ashram to which were related Swami Nirbhayanand and his wife, the saintly pair he met in Jhansi. He found the ashram decorated with festoons, flags and *shamianas*, and hundreds of *sannyasis* who were attracted from several places of India assembled within its precincts. The motto of the ashram was to serve with food any *sannyasi* who happened to visit it. The head of the ashram was Swami Akhandanand, a famous *sannyasi* of the United Provinces. His disciple Swami Satchidanand, a Sanskrit scholar, was the manager of the institution. The ashram had also attached to it a small free Sanskrit *pathshala* for boys.

Swami Nirbhayanand, his wife and a brother of his, Swami Ramanand, who was at the time in the ashram, were also disciples of Swami Akhandanand who had a large following both among the *sannyasis* and the householders. He and his *sannyasi* disciples in their itinerant life, in certain seasons, lived for some period in Jhansi. They had heard of Ramdas from Ramkinkar but had no occasion to see him.

Swami Nirbhayanand had asked Ramdas, when starting from Jhansi, not to fail to visit the Pilikoti ashram. Now Ramdas, entering the grounds of the ashram, mingled with the throng of *sannyasis*. At midday he joined with them in their feast. In the afternoon, taking a walk around the hill, he returned to the ashram in the evening. He occupied for the night a stone bench—a number of such benches had been erected in the yard. The peculiarity with them was that the upper slab was fitted on to the uprights at a slight angle, so as to keep one's head at a higher level when one reclined on it at full length. In the nights these slabs were cold as ice.

As night advanced Ramdas, wanting to rest, covered himself with a part of the only cloth he had, the other part of which being spread on the bench and he lay down. In those days he had very little sleep. An hour later, a young *sannyasi* who had come with two blankets drew his attention. "Maharaj, have these *kambals*; the cold is bitter." By his urging Ramdas vacated the bench and the *sannyasi* spread a blanket on the slab and, after he rested on it, covered him with the other. Everybody is kind to him because everyone is He.

Next day, at daybreak, he went to the river for a bath. The gourd had now become his companion. He came back to the ashram by midday. In the evening the young *sannyasi* who had provided him with blankets the previous night, seeking his society, took him to his *kuti* which stood on the opposite side of the road. Ramdas spoke to him of his meeting with Swami Nirbhayanand and his wife at Jhansi. Then he inquired of Ramdas's name. He gave it.

The night passed. The following day, early as usual, he went to the river for bath and reappeared by noon at the ashram. In the front verandah of a small outhouse a number of *sannyasis* had assembled. As he entered the compound they were to a man gazing deliberately at him and giggling! He was about to walk past them when Swami Satchidanand, the manager of the institution, cried halt.

"Come here," he accosted, beckoning Ramdas into the verandah. He got in.

"We have been contemplating upon the nature of the punishment to be meted out to you," the Swami continued.

One of the saints was holding a stout cane. Smiling, Ramdas took the stick from its owner and offering it to the Swami said: "Here is a stick. Punish Ramdas to your heart's content," and bending down, presented his back for the treatment. All laughed.

"Not that," explained the Swami, "we have hit it all right. You have to stay in this Ashram for one full year. This is the punishment!"

"If Ram does not will it so?" asked Ramdas quietly.

"It is Ram who speaks through us," he rejoined.

"Ram speaks also in Ramdas. He says Ramdas should not agree to your proposal," said Ramdas.

"We shall see about it. We are putting you in a separate room and one of us will mount guard on you. You cannot escape us," he said, shaking his head.

"Ram's will be done," Ramdas replied.

"Now, have you any idea of the charge against you?" he questioned.

"You have already pronounced the judgment. What does it matter whether Ramdas knows or not what the charge is?" answered Ramdas.

"However, I am telling you what it is," he went on: "you have outwitted us for two days. You were with us perfectly incognito. We had heard of you and wished greatly to see you. Hence the punishment for your deception."

(iii) The Test of Self-Surrender

A narrow room was got ready for Ramdas in which he found a wooden cot with a quilt on it, and an earthen pot filled with water. He was handed over to the charge of Swami Ramanand, an old *sannyasi*, who attended to his needs. The childlike nature of the *sannyasis* in this ashram was wonderful. They would frequently come to Ramdas in the room, talk to him and also fondle him, as if he were a child! Here Ramdas had quite a feast of love.

One day, Swami Ramanand and Swami Guptanand, the young *sannyasi* who had supplied Ramdas with blankets on the first night, were seated on the cot beside him. Ramdas spoke upon self-surrender. As an instance, he narrated the episode of Draupadi's predicament when Dushasana sought to disgrace her in the *durbar* hall of the Kauravas. So long as she was crying to Sri Krishna for help, and at the same time struggling to protect herself, the Lord did not come to the rescue. At last, realising her folly, she lifted up her hands in absolute surrender and called Krishna, and that moment He saved her.

When Ramdas came to mention about Draupadi's self surrender in the narration, Swami Guptanand who was listening with great concentration was so overpowered with emotion that he burst into tears. Also Swami Ramanand's eyes moistened.

In Guptanand's company Ramdas, one day, ascended the famous Kamtanath hill which stood in front of the Pilikoti ashram. Some Hindus consider it a sacrilege to tread on the hill which is held sacred, because Sri Ramachandra and Sitadevi are said to have resided on it in the ancient days. The hill was about five hundred feet above its base. There are no structures or any relics of them on the hill. It is covered with wild shrubs and trees of which a certain species bore edible fruits called thendu. While descending, Ramdas ran down a dry water-course, sprinkled with smooth and rounded boulders.

Another day, a *sannyasi* from Kashi took Ramdas out for a walk round the famous hill. On going some distance both sat on a raised stone platform beneath a tree. Here the *sannyasi* confided to Ramdas his condition.

"Maharaj," he said, "I have been for nearly thirty years in this line of *sannyas*, but still my mind is perfectly hopeless. Lust, greed and wrath are as rampant in it as ever. What shall I do?"

"The only way to control the mind and free it from the evils you mention is always to take the Name of God, meditate upon His great attributes and surrender all your actions to Him," Ramdas replied suggestively.

"I have done all that and I have failed," he said.

"You ought to practice in solitude," Ramdas put in.

"Oh!" he cried out, "Don't speak of solitude. I have a terror for solitude. When I am left alone, my mind goes into a whirl of most unholy desires. So I am running after saints. In their society I have peace. But I know, I should not solely depend upon external aids for attaining peace, as such peace cannot be permanent." He stopped and looked at Ramdas for the solution of his problem.

"What you say is right," Ramdas now spoke at length: "God, who is absolute existence, consciousness and bliss, is within you—nay, you and He are not different. Unless you realise Him there can be no true liberation and lasting peace. Please note that the first qualification necessary for the seeker of God is fearlessness. Neither the terror of solitude nor the terror of the crowd should daunt you. But solitude is a great help. Know that God, who dwells in you, is almighty. Seek His assistance by constant remembrance, meditation and prayer. Then the mind is bound to come under control. The evil passions must depart from it.

"Forget not the central truth that God is seated in your own heart. Don't be disheartened by failures at initial stages. Cultivate the spirit of surrender to the workings of His will in you and outside you until you have completely surrendered up your ego-sense, and have known He is in all and He is all, and you and He are one. Be patient. The path of self-discipline that leads to God-realisation is not an easy path. Obstacles and sufferings are on the path; the latter you must bear and the former overcome,—all by His help. His help comes only through concentration. Repetition of God's Name helps concentration."

The *sannyasi* heard Ramdas silently and put no more questions. They retraced their steps to the ashram.

(iv) Ramdas Is a Child of God

A few days later, the same *sannyasi* came to Ramdas and asked: "Don't you know? The great Swami Akhandanandji is here. Have you seen him?"

"To see you is to see him," Ramdas simply replied.

"No, Maharaj, you ought to see him," he said with a serious look. "He is only a few yards from the ashram, seated beneath a grove of trees. He always prefers to stay in jungles and does not like to reside beneath a roof. He is a famous *mahatma*. He is going away tomorrow morning. If you don't have his *darshan* today, you will lose a golden opportunity."

"For Ramdas God is everywhere. He need not go specially anywhere to see Him," Ramdas answered.

"What!" he exclaimed with surprise. "You don't want to see him? You shall go to him," he added emphatically, and taking hold of Ramdas's arm almost dragged him.

"Come, I am also going with you." He was a strong man and Ramdas did not resist.

A few minutes' walk brought them to a large assembly of *sannyasis*, seated beneath the shade of about half a dozen tall, spreading trees. On a cot against a tree sat a *sannyasi* with only a loin cloth or *kaupin* on while all the rest were seated on the ground.

Ramdas went directly to the *swamiji* and placed his head at his feet and sat down on the ground near the cot. Now a stillness seemed to have settled on the gathering. All was silent for a few minutes. The *swamiji* broke the ice.

He said to a householder devotee sitting beside Ramdas: "Ask him if he has any doubts to clear." The *swamiji* spoke in Hindi. The devotee was an English educated man. He interpreted the *swamiji's* question to Ramdas in English, Ramdas's knowledge of Hindi was yet poor. So he, of course, replied in English.

"Ramdas is a child of God and He has long ago removed all doubts of His child." The devotee conveyed to the *swamiji* in Hindi what Ramdas said.

"What is his position then?" came the next question from the *swamiji*.

"His position is this" Ramdas replied, "he is like the river Ganges which, having reached the ocean and become one with it, still continues running towards it."

When the *swamiji* and others heard the reply, a titter went round the congregation. The *swamiji* remained silent.

Then the devotee on his own part put a poser: "What brought you here then?"—a significant question!

"Ramdas came, simply because Ram dragged him here," was the answer, and he looked at the *sannyasi* escort and smiled.

"What is it?" the *swamiji* asked the devotee inquisitively. The devotee explained, and there arose a loud roar of laughter from the assembly.

Then Ramdas suddenly jumped up, and bowing again to the *swamiji* ran a race to his room of the outhouse which he reached in less than a minute.

Swami Ramanand was a simple and kind soul. He looked after Ramdas with great tenderness. He counted on Ramdas's stay in the ashram for a pretty long time. In his own way he was watchful. Ramdas knew that to leave the place with his knowledge was out of question. Ram was bidding him to decamp—but how?

Ram provided the opportunity one day. The sun was unusually hot. At midday, some of the elderly *sannyasis* would have their forty winks. But this particular day the heat of the sun laid prostrate both the young and the old. The outhouse, at about one in the afternoon, resounded with a variety of snores! Swami Ramanand led the chorus.

Ramdas, who was all alive and active, taking the gourd pot in hand, slowly slipped out of the compound on tiptoe. He reached the road making the least possible noise—the *sannyasis* never the wiser. Once on the road, he started on a trot which soon developed into a downright gallop! He ran for a mile and then walked at a brisk pace.

CHAPTER 18: TOWARDS BANDA – BANDA

(i) The Water—Nectar of Pure Love

Ramdas had no idea of any destination and did not care which way he walked. He found himself again in Karvi by evening. Early next morning he was proceeding along the railway lines, treading on the bed of sharp-edged granite bits near the rails. On covering a mile or thereabouts, he came to a level crossing where the railway gate-keeper seeing him, said in a sharp voice: "What is the matter with you? Are you mad? Don't you feel that you are walking on sharp-pointed stones?" Pointing to a road, he added: "Take to that; the road goes straight to Banda."

Following the gate-keeper's suggestion, he moved on to the road and continued his journey. At noon he reached a small village, having on the roadside a few shops. A shop-keeper invited him to his shop. He got in and sat down on a mat. The first thing his eyes fell on, as he entered, was a framed picture of Kali on the wall, decorated with a flower garland. A number of customers were seated in front of him, sipping a clear, transparent liquid from small tin cups. The strong odour was suggestive of liquor. So he was in a liquor shop! It dealt also in *ganja*, for on another side a man having purchased the stuff was preparing a smoke.

The shop-keeper also prepared a *chilam* of *ganja*, and lighting it, offered it to Ramdas. It was taken for granted every *sadhu* smoked *ganja*! He was not used to *chilam* or the country pipe. He apprised the dealer of the fact and begged to be excused.

"I will teach you how to manipulate the *chilam*," he said in a kind tone. In a trice Ramdas was trained. He had a few puffs at the pipe.

An hour later, the kind shop-keeper provided him with a meal. At about three o'clock he left the village and continued the journey. At dusk he gained a small hamlet. On the roadside, below the trees, was an enclosure made of high stone benches. He got a perch upon one of them.

Usually one meal a day sufficed him. He had no craving for food in the night. But today he had a distinct feeling of hunger. The *ganja* smoke, although it did not affect him in any other way, created this feeling. He spoke of it. To whom could he do so but to Ram?

Five minutes had not elapsed when a lad of about fourteen ran towards him and, leaping on the slab on which he was sitting, drew close to him, and said: "I want to give you a meal. What would you have?"

"Rice and milk," Ramdas replied.

Ramdas was not surprised at his offer. His life had been replete with a series of such surprises. Ram's nursing hand was visible to him everywhere. The lad disappeared and returned two hours later. He escorted Ramdas to his cottage, and his kind mother served him with rice and milk. On finishing the meal he regained the seat on the stone slab.

Night passed. Next day he continued his journey. It was midday. The still air was burning hot. He went bare-footed and bare-headed. For him suffering was joy. His supreme indifference to physical comforts had transformed every emotion of his into ecstasy. Thus bathing in the burning glory of the sun he walked on. Now a passing cartman accosted him: "Maharaj, the sun is hot. On your left, a furlong away in the fields, there is a small ashram of sadhu Ramdasji. Go there."

Ramdas, turning to the direction pointed by the cartman, made for the ashram. Here he met a very old *sadhu*. He was, kind and affable. Ramdas had a bath at the well, a simple meal and rest for an hour on a shaky bench. Again he marched on. At sunset he found himself in the midst of a jungle. He always felt a peculiar feeling of exaltation when he was alone in the jungles at night. He repaired to a place beneath a large tree for spending the night. He laid himself down on the rough ground. In less than five minutes, he had a shower of bird's droppings from the branches of the tree. Then he moved into the open and reclined on the soft grass.

The moon was up. Its cool rays illumined the forest. The light filtering through the leaves and branches of the trees formed on the ground below beautiful spangled designs, and the forest seemed as if it were covered with a multi-patterned carpet. The air was cool and a soft breeze was blowing. The silence of the night was broken now and then by the flapping of the huge bats that flew from tree to tree and the distant hoots of owls who were holding their nocturnal discourses. The night passed in wakefulness and bliss.

Next day, again at midday, he was stopped on the road by another cartman who directed him to a temple close by. He said that Ramdas would do well to have the *darshan* of a *sadhu* named Kamtanath who resided in the temple. The time was about one o'clock, afternoon. The temple was about fifty yards from the road. He entered the temple. Everything was still within. There was none inside except a *sadhu* snoring on a cot. He quietly took a seat, a little away from the *sadhu*. The *sadhu* awoke with a start and his eyes fell on Ramdas. Beckoning Ramdas towards him, he rubbed off with his cloth the perspiration streaming down Ramdas's face and arms.

"I have no food to offer you," he said with a smiling face, "you have to be content now with mere water. In the night you shall have a good meal."

Ramdas laughed and replied: "Mere water will do, Maharaj."

"Go and have your bath," he said next.

Ramdas finished his bath at the well and returned. The *sadhu* then, taking him by the arm, led him towards the main room of the temple where gaudily decorated images of God were kept. Then leading him to the narrow passage, he made him sit on a mat. Going into an inner room he brought a bowl of *dal* and a thick *roti*. Sitting down beside Ramdas he mixed the *roti* in the *dal* curry and suddenly thrust a lump of it into his mouth. Ram, indeed, has his own unique ways of feeding Ramdas! As he swallowed, he forced lumps of food into his mouth one after another, until he was overfilled. Coming out they sat on the cot, his arm round Ramdas's neck. He was simply gushing with love.

"You shall stay here for some days. Won't you?" he asked.

"No, Maharaj, Ramdas is starting presently," answered Ramdas in an appealing tone.

"I am not allowing you to go. I want you to be with me for at least four of five days," he said compressing his lips.

To argue with him seemed to be useless. So Ramdas remained silent.

"You see the sun is still hot; have a nap." he said, and lying at full length on the cot fell asleep.

Ramdas waited for some minutes and, finding that the *sadhu* had fallen asleep, slowly got up and walked out of the temple on tiptoe—as he did at the Pilikoti ashram. As soon as he came out on the bypath, he ran at full speed until he gained the main road. A few miles ahead he came across a bullock-cart. At the sight of him a man jumped out of the cart and drawing near him pleaded: "Maharaj, do take a seat in my cart. I cannot bear to see you walking on the burning ground in the hot sun."

Ramdas told him that he was on his way to Banda and his course lay in the opposite direction.

"Then, here, please take this money; it is only one anna and a half the railway fare from a station just a few yards from here to Banda. A train is due in a few minutes. Do catch it." He forced the coins on Ramdas.

Ramdas proceeded to the small station. On enquiry he was told that the fare was two annas. He came out of the station and continued his travel on foot. Before sunset he reached the outskirts of Banda. Here a woman on the roadside had, beneath a tree, a small thatched hut in which she stored drinking water in big earthen pots. She freely distributed the water to thirsty travellers who happened to pass that way.

When she saw Ramdas, she called out: "Mahatmaji, Mahatmaji, come here; have some rest in my humble shed."

He responded to her call.

The kind mother made him sit on a bench and washed his feet and legs up to the knee with cool water from the pots. He also drank the water she offered. It was the nectar of pure love!

(ii) The Militant *Sadhu*

Ramdas was passing through the crowded streets of Banda, when a merchant from his shop called him and said: "Maharaj, only a short distance from the town, in a secluded place, resides a *sadhu* by name Vishuddhanand. The place is called Budh Ram Kuva. He is a pure saint, go to him." He pointed the way through a by-lane.

Ramdas walked in the direction indicated by the merchant, but as he proceeded, in the network of streets, he lost the way. He asked a passerby who said that he would escort Ramdas to the spot. Ramdas followed him. They came to a temple of Mahadev at the foot of a hill, and passing through a high porch ascended the hill. They had to climb a few yards on all fours and come to a flat surface in front of a large shallow cave. A number of people were sitting on the ground. A *sadhu*, a young man in *kaupin*, was standing inspecting the construction of *dhuni* or fire-pit at the mouth of the cave.

Seeing Ramdas he offered an empty gunny bag for a seat, on which he sat. Now the *sadhu's* attention was drawn to a man in the assembly. Flying into a temper he roundly abused the man in coarse language. Ramdas enquired of the escort if the angry *sadhu* was Vishuddhanand.

"No," he replied, "this is Balak Ram Paramhams. Vishuddhanand stays about a mile away from here."

"Can you take Ramdas to him?" Ramdas asked.

"Very well," he answered.

The latter part of this dialogue reached the ears of the irate *sadhu*. It tended only to fan the flame. He now emptied the vials of his wrath on Ramdas's escort.

"What?—you are going to take the *sadhu* away. Get away from here, you fool; leave this instant." and he raised his right leg towards him for a kick. The frightened escort ran down the hill and disappeared.

"Maharaj," the *sadhu* said turning to Ramdas, "do remain here; I shall see that all your wants are met."

Ramdas submitted, but made him understand that his wants were few and that he would prefer to live there on mere milk diet. A merchant named Seth Moolchand furnished the *sadhu* with food twice a day. A small boy was employed for fetching the meals. Night came on; the crowd dispersed. About an hour later, the boy turned up with the meal as usual. The *sadhu* had another guest who now issued from a hole on the left side of the large open cave.

"Tapaswiji, hurry on; dinner has arrived," said the *sadhu*, Balak Ram.

Tapaswiji was a man of about thirty-five with a stout and well-built body, besmeared with a thick layer of ashes. He had a stout coir rope round his waist and wore only a *kaupin*. His matted hair was coiled up into a crown on his head. He held in one hand a *yoga-danda* (or arms-rester) like a cross, and in the other a *japa-mala* of *rudraksha* beads.

They sat down for the meal and asked Ramdas to join them. He excused himself. Balak Ram tried to persuade the boy to fetch some milk for Ramdas. He demurred and said that he did not know where to get milk from.

"Never mind," put in Ramdas, "Ramdas is not hungry: he will be satisfied with a tumbler of water for the night."

The meal over, the *sadhus* prepared *ganja chilam* and Balak Ram appealed to Ramdas to share with them a smoke. Here again he declined their offer with thanks. He was silent and watchful. The *ganja* intoxication made the *sadhus* drift into strange and irrelevant talks.

Ramdas stopped on the hill for about a fortnight and the short stay was crowded with thrilling and amusing incidents. The hill was called Bambeshwar Pahad. Except for a sprinkling of shrubs and two or three trees, the hill was arid and rocky. So there was scarcity of water on Bambeshwar Pahad. Water had to be carried up from the temple well down below.

Balak Ram Paramhams was a young man aged about thirty-two possessing a lithe and upright figure. His lower jaw and the compressed lips showed determination. His eyes were tender and his face was suffused with smiles when he was not in fits of temper, which would sweep over him as the raging tempests, only to be followed by calmness and a clear sky. At heart, Ramdas could discern, he was soft and compassionate. For lack of proper discipline and society he had a mind riotous and uncontrolled. He had a recoil from the unrealities of the world and his dispassion was admirable. The only method he employed to subdue the cravings of the mind was *ganja* smoking, but the stuff would only raise the very spirit of wrath in him. One predominant trait in him was a passion to serve saints. By such service alone, he firmly believed, one would attain liberation or *moksha*. His one message to all those who came to him was to use their wealth for the service of *sadhus*. His ambition was to make the hill a home of *sadhus* and for himself to be their servant, and the worldly people the suppliers of the necessaries for such service.

He was militant in his ways with the visitors, and with the whip of his tongue he would lash them. A specimen of the manner in which he talked to them will be related here. One day, it appears, he sent for the Deputy Collector of the district who was in Banda at the time. He was a Hindu. The poor officer, having a religious turn of mind, not knowing what was in store for him, obeyed the call of the *mahatma*. He came to see Balak Ram at the close of his office, in his usual office dress. The officer bowed to Balak Ram and sat down.

Now Balak Ram, taking a full survey of the man in front of him, rolled out his tongue to lubricate it. He was gifted with eloquence combined with vehemence so that he could reduce his adversary to pulp.

"Ha, ha," he began derisively, "what a fine *pheta* you do wear!—a well-ironed long coat, clean white trousers, superior English boots and a fashionable cane into the bargain. Luxurious dandy that you are! How much precious money are you wasting on these foppish things? You think you are very clever, because you have these adornments. Fool, do you still believe in wallowing in dirt like the filthy worm, toiling and moiling from morn to eve to procure these baubles and steep yourself in the enjoyment of selfish and sinful desires?"

"Beware," he continued: "death like a huge cobra is ever stalking behind you, waiting at any moment to swallow you up. Have some thought about what you are here for. The only way for you, mud-worms, to attain salvation is service of the saints. If you don't do this, you are done for. If you have any money about you, shell it out."

The dazed and perplexed officer said that he would send some money on reaching home, and mumbling some excuse sneaked away. The money never came. Thereafter Balak Ram sent for him half a dozen times. The officer did not, of course, turn up!

(iii) The Way to Peace

School boys have a fascination for *sadhus* and *mahatmas*. They can have good fun in their company. They watch and then imitate the curious antics of the *sadhu*-world. The whims, caprices and eccentricities of this race of religious mendicants are for ever a matter for close observation on the part of the youngsters. Because here they witness a delectable show without payment of any fee. Not so with Balak Ram. No doubt he had a great love for boys, but they had to pay dearly for both the show and the love he bore for them. When the school hours were over, a company of boys would crawl up the Bambeshwar hill. Now Balak Ram had with him a dozen well-sized earthen water pots handy.

"Sonnies, O dears," he would call them. He had the trick of forming his thin lips into the shape of a flattened funnel to show his endearment. "Will you not get me some water from the well below? Here are the pots, one each—clever fellows—you can do it in a twinkling; yes, dears."

Such were his insinuating and coaxing ways! Once Ramdas was the spectator of an incident like this. A batch of six boys was egged on to fetch the water and were provided with pots. Of this batch two boys could alone come up safe with the pots, while the others carried with them either the broken necks or bottoms of the pots. At the loss of four pots in one experiment Balak Ram's monkey was up. His smiles disappeared and, looking sternly at the four delinquents, he bellowed forth: "Do you think—you rogues—that the pots belonged to your grandfathers! I paid hard cash for them. You broke them, careless imps! Go immediately to your parents and get me one anna and a half each. Run away, quick. You must be back with money by nightfall."

The boys skulked away never to show their faces again! Another day a fresh batch came and the same story was repeated.

Balak Ram was worrying for some days over a certain overseer who had yielded up a couple of rupees at his first onslaught of abuse, just as in India a milch buffalo does not yield milk unless beaten on the back by the stalk of the plantain tree. He was keen on giving a second trial to the overseer, but the overseer knew better. Every messenger sent by Balak Ram returned to report that he was not to be found. So far as Balak Ram was concerned, the Deputy Collector had proved an utter failure—no scent of him again!

One night Ramdas asked him why he treated the visitors with harsh abuse, and he replied with a sniff of contempt: "You see, sweet words and arguments are not for donkeys. They need a stout stick to make them work. So with these selfish and ignorance-ridden folk. I mean well of them; their hide needs hammer blows to awaken them."

"You are mistaken," Ramdas then told him, "there is no power on earth greater than love. By mildness and gentleness you can conquer the world. You are out as a *sadhu* to know God. God is love and peace. An abusive tongue and a mind filled with wrath are signs of ignorance. Until love, compassion and forgiveness dwell in your heart and perfect peace in your mind, you cannot realise God."

"Oh! how your words heal me; make me a better man," he cried out passionately. "I know I am full of defects. I wanted you to remain with me only for this reason. I wish earnestly to be benefited by your society."

Now the Tapaswiji drew his attention to the fresh-lit *chilam* of *ganja*. The conversation broke off.

Ramdas made him understand on several occasions, when he was using harsh language with the visitors, that he would prefer bidding him goodbye to remaining with him to hear his abuse. He was averse to losing Ramdas. He loved and adored him. Many a time he curbed his tongue lest Ramdas should slip away from him.

Things nearly approached a climax one night. Balak Ram had kept a rupee in some crevice within the small cave. That afternoon he looked for the coin but could not find it. The boy, the food carrier, used to sweep the floor of the cave. Suspicion fell on him. The boy was absent. Balak Ram fumed with rage.

"Let the boy come. I shall take proper account of him—the blackguard!" he rang out.

As usual, at about eight o'clock, the boy came with the night meal. The moment he lowered to the floor the vessel of food, Balak Ram caught hold of the boy's arm in a firm grip and shouted: "You thief, where is my rupee?" Looking at Balak Ram's fiery eyes and menacing tone, the boy trembled.

"I do not know, I have not taken it," replied he in a whining voice.

"Liar!" roared Balak Ram, "having committed the theft, you dare to tell a lie on top of it. You are not fit to live; if you are allowed to, you will turn into a regular budmash. I shall presently strangle you to death," Suiting action to his words, with a murderous fury, he closed his fingers on the boy's throat.

At once, Ramdas going forward told him: "Look here, Ram, Ramdas is off. He cannot any longer remain with you." He suddenly jumped past a rock in order to go down the hill.

Balak Ram releasing his hold on the boy's throat ran after Ramdas and falling at his feet said: "Forgive, forgive me; I forgot myself. I shall never harm the boy; do return."

Ramdas returned. That night also he had plain talk with him.

"You must control your temper, Ramji," Ramdas said, "and not allow it to run amok as you did a little while ago. In your rage you would have killed the poor boy. You think you are trying to mend the ways of others while your own are not straight. Have you heard the saying: 'Physician, heal thyself?' This very appropriately applies to you. You are recklessly wounding the feelings of others by your vituperative speeches. No, you should not go on like this. People come to you to know the way of peace and what do you give them?—a shower of abuses. Infinite love dwells in your heart, but you are submerging it in a storm of unbridled passions."

"Oh! do I give pain to people by my words?—how I wish I should not! I did not know I was such a tyrant. I mean always well. Oh! heartless wretch that I am!" he uttered with a deep touch of remorse, and covering his eyes with both hands wept bitterly. Then he pleaded: "Show me a way to control this insane mind. At times it burns like a furnace and my head seems to be splitting. Oh! show me some way."

"For control of mind the best method is repetition of God's Name," advised Ramdas. "Keep the Name always on your tongue, talk little, have proper food. Above all, give up *ganja* smoking. This habit has been the ruin of you."

CHAPTER 19: BANDA – GOHKARPARVAT

(i) Nothing Is Impossible for God

Tapaswiji had left the hill, the day following the night that Balak Ram attempted to strangle the boy-servant. The boy had also disappeared. For want of a servant it was now difficult to get meals from Seth Moolchand's. Ramdas was going on milk diet, and some devotees brought him milk regularly morning and evening. Now Balak Ram also shared the milk with him. Balak Ram commenced repeating the Ram *mantram*. For two days he remained quiet. He was free from fits of temper. *Ganja* was eschewed. He talked very little. He was resigned and peaceful. On the second day he said that he felt hungry.

Straightaway, Ramdas with an escort proceeded to Budhram Kuva where *sadhu* Vishuddhanand resided. At the sight of him the *sadhu* went into ecstasies. He welcomed him with a fond embrace. He was an old man, lean and tall, with a long white beard and hair reaching his shoulders. He wore only a *kaupin*. Ramdas told him that he had come to beg for a meal for the sake of Balak Ram.

"I would allow you to carry food to him," he said, "only after you have had your meal here."

He was an active old man. Within half an hour he cooked a simple meal of soft *rotis* and *dal*. Then he took Ramdas to a well. The place was named after the saint at whose instance the well was dug. Before Vishuddhanand came to occupy the place, there lived a *sadhu* who went by the name Budhram. Hence the name Budhram Kuva, that is, Budhram's well.

As an Indian mother washes her child, so Vishuddhanand bathed Ramdas with his own hands, drawing water from the well. Then feeding him with a plain but wholesome meal he had prepared, he permitted Ramdas to leave him, carrying a meal for Balak Ram. Balak Ram took the food. In the evening his craving for *ganja* returned, and unable to resist he smoked it again. God's Name left his tongue, the old temper subdued for two days once more raised its vicious hood.

The following day, he proposed to have a *Ramlila* performance at the cave. It is a religious function in which two men sing alternately, to the accompaniment of musical instruments, the exploits of Sri Ramchandra. These performances are popular in the United Provinces, and hundreds of people assemble on the occasion. Balak Ram, since morning, was trying to persuade the visitors to arrange for the function, but none would take any interest in the matter. He was sorely upset and disappointed.

At midday, Ramdas was lying down in the small cave, when the *pujari* of the Mahadev temple, a frequent visitor, came up: "*Pujari*, you must somehow manage to have *Ramlila* performed here tonight," said Balak Ram.

"Maharaj," he replied, "I am a poor man. The performance will cost ten rupees. I don't see how I can collect so much money."

"No, no, *pujari*, I am bent upon it. Do arrange any way," insisted Balak Ram.

"You are asking me to do the impossible," pleaded the *pujari*.

Ramdas in the cave was listening to their conversation and, at this juncture, spoke: "*Pujari*, nothing is impossible for God. Why do you think you are the doer in any matter? Take it that you are merely His instrument and set about this business, and God will crown your efforts with success," assured Ramdas.

"Well, if it be Mahadev's will let it be done. I feel now I can be a tool in His hands in this affair. I am going," and he left.

Balak Ram had still his doubts; time passed. It was nearing five o'clock and he remarked in despondent tone: "Maharaj, there is no hope of *Ramlila*. The *pujari* is not to be seen."

"There is yet time; don't be impatient," said Ramdas.

Ten minutes had not elapsed when half a dozen men arrived, carrying with them all the necessaries for the *Ramlila* performance—rugs, carpets, flowers, gas lights, sweets, *agarbattis*, fruits, festoons, and other articles. A party of musicians also came with their musical instruments. Now Balak Ram's face brightened.

"Maharaj," he said to Ramdas, "will you kindly go to Vishuddhanand and fetch him? His blessed company is also needed at this function. He will come only if you invite him personally."

Ramdas accordingly started and went to Budhram Kuva and begged the old *sadhu* to grace the performance with his presence. He agreed and both reached the cave on the hill by seven o'clock. Meanwhile, the place at the front of the cave had been beautifully decorated. The rugs and carpets were spread on the floor and over a hundred persons of both sexes had assembled, and the gas lamp was shedding its brilliant light on the scene. The *pujari* was busy arranging things.

Balak Ram, Vishuddhanand and Ramdas sat in a line at the mouth of the cave and the *Ramlila* celebration commenced. The singers possessed a sweet voice and the air thrilled with their music. The performance continued till one o'clock when the crowd dispersed.

(ii) The Absolute Fast

On the day following the *Ramlila* performance, Ramdas roamed over the Bambeshwar hill and came across another cave, a few yards above the one occupied by Balak Ram. It was made up of large blocks of rock leaning against each other forming below a big cavity, having an opening right at the top where the rocks met. The entrance to the cave was a narrow passage through which one could not pass abreast. One had to force oneself sideways.

He went inside and saw that the space within was sufficient to accommodate one person. Caves exerted a strange influence on him. The moment he saw one he would decide to spend some days in it. This cave also appeared to invite him for a stay, but on condition that he should remain in it without food and drink, not even water, observing at the same time the vow of silence.

Going down to Balak Ram, he said: "Ramji, a little way up there is a cave. Ram wills that Ramdas should dwell in it and go on an absolute fast. He should not drink even water, and should hold perfect silence."

"For what period is the fast to last?" questioned he.

"Ramdas has no idea, Ram will determine it," Ramdas answered.

Balak Ram obtained through the visitors a basketful of cow-dung and, having the inside of the cave well swept, smeared it with a layer of it. After the floor was dry he spread on it a torn mat he had. In making these arrangements Balak Ram manifested great enthusiasm. In the evening Ramdas occupied the cave. He sat up on the mat in utter darkness, mentally repeating the Ram *mantram*. Where the rocks that formed the cave met were deep recesses filled with dry leaves. In the darkness the rustling noises produced by creeping creatures living in these recesses would fall on his ears. Sometimes he would feel they were crawling quite near him. Fear had gone out of his life. He was calm and undisturbed. An upward glance revealed the distant blue heavens, glittering with twinkling stars through the angular opening, at the summit of the cave.

The day dawned. Balak Ram came to see him and remained for a few minutes. Seeing Ramdas silent and indifferent he left. The day passed. The time was mid-summer. Summer in the United Provinces is attended with extreme heat. From ten to five during the day the sun was belching forth fire. The rocks of the cave exposed to the direct blaze of the sun would burn with intense heat. Fiery breezes were blowing into the cave through the narrow entrance. Ramdas scarcely moved from the mat. The second day passed.

On the third day he rose above body consciousness, and his experience was that he felt a solemn blankness in existence. A stillness and peace pervaded his being. He was now mostly lying down on the mat flat on his back. He had not a wink of sleep and his eyes were ever open, even in the nights, for he could not keep them shut long. Neither weakness nor pangs of hunger affected him in the least. Balak Ram was paying him a visit every morning. He thought that the fast was for his sake. He hoped that by Ramdas's austerity he would attain liberation. Ramdas did not know nor did he care to know the why and wherefore of the fast. He simply observed it by Ram's will.

At midnight, on the third day, Ramdas was sitting on the *asan* when suddenly a thunder crash was heard and for a quarter of an hour it rained in torrents. The rain pouring down the opening at the roof of the cave, directly fell on him as though he were seated beneath a waterfall. He was wholly drenched and the cave was filled with water to the height of an inch. He budged not. His only cloth and the mat were thoroughly soaked. Next day the heat of the sun was as rigorous as ever, and so, by noon, the water in the cave dried up; so also the cloth and the mat.

The news of the fast spread in the city of Banda. People in large numbers mounted the hill to see him. Many of them came only as far as the lower cave and after inquiries with Balak Ram returned, while some ascended to the upper cave in which Ramdas lived. They would only peep within through the narrow passage, but none dared to enter. They displayed superstitious awe.

However, in the afternoon, a man boldly came in. Ramdas was reclining. The visitor sat down at first at his feet and slowly commenced massaging his legs. Then drawing near Ramdas's face, he burst into tears. He wept like a child. Brushing aside his tears by the sleeves of his coat, he spoke: "Maharaj, I am a poor cobbler. I do my work on the roadside. One of my customers, who came to me for repairing his shoes, narrated the story of your fast. He said that you had even eschewed drinking water. The news terribly upset me. I thought: 'How could I go home and take my dinner, knowing that there is one on the hill who is starving?' My mind revolted at the idea. Dazed and bewildered I at once threw down the work and ran up here. Now, my resolution is this: until you take food I am determined not to have it for myself. I prefer to fast with you. Till then, I am also going to stick to this cave."

His speech struck a chord in Ramdas's heart which was silent during the fast and set it vibrating. His whole frame responded to the thrill that emanated from it. He suddenly sat up with a bound and, placing both his hands on the shoulders of the cobbler, asked: "What do you want Ramdas to do?"

"Take food, of course," he replied.

"Well, get him something then," Ramdas said.

"I shall bring whatever you want," he answered eagerly.

"A cup of milk," Ramdas suggested.

At once the cobbler friend left the cave and reappeared in ten minutes with a bowl filled with milk. He was panting which showed that he must have run to and from the bazaar.

"Here you are, Maharaj," he said and offered the milk. Ramdas drank it.

(iii) Balak Ram, the Prodigal

The fast broken, Ramdas immediately abandoned the cave and came down. Balak Ram was surprised to see him.

"Ramji," Ramdas told him, "Ram commands Ramdas to quit the hill and depart from Banda; he is off."

"Fine, I would also follow. My place is with you. I cannot give you up," he replied.

Ramdas dissuaded him, but he was obstinate. Both descended the hill and he directed Ramdas to the house of Seth Moolchand. The seth and his wife welcomed them with great joy. Ramdas proposed to leave Banda on foot for Jhansi, early next morning.

"Swamiji, I shall take you to Mahoba," interposed and urged Balak Ram. "About three miles from the town is a place worth visiting—of hills and jungles. It is considered to be a *tapobhumi*. It is called Gohkar Parvat. I had occasion to live on the hills for some months. Now we shall proceed straight to that spot, not on foot but by railway."

There was a night train running to Mahoba, and Ramdas suggested departure by that train. Meanwhile, a large number of people had gathered in Moolchand's house for the *darshan* of the *sadhus*. Among them was the devout sister of Moolchand. She came forward.

"Maharaj," she said, "I have a humble appeal to you. I beg that you may postpone your journey till tomorrow night. My prayer is that you should both grace my house with your presence tomorrow for the midday meal."

Ramdas accepted her invitation and Balak Ram followed suit. The night was passed in the front-yard of Moolchand's house. The following day, at eleven o'clock, Moolchand's sister came to escort the *sadhus* to her house. She was the wife of a rich merchant.

The *sadhus* were taken to a room on the upper floor of her big house. Seated, side by side, they were served with meals. They were fed on choice dishes. The mother was all love. The meal over, she requested Ramdas to enlighten them with a discourse on *bhakti*. All the ladies of the household assembled in the room to hear him. Although his Hindi was poor he would grow eloquent when he talked on religious topics. He spoke for nearly an hour. He intermingled in his discourse many *puranic* episodes describing how in the life of devotees, after a keen struggle, *bhakti* triumphed. In short he held out devotion to God as the one purpose of human existence. The listeners were touched by the talk and tears of pure emotion flowed down their cheeks.

Now, he was about to start when Balak Ram beckoning him to be seated a few minutes more, said: "I have also a few words to say"—then turning his gaze at the hostess, "Twenty rupees down for *sadhu seva*—at once, quick," and raising his right hand high in the air he brought it down striking the floor with his palm. The kind hostess and other ladies were struck dumb at this sudden demand.

"Mataji," said Balak Ram, "why do you hesitate? Come along—no time to lose; twenty rupees down."

The bewildered mother left the room and reappearing with the money placed a pile of twenty rupees in silver in front of the *sadhus*. Balak Ram at once closed his fingers on the pile and holding the amount in his hand got up.

"Swamiji, let us now go," he said turning to Ramdas. They went out and reached Moolchand's house.

Balak Ram, now a master of wealth, set about discovering ways and means of spending it. He called a visitor to his side and said: "Here are six rupees; get me from the bazaar orange coloured cloth sufficient for a gown, and also a tailor." The visitor left with the money.

"Now, you there," he called another, "here, two rupees; bring me two rupee worth of *charas* (extract of *ganja*)." The second visitor was also sent away on his errand.

In a couple of hours he had the long loose gown decking his body and had a few full doses of *charas* smoke. He had still eleven rupees left. The coins jingled in his hands and he was laughing most benignantly.

"Swamiji, let us take a round in the bazaar," he suggested.

A party started consisting of Balak Ram, Ramdas and three or four others. He strutted in the streets as if he were "the monarch of all he surveyed." His outstretched arms moved to and fro, his shoulders rose and fell at every stride, his legs wide apart tramped with a measured and proud pace; his head, seemingly poised on a loose pivot, moved like a pendulum from one side to the other. His whole bearing showed that he wanted to impress upon the ignorant world that a great personage had been gracious enough to bless the streets of Banda with his holy tread! In the thickly crowded bazaar people made way at his approach. Many bowed and prostrated before him. O! Ram, what wonderful masks you put on!

Balak Ram descrying an umbrella shop got in and came out with a fashionable umbrella worth three rupees. Next, entering a shop of footwear, he purchased a pair of shining shoes and a pair of socks, striped yellow and red.

Now he flourished the umbrella in his right hand, and as the shoes were of a size too small for his feet he hobbled along, adding to the majesty of his gait. Merchants in their shops forgetting for a time to attend to their customers, gazed on Balak Ram in wonder, not unmixed with awe. At last the party arrived at the point from which they started, that is Moolchand's house.

"Curses be on the bootmaker," he shouted.

Sitting on a bench he asked one of the devotees to pull out his shoes at once. One of the party removed the shoes from off his feet, as also the socks. When Balak Ram raised his heels what did he see?—two blisters as big as marbles!

"The blackguard!" he cried out in rage, "he cheated me downright. He shall not go scot-free; come on, let us go to him; I would have a good pull at his long beard."

The party started again, now on an adventure. He made one of the party carry the shoes. Giving up his lordly gait Balak Ram was now hurrying on at a brisk pace. His hands were presumably itching to have a tug at the Muslim's beard! They came before the shop but it was closed. In the intoxication of *charas*, Balak Ram did not remember the shop from which he had made the purchase. Adjoining the closed shop was another dealer in boots and a bearded old man was seated at the counter. Balak Ram approached him, and was about to give a full and free play to his well-trained tongue when Ramdas pulled him by the sleeves and warned him: "Look here, you are about to tear up the wrong man. It is from the closed shop that you bought the pair of shoes. Let us be away."

The party turned back. Balak Ram was fuming like a suppressed volcano. All the way he had conjured up a charming array of choice epithets to be shot at the shopkeeper, but all went in vain! His chagrin was great. But he made good the loss to some degree. He stood before the closed shop and delivered himself of the invective on the absent bootmaker, dragging into it also his ancestors and descendants, resolving them all finally into one lump of the most despicable piece of humanity. On their way back to Moolchand's house, in a rumbling sound like slow thunder, he further gave vent to some newly remembered choice bits of billingsgate.

(iv) Cause of Toothache

By the night train Balak Ram and Ramdas started from Banda and reached Mahoba early the next morning. In the bazaar they were greeted by Balak Ram's old friends. Of these two, Bahadur and Jagannath were most assiduous in their attention. In the evening, they proceeded to the Gohkar Parvat. When leaving the town, Balak Ram divested himself of the long gown and presented it to a friend in the bazaar. Similarly, the umbrella and the shoes were also given away. He remained in bare *kaupin*.

The Gohkar Parvat was made up of a series of mountains, some low and others high. The mountains were formed of huge black boulders piled up together. Here tall trees were sparse, but the hills were covered over with a thick growth of shrubs and grass. At a lower level, around the extensive area of the hills, were small lakes bearing on their placid bosom red and white lotuses. As they climbed the hills, they reached a central piece of level ground, enclosed all round by lofty hills. Right in the middle of this level ground was a heap of giant rocks, about a hundred feet high. At the base of this pile was a cave like a cubical room. Now a difficult ascent, a few yards upwards, revealed another spacious but very low compartment between two broad and flat rocks. In this compartment was another recess which could just accommodate one person. The compartment and the recess were so low that one could move in it only on one's haunches. This rocky upper chamber was occupied for the night.

Balak Ram's temper was as bad as ever. At the least provocation he railed violently at the visitors. When alone with him, Ramdas again talked to him of peace. In response he resolved that he would from the ensuing day observe perfect silence, live on mere milk diet, and not quit the chamber for seven days. He also desired to remain quite solitary and to allow no visitors to come up except Ramdas. The latter undertook to carry for him from below milk, water, etc. He also appealed to Balak Ram to go on with the repetition of Ramnam.

Next day Ramdas took his position under a slanting rock at the base of the hill. The visitors commenced to pour in. They demanded to see Balak Ram. Ramdas explained to them the situation as it stood. They were much disappointed and grumbled. He discharged the duty imposed on him; that is, on the one hand of persuading the visitors not to climb up the hill to see Balak Ram and, on the other, of carrying food and water to him in his solitary cell.

One thing has to be noted that this part of the hill was bereft of water supply. There was neither a spring nor a well. Water had to be brought from a well nearly two miles from the cave. The kind friends Bahadur and Jagannath arranged for the supply.

One night Ramdas discovered Balak Ram lying down on a flat rock, at the top of the cave, moaning and crying with pain.

"What is the matter with you, Ram?" Ramdas asked, approaching him.

"Maharaj, I have a severe attack of toothache. I cannot bear the excruciating pain," he sobbed.

Ramdas passed his hand over him soothingly, when he added: "Do you know why I suffer like this? I shall tell you: I can well understand that it is all due to the curses of my wife and children whom I have deserted."

"Lord!" Ramdas exclaimed, "if that be the case why not return to them?"

"Impossible," he jerked out: "I have absolutely severed myself from them, leaving no hope of return."

"There is no such thing, Ram. You can yet go back to them if only you make up your mind," Ramdas assured him.

But Balak Ram was firm in his convictions. Soon after this he fell asleep and the following day he was free from pain.

Day after day passed. The visitors from the city, who came in large numbers, clamoured for Balak Ram's *darshan*. They in a way accused Ramdas of being at the bottom of the affair. But he took their remarks in good part. Balak Ram, on the other side, was also growing impatient. He struggled with his mind which revolted against the restrictions imposed on it. On the fifth day, a large crowd of devotees at the foot of the hill raised a hue and cry, and the noise reached the ears of Balak Ram in his seclusion. Out he came like a prisoner set free, and jumping from stone to stone was in a minute in the midst of the crowd. He received from the mass a loud ovation.

For a few minutes he was mild, cheerful and smiling. The passion that lay dormant for five days once more raised its hood. Now its venom flowed with unabated fury, in a torrent of abuse on all the people assembled there. At this the crowd slowly melted away and dispersed. The majority skulked away to their homes. A few remained who tolerated and loved him, in spite of his violent nature. Many of his admirers knew that his outbursts were not to be taken seriously and that his heart was tender, compassionate and loving. Ramdas once observed him fondling a baby. He was simply lost in raptures when he was in its society. He was an avowed enemy of falsehood, deceit and greed. Towards these his attitude was most violent and uncompromising.

On the evening of the same day, when Balak Ram became free from the restrictions of his vow, Ramdas expressed his wish to leave Mahoba that night for Jhansi. Balak Ram remonstrated, wept, caught Ramdas's feet, appealed and did his best to detain him for a longer period. But Ramdas was so firm in his resolution that Balak Ram could not move him this time. Accordingly, he started by the night train from Mahoba and reached Jhansi next morning.

CHAPTER 20: MOUNT ABU

(i) Sri Shanti Vijayji—A Pure Saint

Ramdas again occupied Atkhamba on the bank of Lakshmi-talao. On the day of his arrival he had an attack of high fever which lasted for three days. Ramkinkar attended on him. He grew extremely anxious about Ramdas and sometimes wept when he had very high fever. Ramdas refused to be treated with medicine and suggested a fast for a day or two. At first Ramkinkar opposed the idea but had to yield when he saw the fever continuing. A two days' fast cured him of the malady.

Here Ramdas received an invitation from Mother Elizabeth, the English lady, who was then living on Mount Abu. He made up his mind to visit Mount Abu. Ramkinkar and other friends of Jhansi proposed that he should have an ashram somewhere in Bundelkhand. After some discussion they fixed Gohkar Parvat as a place suitable for such an ashram. They insisted upon his return after the visit to Mount Abu. Ramcharandas also came to Jhansi about this time. He requested again that he be allowed to keep Ramdas's company. The latter asked him to go in advance to Mahoba where he would meet Ramcharandas on his return from Mount Abu. Ramdas once more met Swami Nirbhayanand and his noble wife at their *kuti*. Before leaving Jhansi he had his last dinner with them.

A wire had been sent beforehand to Mother Elizabeth of Ramdas's coming. In due time, he reached Abu Road station. Raja Ram's *sepoy* was awaiting his arrival. By motor-bus, Ramdas with his escort went up Mount Abu about twenty miles. At last he came to the bungalow of Mother Elizabeth. She had at the time two prominent guests—the Thakore Saheb of Limbdi and Sir P. Pattani, Dewan of Bhavnagar State.

Mother Elizabeth greeted Ramdas with manifest joy. A room in her villa had been prepared for him. Next day the party was joined by a saint of Jamnagar, Ramprasad. Ramdas preferred to live on milk and fruit diet. He would sit at the mother's table in the company of her distinguished guests for taking his milk and fruit. The mother was overwhelming in her love and kindness. She would almost feed him with her own hands. He remained at Mount Abu for about twelve days. He would here chronicle only one or two important incidents during his short stay on the hill.

He was ever having the Ram *mantram* on his lips. The room in which he dwelt was ringing with its sound. Now Mother Elizabeth had engaged some masons to raise a compound wall round her house. They were working about twenty yards from his room. One day the mother came in a hurry to him, and asked: "Ramdas, have you taught the *mantram* also to the masons? I hear them repeating it while they are at work."

In fact, the *mantram* was automatically uttered by all in the compound. In the nights after three, Pattani Ram—so he was named—was heard singing the *mantram*. He had a suite of rooms close to Ramdas's. The brahman cook and *sepoys* of Raja Ram and other servants were also found singing the *mantram* to themselves. Once when the mother with Raja Ram, Pattani Ram and Ramdas was motoring towards the famous Dilwara Temple, the car was ringing with the loud music of the *mantram*; every occupant of the car was singing the *mantram* at a high pitch. It caught everybody like a contagion.

The Dilwara Temple which they visited was a very picturesque edifice carved in white marble. The sculptor has freely lavished all his genius and skill in making the temple a unique piece of architecture. As you entered, you came upon a quadrangular set of structures with a central block in which the main image of Mahavira, the great saint of Jainism, was installed. The quadrangles consisted of long verandahs, open inside, having on the walls, ceiling and pillars exquisite carvings of emblems and designs with the figures of nude Mahavira at intervals in the niches on the walls. The cupola of the central dome was also a wonderful piece of sculpture, carved in artistic devices.

The Jain saints, who resided within the temple, were kind enough to take Ramdas round and show the interior of the shrine. At its front, there was a small structure of marble with a number of caparisoned elephants, fashioned out of pure white marble, and on the decorated howdahs of these elephants were seated effigies of ancient Jain kings.

Mother Elizabeth looked upon a Jain saint, Sri Shanti Vijayji, who lived in one of the caves of Mount Abu, as her *guru* or spiritual teacher. Once she had proposed to take Ramdas to him, but he evinced no enthusiasm in the matter, and the idea was dropped. But suddenly one morning the *mahatma* himself turned up at her villa. The mother introduced Ramdas to him. He was seated on an *asan* on the floor of one of her rooms. Ramdas going up to him embraced him with great joy. He returned the embrace with as much delight. Then Ramdas sat beside him. He was humility personified. He was a stout and short figure with full black beard.

He wore only one cloth across his shoulders. The cloth was at places torn and dirty. His eyes had a distant look of meditation. He radiated purity and peace. Ramdas had no talk with him. He could speak only in Gujarati and Ramdas was a stranger to that tongue.

(ii) Knowledge Is to Know You Know Nothing

One day the mother took out Ramdas for a walk on the hills and she showed him the extent of her property. She said: "I always like the society of saints; any other kind of company jars me, especially of householders who are immersed in worldly things." In the course of the talk, Ramdas had to say: "Mother, Ramdas's weak body may not live long. There is a presentiment that it is to drop shortly."

"Don't you say so, it has yet to do great things," she returned. The period taken up by the walk was about half an hour, after which they retraced their steps to the villa.

The mother wished in her heart that he should eat meals prepared by her hands. Her silent wish strangely produced a response in him. He involuntarily requested her to feed him with food cooked by herself. With the greatest delight and overflowing love, she got ready some wheat *rotis* for him which tasted quite heavenly.

Another day a *sepoy* of Raja Ram, a kind friend, took him out for a stroll. He asked the friend to lead him to a solitary place, away from the haunts of men. But being of an officious nature, the *sepoy* escorted him to a distant cave occupied by a *sannyasi*. In the midst of a jungle he found himself in front of a large wide open rock-cut cave. In it was seated a young *sannyasi*, clad in ochre coloured cloth, clean shaven, with a number of books scattered beside him.

The kind friend whispered into Ramdas ears: "This is Swami Kaivalyanand." Ramdas went up to the *sannyasi* and prostrated before him.

With a look of surprise he asked: "To whom are you offering this salutation?"

"To Ram," Ramdas replied. "Who are you?"

"Ramdas."

"Ramdas, Ramdas, funny ain't it? There is only one Truth. Why do you assume this false duality?"

"It is Ram himself, being One, has chosen to be many."

"Wrong, He is always one; many is false, is illusion," he said.

"Truth has become God and His devotee for the sake of *lila* or play."

"Why play?" he asked.

"For love and bliss; so, when Ramdas prostrates before you, it is yourself who do it in the form of Ramdas," Ramdas rejoined.

"Bosh, there is only one, never two."

"To whom are you talking then, Swamiji?"

He reflected for a while and replied, "To myself."

"Exactly—you assume there are two, although in the light of absolute Truth there is only one."

"No, no—no realised man believes in duality."

"What of Tulsidas, Surdas, Kabir, Samarth Ramdas and many others?"

"Oh!" he laughed, "they had not attained *jnana*. They were struggling still on a lower plane!"

"But their teachings and works show that they possessed high illumination. They held out *parabhakti* as the highest realisation," Ramdas rejoined.

"I maintain they were ignorant folk," and, taking a book from the pile near him, he added, "brush them all aside, here, take this book and read; you will understand things more clearly."

"Ramdas does not need to understand. Knowledge has been defined to him as that state in which you know that you know nothing."

"Well, well, I say read this work; it is written by me."

He pressed Ramdas hard to accept it. A glance at the book revealed its title and its author: "Will to Satchidanand by Swami Kaivalyananda, M.A." Ramdas took leave of him after his usual way of a parting *dandavat* at his feet. He carried the book with him.

Again Ramdas, in the company of the same *sepoy* friend, visited the Ram Mandir of the place. Here he met many Vaishnav saints who treated him with great kindness. While returning they passed through a road beside a large lake, sparkling with limpid blue waters. On the bosom of the lake were seen Europeans, in their bathing dress, rowing in pleasure boats. Mount Abu is a beautiful place, cool even at midday in the summer. The sceneries and landscapes are charming. The air is pure and refreshing.

(iii) The Mother's Love Prevailed

On the following day, at the morning meal, Ramdas announced his desire to leave the place for Wadhwan and Limbdi wherefrom he was receiving repeated calls, the last being an urgent telegram.

The mother was greatly upset by the news. She appealed to him to remain for some days longer and looked to her guests for their support. They also, at her pressure, tried to persuade him to stay.

"Ramdas" said the mother, "the heat in Limbdi nowadays is terrible. We hear reports that even birds drop down from the trees and die on account of unbearable heat. You should not go into a fiery place from the cool heights of Abu."

"Mother," Ramdas replied, "love knows no discomfort. The people of Limbdi and Wadhwan are very anxious to have him with them. It is their love that calls him so imperatively."

"No, you shall not go. I am your mother; I would take care of your frail body. It needs rest in a cool climate. Please don't go."

Ramdas was adamant. He left the table and went out to the verandah. The mother ran after him and with folded hands said: "You must, Ramdas, stay with us for at least four days more; don't say no. I depend upon you. You will oblige me so much." Ramdas stopped and was silent for a tense minute. The mother's appealing eyes changed the side of the balance.

"All right, mother—for four days more," said Ramdas.

When she heard the reply she went into ecstasies. She skipped with joy and rubbed with her hands his two palms which he had held up in the mode of salutation. What a glorious heart she possessed!

Many prominent men who had come up to Abu for the summer visited Ramdas in his room and held long conversations with him. Love poured in on him from all sides. Amongst them there was also a saint named Ramprasad, from Jamnagar who lived in a small detached house, close to Mother Elizabeth's villa on the same grounds. It appeared he had founded an orphanage in Jamnagar in which the poor and helpless children found rest, training and food. The saint had expressed a desire that Ramdas should pay a visit to the orphanage, but Ram did not afford him an opportunity for fulfilling his wish.

On the day previous to his departure, Raja Ram suggested that as he was to return to his state four days later, it would be as well for him to travel in his company. As an inducement he held out: "Ramdas, I am going in my special saloon car and you can also travel in it."

"Ramdas's departure tomorrow has already been fixed; he cannot change it. He travels always third class. Even if he were to travel by the same train as the one you were to go by, he would prefer a third class carriage to your well-furnished saloon," replied Ramdas.

Raja Ram became silent. Now the mother wished to have somebody to escort Ramdas as far as Wadhwan. He made her understand that an escort was quite unnecessary as, being a *fakir*, he was accustomed to travel long distance alone.

"No, Ramdas, for my satisfaction I would send with you Raja Ram's *sepoy*," she said.

Raja Ram also agreed with Ramdas that there was no need of an escort for him. But the mother was unshakably firm in her resolution.

Next day the kind mother motored him and the *sepoy* to the bus-stand. She made him sit comfortably in the bus. As the bus moved she turned back in her motor and cast a last lingering look from eyes that were moist. She must have felt the separation very keenly. O! mother, what infinite love you have in your bosom for your child, Ramdas!

The *sepoy* friend, who had a basket of fruits kindly provided by Mother Elizabeth, led him to a third class compartment and was about to open the door of the carriage when a *sadhu*, sitting near the door, shouted that there was no room in the compartment. He firmly pulled the door inwards to prevent its being opened. But the *sepoy* friend, a strong man, opened it in spite of the resistance and asked Ramdas to get in. When he was entering, the *sadhu* stretched his arm in front to obstruct his ingress. But the *sepoy* coming up brushed his arm aside and made way. Both found seats in the train. There was room sufficient not only for two but for ten!

In the carriage there were about a dozen *sadhus*. The train moved on. It reached a catering station where it would halt for over half an hour. Here the *sadhus* ordered for purees and curry from the platform vendor of eatables. Now they were busy with their meal when a passenger got into the compartment with purees and curry, of course, for his own dinner. The moment he entered, the *sadhus* rose as one man with their sticks in hand and threatened him to leave the carriage at once: "You polluted wretch! how did you dare to get in with your meal in this compartment in which we, *sadhus*, are eating? Get down at once or we shall belabour you with our sticks."

The poor passenger, like a frightened rabbit, jumped down to the platform and made his way towards another carriage.

"This is *sadhuism*, maharaj," remarked the *sepoy* friend to Ramdas.

CHAPTER 21: WADHWAN – IN THE TRAIN

(i) Bala Mandir

A wire had been sent to Dr. Shukla of Ramdas's coming. Dr. Shukla, Chunibhai, Maganlal, and others met him at the Wadhwan station. This time he stopped at Dr. Shukla's house. He and his wife were supremely happy to see him. He spent here only four or five days. The days had a crowded programme.

Visitors came in large numbers to see him. They put him questions on devotion and on the efficacy of God's Name. He was kept busy placing before them his own experiences. He said in reply to a question: "To control the mind, the best and easiest method is to repeat constantly God's Name. Concentration is attained by fixing the attention on the sound of the Name. As the mind is concentrated there must follow meditation upon the glorious attributes of God. Continuous practice of utterance of the Name and meditation stops the restlessness of the mind and merges it into the blissful, eternal and universal Self. God-remembrance is not possible unless you have an intense longing to realise Him. This intense desire is called *bhakti*. This longing must so seize your mind that you should feel a sensation of acute pain when you forget God on account of selfish desires. Your actions should also go to purify your mind; i.e., they should be done in a spirit of *nishkama*. Purity of mind means freedom from lust, wrath and greed. For, a pure mind alone can see God. Concentration itself is purity. Forget not that the God that you seek is within yourself."

One day Ramdas was taken to the State Bala Mandir where children ranging from one and half year to about four years of age received instruction. When he visited the school they had over a hundred children. As soon as he entered the *mandir* and saw the little ones, his heart bounded with untold joy. He directly went and sat in their midst. Instead of feeling shy in the presence of a stranger, they accepted him as one of them. They came and sat on his lap and sought to climb up his shoulders, all the time uttering the name "Sitaram, Sitaram." They were perfectly friendly and quite jolly. Then they gambolled round him singing in great glee. It was an unique experience, full of bliss.

The teacher, a quiet and kind soul, made them dance in a circle with small sticks in hand to the music of "Om Sri Ram Jai Ram Jai Jai Ram." They were provided with small low desks having drawers in which they kept their writing materials. Ramdas saw their first attempts at letters and drawings. They had also varieties of game on the kindergarten system. They were taught to do things in simple and quiet ways without their playful, child-like nature being hampered. He saw a tiny girl of about two years sweeping the floor, on her own initiative, very carefully. The teacher said that she was the most intelligent child of the lot.

In memory of the visit, Chunibhai had arranged to distribute to the children milk and sweets. There was a separate room for feeding them. Here were placed in line low wooden stools as is the fashion in Hindu households. The children took their seats. Some of them were engaged in serving the rest with eatables. Before each child a china saucer was placed by the serving children, and then a bit of sweetmeat was gently placed in it. The whole proceeding went on so quietly that there was not the least bustle, confusion or unusual hurry. A small cup of milk was also placed beside the saucer.

There was perfect order and serenity. When everything was ready till then the children waited patiently and all children were in their seats the teacher uttered a prayer which was repeated by the children in chorus. At the close of the prayer they commenced eating. They handled the cup and saucer very gently. It was all a charming sight.

Next morning the instructor got the whole party of children at Dr. Shukla's and made them sing and dance in a ring to the music of Ram *bhajan*. At the close of the performance they were again given milk and sweets. Bala Mandir was under the direct control and management of the Wadhwan State. Cushioned four wheeled carriages, drawn by horses, were provided for the institution to fetch the children from the respective homes to the school, and then take them back after school hours. It was a free school and tiffin was given to the children in the school at State expense. The school hours were from eight to eleven in the morning.

Another day he visited similar institution outside the city, started in the name of Mahatma Gandhi by a rich man. Here also the tuition was given to the children almost on lines similar to those in the Bala Mandir. The peculiarity of both the schools was that the teachers talked to the little ones very gently and in whispers. No harsh or loud commands escaped their lips. The teachers were so kind and friendly to Ramdas. After distribution of sweets he closed his visit to the second school.

Jivraj Baloo, a *sadhaka*, would constantly come to him. He had retired from worldly life and was living for his *sadhanas* in a solitary spot in the midst of fields outside the city. Here he had a small *kuti* in which he dwelt. He asked Ramdas to pay a visit to his *kuti*. The Dewan *saheb* was also invited. So both drove to the *kuti* in the Dewan's carriage. Jivraj Baloo embraced Ramdas and was extremely happy to have him there. The host then gave the guests a treat of milk. Ramdas was then asked to deliver a discourse. He spoke for about half an hour. It was followed by music. Jivraj sang some songs composed by himself.

In the evenings at Dr. Shukla's house Chhotabhai would entertain the assembled devotees with music playing upon the *dilruba*—an Indian musical instrument.

(ii) Worship of Boot-Kicks

As on the previous occasion, Ramdas occupied Kantilal's house in Limbdi. The eagerness of the people of Limbdi to behold him again was so great that no sooner had he arrived there than hundreds of them visited the house. The same programme, as at the last time, was gone through in almost all its details.

Dr. Shukla, Chunibhai and Chhotabhai came down everyday from Wadhwan to see him. Ramdas was continuing his milk diet. He had invitations from Ugarchand Seth and Mohanbhai, the noted merchants of Limbdi. The old sugarcandy mothers were filled with no small joy to have him again in their midst. One of the old ladies by name Gangamai aged over seventy years would crawl up the staircase with great difficulty, and coming to him would thrust in his mouth a piece of sugarcandy and embrace him. Indeed wonderful was her devotion!

After a few days' stay in Limbdi, he received a command from Ram to leave the place for Gohkar Parvat, en route Jhansi.

He entrained for Jhansi. When travelling via Ujjain, several changes had to be made. At Bina he had to get into a train running to Jhansi. The time was about ten in the night. When he was entering a carriage, a Mussulman obstructed him but he slipped in. He had a single ochre-coloured cloth, as usual, wound on his body, and a ticket tied to its corner. Now the carriage was full of

Muslim passengers, and everyone was lying down at full length on their beddings, leaving no room for any other passenger. However, he got a perch at the feet of a Muslim who was a short-statured man. The train moved on. At the next station, a number of new passengers poured into the carriage, all Muslims. They had to stand in the narrow passage between the seats; not a single sleeper made room for them. Ramdas felt he could abandon his seat for one of them and quietly slipped down to the floor of the carriage and sat there. The place vacated by him was at once filled up.

At the next station a fresh batch of passengers came in; again all of them were Muslims. The rush was now so great that they began tramping through the passage with their heavy boots in search of seats. Ramdas like a rabbit crouching on the floor received their kicks with no small delight. He rolled down and twisted his body into the figure 8 so that he could take up the least room. Station after station new passengers got in. They crowded the carriage to well-nigh suffocation. Some sleeping passengers had to sit up, because they were forced to. So Ramdas was treated with boot-kicks from all the four sides! The Muslims who were seated had to knock against him when changing the position of their legs. The standing friends in the passage close to him added their share. His only cloth covered him from head to foot. He looked like a cloth bag on the floor!

Now he spoke to himself: "Ramdas, you were receiving worship at several houses of devotees with flower garlands, sandal paste and lights. That was one kind of worship. Now here you are getting another kind, with boot-kicks! Both are same to you."

He enjoyed the fun. Morning dawned. The crowd in the train thinned. The place on the bench that he formerly occupied fell vacant and he jumped into the seat. Now a bearded old Muslim, sitting opposite, with reddened eyes and grisly beard and moustache on ends, forcibly pulled Ramdas's arm and said in a tone of command: "Get down, sit on the floor."

Ramdas stuck to his seat while another Muslim by his side, espousing his cause, rebuked the old Muslim for his gratuitous insult to Ramdas.

"*Sadhu*, you sit where you are. Don't move; the old man must be mad." The old Muslim calmed down.

CHAPTER 22: GOHKAR PARVAT

(i) Reckless Activity

Ramdas arrived at Jhansi. At the station he was welcomed by Ramkinkar and Mahadev Prasad. The latter embraced him and wept through joy on beholding him once more. He was put up again at Atkhamba. After two or three day's stay, he left Jhansi in the company of Ramkinkar and Chhedilal, also an earnest and loving soul. The Mahoba friends were intimated by wire of his coming. So about a dozen of them including Ramcharandas were eagerly looking for the arrival of the train at the Mahoba station. On alighting, the party was enthusiastically welcomed by the friends and were led to the city, and for the night they occupied the Mahavira's temple situated outside the town on the way to Gohkar Parvat. Next day, they ascended the Parvat and reached the caves in which he had lived on a former occasion.

A brahman boy named Kallu undertook to cook for him, and Jagannath supplied provisions. Two or three days later, a *sannyasi*, Bhagawan by name, whom he had seen before in Chitrakut Pilikoti Ashram in the *mela* of *sannyasis* during the Ram-Navami festival, came to stay with him. Bhagawan was a pure-hearted and simple *sadhu*, extremely quiet and taciturn. His great love for Ramdas made him stick to the place. Ramcharandas was of course there. For nearly four months Ramdas lived on those hills.

In the company of devotees who used to come in large numbers from the surrounding villages, Ramdas would dance to the loud and measured repetition of Ram *mantram*. The whole stay was a period of unique spiritual ecstasy. He would feel, when about fifty men were dancing with the sweet music of God's Name, as though the whole universe was dancing too. Dance for hours did not in the least fatigue him. Bhagawan, who was not till then accustomed to dancing, also joined them. Whoever newly came to the hills could hardly resist dancing. God's name resounded through the hills, producing an atmosphere pregnant with blissful thrills.

In the nights some devotees who possessed a sweet voice sang to the beats of a hand-drum, songs of Kabir and Banarasi. The *kirtan* would proceed far into the night, till two or three early morning. Ramkinkar, finding the hill awe-inspiring, especially when he was told that tigers roamed about in the nights, refused to stay with him and returned to the town with the visitors. Within three or four days, his leave having expired, he left for Jhansi. Chhedilal continued his stay for a week at the expiry of which he also returned to Jhansi. He had remained on the hills day and night.

Ramdas was, during the day time, like a frisky monkey. He could not stand quiet. He would either dance or run. When he was not engaged in dance he would run up the surrounding tall hills like a squirrel. He used to feel his body extremely light, and the divine *Shakti* was coursing through his frame like the lightning current. When he reached the top of the hill he would cry out in a high pitch: "Hari Om," and the sacred syllables would reverberate through the hills. Every hill would echo back the sound of "Hari Om" in a distinct and ready response, filling the air with rapturous harmony.

Ramdas would be followed in his race uphill by Ramcharandas, Jagannath and one or two others. The ascents were perilous and few dared to follow him. While descending, it was not by creeping down that he would come to the bottom. He would jump from one rock to the other. At times he would recklessly take leaps over fifty feet, but every time he alighted on the lower rock safe on all fours like an ape. Life and body were held by him light as straw. In spite of the incessant activity to which he subjected his body, he never knew exhaustion. He was as fresh and vigorous as ever.

In the wanderings on the hills with friends, he once came upon a gigantic stone image of a three-headed God, leaning against the side of a hillock. The ruins around showed that in olden days there was a temple here for the huge stone idol. He was urged from within to climb to the head of the image which he did with lightning rapidity, and on the broad crown of its head he danced with untold delight.

The party had another addition of a Vaishnava saint, Vaijnath.

He would remain at the base of the cave with a fire before him telling his beads all the night. One of his disciples, an elderly mother, would come to the hills during the afternoons and entertain them with the charming songs of Mirabai. Her devotion was so great that when she sang, tears of ecstasy would course down her cheeks, and her face would be aglow with spiritual light.

The devotees hoisted on the hillock, on which Ramdas lived, a gigantic flag, ten feet by ten feet, containing in big Hindi characters the Ram *mantram*, "Om Sri Ram Jai Ram Jai Jai Ram." The flag was visible for miles from the hills.

It was a dark night. The rain was pouring and the air was chill. About ten o'clock, when the party of singers were deeply engaged in *kirtan* and Ramdas was occupying the small interior cave, a young, educated and well-dressed man turned up with an escort. Coming to Ramdas he fell at his feet and said: "Swamiji, I am on my way to Cawnpore from Chhattarpur. I heard of you and have come for your *darshan*, having broken journey at Mahoba. Pray have your *kripa* on me."

He received from Ramdas, then and there, the *upadesh* of Ram *mantram*. When all were silently sitting, three big centipedes appeared on the scene. They were moving about freely. A lantern was burning in the centre of the group. One of the centipedes approached the young man whose name was Ramchandra Gupta. He was shrinking from it, when Ramdas asked him not to be afraid of it, and assured him that it would do no harm. One of them actually passed over the lap of Ramdas in quite a friendly manner. Shortly after this Ramchandra left.

(ii) Alone on a Dreaded Hill

Ramkinkar had specially accompanied Ramdas to Gohkar in order to arrange an ashram on those hills. He had collected over two hundred rupees for the purpose. Ugarchand Seth of Limbdi had also contributed to the fund. The prospect of having a *kuti* on those dreadful hills did not appeal to Ramkinkar, but he could not object as Ramdas had pitched upon the place. He gave some amount to Jagannath and instructed him in the first place to dig a tank for water.

There was an attempt made by Balak Ram, when he lived there, to sink a small tank, but the work had to be given up for want of encouragement. Now it was proposed to deepen the same pond and build up the sides with stones and mortar. Coolies were engaged for the work, and on digging a few feet a spring was lighted upon, which supplied the small tank with water. The work was going on when one of the friends quarrelled with Jagannath, who managed the work, over the wages paid to the coolies and the work stopped, never to be taken up again. Ramdas dropped the idea of having an ashram there.

Ramcharandas, then only a lad of about eighteen, was perfectly fearless. One evening, as the sun went down, Ramdas asked him to go and sit for the night in a cave on the hill opposite, the biggest of the lot. The leopards and tigers have their home in the caves of this hill. He cheerfully obeyed Ramdas.

"Look here, Ram," Ramdas told him, "you have to sit in utter darkness in one of the lairs of the tigers. You should never have a wink of sleep for the night. Repeat the Ram *mantram* without stopping and you have no fear—go." He went.

The night passed. At daybreak Ramdas came out of his cave and saw Ramcharandas descending the hill which he had occupied in the night. When he approached Ramdas he asked him: "Ram, were you not afraid in the night?"

"Not in the least," he replied.

"How is that? Ram *mantram* perhaps never left your lips."

"Not only that," he said, "I was there in accordance with your command, and so I was perfectly certain that no harm would befall me." Wonderful was the faith of the boy!

About this time, Ramcharandas was reading a Kanarese translation of Vedantic works. He came to Ramdas one day and said: "Swamiji, Vedanta declares everything is Brahman. Then, when I am Brahman Himself, where is the necessity for *sadhana* on which you lay so much stress?"

"True, Ram," replied Ramdas, "everything is Brahman, but this has to be realised; merely saying that you are Brahman cannot make you realise the truth. You ought to experience that state, rising above all sense of duality by freeing your mind from illusion. Your 'I', should no longer be the local, narrow individual 'I' but the universal, eternal and absolute 'I'. To realise this ineffable, perfect state, *sadhana* is necessary. Mind and its desires have to be conquered by concentration and purification."

"When there is nothing but Brahman who is to do *sadhana*?" Ramcharandas put in.

"You will know. Experience will teach you that the *jiva* has a false existence; still it exists encompassed by darkness and ignorance," said Ramdas.

He was not convinced; but it was not long before he was. He gave up repetition of God's name and early rising. He slept like a log till late in the morning and again in the noon he slept for long hours; the result was that he was seized with unusual hunger. Stealthily he would go into the bottom cave, which was used for a store, and mixing large quantities of a mingled food-stuff called *satua* with water, he would quietly eat it. This he took in addition to the usual food with regard to which a fight ensued between him and Kallu the cook who complained that Ramcharandas would eat up all the *rotis*, leaving him nothing. One morning he appeared before Ramdas with a mottled face, full of red eruptions.

"What is the matter with you, Ram?" Ramdas asked.

"Don't know, I feel also feverish," he replied with a wry face.

"It is all due to over-eating, *satua* has manifested itself on the face. Is it not so?" Ramdas said laughing.

He was as quiet as a mummy. Then he crouched near Ramdas in the tiny cave which he occupied, fully covered with his cloth, but shivering with high fever.

"Ram, are you not Brahman?" Ramdas asked.

"Swamiji, now I know I am not. A wonderful way of teaching you have!"

"Ramdas is not teaching. It is Ram who teaches you. Do Ram *bhajan* and everything will be all right." Ramdas assured him.

Next day he went without any food, and on the third day he was all right. He took up again the Ram *mantram*. One day a complaint came to him from Kallu who said that Ramcharandas was worrying him for the brass cup which he (Kallu) had somewhere mislaid.

"Yes, Swamiji." grumbled Ramcharandas, "it was a cup which was such a nice fit to my *lota*; I want it."

"Ram," Ramdas asked "whose cup was it?"

"Mine," rejoined the boy.

"Nothing is yours, Ram. Everything is God's; it came from Him and has gone back to Him, so don't fret," said Ramdas.

"Very fine consolation," he said with a tinge of regret for his loss.

Thereafter he slept over the matter. One day he said that he was going to Chhattarpur to stay for some time with Balak Ram who was holding his *durbar* on one of the hills of that state. Ramdas was receiving invitations from him repeatedly. Ramcharandas had heard of the ways of Balak Ram. So he did not want to take with him his new *lota* which he loved so much.

"Swamiji, I leave the *lota* with you. I shall return in a few days," he said, and left.

Meanwhile, during his absence, two *sadhu* lads paid Ramdas a visit. One of them had a water vessel while the other was without one. The latter appealed to Ramdas to provide him with a *lota* since a *sadhu*, he added, should not go without a water vessel. Ramdas had at hand Ramcharandas's *lota*. He took it and passed it on to the boy. The boys departed, the one who got the *lota* quite joyfully. Four days later, Ramcharandas returned but not quite happy. Balak Ram's society was anything but exhilarating to him.

At first sight Ramdas told him: "The *lota* you had, and which Ram gave you, has been taken away by Ram. What do you say?"

He blinked and then smiled, because he had held that Ramdas's decisions were final and not to be questioned. He had always submitted without a word. He had some friends in the town among whom was a rich merchant. He visited him that very day and returned in the evening with a brass *kamandal* and a large cup to fit its mouth.

"How is this, Swamiji?" he said, pointing at the *kamandal* which he poised in his hand stylishly.

"Grand, simply grand," replied Ramdas laughing.

Amongst the daily visitors there were two weavers. They presented Ramdas with a piece of pure *khaddar*. One of them who came in the evening overstayed. There was the usual *kirtan*. The pious weaver was so much absorbed in the music that he lost all account of time. It might have been past midnight, when he suddenly came to himself and exclaimed: "Oh! I meant to return home early in the evening. Now my people at home will be very anxious about me, since I have stayed away for the night. I am scarcely absent from home after dark without their knowledge."

"Well," Ramdas suggested; "you may go home at once."

His house was at a distance of about three miles from the hills and his way lay through the jungle. The night was pitch dark and the wild beasts freely roamed in the jungles at that time of the night. He hesitated to venture out. But Ramdas assured him safe journey provided he kept Ramnam on his tongue. The weaver, a man of faith, boldly acted upon Ramdas's word and left the hills.

In the evening next day, he turned up and said that Ramnam had made him perfectly fearless the previous night, and he reached home without any mishap on the way.

(iii) God Is Giver and God Is Receiver

In the nights the tigers were freely roaming in the woods surrounding the cave. With a party of select few Ramdas started the next day in quest of tigers in their caves so that he could come face to face with them. He rummaged cave after cave in the hills. Marks and traces of their close vicinity were seen, but no animals could be discovered. He dived boldly into the dark depths of the caves and shouted at high pitch "Hari Om" so that they might come out and give him *darshan*! But none appeared. The quest had to be eventually abandoned.

Now Ramdas was bid by Ram to observe a fast and undertake a vow of silence. He lived for a week on milk diet. Silence on the part of Ramdas sorely affected the *sadhu* Bhagawan. He wanted always to hear Ramdas talk although he himself usually spoke very little. He suddenly made up his mind to bid adieu to Ramdas and the hills. He departed. *Sadhus* come and go according to their sweet will. They are free children of God.

During the period of silence and fast, two *sannyasis* visited Ramdas. One was a tall old man of over sixty. In spite of his age he had walked three miles, over the hills and through the jungle from Mahoba to see Ramdas. What love they bore for this child of God! And the other was a bright looking stout young man. He had brought with him from the town a party of devotional singers with harmonium and drums. Before starting the *kirtan* he remarked: "I am not a believer in all these ways of *tapasya* and vows. I like music relating to the praises of God and on hearing which I go into ecstasy and it is true joy." Some beautiful songs were sung by the *bhaktas*. After a meal the saint left the place.

Among the visitors was also a *sadhu* by name Vichitranand, a simple and child-like saint but his body was dry and emaciated due to excessive *ganja* smoke. He had composed some touching Hindi devotional songs which are popular in Mahoba. He lived alone in a *kuti* near the town. He came frequently to Gohkar Parvat.

One afternoon, quite a crowd of devout mothers presented themselves at the base of the rocks clamouring to see Ramdas. In response to their call he came down from the cave. At the sight of him they were extremely delighted. Some of them massaged his legs with overflowing love. They had brought milk and eatables with which they fed him. They remained for an hour and then departed.

Another day, two European missionaries came in search of him. They could find him out only with great difficulty. In the course of their talk they emphasized the personal aspect of God as the whole truth. Ramdas confessed his faith in a God who is both personal and impersonal. He added that one could not know the glory of the supreme Person without realising His impersonal aspect as well. They expressed doubt in the truth of his statement. Without pursuing the subject further, they took their leave and returned to the town.

Now an event occurred which caused a good deal of disturbance among the friends. One morning, as customary, Kallu, the cook entered the lower cave to bring out the vessels for cooking. The vessels, new set of which had, a short time before, been purchased for the use of the *sadhus* on the hill, were kept in the lower cave which had, of course, no door. All the *sadhus* and friends retired to the upper cave in the nights. Now Kallu discovered that the vessels had disappeared. He ran up to Ramdas in a state of alarm and said: "Maharaj, the cooking utensils have disappeared. Somebody has stolen them away."

"Good," Ramdas replied quietly, "the man who took them is evidently more in need of them than we are. It is all right. Ram gave and Ram has taken away."

He stared at Ramdas with perfect blankness when he heard his cool words. Immediately, leaving the hills, he ran to Mahoba and spread the news of the lost utensils and Ramdas's comment on the loss. The friends who had supplied the utensils understood what his words meant and at once substituted the lost vessels by some from their own homes for the time being. A police Sub-Inspector, who loved him greatly, used to come often to see him on the hill. He had also heard the news of the loss of vessels. That afternoon he specially came to make an enquiry into the matter. He questioned Ramdas on the subject.

"Ramji, nothing is lost or stolen," Ramdas said. "It was Ram who furnished him with vessels. It is Ram again who has taken them back. He took away His own things. So, there is no question of loss or theft; therefore, no case against anybody."

The surprised Inspector laughed and remarked: "If all were to follow your principle my job would be gone."

Ramdas's stay was now coming to a close. He had in hand three invitations, one from Chhattarpur, the second from Lalitpur from Triveni Prasad, and third from Cawnpore from Ramchandra Gupta.

The day of departure from Gohkar was a notable day. There was a *mela* held on the hill in commemoration of a deceased Muslim Pir who had *Samadhi* close to the base of the pile of rocks. A Muslim saint occupied the cave on that day. Both Hindus and Muhammadans streamed into the place in thousands for the *darshan* of the saint. Fairs were held and there was great din and bustle. Ramdas along with others took the *darshan* of the saint. The Muslims showered their love on him by embraces.

CHAPTER 23: LALITPUR – RAJGHAD – CHHATTARPUR

(i) Trust in God

Leaving Gohkar Ramdas came to Koteshwar in response to the invitation of Seth Jwaharilal who owned a rock temple of Koteshwar Mahadev. A *murti* of the God was installed in a large, spacious natural cave, attached to which were built some structures for the accommodation of *sadhus* and visitors. The place was only about two furlongs from Mahoba. Ramcharandas had spent some months in this temple under the kind fosterage of Jwaharilal. Ramdas remained here for a night and a day and the Seth arranged a dinner for thirty persons in the *mandir*. It was a most happy occasion.

In the evening he was led in procession through the streets of Mahoba with Ram *bhajan*. Some friends took him to their houses where he was treated with great love. Lastly he visited the house of Jagannath.

Leaving Mahoba Ramdas arrived at Lalitpur. Triveni Prasad who met him at the station escorted him to his spacious house in the town. Here he remained for four days. Crowds of friends came to see and talk to him. A *Ramlila* performance was held in the house. In the evenings Ramdas and Ramcharandas would dance on the front terrace of the house, singing God's Name.

One day they had a walk to the neighbouring river on the banks of which were large flat rocks called Shitapahad. Here the current of the river was very swift as it had to rush down a sudden incline. Near the banks there was no current, and here Ramdas and Ramcharandas descended for a bath.

"Swamiji, we shall make an attempt to cross the river," suggested; Ramcharandas, "let us do it hand in hand".

And he dragged Ramdas with him holding him by the hand. Ramdas submitted to his pull. When they neared the current they found it hard to stand firmly on their legs, being worked on by the furious rush of water. Still they struggled on and on until they felt they were about to be swept away. Ramdas stopped.

"Ramdas is not afraid of the dissolution of the body, Ram," Ramdas said, "but to go any further means certain death by drowning, and Ram says the time for it has not yet come. Ramdas has yet to continue service of the Lord to whom he has dedicated himself; so also you. Hence let us turn back."

"No, Swamiji, we shall pass through," cried the intrepid boy. For him death was of no account. His fearlessness was admirable. But Ramdas would not permit him to proceed further in the current.

"You may return, Swamiji," he said, "I shall venture forward and reach the other bank."

Ramdas banned him from the adventure. So both retraced towards the flat rocks where Triveni Prasad and others were keenly watching their movements.

Ramdas's stay in Lalitpur was during the monsoon. One day, one of the devotees named Karta Krishna, who paid him daily visits invited him, Ramcharandas and Triveni Prasad to his house for the midday meal. For some days it had been raining heavily, and there was an unusual downpour on that morning. The streets were muddy and cold winds were whistling through a drizzle. Tramping along many a circuitous street, they at last reached a dark lane in which the devotee lived.

Karta Krishna, who was a young man, dwelt with his family in the upstairs rooms of a line of petty shops, situated on the roadside. A rugged flight of steps led them up to a narrow terrace from which a low door opened in to a small rectangular room. When they entered it, the first thing that struck them was the full blaze of sunlight descending from above, as though a large portion of the roofing was made of glass. But a look upwards revealed the fact that the aged roof had extensive gaps through which rain and sun found easy access into the room. The morning rain had drenched the mud floor, and about an inch of water had collected on it. In a corner of the room, beneath a part of the roof under better repair and against the wall, stood a coir cot on which was lying a lad scarcely six years of age, enveloped in a thick cotton sheet. A small girl was in attendance.

Ramdas proceeded directly towards the cot and sitting at its foot, placed his hand upon the forehead of the boy. It was burning with high fever and the little patient was tossing from side to side in a delirious condition. Cold blasts charged with rain were sweeping over him through the openings in the roof. Besides this garret which was the only living room of the family, they had adjoining to it a five feet square dark hole which they used as kitchen.

Now came out from the kitchen a young woman with a baby of a few months in her arms. She was the wife of Karta Krishna and mother of the sick lad and the child in her arms, the nursing girl being her sister. Naturally, there was deep anguish on the face of the mother, and as she approached Ramdas and fell at his feet, she wept bitterly. The tale of woe could not be more effectively expressed. Ramdas said within himself: "Here it is, O Lord, Thy presence is needed. Thou art the friend of the helpless. Hasten, O Lord, hasten to the rescue!"

Ramdas then assured the mother: "O mother, have trust in God. He may try us, but He never abandons us. Depend upon Him. Give up your sorrow."

At these encouraging words, which proved as healing balm to her lacerated heart, she lifted herself up and faced Ramdas with a smile.

"O Swamiji," she cried out, "I place perfect faith in your words. I look upon you as God Himself who has come to us, in our distress, in response to our prayer."

Karta Krishna was a poor clerk in Government service whose low salary was hardly sufficient to maintain his family decently. He was paying a rental of three rupees per mensem and more than this, for a better set of rooms, he could not afford. The landlord would take no heed of his repeated appeals to carry out repairs to the roof. Doctor?—where are funds to go in for that precious help? God is the Master Doctor of the universe. He demands of us no fees, but child-like faith. We give Him this, which costs us nothing, and He delivers us from all the ills of the world.

The kind mother had prepared some choice dishes for Ramdas. He, Prasad, and Ramcharandas partook of them and left the place. Next day Ramdas bade adieu to Lalitpur. The last he heard of the boy was that the fever had left him. How kind and merciful God is!

A sequel to this pathetic story has to be narrated here although chronologically its place is elsewhere.

A year passed. After wandering through many parts of India, Ramdas returned again to Jhansi. Karta Krishna was there at the time when Ramdas was stopping in the Ram Mandir. No sooner did the devotee hear of Ramdas's arrival than he ran down to him and insisted upon his visiting his house since his wife was so eager to see him. The latter went with him.

Ramdas met the mother at the entrance of a neat little cottage. Her small girl baby had grown up and was seen crawling on all fours quite healthy, and her boy was jumping about, strong and active. On the face of the mother was beaming the light of cheer and contentment. She welcomed him with unfeigned joy. The children got upon his lap and played and laughed with him. The house they lived in was more spacious and well protected against inclement weather. But with all this there seemed to be something amiss with Karta Krishna. The world is indeed a curious place and man's mind is more curious still. Complete satisfaction and freedom is not for him so long as his mind is subject to fits of temper.

Next day, early morning, Karta Krishna met Ramdas at the *mandir*. Some anxiety appeared to be weighing on his mind.

"Maharaj, I pray to you to get me transferred from here to some other place. I am tired of the present office."

The way how he appealed to Ramdas showed that he firmly believed that Ramdas was the sole dispenser of all things in the world. Ramdas interrupted and told him in plain language: "Look here, Ram, Ramdas is only a humble servant of God. All things happen by His will. No doubt the Master dwells in the servant but don't mistake the servant for the Master. If Lord wills, nothing is impossible. By the way, what is it that ails you?"

Karta Krishna continued: "The fact is my superior officers and co-clerks in the office are harassing me. They have all conspired to make my life utterly miserable."

Ramdas, after a short pause, spoke as follows: "Now listen, beloved Ram, bring back to memory your days in Lalitpur a year ago. What was your condition then? It was simply unbearable. God in His mercy delivered you from it. He has brought you here, provided you with a good house and is keeping your children in sound health. Now you speak of your office troubles. Nothing is wrong with the office. People dislike us because our own attitude of mind towards them is not right. Love can never beget hate. On the other hand, distrust and hate breed every kind of evil. Give up fretting. Be reconciled to the lot that God has chosen for you. Be tolerant and patient. Above all, be humble, kind and forgiving towards all in your office—nay, towards all in the world. With a mind whose passions are uncontrolled, wherever you may go, you can never know peace. You will then be only ceaselessly fighting with the world and find no haven of rest and contentment. Look within yourself. Surrender to the will of almighty God. Humble yourself before Him and extend your love and sympathy towards all beings. Take it that God does everything for the best. If you are obedient to your superiors and kind to your co-clerks, they are bound to change their attitude towards you, and then you will find the very office from which you desire to run away a delightful place for work. Kindly come to Ramdas again day after tomorrow and report to him how matters stand with you. But do act as Ramdas has told you." He left Ramdas.

The other clerks of his office who were also visiting Ramdas informed him that Karta Krishna was a very short-tempered man and would be always picking quarrels with everybody in the office.

As requested, Karta Krishna turned up on the due date. He came with a bright and joyous face.

"How are you getting on?" Ramdas asked.

"I followed your advice, Maharaj," he replied, "and the result has been marvellous. There is an entire change in my office mates in regard to me. My officers have been kind and good, my colleagues helpful and friendly. Oh! how happy I am! I do not want a transfer."

"Ram," Ramdas said, "the change is in you. The whole world is good to us if we are good. If we love the world, we may be sure, in return we shall receive nothing but love from it."

Now to resume the thread of the narrative, Ramacharandas was unduly attached to the new brass *kamandal* and was also carrying a good many spare clothes presented by friends, besides a small amount of money. Ramdas had often advised him not to carry money and other superfluities. But his accumulative tendency was so hard to put down. Ramdas had received an invitation from Chhattarpur. He was about to start, when he told Ramcharandas to give up the *kamandal* and the spare clothes, and then only follow him. He obeyed most reluctantly.

They took seats in the train running to Mahoba, for the way to Chhattarpur lay via Mahoba. In the train, Ramcharandas who, as already stated, possessed some money, started purchasing eatables at every station from the sweetmeat vendors. He fell to continuous eating forgetting Ramnam. Ramdas found sitting opposite to them a *sadhu* with a famished look.

"How much have you got, Ram?" Ramdas asked turning to Ramcharandas.

He looked frightened at the question, for he could understand what Ramdas's question meant.

"Here it is," he said opening a knot in his cloth. The amount was three rupees and odd annas.

"Hand over the amount to the *sadhu* sitting in front of us," Ramdas said to Ramcharandas. He immediately obeyed. The money transferred, he was indeed free.

"Now, give some respite to your stomach and brisk work to your tongue by repeating God's Name!" Ramdas hinted. Till they reached Mahoba the Name rolled on his tongue incessantly.

(ii) Balak Ram's Rage Against Shiva

Arrangements were made by Bhavani Prasad, father of Ramchandra Gupta of Chhattarpur, to take Ramdas to his place. Ramdas started by motor-bus, and Vaijnath and seven others from Mahoba also accompanied him. At Chhattarpur Ramdas and the party were lodged in the Radhakrishna temple near the city. Bhavani Prasad, an old man, welcomed him with inexpressible delight and attended to all the needs of the guests. Ramdas preferred to live on milk diet.

Bhavani Prasad, a retired Government Officer, and an earnest soul, was struggling keenly for God-realisation. His favourite reading was Bhagavad Gita which he would go through with all faith twice every day, besides the telling of beads all the day. His wife was also a great lover of saints. His elder son Gulab Rai was the secretary to the Maharaja of Chhattarpur.

On the second or third night of his stay in the *mandir*, Ramdas had an attack of malaria. He used to feel unusual ecstasy when he had high fever. He could not control himself. He would dance wildly taking God's Name. Bhavani Prasad and Ramcharandas would beg of him not to exert himself in that state and would almost forcibly make him lie down on the cot provided for him. The fever lasted two days.

A devotee from Navagaum, a village fourteen miles from Chhattarpur, came to take Ramdas to his place in order to introduce him to his ailing brother. Ramdas found the sick man in the last stages of consumption. He was reduced to a mere skeleton and his relations, having given up all hope of his recovery, desired to have for him the *darshan* of Ramdas before he passed away. Ramdas remained in Navagaum for a night, and then returned to Chhattarpur.

Balak Ram, who lived in Chhattarpur for sometime, had left the place and gone into the interior, about twenty-six miles away to occupy a hill-top called Rajghad. An invitation also came from Ramchandra Gupta to go to Cawnpore. On top of it all, a wire was received from Triveni Prasad urgently calling Ramdas again to Lalitpur, just for a day.

About noon, one day, Ramdas suddenly proposed to leave for Rajghad. The sky was dark with clouds and there was a drizzle. Ramdas walked straight out of the temple and proposed to cover the distance on foot. Ramcharandas also got ready, but what of the others? They looked askance at each other and demurred. The prospect was not alluring. The way to Rajghad lay through a dense and extensive jungle. There were no villages for halts. The other friends including Vaijnath shrank from the adventure and expressed their decision to stay behind.

Bhavani Prasad coming to know of Ramdas's determination sent his son Gulab Rai to persuade him not to start in that weather. Gulab Rai found Ramdas was fixed in his resolve and could not be moved.

"Please wait for five minutes, I will return presently," he requested and disappeared.

Within five minutes a brand new motor car was standing at the entrance of the temple. God's ways are wonderful! Ramdas got into the car, and funnily enough all the friends who had hesitated to walk with Ramdas also scrambled in—Vaijnath and all! Gulab Rai requested Ramdas to pay a visit to the owner of the car who was at that time laid up with a severe attack of typhoid fever. Ramdas agreed. The car stopped at the sick man's door and Ramdas with the party entered the house and found the patient in a state of delirium. Ramdas sat beside his bed and, passing his hands over his head and body, assured him that he would be all right. The people of the house offered Ramdas some milk to drink. He drank a part of it and gave the rest to the patient. Then he left the house and all got into the car again. It started and as it came upon the lonely road outside the city, it flew like wind in spite of the rugged condition of the jungle road.

By three o' clock the car reached the bottom of the chain of mountains called Rajghad. Alighting, the party made for the place where Balak Ram lived. They had to ascend a flight of rocky steps, over a hundred in number, before they came to a flat projection of the mountain where Balak Ram had made his abode. No sooner did Balak Ram see Ramdas than he fell at his feet, weeping through excessive joy, and embraced him again and again. Balak Ram had been living in a small shed hoisted on four strong posts, about ten feet from the ground similar to the country watch-towers in the corn-fields.

At the edge towards the hill, which extended high above the level of the place, was seen a *Shiva-linga* which was partly within an excavation on the hill-side. A diffused water spring at the top of the hill was dripping down its edges in tiny streams forming into a pretty thick jet which poured on the head of the *linga* continuously day and night. At the outer end of the flat ground was a leaning stone-bench all along the edge.

"Last night was a terrible period for me, Swamiji," Balak Ram recounted. "I was in utter despair. In spite of my herculean efforts God would not give me *darshan*. I flew, into such a rage against Shiva that I ran wild and madly kicked at the *Shiva-linga*, struggled hard to uproot it from its seat and throw it down the hill, but I could not move it. It was so firmly fixed in the ground. Next I remembered you. I called you aloud "Ramdas, Ramdas, Ramdas!"—I went on at the highest pitch of my voice for nearly half an hour and stopped through sheer exhaustion. After all, in response to my insistent call, you have come. You are my God."

"Ramdas is only a servant of God," Ramdas assured him, "who is dwelling in the hearts of us all, and he goes from place to place in obedience to His command."

(iii) God's Act—Miraculous Cure

As the shadows of the evening closed upon the scene, all the friends, except Vaijnath and Ramcharandas, went down the hill to spend the night in the village at the foot of the hills. Balak Ram had a lantern which he lit when darkness set in. The mountain was clothed with a dense jungle of gigantic trees. The beasts of prey came out of their lairs and set forth their hungry roars which could be heard distinctly from all sides.

Before dark the party of four had climbed up to a higher position on the hill. The way to it was eminently slippery and dangerous. Here was a cave-like room, constructed of the bricks, in front of which was a narrow passage, and that was all the space available for their occupation.

"Swamiji, this morning I was so sure of your coming that I had smeared the inside of this cave with cow-dung so that you might occupy it," said Balak Ram, and added, "I beg, Swamiji, that you stay with me for some days."

"No, Ram, that cannot be," replied Ramdas: "you see so many friends have come with Ramdas to take him back, and the motor-car is detained specially for his return journey."

"You should not go," he persisted, "let the friends go back. I will have you alone with me. After a few days I shall arrange for a motor-car for you to go." he appealed, wept and fell at Ramdas's feet.

Then Ramdas told him that he would stay on certain conditions, and if any one of them was broken, he would go.

"I shall see that your conditions are faithfully fulfilled on my part," he promised.

"Now the conditions are: So long as Ramdas is with you, he will not leave this elevated place. Second: he will occupy the cave in the nights. Third: he will live merely on water diet. Fourth: he will observe the vow of silence. Do you agree?" Ramdas stipulated.

He gladly accepted the conditions because he believed that by Ramdas's *tapasya*, his own uncontrolled mind would attain peace. Till late in the night the talk went on. They had rest for only two or three hours in the morning. Ramdas slept in the cave-room.

Next day all went down to the lower stage where the *Shiva-linga* was installed. Ramdas remained near the cave. At about eight o'clock the party from the village came up headed by Bhavani Prasad. He brought with him food consisting of purees, curry and milk to suffice all the members of the party. Balak Ram explained to them at Ramdas's request, the latter's resolution to stop with him for some days and also about the conditions. So he asked them to leave the hills without Ramdas. The friends remonstrated. They said with one voice that they would not go except with him and also would not take food unless he shared it with them. He could hear their talk and see them from above. They pressed Balak Ram to bring him down. Balak Ram was in a dilemma. He had given word that he would not be a party to the breaking of the vows. The situation was extremely awkward for him. At last he had to yield. He came up and led Ramdas down. Then the party sat for dinner. Balak Ram with his own hands mixed a puree in milk with sugar and offered it to him. He ate—three vows broken—and also broke the last with the remark: "Ram, all the vows are broken and you are the cause. So Ramdas takes it that he is allowed to depart with the party."

"No, no, Swamiji," Balak Ram cried out with frightened and grieved tone. "You may observe the vows after they are gone."

At this stage, Ramcharandas who was dead against Ramdas's stay with Balak Ram, made a sign to Ramdas not to yield to his persuasion. At this Balak Ram got terribly enraged with Ramcharandas, and with a loud voice said: "You dare to instigate Swamiji not to stop here! May the curses of Shiva be on your head!"

Ramdas immediately replied: "The curses of Shiva be on Ramdas's head and not on Ramcharandas's since Ramdas's head is smooth, being bald, and therefore can accommodate any number of curses." Ramdas got up to start while Balak Ram wept and rolled on the ground to prevent him from going.

"Control your anger, Ram," Ramdas said, "repeat Ram *mantram*."

The party left the hills and returned to the motor-car. They reached Chhattarpur by midday. The motor-car drove directly to the door of its owner who was ill. Ramdas went in to see him. He was sitting on his bed, still weak but entirely free from fever. He shook with emotion on seeing Ramdas. He was offered some milk which he again shared with the patient and was about to leave him, when he called the motor-driver and instructed him to keep the motor-car exclusively at the disposal of Ramdas so long as he remained in Chhattarpur. He also refused to accept any fare from Bhavani Prasad for the journey to Rajghad.

Ramdas requested the friends that had hitherto followed him to return to their place, leaving him and Ramcharandas to proceed to Cawnpore. The same car took them to Harpalpur station where they caught a train for Banda for the *darshan* of Vishuddhanand.

CHAPTER 24: CAWNPORE – IN THE STEAMBOAT

(i) God Cannot Be Proved by Arguments

Ramdas spent about five days with the *sadhu* in Banda. He was supremely delighted to see Ramdas again. He used to make Ramdas sit on his raised *asan* and, squatting in front of him, read out passages from Yoga Vasishta and compare with Ramdas's state the description given therein of a liberated soul. He would exclaim with great glee: "Your life is moulded exactly after that of a *jivanmukta* as delineated in this work." He took Ramdas to the city and presented him to his disciples. Jagannath of Mahoba came here on a visit to see Ramdas. On the third day Ramdas had another attack of fever which lasted for one night.

One evening a man came running to the *kuti* and told the *sadhu* that there was a likelihood of bloodshed that night in Banda. Two processions, one of Muslims and the other of Hindus headed by Swami Satyadev, were to pass the same road from opposite directions. Preparations had been made on both sides for a fight. They had armed themselves with *lathis*. The tender heart of the *sadhu* was touched by the alarming news. He drew a long breath and sighed.

"Maharaj." then Ramdas spoke, "there will be no fight and no bloodshed."

He looked at Ramdas and smiled and said "Amen." He became cheerful again. At eleven o'clock a messenger came from the town, bringing the tidings that all went well with the processions. There was no brawl between the parties. They passed on the same road, side by side, without any friction.

"God be praised," uttered the compassionate old *sadhu*. Taking leave of the *sadhu*, Ramdas and Ramcharandas started from Banda and arrived at Cawnpore where they were received by Ramchandra Gupta at the station. Gupta had arranged for their stay in a Shiva Mandir on the banks of the Ganges. Here fever again made its appearance. Gupta was a student of the local college of commerce. Hundreds of students of the college came to see Ramdas. Fever did not prevent him from having free talks with them. They would put him all kinds of questions and he was ready with replies.

One night a number of students, headed by a leader, came to interview Ramdas. They belonged to a sect called Charvak, allied to materialism. Their leader discussed till one o'clock contending that the body was all and that life was intended only for material enjoyment. Everything was merely nature and its work; there was no such thing as soul, spirit or God as controller of the worlds.

Ramdas told him at last: "Friend, Ramdas cannot prove to you by mere arguments the existence of God, nobody can. Ramdas from his own experience can boldly assert that there is God. Until you yourself get the experience, it is natural that you should deny Him. But a time will come when you too will have faith in Him."

Ramdas's stay in Cawnpore was only for four days. From Lalitpur, Triveni Prasad explained by letter that his second call was due to the local *munsif* who had missed him, owing to his ignorance of Ramdas's arrival at Lalitpur at his first visit, and who was now anxious to see him. Ramdas proceeded, therefore, with Ramcharandas again to Lalitpur. The fever continued. This time they were put up at the *munsif's* house. He and his wife were extremely kind. They tended him as though he were their child. Here Ramdas met Ramkinkar of Jhansi.

After a couple of days they left Lalitpur direct for Bombay. In the train they met a Sikh who was also going to Bombay. All through the journey he looked after Ramdas with great tenderness, attending to all his needs. As they neared Bombay, the compartment in which they sat was vacant except for the three. Ramdas was sitting in a corner and Ramcharandas leaned out of a window. Everybody was silent in the compartment. Suddenly, Ramcharandas came bounding to Ramdas and said with surprised looks: "Swamiji, some one has just been uttering in my ears Ramnam; I distinctly heard it. Who did it?"

"Ram, Ramdas never moved from his seat, so also the Sikh. It must be Ram, and who is there other than He?" Ramdas replied.

At the Victoria Terminus they met Sanjivarao who was awaiting their arrival. They drove in a victoria to Sanjivarao's quarters at Gamdevi.

(ii) God Is Providence

The fever continued to appear every third day for about four or five hours in the evening from four to eight or nine. Sanjivarao and his wife grew anxious about him. Often in the evenings, on the fever days, he would be talking on *bhakti* and *vairagya* to the mothers who used to visit him at that time. He was reading out bits from the "Rambles in Vedanta" by B. R. Rajam Iyer. When he was narrating the life of Nanda, the pariah saint, from this book he would go into ecstasies. The life presents the unique devotion of an outcast saint who was completely merged in divine consciousness. The hearers would also become blissful.

In the night Ramdas would, in spite of fever, talk long and spontaneously, expounding the greatness of *bhakti* and of the inestimable power of God's Name. A doctor friend, who had great love for him, would pay him visits. He proposed to give him an injection for the fever. Ramdas would not have the treatment. But Sanjivarao and his wife were persistent. They would have him take some medicine. At their pressure he drank twice a day a bitter mixture and every time, when he did so, he remarked that the medicine was so very sweet! The mother—Sanjivarao's wife would be surprised to hear him say so. Ramdas would only laugh. All the same the fever persisted.

"The fever refuses to leave," Ramdas observed, "because you have made him a welcome guest by feeding him with fine things. The small quantity of the bitter medicine has no effect on fever while he is well served with tasty sweets and other kinds of food three or four times a day! So long as you feed an undesirable guest he will certainly stick on. But the moment you starve him he will without your bidding make himself scarce. So allow Ramdas to go on a fast for some days. He will live merely on milk." At first the loving pair objected to the proposal, but at last yielded. A four days' fast and the fever-guest took to his heels.

Invitations came from the Sholapur District, but God willed that Ramdas should proceed to Mangalore. So he and Ramcharandas boarded the steamboat sailing for Mangalore port. Ramcharandas was busy exploring the ship for tiffin-shops. At about nine o'clock he turned up with a bright face and said: "Swamiji, there is on the boat a coffee-hotel in which all kinds of eatables are sold. (Here his mouth involuntarily watered, and he had to drink off the nectar before he proceeded.)

The hotel man says that he can also provide meals if we place an order with him beforehand—each meal costs six annas only."

Now Ramcharandas had money given him by Sanjivarao for expenses on the boat and at landing. He made a sound of coins to show that there was no dearth of funds.

"Right ho!" Ramdas replied laughing, "place at once an order for two meals for midday. Fire away."

He bounded with joy towards the tiffin-shop and personally supervised the cooking of the meals. He was himself something of an expert in cooking which art he exercised by making experiments of his dishes on Ramdas when he travelled long distances with him!

At about twelve o'clock he came to take Ramdas for meals. It was a simple but wholesome meal. After the meal Ramdas returned to his seat while Ramcharandas remained behind, talking to somebody. A little later he also came, but this time with a worried look.

"What is wrong with you?" Ramdas questioned.

"Some men near the tiffin-shop saw us taking meals," he answered and remarked to me: 'Although *sadhus*, you are very particular about meals. Eating seems to be the predominant *sadhana* of your *sadhu* life.'

"Ram," Ramdas said with a laugh which he could scarcely repress, "the food was delicious. So also, why not find the same taste in this sweet remark?"

He never ordered further meals, presumably because the bitterness of the remark outweighed the taste of the meal!

On the way, when the steamboat was still moving, two mothers gave birth to twins. They were third-class passengers and the accouchement took place on the deck. There were among the passengers also a doctor and a nurse who attended on the mothers. In the mid-sea, even in such a contingency, God provides necessary assistance. Hence God is called Providence.

Ramdas and Ramcharandas on arrival at Mangalore were put up at Sitaramrao's house. An invitation came from Kasaragod to attend the closing day of a nama-saptah held in the house of T. Bhavanishankarrao, a relation of Ramdas's old life. He and his house-people had undertaken to repeat the Ram *mantram* thirteen *lakhs* of times within a week, and in the *japa* children and servants had also joined.

About this time Ramdas had a visit at Mangalore from Savoor Shankarrao who held English degrees and was then a professor in the Presidency College, Madras. In spite of his great learning and attainments, Ramdas found him to be a simple, humble and pious soul. He conceived a great love for Ramdas at first sight and frequently courted his company. The very talk of God would work on his emotions and bring tears into his eyes. He joined Ramdas at the Nama-Saptaha. Ramdas spent a most blissful time for about two or three days on this occasion. The *japa* had exceeded fifteen *lakhs*. The zeal, even of the youngsters to make up the highest possible number of *japa*, as their quota, was admirable.

Ramcharandas who was also present at the religious function was asked by Ramdas to go back to Mangalore, and to have resort to solitude for *japa* and meditation. Accordingly he left Kasaragod for Mangalore.

A saintly soul from Kallianpur was in Kasaragod during this time owing to the illness of his grand-daughter. He took Ramdas to see the girl. The little girl had great love for Ramdas. She was overjoyed to behold him. She narrated in her own innocent way that she had a vision, on the previous night, of Rama and Sita. The girl recovered soon after this.

Ramdas also paid visits to Gurudev whose body was weak and worn out by the infirmities of old age. He was living with his son Anandrao. He was then past eighty years of age. He was perfectly calm and peaceful, and the worries of life had ceased for him. Ramdas having received an invitation from Sanjivarao of Ernakulam left Kasaragod for that place.

CHAPTER 25: ERNAKUlAM

(i) Friend of Bird and Beast

At Shoranur Ramdas met Sanjivarao who had come to escort him. For the first few days he was put up at his house. Now remittance and a telegram came from Madhavrao Kulkarni of Anjangaum, requesting him to start immediately so as to be present at the religious celebration held annually in his house. But owing to the indifferent health of Ramdas, due to frequent attacks of malaria even after reaching Ernakulam, the friends here resolutely stood against his travelling to such a distant place as Sholapur. He had to submit, and the money having been returned, Madhavrao was duly informed by the friends through a joint letter that Ramdas's then condition of health did not permit of his travelling and that he needed perfect rest for some time. Ramdas proposed to Sanjivarao to provide him with a dwelling place outside the town so that people who wanted to see him might visit him there and have talks with him. Soon a house about a mile from the town was pitched upon for his stay.

A day prior to his shifting to this house, a friend, a pious brahmin, came to see Ramdas at Sanjivarao's abode. Ramdas was sitting on a chair facing the entrance in the front room. The time was about eight in the morning. The brahmin ascended the first front step and stopped suddenly and stood stock-still like a statue, gazing at Ramdas. He possessed large eyes which looked at Ramdas with a winkless stare. A minute or two later he came inside and took a chair beside Ramdas. He was still gazing on Ramdas. For five minutes there was complete silence. Then he broke out into speech.

"Do you know," he asked, "why I stood on the steps gazing on you so intently? I shall tell you. I beheld a strange phenomenon. The moment my eyes rested on your figure I saw a brilliant flame of light all around your body. It was a pure dazzling light. I was transfixed at the sight. The light was there for a few seconds and it vanished, and then I entered the room."

Ramdas shifted to the house outside the town. It consisted of three small rooms and an open verandah. The house was situated in the middle of a garden of coconut palms. Ernakulam is a sandy place, being close to the Arabian sea, the shores of which are studded with beautiful coconut groves. The main produce of the land is coconut out of which oil and other foodstuffs are extracted and exported in large quantities.

In the evenings and mornings visitors used to come to his retreat to see and have talks with him. They would put him questions on religious subjects and he would, drawing upon his experiences, attempt to elucidate them. High Government officials, *vakils*, and professors would also give him the joy of their society. The neighbourhood in which he lived was of Christians whose fowls and goats that wandered around had free access to the house. He would feed them with plantains and grains which he received as presents from the visitors. The pregnant hens would lay their eggs on his bedding at day-time, believing that they would be safe there. They clearly exhibited an anxiety to preserve and protect them from their marauding masters who would deprive them of their offspring still in the egg.

But the sons of these masters came to the house in search of eggs and would carry them off. One day a poor hen missed her egg from the bedding of Ramdas on which she had laid it. Ramdas at the time was sitting outside in the verandah. He was alone. The hen directly came to him with questioning looks and cried "Ko-Ko-Ko"—meaning: "What became of my egg that I laid on your bed?"

"Mother, what can Ramdas do?" Ramdas replied. "The sons of your masters come here and take away your eggs in your absence."

The same story would repeat itself again and again. When Ramdas was one morning feeding and talking to some goats, two Christian padres came to see him. Observing Ramdas's friendly intercourse with the animals they spoke of the famous Saint Francis of Assisi whose life, they said, was similar to the one which Ramdas led.

The Lord, through the friends at Ernakulam, willed that Ramdas should write this narrative in continuation of the first book "In Quest of God." He was provided with the necessary writing materials. Ramdas commenced to put down on paper the story of his life, but gave it up after inditing a few pages. He had then, at the outset, jotted down the main points of the narrative on a scrap book, and these notes, which were preserved, are utilized now for reference.

Here Ramdas was again joined by the *raja yogi* who had instructed him in the practice of *pranayama*. Among the visitors was a prominent Malayalee *vakil*, Narayana Menon, who took it into his head to adopt *sannyas*. He also received initiation into the practice of breath-control, and the *raja yogi* began to deride at all other methods of concentration.

Ramdas was holding up the repetition of God's Name as the easiest and best path to reach God, while the *raja yogi* openly condemned this method and spoke of it disparagingly to the visitors on whom Ramdas was impressing its importance. There was a clash. The visitors were perplexed and Ramdas was at his wit's end and submitted to the will of God, and God solved the problem in His own inscrutable manner. The *raja yogi* was residing in Ernakulam for a pretty long time, even before Ramdas visited the place, and he had freely and indiscriminately instructed many people in this practice, with the result that it worked a good deal of harm among them, and there was a rush of these poor unlettered folk to this house, where, they had heard, the *yogi* stayed. They complained of heart palpitation, cough, loss of memory, wasting disease and what not! This storm cooled down the ardour of the yogi. He stopped urging his pet method and also giving instructions relating to *pranayama*.

(ii) Qualities of a *Sadhu*

About this time another *sannyasi* turned up. He entered the house, and seeing some plantains in a cupboard helped himself to them, and then coming to Ramdas, said: "I want a bath; get me some hot water ready, at once." Now there was no arrangement in the house for heating water. Ramdas and the yogi used to have cold baths. Ramdas made him aware of the situation.

"No excuses," he shouted, "hot water, quick. I have had no bath for several days. You see, I insist on having it here and now."

There was an earthen water-pot. The *yogi* quietly mounted it on three stones which he fetched from the compound, and with dry coconut branches lit a fire and the water was heated. Ramdas and the *yogi* then gave him a bath. The *yogi* washed his dirty clothes. The whole thing was performed by both in the best of humour. After bath he commanded: "Where is the meal? I am hungry."

The meals for Ramdas and the *yogi* used to come from the city at twelve midday. The time then was ten o'clock. He was told about the time of meals. Ramdas was prepared to forego his meal for the *sannyasi* for that day. So he asked the friend to wait till the meal arrived.

"I cannot wait," he said, "I am going out. I will try to get food somewhere in the town." Saying this, he walked away. At twelve the meals arrived. Ramdas proposed to the *yogi* to wait for some time, as there was a chance of the *sannyasi* turning up. They waited for nearly half-an-hour but the *sannyasi* did not put in an appearance. The *raja yogi* suggested that they might finish the meals so that the carrier might not wait for the vessels very long, and added that the *sadhu* might have procured food in the city. So they took their food.

Just after the meal was over and the vessels were cleaned, the *sannyasi* entered the house with hasty and eager steps and directly went to the room where the dinner was served, and there he found nothing but a most tantalizing after-dinner smell of food, at which he sniffed.

"Where is food for me?" he bawled out. He gave such a furious stare at Ramdas that if he could swallow up Ramdas by his gaze he would certainly have done so that instant.

"Fine fellows! You have eaten everything and left nothing for me?" he spoke with withering scorn.

"You too shall have your meal, swami, but since you did not come in time, you will have to wait another half-an-hour," Ramdas replied. He then instructed the meal carrier to run at once to a certain friend's house and fetch double meals. The obliging young man, in half-an-hour, brought a sufficiently large quantity of food, and the hungry *sannyasi* had a satisfactory meal.

The *sannyasi* stayed for the day. That evening visitors poured in as usual but when they saw the *sannyasi* there, they manifested uneasiness and anxiety. Two early visitors spoke out their mind in his presence, and said: "This *sannyasi* is a great pest. He comes to our houses and worries our lives out of us. He is not satisfied with mere food. He also wants money. We poor people cannot afford to meet his demands. Further he threatens to hurl curses at us. We do not set much value on his curses, but his behaviour is quite intolerable. We would have dealt with him in a drastic manner, but we respect the colour of the cloth he wears."

While this open indictment was made to his face, the *sannyasi*, with one leg resting in a lordly style on the other and his right hand twisting one side of his moustache, was smiling most approvingly as though he were listening to some glorious exploits of which he was the hero. Ramdas then briefly spoke to him about the true qualities of a *sadhu*.

"If a *sadhu* were to remain for a long time at any particular place, he must live outside the town and go to it only to receive his *bhiksha*. He must never harass the householders. He must cultivate patience and forgiveness. He must never enter their houses without the permission of the master of the house. He should not ask for money, but be satisfied only with the food that is offered to him. To wish ill of anybody or heap curses on anyone is quite contrary to the principles of a *sadhu*. When he wears the *sannyasi* robes, he should never by his conduct disgrace the cloth. The cloth stands for absolute renunciation. If he finds himself unfit for it, he must never adopt it, or, if he has taken to it through an error of judgment, he ought to give it up as soon as he discovers the mistake, lest people be deceived by his appearance.

"He must never frequent the bazaars. He must adhere to his solitary abode and do the necessary *sadhanas*, or enlighten those who go to him for spiritual help. If his trust in the supreme

Truth and his confidence in his own desireless efforts are weak and, as a consequence, he cannot progress towards a life which is self-sufficient and independent, he would do well to abandon the *sadhu's* garb and life and take to any honest profession for his living, suited to his nature. To be a pest and burden to society is to court evil for himself, besides being a nuisance to those who come in contact with him."

The *sannyasi* listened with eagerness and concentration to Ramdas's speech, a smile playing about his lips. In the night the *sannyasi* was given a cloth to cover himself. Early next morning, as he got up from the mat on which he was lying, he said that he was leaving Ernakulam that day, and taking the cloth with him left the place and did not come again.

(iii) Your Body Is His Expression

Now Ramcharandas, who was for some time roaming in some villages of South Kanara, thought of travelling towards Northern India. As he desired to see Ramdas before finally leaving the south, one day he suddenly turned up at the retreat. Ramdas was happy to see him.

In the course of conversation with him Ramdas spoke to him of the divine vision: "God-vision is nothing but to realise and feel His presence within yourself and everywhere about you; because God is an all prevailing spirit, permeating the entire universe. The manifested worlds are not different from Him, since they are but His own expression in terms of name and form."

But the boy was not impressed at this presentation of Truth, and he said in a tone of utter dissatisfaction: "Swamiji, I would have nothing of your *nirguna* or impersonal aspect of God. I want to behold Him as *saguna*. I crave for the *darshan* of the Ram *panchayatan*; i.e., as Rama, Sita, Lakshman, Bharat, and Hanuman. You are always harping on the same tune—His formless aspect."

Ramdas smiled and replied: "The *saguna* you are after is an image of your own mind and it cannot satisfy you. You ought to rise beyond all forms of sight and mind. The true *saguna* or body of the Lord is the universe itself in which He is immanent and by His power He is causing, in this manifestation, birth, growth, and dissolution of all beings and things. He is also transcendent as pure spirit. Your body is one of His expressions. Your activity has its inception in the infinite power of God. Don't be deluded by a desire to behold things which are conditioned and momentary—mere phantoms of your mind. Have the true longing to realise your immortal nature and your union with the omnipotent and omnipresent God, who is the supreme Lord of the universe. Purify your mind and heart by proper discipline and entitle yourself to this glorious vision, and attain perfect freedom and eternal bliss."

Ramcharandas remained silent. A short time after this he took leave of Ramdas.

CHAPTER 26: ERNAKULAM – ALLEPPEY

(i) What Do You Make of It?

A humorous and instructive story in the life of a high official of Ernakulam may be cited here. The incident was related by the official himself who was a sincere and pious soul. He narrates: "I am earning a sufficiently large salary for the upkeep of my family, but cupidity is one of the greatest failings to which human nature is subjected. Craving for wealth is an insatiable fire. The more you feed the fire the more furious it grows. My wife is a devout soul. She would always be praying to the Almighty to bestow on me a higher post than I now hold so that I might draw a larger salary. But her appeals remained unheeded. So one day she proposed to perform a special propitiation of the goddess of wealth in order to induce her to yield her favour. She got a clay image of the *Devi* made and installed it in the room in which the family deity was worshipped. When I asked her for the reason, she said that she intended to worship the new image with a view to my being granted promotion. She added that she had warned the goddess that if she did not fulfil her wish in a month's time she would abandon her worship. A month's time and notice for the poor goddess!

"Worship went on from day to day with great assiduity and offerings of choice *prasad*. I was not particular about the number of days she performed the worship. One day I found the place empty. The image was not there. I called my wife and questioned her about the disappearance of the goddess.

"'I have done with her,' she replied with a look of disgust. 'I did all I could to please her but she has not granted my prayer. The month has passed away and no sign of your promotion. I have thrown her out.'

"Later, I discovered the rejected image lying piteously in a heap of rubbish in a pond, at the back of the house! Wonderful indeed is her *bhakti*! What do you make of it?" The listeners broke out into a loud laughter.

The *raja yogi* was growing cooler everyday, because more sufferers from the effects of the *pranayama* practice poured in. Ramdas was consulted in the matter by these people and he advised them point-blank to put a stop to the practice altogether. About the same time he received complaints on the same subject from Bangalore and South Kanara where this practice had been widely disseminated by other yogis of the same ilk.

Ramdas could not remain unconcerned any longer. He was made to write a strong article, which was published in newspapers, warning the people neither to take up nor prosecute, if already adopted, this practice, if they were not prepared to fulfil the other conditions of the yoga, as it would otherwise cause incalculable harm to them. Ramdas also spoke about the matter to the *raja yogi*.

"You have observed, Ramji, what mischief this practice of yours is causing to those who cannot observe the other rules which necessarily go with the yoga discipline. So you will do well in future not to initiate indiscriminately everybody who comes to you without judging whether he or she is fit for it or not."

Now about the *vakil* who was preparing for *sannyas*. He broached the subject to Ramdas. The latter discouraged him and said: "If you are so anxious to dedicate yourself entirely to God, you may retire from public activity and have a small *kuti* on your landed property and lead a life of contemplation and meditation on God. Don't think you can attain God merely by donning the orange robe."

He replied that he had once for all decided upon taking *sannyas*, and that he was determined about it.

"God's will be done," Ramdas submitted.

He was an elderly man of means having a family. One night he came with a set of ochre-coloured clothes and said to Ramdas: "Swamiji, I have made all arrangements for the maintenance of my family and have made over all the rights of my property to the proper persons. I am free. Tomorrow I will leave Ernakulam. I wish to travel from place to place without funds as you did during your first year's itinerant life as chronicled in your book 'In Quest of God'."

Next day he left Ernakulam. The *raja yogi* accompanied the *vakil*—an opportunity which he could not miss of getting out of the unpleasant situation in which he found himself. Ramdas learnt that the *vakil* had after a few months' wanderings returned to his professional work. Now he is intimately associated with the activities of Anandashram.

Once again, the old malaria that had left Ramdas for a few months made its appearance. Ramdas began to have periodical attacks of fever.

Sanjivarao and his family were all love and kindness to Ramdas. The Ram *mantram* had so firmly captured Sanjivarao that he would not forget it for a single moment. This always happens when it once takes possession of the mind. Even when you are busy with work, the *mantram* would be unconsciously revolving in the depths of the mind and automatically. Such was the case with him at the time. He was experiencing the opening of the fountain of joy and peace within him. This was all apparent from his serene, radiant and blissful face.

News came to him that Ramdas's daughter by the old birth, Ramabai had been betrothed to Chandrashekarrao, son of Ramdas's sister, and that the marriage was to take place in a short time in Kasaragod.

(ii) A Christian *Sadhu*

Mark Sanjivrao was Ramdas's cousin by the old birth. From early boyhood he and Ramdas were great chums. When he was still young, he renounced the Hindu faith and embraced Christianity. The great Christ, as a supreme ideal, fascinated and captured him, and as an earnest seeker of the everlasting life, i.e. the kingdom of God, he became Christ's disciple. The friendship between him and Ramdas continued unhampered. Ramdas admired his courage in taking a step which threw him into odium and made him an object of ridicule from the Hindu public. He bore the cross of persecution calmly because he had the courage of his convictions. He associated with pure and saintly souls amongst the Christian missionaries and imbibed from them the spirit of a dedicated life.

Ramdas's new birth and purified vision had brought about a momentous change in his life. On his return after a year's absence from South Kanara, Mark Sanjivarao paid a visit to him, and Ramdas felt great joy on seeing him. Now his love for Ramdas had increased a hundredfold. He was instrumental in bringing Ramdas in close touch with the sublime teachings of Christ in the New Testament. Ramdas had no predilection for any particular creed or religion. He held in the highest veneration the founders of all the great religions of the world, Sri Krishna, Jesus Christ, Buddha and Mohammed. Now Ramdas knows that these great ones are the torch-bearers of Truth who show to the deluded souls the path to the supreme Reality, a Reality which is revealed by these torch-bearers.

Mark Sanjivarao was a preacher of the Christ's Gospel and his sphere of work covered an extensive field. He came to Ernakulam on his way to Alleppey and Kottayam in the Travancore State. He paid a visit to Ramdas in his retreat and proposed to take him to these places. Ramdas at once fell in with the idea. They started and reached Alleppey in due time. Here they were put up in a commodious building called the Christian Institute. In the Institute, Ramdas came in touch with two self-sacrificing Christians, *sadhu* Mathai, an elderly man, dressed in ochre-coloured robes, and Thomas, a young man. Both of them showed great love for Ramdas. Thomas was quiet in his ways whereas Mathai was not; he set about hammering into Ramdas Christ's teachings as the only true revelation of God. He worked at the proselytism in season and out of season with all the ardour of a Christian missionary. Ramdas told him finally: "God has given Ramdas's head a permanent shape. You may hammer on as much as you like but you cannot change its shape into what you wish it to be!"

Mark Sanjivarao, who was watching, burst into roars of laughter. He would ask Ramdas humorously: "Has Mathai been able to change the shape of your head?"

"Mathai cannot perform the impossible. Ramdas's head is cast in such a mould that a permanent shape has already been given to it," Ramdas would reply. And they would laugh. Whenever Mathai approached, Ramdas would remark: "The hammer has come." At last Mathai gave up his futile task and Ramdas concluded that the hammer had broken!

Those were jolly days that Ramdas spent in the Institute. In the spacious upstair rooms of the building, Ramdas freely frisked, danced, jumped, and ran about like a playful kid. Sanjivarao remembered Ramdas's oft-repeated expression, 'wild joy.'

Sanjivarao delivered in the Institute two sermons on "Why I became the disciple of Christ." After a few days' stay, Ramdas with Mark Sanjivarao and Thomas proceeded to Kottayam. On the day he reached the place, he had an attack of malaria. He was accommodated in the house of a pious Christian who was all hospitality and kindness. The fever continued only for one night.

The following day a lecture by Sanjivarao was announced to the public. The local YMCA building was the appointed place for its delivery. A resident missionary was in the chair. There was a crowded audience. Next morning, Ramdas, of course in the company of Sanjivarao, visited the Christian High School. The Principal, clad in *khadi*, offered Ramdas a glad welcome and arranged for a speech to the students by Ramdas. The latter spoke in English on "God is Love" as revealed in the teachings of Jesus Christ for half-an-hour. The Principal interpreted the same in Malayalam to the assembled students.

In the evening there was another lecture by Sanjivarao at the YMCA At the pressure of the friends, Ramdas spoke for about fifteen minutes before the regular speaker took the platform. Ramdas dealt with the unity of religions and pointed out that in their teachings all the great incarnations of the world of different ages perfectly agreed. Next followed the speech of Sanjivarao. This time there was no president. The president was God Almighty who was seated in the hearts of the speakers and the audience themselves.

After a couple of days they returned to Ernakulam. Now Ramdas got the idea of visiting the ensuing Kumbha Mela of Hardwar. The prospect of seeing the Himalayas again made him quite enthusiastic. But before proceeding towards the north, he left Ernakulam with the intention of paying a visit to Kanara.

CHAPTER 27: KASARAGOD – SWARGASHRAM

(i) Ramdas Beholds Rama and Sita

When Ramdas arrived at Kasaragod, he came to know that Ramabai's marriage was to be performed in a week's time. Anandrao, who was extremely kind to Ramdas in every way, had undertaken to have the celebration at his house. Ramdas stayed for the time being in the small room of his office. The preparations of the marriage went on. On the appointed day the house and the *pandal* were quite full of visitors. Ramdas was, all through the performance, an unconcerned witness of the wedding ceremony. He utilized his time in playing with the children. Once, when the bride and bridegroom were seated in the decorated *mandapam*, Ramdas was questioned as to who they were, and he made the ready reply: "Ramdas beholds Rama and Sita in the pair."

The outstanding feature of the ceremony was the feeding of the poor at the close of it. Nearly three to four hundred people were provided with a sumptuous feast. Anandrao and his wife conducted the celebration. A few days later, Ramdas left Kasaragod for Mangalore where he spent a few days. Here again he met Mark Sanjivarao with whom he read some religious books at his rooms in Balmatta. Sanjivarao also introduced Ramdas to a Christian missionary couple. He took great interest in presenting Ramdas to the Christian world.

Krishnarao, father of M. Bhavanishankerrao, who was then in Mangalore, came to Ramdas and proposed to escort him to Bangalore. They travelled by motor-bus via Mercara. One evening they found themselves in that hilly tract. There was a drizzle. Ramdas was made to sit in the motor-agent's tiny office. Where to spend the night? The question was sorely troubling Krishnarao, as he wished to find for Ramdas proper accommodation for the night. But God had provided against every contingency. When dusk was approaching, a man whom Ramdas had never seen before coming to him fell at his feet and said: "Swamiji, it will give me no small delight if you will be pleased to grace my house. I had been so keenly longing to have your *darshan* and God has granted me this blessed opportunity. Pray do come with me."

Ramdas agreeing, the friend took him to his storied house. His family members were away and he was alone with a servant. He made Ramdas sit on a deerskin *asan* and introduced himself as thus: "Swamiji, my name is Madhav Kamath. I have read your book, 'In Quest of God' and have seen your picture in it. From the likeness you bear to the photograph I saw in the book, I could recognise you at once. Ever since I perused this book I was intensely desiring to see you. God heard my prayer and has sent you here for my sake."

As he spoke his throat grew husky with emotion and from his large eyes poured a stream of tears. He embraced Ramdas repeatedly in a state of ecstasy. He asked Ramdas to place his hand on his head which Ramdas did, and Madhav Kamath rolled on the floor in a trance-like condition. They went on talking till late in the night. He showered torrents of love and kindness on Ramdas. God in His own inscrutable ways looks after Ramdas with all tenderness and care.

Next day Ramdas started with Krishnarao. At Bangalore Ramdas was welcomed by Bhavanishankerrao, Sitabai and others of his household with great joy. Ramdas spent a few days here. Bhavanishankerrao, who was also eager to attend the Kumbha Mela, accompanied him. In due time they reached Bombay and were received at the station by Sanjivarao who escorted them to his house. Sanjivarao and his wife were as overflowing with love as ever. Ramdas stayed with them for about three days and then, with Bhavanishankerrao, he journeyed towards Jhansi.

In Jhansi they resided in the same Ram Mandir which he had occupied on previous occasions. All the old friends crowded into the *mandir* to see Ramdas. Ramkinkar found great happiness in serving the guests. Ramdas also met Ramcharandas who was awaiting his arrival in Jhansi.

The one prominent feature of his stay in Jhansi on this occasion was that he ate food from the same plate with friends drawn from different castes. Even brahmins joined them in the promiscuous dinner. Ramkinkar, a brahmin by caste, at first mildly resented the onslaught on the age-long custom, but in the end he yielded on account of his high esteem and love for Ramdas.

After a short stay in Jhansi, Ramdas with Bhavanishankerrao and Ramcharandas departed for Hairdwar. Haridwar is at the foot of the Himalayas, a noted place of pilgrimage for Hindus. Here, once in twelve years, a mammoth gathering is held to commemorate the occasion of the devas drinking the nectar procured from the churning of the ocean. The festival is called "Kumbha Mela."

The party stopped at Haridwar for an hour or thereabouts and then directed their steps upwards towards Rishikesh which lay at a distance of about fourteen miles from Haridwar. They travelled on foot. In the evening they reached the banks of the Ganges in Rishikesh. Crossing the river, where it was shallow, they came upon a vast sand bed which Ramdas selected as the most suitable place for their night halt. It was at the edge of a range of majestic heaven-kissing mountains. As night approached cold winds swept over the sand bed on which they had camped. There was a fallen tree close by. A fire was lit by setting fire to a dry branch of this tree.

The wind developed into a gale which blew furiously, carrying with it loose sand from the surface of the river bed. The situation became quite ticklish, and Ramdas laughed with unusual glee, at the ineffectual efforts of the party to cover themselves with blankets against the sand-storm. The night passed without a wink of sleep. When the day dawned the devil of the storm was laid. The morning presented a calm and bewitching sight. The twilight spread its enchanting glow on the tall hills full of vegetation. Stillness and serenity reigned everywhere and the soft bracing breeze played on the scene which had assumed a menacing and troubled aspect the previous night.

At midday they ate meals procured from the *annakshetra*s of the place, and towards evening they crossed the river and reached Swargashram. On the left bank of the river Ramdas observed a neat building going by the name 'Ramashram.' The ashram was built in memory of the great and renowned Swami Rama Tirtha. Another time Ramdas had an opportunity to enter this ashram. A portion of it was then used as a post office and the rooms inside were filled with book-cases containing a vast collection of religious literature in Sanskrit, English and other languages.

(ii) The Boy Gets His Monkey Up

Swargashram is an extensive garden at the base of the Nilkant hill, close to the banks of the Ganges which is running down at its front. In this garden, in three rows, are situated about two hundred *kutis* or tiny single and double room structures at twenty yards from one another. These are intended for the occupation of *sadhus*. There is also an *annakshetra* in the compound for supplying the *sadhus* with food twice a day.

The *kutis* were all full. There was no vacant *kuti* for their occupation. They at first settled themselves below a tree and decided upon spending the night there. But a kind Bengali *sannyasi* managed to procure for them a double *kuti* by a mutual arrangement with its then occupant. So they shifted to the *kuti*.

There were yet ten or twelve days for the Kumbha Mela celebration at Hardwar. *Sadhus* and pilgrims had commenced to pour in, in large numbers, from all parts of India. Ramdas lived with the friends in the *kuti* for a couple of days. They obtained their food from the *annakshetra*. The food was shared by the three together from the same plate or leaf just as the Muhammadans do. One day Bhavanishankerrao and Ramdas finished their meal earlier than usual, and Ramcharandas was still busy munching the select bits of *rotis*, quite in a leisurely fashion. A poor sweeper at the door of the *kuti* was anxiously waiting for the remains of the food, because the food the three got was more than they could eat. Seeing the eager and hungry look on the face of the sweeper, Ramdas said to Ramcharandas: "Ram, that poor man must be very hungry; give him some *rotis*. There will be anyhow a surplus left."

Ramcharandas went on eating without heeding Ramdas's words. Ramdas again repeated his suggestion. Still the boy gave no heed. For the third time Ramdas repeated his request. Now the boy was roused to anger. He looked at Ramdas for a few seconds with a steady glare, his eyes red with anger, and he growled: "What! you would not allow me to eat in peace? What is the sense of your bothering me like this?"

At this outburst Ramdas could not resist exploding into laughter, whereas the boy unconcernedly went on cramming down *roti* after *roti*.

One day Ram willed that Ramdas should visit Vasishtashram. Ramdas proposed to go there alone. But Ramcharandas and Bhavanishankerrao insisted upon accompanying him. So the trio started together one early morning. The route to the ashram had been described to them by many *sadhus*, who were consulted on the subject, as extremely perilous, and none of them could tell where exactly it was. Crossing the river Ganges by boat the suspension bridge having broken down during the floods—they came to the other side; i.e., the left bank of the river. Here they refreshed themselves with a cup of milk at the milk-vendor's. Ramcharandas carried with him a *jholi* or arm-bag containing some food-stuffs and vessels.

CHAPTER 28: HIMALAYAS – VASISHTASHRAM

(i) Upon the Precipitous Rock

Now, they set out on the journey, trusting solely in divine guidance. At first a shopman pointed out the direction they had to take. They passed through several fields and then waded past the thick growth of a jungle. As they emerged from it they came upon the bank of the Ganges. Here they met a cultivator who directed them to proceed along the river bank. At the same time, he also warned them that there was no beaten track to Vasishtashram and that, without a guide who knew the route, it would not be possible for them to reach the place. The distance to be covered was over twenty miles. God was their guide. They went forward.

The bank of the Ganges was strewn with big boulders, and they had to pass over these stones by jumping from one to another. They trod on thus for about three miles, when they came face to face with a sloping projection of a hill or headland at the edge of the river. So, here, further progress was cut off. They had then to climb the mountain to their left and pass through a labyrinth of trees, shrubs and creepers for about a mile. Then after a short descent they came again in sight of the river bank. While journeying over the mountain, they had to traverse through a tract called Brahmapuri which they did not notice at the time. On the banks they continued their journey again skipping from boulder to boulder. They went on like this for about two miles.

Here an accident happened which partly disabled Bhavanishankerrao. The jumping feat sprained his ankle. So he began to slow down. Ramcharandas kept him company, whereas Ramdas was running in advance. Ramdas stopped at a spot where further progress was again cut off, as in the last instance. But the promontory this time was not a slope. It was an upright precipitous rock with slight ridges on the flat surface, facing the river. The mountain forming this rock was shooting straight up to a great height; so there was no means of climbing it sideways. The only path was to crawl along the brink of the rock, trusting hands and feet on the uneven furrows upon the vertical surface of the menacing cliff. Down below was rushing in high current the Ganges. A slight slip from the rock meant a fall into the foaming eddies of the river.

This was the situation that confronted him. After waiting for about half-an-hour, he was joined by the two friends. The condition of Bhavanishankerrao's foot was bad, and he was suffering from great pain. They discovered the danger and difficulty in the way of further progress. Ramcharandas suggested that the only alternative left was to return, and Bhavanishankerrao gave his silent vote in favour of the proposal. But Ramdas had to obey the will of Ram which was that he should brave the perilous path. He told the friends of this decision. Ramcharandas was against it and declared that it was sheer madness to venture upon an inaccessible path. Ramdas had no argument to offer. He only replied that the inner call of Ram was insistent and he must obey it, madness or no madness.

While Ramcharandas was still expostulating, three mountaineers, two men and one woman, were seen creeping along the same precipice towards them, coming from the opposite direction. After they had crossed over, Ramdas started up and was about to proceed towards the fascinating rock, when the mountaineers shouted: "Beware, don't attempt the feat because we could do it. We are hill-people trained to such climbing from our childhood. Your case is different. You run a grave risk. Be advised. Don't, for God's sake, be fool-hardy and throw away life."

"Swamiji," Ramcharandas spoke again, "what the man says is perfectly right; do please give up the idea."

Ramdas, feeling amused by this talk, coolly replied. "Well, Ram, did you not observe that the feat was successfully accomplished by a woman while God has made us men and we hesitate?"

At this pointed remark Ramcharandas flared up. His mettle was roused and the boy retorted: "You know, for myself I don't mind casting my lot with you, but what of Bhavanishankerrao? You are aware that as his foot is not all right he cannot make the venture."

Ramdas was adamant. He was urged on from within. He could not withstand the stern command. He rushed to the precipice. His nimble body mounted the rock. His fingers held on to the slits on the rock; his toes rested on the cracks, his breath suspended, he crept on and on—a tense ten minutes' job and he was on the other side, at the top. He could see the two friends sitting on the sands on the opposite side. He now wildly beckoned them to follow him. Ramcharandas suddenly disappeared from his view. He was making the attempt—ten minutes, and Ramcharandas was beside him. But Bhavanishankerrao was still where he was sitting. Surely he too would have come up had his foot been sound. Now Ramdas realised the situation.

To leave Bhavanishankerrao alone, maimed as he was, and that too half-way in a strange place, was not proper. He was unused to such adventures.

Now, turning to Ramcharandas, Ramdas said: "Ram, Bhavanishankerrao cannot be left behind alone with a sprained foot. You ought to return to him and escort him back to Swargashram. As for Ramdas, there is no retracing; he must proceed in search of Vasishtashram. It depends upon Ram if you will ever see him again. He is going to lose himself in the bewildering maze of the Himalayan hills and forests."

Ramcharandas had to retreat. He joined his companion on the other side and both together started back to Swargashram. Ramdas was now alone. It must always be understood that Ram ever kept him company. He ran on, dancing on the banks of the Ganges. He rounded a curve of the bank and rushed on for about half-a-mile only to meet again another headland. He looked aloft and discovered about fifty feet uphill a hollow—a wide gaping cavity in the hill. To cross the hill at the sharp edge of the river was out of the question. He now ascended the slope on all fours, and creeping up like a mouse came to the hollow. It was a shallow cave. On entering it he found that he could just stand erect in it. In the interior at its roof was a huge honeycomb. He found thousands of bees humming around their picturesque abode. The sweet music of their buzz filled the cave. He listened to it for a time in rapture. Emerging, he looked at the prospect. The giant rock to be traversed in front was very smooth and slippery. It extended over a hundred yards. What was to be done? Ramdas spoke: "Ram, now it seems to be Thy will that Ramdas should not visit Vasishtashram, although it was by Thy will he started on this adventure. What does it matter to Ramdas if he should not? He will return by the way he came."

He felt no sense of disappointment. He climbed down to the bank of the Ganges, and turning back kept running close to the water-side. He had not gone fifty yards when he came upon a sight which arrested his further progress. A human skeleton was lying before him at the edge of the waters. From its size it appeared to be of a boy, still in his teens. It was a fresh skeleton and the natural gloss was still on the bones. Except for a few patches of skin and hair on its skull, the rest of it was clean stripped off all flesh.

Hitherto silent, Ram now addressed Ramdas: "Ramdas, do you see the skeleton—a mere inert mass of bones? Your body too is made of the same stuff and a similar fate awaits it. The body is a transient, perishable thing. You have no reason whatever to be proud of it. The only purpose for which it is granted to you is to utilise it for My service, until it falls off and is reduced to the same condition as this worthless skeleton."

Ramdas took the lesson. Ram is the greatest teacher of the world. As occasions require He would assume any part he chooses. He is a consummate actor and a master of all arts.

(ii) You Are in the Hands of God

Now Ramdas further retraced his steps and neared the precipitous rock where he had separated from the two friends. As he was making for it, a voice called from the river-side. He halted and saw two mountaineers (certainly, it was Ram in those forms) filling their pitchers with water at the river. One of them came towards him and enquired whither he was going. Ramdas told him that he wanted to visit Vasishtashram, but since Ram had not shown him the way he was returning. Ram's ways are wonderful!

The man said: "Vasishtashram is still far away. There is no path by the bank of the river. You have to climb the tall mountain in front. Thereon you see a foot-path in the midst of the jungle. You must take it. On reaching the top, you should descend to the other side where you will observe from a distance the dome of a *mandir*. Taking it as your mark, you should proceed towards it, and you will reach Shivapuri, a small village in which the temple stands."

He pointed again to the foot-track; a thin streak of it could be seen on the high mountain. Ramdas at once ran on to it. Up and up he climbed. It was a steep ascent, but Ramdas did not stop even to take breath. The divine power in him had gifted him with marvellous agility and unusual endurance. An hour's walk brought him to the summit wherefrom he could observe the dome of the *mandir* referred to by the mountaineer. Here commenced the descent. It must be noted that the mountain was covered with a dense forest. On occasions he had to wriggle through the mazy growth of shrubs and trees. He ran down the incline at full speed. At the bottom he met again the welcome river. He drank to his fill its nectar-like water, and proceeded to Shivapuri which was now close by.

Ramdas found in the village, besides the temple, only about five or six huts of cultivators. One of the cultivators, seeing him, invited him to his hut. Ramdas entered and sat on a mat spread out for him. He beheld a bonny baby playing near a grinding stone. He got the baby at once on his lap and began to fondle and laugh with it. The cultivator and wife were tenderly watching him as though a new child had come to them to play with theirs. Now he told them that he was on his way to Vasishtashram. Both of them gazed at him with wonder. He was not only alone but had nothing with him except his long coat of *khaddar*, a cheap sweater as underwear (which he handed to the cultivator friend before leaving the place) and a piece of blanket.

"Look here, Sadhuji," the cultivator said, "it is getting dark (it was then about half-past-six, evening, when Ramdas reached the village); you may occupy the temple for the night. My wife will send you some *khichdi*. As for your trip to Vasishtashram I do not know what to tell you. There is no proper route to it, and without a guide you cannot dream of reaching it. I know people of your sort cannot be persuaded to give up the venture. So I would tell you this much. Go along the bank for about two miles and you will see on the opposite side of the river a projecting group of trees bending over the river. Mark this spot. Just facing this clump of trees, on your side of the hill, you will discover a footpath. Here, abandoning the river bank, take to the footpath and climb up the hill. Further, how shall I instruct you? You are in the hands of God and He will see to it."

With these words he accompanied Ramdas to the *mandir* where he left him. In due course the *khichdi* came. It tasted heavenly for it was full of *prem*—love.

The interior of the temple was about seven feet square. Its spire rose high up in the air. The whole structure was built on a raised stone platform. The doors were open. The last streaks of light of the dying day entering the temple displayed to Ramdas's view a number of small brass images of God on a low, wide stool, standing against the back wall of the temple. On the wall, over the images, on two pegs was also hanging a coarse red Kashmir shawl. As evening approached cold had set in. Ramdas spread the blanket he had brought with him on the floor, and removing the temple shawl covered himself with it and lay down. Indeed, the divine Mother of the universe is ever watchful to protect Her children. No sooner had Ramdas closed his eyes than he heard somebody stepping into the temple. Ramdas opened his eyes and sat up to find a man sitting before him. In the dim light the features were not visible.

"I am the *pujari* of this temple," he introduced himself. He scrutinised Ramdas closely, then touched and felt the shawl, and then looking at the pegs on the wall he exclaimed: "So you have taken the shawl. It belongs to Thakurji,"—meaning God.

Ramdas then put him a simple question: "Can you show Ramdas where your Thakurji is?"

At once he cried out: "I beg your pardon, blind fool that I am. You are He, you are He. You have every right to use it, Maharaj." Instantly, he was all kindness and love. He further said: "May I get you something to eat? I have food ready in my house. It will be no small joy for me to feed you. Pray accept my humble fare."

"Ramji," Ramdas replied, "Ramdas has already had his meal. Thanks for your kindness. You are Ramji indeed." He then left Ramdas.

Ramdas, rising early next morning, left Shivapuri and proceeded on his journey along the river bank. The sign pointed out by the cultivator was missed. About three miles' tramp brought him to a spot where further journey was cut off. He attempted a cliff, but had to give it up, for it was too steep and had absolutely no supports. He stopped and spoke to Ram: "Ram, you are playing a funny game with Ramdas. Do as you will. Ramdas returns. If he were asked why he did not reach Vasishtashram, he would plainly say that you fooled him and sent him back half-way." It was all Ram's will—Ram's play.

Once again, Ramdas retraced his steps and by about nine o'clock reached Shivapuri again. He had no prompting to go to the village and so continued his journey. He passed the river-bank by the village but had not gone a few yards, when he met two mountaineers, forms of Ram—all forms are His—coming towards him from the opposite direction with two empty kerosene tins tied to their backs. They were tall young men. They saluted him "Ram, Ram" and questioned him as to where he was going and what he was about. He explained to them his object of visiting Vasishtashram, how it was thwarted and of his final retreat to the plains.

Now one of them said: "Turn back again: we are going with you, our way also lies towards Vasishtashram. We can escort and guide you along."

Ram, what a fast and loose player you are! The friends were quick trampers accustomed to hill climbing. So they thought it would be as well to make Ramdas walk before them so that he might not lag behind. But the power of God was tingling in Ramdas's veins. He skipped, danced and ran. The friends followed as best as they could. Now began an ascent on the hills. Here again his speed was as fast as ever. He was running up like a squirrel. After covering some height he halted and looked back. The two friends were still about forty or fifty yards behind, tearing along in hot pursuit. They waved their hands and hallooed him to stop.

They came up to him gasping for breath, and peering at him with a curious twinkle in their eyes said: "You are not an ordinary fellow. You well-nigh knocked the wind out of us. No good to have you in front. Henceforth you shall follow us." At this, Ramdas could not resist laughing, in which they heartily joined. So he had to go behind them. The gallop was now reduced to a trot, and when close to their back he would jump like an India-rubber ball. The play of *Shakti* in him was irresistible.

At about one o'clock in the afternoon, the party reached the summit of a high mountain where there was a long narrow hut, peopled by cultivators and their cattle. The sun was hot and so the friends proposed to have some rest at this place. In a small outer hut Ramdas was asked to sit on some hay which was spread on the floor. The friends went inside the large hut and prepared, from the provisions supplied by the hospitable dwellers of the hut, meals consisting of rice, vegetable curry and curds. When things were ready he was asked to join them, and he had a refreshing dinner. It was the fare of the gods of which he partook there, so simple, clean and delicious. Altogether, after an hour's rest, he continued the journey with the two friends again. Now the path was through brambles, heaps of dry leaves and a network of trees and creepers. It was a gradual descent and at about six o'clock the trio sighted the river-bank again. One of them said: "We are now very near to the Vasishta cave."

"Where? Where?" cried Ramdas in irrepressible glee. They came on the bank. "There," pointed the finger of the friend towards the yawning mouth of the cave at some distance. Now Ramdas could not resist; he rushed in the direction like wind leaving the friends behind. At the entrance of the cave he found standing a tall thin *sadhu*, wearing only a *kaupin*. Ramdas had been told by the friends, who guided him, that the cave was occupied by a *mahatma*.

Directly he saw the *sadhu*, he ran towards him and prostrated at his feet. The *sadhu* did not seem to like this mode of salutation. He remonstrated by the gesture of his hands. He entered the cave and Ramdas followed him. It was a large and spacious cave about ten feet high and fifteen feet wide and twenty feet long. As Ramdas stepped in he observed at the left-hand corner a number of tins arranged in a line. The floor was covered at the front by two gunny bags and by a wide, white quilt at the further end which served as the *sadhu's* seat. In the centre of the cave there was a small fire-place or *dhuni*. At the mouth of the cave, on the right, there was a neatly stacked pile of firewood. Ramdas sat down on one of the gunny bags and the *sadhu* occupied his seat. By this time the friends who guided him also arrived. They remained for a few minutes and then taking leave departed. Ram after all brought His child to the ashram.

CHAPTER 29: VASISHTASHRAM

(i) The Cup of Milk

Now the *sadhu* looked at Ramdas and asked: "What brought you here?"

"Ram has brought Ramdas here to see the cave and also for your *darshan*," replied Ramdas.

"Have you had any food during the day?" he enquired.

"Yes" said Ramdas, "the guides who escorted him hither have been kind enough to feed him on the way."

Now staring at Ramdas more closely, he asked: "Is this all you have got about you? Do you possess any money?"

"No, Ramdas has no command from Ram to carry money with him," answered Ramdas.

"In that case, you have come here to starve," said the *sadhu* deliberately. "Now listen," he continued, "I shall tell you how matters stand with me. I am neither a *sadhu* nor a *mahatma*. I am a simple *vaishya* merchant. I occupy this cave for three or four months in the year. It is not possible to remain here during the rains when the river swells and her water inundates the cave. The rest of the year I spend in my native place, in the plains. There I engage myself in some trade and collect profits amounting to about two hundred rupees with which I come here. I am not beholden to anybody for anything. I spend my own money to meet my wants. For a month past I have been living merely upon milk diet. I take daily not more than three-quarter seer of milk which I procure from the villages on the mountains.

"A man from the village brings me milk at noon every day and I pay him down cash for it. Do you understand? If you would have any food you ought to climb up the hills and get *bhiksha* from the villages. To go up and down for it will absorb most of the day, and at that rate it would not be worth your while to stay here. So I would advise you to leave this place as early as possible. What are your plans? How long do you intend staying here?" he questioned.

"Ramdas has no plans," he replied. "He does not know how long Ram wishes him to stop here. All depends upon Him. As regards food, Ramdas is averse to taking solid food at any place where he wants to devote all his time to God, in wakefulness and meditation. Since God has granted him the staying power, even on water for some days, he would prefer not to climb the hill in search of food."

The *sadhu* was roused by this reply. Intently gazing on Ramdas, he said derisively: "Enough of your gab. I have known many *sadhus* of your type who speak glibly of water-fast, but could not observe it for a single day. None of your bragging to me." Ramdas could clearly see that Ram was at His old game again. "Well, you say," he went on, "you would not take solid food, that means you are for liquids, eh!"

"Quite so, water only or milk if Ram provides," quietly rejoined Ramdas.

The *sadhu* burst out: "Ah! there you are. Now the cat is out of the bag." Now bending himself towards Ramdas and pointing his long forefinger at him, with looks full of contempt and words tinged with sarcasm, he spoke: "Have you come here to share a part of my daily drink of milk and starve me to death—is that what you mean?"

Ram, what a consummate actor You are! As is the master so is the servant. Ramdas, who learnt all this art at Your feet, can meet You on Your own ground. The play was now assuming a beautiful turn.

Ramdas coolly replied: "Ramji, it is far from Ramdas's wish to have any share of your milk. If Ram, who is all love, provides, he would have milk, but if He chooses not to, he will be content with mere water which can be had in plenty from Mother Ganga."

"We shall see, we shall see," he interrupted. "Now for the night, which is fast approaching, I shall show you two caves, come out," and he arose and went out, "you may occupy any one of them."

He took Ramdas out into the open and pointed out two small caves, one to the left and the other to the right of the big cave in which he lived. Ramdas selected the one to the left. It was just sufficient for one to stay in and, moreover, the floor was covered with a layer of hay. When Ramdas got in he found the cold within was severe, as though all the cold from outside had found its hiding place within the cave at the approach of night.

"You may occupy it afterwards, come with me to my cave. There is still light. We can sit together for a while," he said, and Ramdas, accordingly, followed him to his cave.

From one of his tins the *sadhu* took out some lumps of sugar and dissolving them in a brass cup of water offered the syrup to Ramdas. Ramdas drank the sweetened water. Then he prepared a *chilam* of tobacco and ascertained if Ramdas smoked. Ramdas said that he had no objection to smoking when Ram supplied.

"You are a wonderful fellow," he exclaimed, "you are used to smoking, and still you don't carry any smoke with you!"

Ramdas explained that he was a slave only of Ram and not of any habit. Then he drew in a few puffs at the *chilam*. It was now getting quite dark. The *sadhu* had lit a small earthen lamp poised on a wooden stand. Ramdas now stood up and walked out of the cave to proceed to the small cave he had decided upon occupying, when the *sadhu* stopped him saying: "Tonight you may stay with me. From tomorrow you can live in the other cave."

Ram was kind indeed! Ramdas had really a great desire to remain at least for a night in the big cave which is the famous Vasishta cave. He returned and took his seat again by the side of the *sadhu*. Thereafter there was no talk. He sat up for about two hours in silence and then, taking the *sadhu's* permission, laid himself down. All the night he was half awake. The *sadhu* also never slept. He reclined against a cushion and at short intervals he was busy smoking his *hookah*, and was also now and again throwing a lump of sugar into his mouth.

The night passed. At daybreak Ramdas rose and sat up, but he felt no inducement to move. After some time, the *sadhu* suddenly flared up and said in a harsh voice: "Get out, what are you doing here? Go to your cave. I wish to go into *samadhi*."

Ramdas quietly slipped out and directly entered the small cave in which he remained unmoved for the whole day. At about eleven o'clock noon, two men passed by the cave carrying milk for the *sadhu*. Half-an-hour later, one of them came to him with a cup of milk. He said that the *sadhu* in the cave had requested Ramdas to accept it. Ramdas now played his part as artfully as Ram played His. He refused to have the milk and asked the man to take it back to the *sadhu*. Thereupon the *sadhu* came in person with the milk-cup and approaching Ramdas pressed him to drink.

"Maharaj," Ramdas said, "excuse Ramdas. How can you expect him to receive a share of your milk which is just what you require for yourself for the day? You may remember how you warned him when you said: 'Have you come here to share my daily drink of milk and starve me to death?'"

At this straight talk he winced and lowered his eyes, but still he pressed again.

"I appeal to you," he cried. "I want you to take this milk. I have mixed ample Gangaji's water with it. For me there is a sufficient quantity left."

"It is clear, Ram wills that Ramdas should live upon water diet for some days, but since you are so insistent, in the present instance, Ramdas accepts your milk on condition that he should not be offered again, and even if you do, he would not have it by any means."

The *sadhu* excitedly said: "All right." Ramdas drank the milk.

(ii) The Vision of Christ

Till evening Ramdas stuck to the cave. When night was drawing near, he found the *sadhu* popping in his head at the mouth of the cave and shouting out: "Would you like to come to me for a smoke?"

It was evident that he wished to have Ramdas's company. Ramdas accordingly followed him to his cave. He offered Ramdas some puffs of his *hookah* and a cupful of sugar-water. There was not much of talk. Before it became quite dark, Ramdas left him and returned to his cave. The cold in the cave at night was very intense. He covered himself with the piece of blanket and sat up. About two or three hours after midnight, he was prompted by Ram to go to the *sadhu* for a live cinder. There were dried pieces of timber lying about in front of the cave. He thought of making a fire. In fact, he could bear the cold. Yet, why this idea of a fire? Ram, you want some fun perhaps, else why do you egg him on to this? He crept out of the cave in the darkness, came to the other cave and entering it called out: "Maharaj, will you kindly spare for Ramdas a bit of fire? He wants to light up a fire in his cave."

"Eh!" he snarled, "you can't endure the cold and you want fire. You are climbing down, my boy. Here, take it."

Ramdas got a live cinder and returned to his cave. While he was doing so, he heard the *sadhu* muttering something in his own peculiar mocking tone, and Ramdas could not help chuckling within himself: "Ram, you are a downright joker!" The fire was lit, and he burnt all the firewood he could scramble together in the dark.

Morning dawned. Ramdas walked out of the cave. The morning light presented to him a most bewitching scene. The river was flowing at a distance of about twenty yards from the cave. A number of huge rocks were scattered over the bank of the river. He got a perch upon one of these rocks to view the enchanting scene before him.

From between a chain of tall, heaven-kissing mountains the glistening waters of the Ganges were gushing down past the caves. The mountains were clothed with dense vegetation and it looked as if a multi-coloured carpet was spread over them. Orange-hued clouds were slowly moving in the sky, on a background of pure blue. Stillness, coolness and grey mist pervaded the whole atmosphere. Ramdas's soul thrilled with inexpressible delight. For a while, all account of time, place and circumstance was lost. No wonder, Vasishta selected this spot for his ashram. To breathe that air is meditation itself. Your entire being remains merged in the infinite existence of God's own being. You are simply intoxicated with eternal peace and joy.

Except going up to the river twice or thrice a day for drinks, Ramdas spent all his time on the rock. As night was throwing her dark mantle on the scene, he returned to his cave. For the first night in the cave he had some sensation of cold, though he could endure it. During the subsequent nights he was entirely free from its effects. As usual, the second night also passed in a half-wakeful and blissful state. In the morning, again he was found on the rock. When the sun had risen high up in the heavens, he observed a hill-man standing before him.

He questioned: "Is it true that you are bent upon starving yourself to death?"

Ramdas had no reply to give. He only smiled. The man gave him some half-ripe berries. They were hard and yet, for the sake of the love with which they were offered, Ramdas put them into his mouth, chewed them a little and then threw them away. Now the *sadhu* from the other cave also came to the scene, and staring at Ramdas said: "You have come here not for yoga but for *atmaghata*, downright fool that you are!"

At this fresh fling, Ramdas's risibility was again excited and he burst into a hearty laugh.

Then Ramdas addressed him: "O Ram, having brought your child here you are making him fast, and, on the top of it all, you are calling him a fool. Well, do as you will."

Here Ramdas discovered the truth of the saying "Man is God playing the fool." The *sadhu* was uncontrollable in his rage. He could not speak more. He turned round and went back to his cave. Another day passed. The *sadhu* was careful thereafter to avoid Ramdas. Days were spent on the rock, and nights in the cave. Thus passed three more days.

Now the memorable night. It was on the fifth day, maybe after midnight; the nights were pitch-dark. Ramdas usually sat up the whole night in the cave. The cave was suddenly lit up by a strange light. Ramdas saw seated before him, on the floor about three or four feet from him, the figure of a man. His face was dazzling with a heavenly splendour. The features were fine, regular and beautiful. There was a short, black, glossy beard and moustache on the face. The lips were crimson red, revealing milk-white, lustrous teeth. Soft shining black curls flowed down his shoulders. He wore a long, dark, chocolate-coloured robe or gown with wide, loose sleeves. What fascinated Ramdas were his eyes. They were scintillating like twin stars. The rays they were emitting were filled with tenderness, love and compassion.

Ramdas gazed on them, charmed and delighted. It struck him: "This is Jesus Christ." There was another beside him, but Ramdas's eyes were not for him, although he was aware of his presence. He might be a disciple. Now Christ's lips moved. He was speaking. Ramdas listened, but could not make out what he said. The language sounded strange and unknown to him. For, perhaps, a minute he spoke; then the vision vanished, while the glow of light remained in the cave for some minutes more. Ramdas was completely immersed in ecstasy and only came to external consciousness after broad daylight.

(iii) Selfishness—Root of All Ignorance

Ram now made him understand that his stay at that place was coming to a close. He had no thought of the definite hour for starting. Until three o'clock he remained, as usual, on the rock in the open air.

Ram within told him: "Five days' fast has weakened your body, and so you are not fit to travel back to Swargashram. Go to the *sadhu* and request him to feed you with *roti* and *dal*; then start."

Ramdas directly went up to the *sadhu* in the cave. The *sadhu* showed surprise at the sight of him. With eyes dilated, he looked at him and shook his head questioningly. Ramdas observed a marked change in him. His face was pale, dry and careworn. His frequent ebullitions of anger must have worked havoc with him.

Ramdas: "Maharaj, Ram wills Ramdas should now take leave of this place, but since his limbs are weak, owing to the fast, he has come to beg of you to feed him with *roti* and *dal*, so that he may gain sufficient strength for his return journey."

For a while the *sadhu* was perfectly silent—then a smile beamed on his face. First, he mixed some sugar in water, and making Ramdas drink it asked him to follow him. He took Ramdas out and both walked to the foot of a mountain, a furlong away. There, at a small stream of water flowing downhill, they found five sturdy mountaineers at work. They were turning wood on a lathe contrivance by water-power—a crude wooden wheel revolving on a long spindle, at the end of which was fixed a round log of wood. With sharp edged tools they were working at the wood, turning out beautifully-shaped vessels. The *sadhu* approaching them said: "Look here, here is a *sadhu* who has been fasting for five days; he wants food. I have no food-stuffs with me. Will one of you run up to your village on the hills and get me victuals for one meal? Here is money for the purchase of the things," and he produced some coins.

They glanced at Ramdas and, turning to the *sadhu*, said: "Out of the stock of wheat-flour, *ghee*, and *dal* we have with us, we can spare for him a meal, but we will not accept any price for them."

The *sadhu* remonstrated: "That will not do. You shall accept the price of the things you give. I wish to feed him at my expense."

So he persuaded them to take the price. They returned to the cave with the articles. The *sadhu* was a quick and neat hand at cooking, and, in less than half-an-hour, he prepared four *rotis* smeared with *ghee* and a curry of green *dal*. When he was at this task, he chose to have a few words with Ramdas.

"Nice fellow you are! These five days you have been frying me as I am now frying these *rotis*. Your fast has created a flutter in all the villages over the hills, wherefrom so many people brought milk and foodstuffs for you, while you were sitting on that rock oblivious of everything. I sent them all back, for I dared not go and tell you. You denied me even the pleasure of feeding you with milk."

Here Ramdas interrupted him: "What! Maharaj, why shirk it? You have brought it about by your own words."

At this he cried out impatiently: "You fling it at me again and again!"

Ramdas looked straight at him, and the *sadhu* cowered beneath the gaze. Then Ramdas said: "Maharaj, please listen. Ramdas is a humble servant and an innocent child of God, and he came here by His will alone. It is again He who prompted him to fast during these days. Ramdas never expected you to feed him. From the very first you thought of driving Ramdas away. You tried to frighten him, but Ramdas could not be frightened. You spoke harshly to him, but Ramdas could not be scared. You denounced him, and yet Ramdas remained good-humoured and calm. This is on one side. On the other, you were extremely kind to him. You compelled him to drink milk on the first day. You granted him the happy privilege of staying for a night in your cave. You regaled him with sweet drinks and tobacco, and gave him fire even at dead of night. Your appearance shows, because of this fast, you have been feeling anxious about Ramdas. Ramdas knows that this is all Ram's play. Kindness and harshness are the same to him. He does not know what yoga or *atmaghata* means. He is a simple believer in the all-powerful Name of God. It is that Name that has brought Ramdas face to face with Him."

Here the *sadhu* broke in: "That you do not know yoga, I cannot now believe. I admit I made a mistake. I ought to have known better by the colour of your cloth. I have a perfect dread of *sannyasis*. Fasting is no good for you any longer. It brings you down to *tamoguna*; otherwise you would not have talked as you have done."

Ramdas replied: "Ramdas does not know how any *guna* works in him. He does everything by Ram's will. Even now he is talking by His will alone. Ramdas has neither hatred nor love for anybody. Whereas he had been tutored by Ram that selfishness is the root of all ignorance in this world; it is the cause of all misery and pain. By surrendering to the Lord of the universe, the supreme Master of our being, we can eradicate the ego sense, get enlightenment and attain eternal peace and joy. This blessed cave is the abode of the *rishis* who realised the grand Truth. The atmosphere here is thrilling with the fervour of their *tapasya*. Living in it let us not forget the aim and goal of life; viz., the realisation of the Godhead within and without us."

CHAPTER 30: RETURN JOURNEY

(i) God Is an Ocean of Compassion

By this time the *rotis* and *dal* were ready. The *sadhu* procured some large leaves from the shrubs outside, and packing the food in them he called for the spare *kaupin* of Ramdas, and fastening the parcel with it, handed it to him saying: "Go to the bank of the river, eat as much as you need and pack up the remaining food which will serve you on your way. After you have finished, I will escort you to the edge of the river where you will find a man with a raft. He will take you across. You can journey back by a new route, along the other side of the river."

Accordingly, Ramdas went to the riverside and sitting on a stone could not consume more than a quarter of a *roti* and a small quantity of *dal* with it. The rest he tied up again and prepared to start. The *sadhu* took him to the raft and instructed the raftman to row him across the river. Ramdas boarded the raft and the *sadhu* returned to his cave. The current in the river was very strong, but the raftman was equal to it. He rowed on. In midstream he asked Ramdas what he was carrying in the parcel. Ramdas told him that it was *dal* and *roti*. Then, with a bright smile he said: "I am so hungry, I shall thank you if you will give the food to me."

Ramdas needed no asking twice and no thanks. With the greatest delight he passed on the parcel to him. Ramdas now understood that Ram wanted him to carry it for the sake of the raftman.

Ramdas arrived at the other bank. As he proceeded on the sands a few steps, he found an old man chopping a fallen tree with a hatchet, for making a post. Ramdas went up to him and sat beside him.

"Ramji," Ramdas asked, "will you please show Ramdas the way that leads to Swargashram?"

The kindly old man stopped his work and looking up at him, said: "Swargashram is far, far away. There is no beaten track or cut-out path. You have to go from stage to stage, making enquiries on the way. Darkness is already at hand. So you cannot think of starting on your long journey now. You go by the path I am showing you. A mile uphill you will discover two houses, surrounded by cornfields. You take refuge in one of them. The people over there will gladly give you shelter for the night. Tomorrow morning you may start on your journey."

He pointed at a thin zigzag foot-path, going up the hills in the midst of a dense growth of trees. He climbed up and, on ascending about a mile, found himself on a vast area of green fields, the mountain rising still higher in the background. He noticed two small houses, about forty yards from each other, standing in the midst of the fields. He passed through the fields towards one of them. In the front of the house there was a raised platform of wooden planks supported by stout stumps of trees. He got upon it. Beside two lads, a middle-aged man and an old man were squatting upon it. The latter two were busy mending a torn blanket. When they saw him the middle-aged man rose, and procuring from the house a black rug, spread it on the floor and beckoned him to sit on it. He sat down. He asked where Ramdas was coming from and whither he was bound. Ramdas replied that he was hailing from Vasishtashram and was on his way to Swargashram.

The middle-aged man: "You must have then met the *sadhu* who lives in the cave. He does not let any other *sadhu* stay at the place. He makes it a point to drive him away. He is harsh and cruel."

Ramdas said: "Externally he may appear to be harsh, but he has a soft heart. God's *lila* is wonderful! He plays in various ways. The *sadhu* fed Ramdas with *dal* and *roti* before leaving the ashram. In many ways he was kind and loving to him."

He replied: "This is strange. We have found him far from kind and courteous. However, by the way, for the night what shall we offer you?" After a pause of moodiness, he said: "Here I have a number of cows," pointing to a herd of cows resting in an open enclosure, facing his dwelling, "but I count it a misfortune that at the moment none of them is yielding milk, or I should be so happy to feed you with milk."

Again after a moment's thought, he called his son—one of the lads and asked him to run to the neighbouring house with a pot for some milk, and spread two thick blankets on a coir cot, the only furniture in the house, and lighting up a fire in front of it, asked Ramdas to enter and occupy it. He made him lie down and began to massage his legs.

He addressed Ramdas, his heart welling up with love: "You are veritably Ishwara who has come to my humble abode. I am only a miserable samsari, lost in the whirlpool of *maya*. I have been crying to God to grant me peace and He has, in answer to my prayer, come to me in your form. God is indeed the very ocean of compassion and mercy."

Ramdas rejoined: "Hare Ram, this is all your *lila*. Ishwara is the friend of the helpless and servant of His devotees. Ramdas is only a child of God. Thou art He indeed who is deluging him with Thy unbounded love."

Ramdas cannot find words to express with what motherly kindness and care he tended Ramdas. His daughter aged about twelve prepared the food, his wife being no longer in the land of the mortals.

The interior of the hut was dimly lit by a log of fire. The host left Ramdas and returned with a wide-mouthed cup of hot milk and a soft *roti* which he minced and mixed with the milk. Meanwhile, he picked up some white things from a full basket close by and offered them to Ramdas.

"Eat them," he said.

Ramdas pressed them between his fingers and felt them soft. In the dim light he could scarcely make out what the pieces were. Ramdas put a piece into his mouth. It was so delicious to the taste.

The host: "It is *kand*, a root that you are eating. It is boiled. We obtain it in these parts in plenty."

Ramdas: "Ramji, Ramdas would prefer to eat two more pieces of this root and must be excused regarding *roti* and milk."

"No, no," he lovingly remonstrated, "you shall have both. You may do justice to as much *kand* as you like, but you ought to drink also milk in which I have mixed up *roti*."

Ramdas had to drink milk thickened with *roti* as also eat some more bits of *kand*. Then all the inmates had their evening meal. Far into the night the happy talk of God, *bhakti*, *prem*, and *anand* went on. The host was all the while in ecstasy.

After a couple of hours' sleep, Ramdas awoke in the morning and started on his journey. The host was inconsolable. With tears in his eyes he appealed to Ramdas to stay with him a day longer.

But Ram's command to Ramdas to leave the place was imperative. He gave a parting embrace to the kind host when he said: "You see higher up on the hills a small patch; it is a group of huts. Keeping the sign in view, walk up towards it. You might reach there at midday, and the hospitable people of the village will look to your wants."

Traversing through forests and valleys, Ramdas reached the village, when the sun had risen right overhead. Here too, the villagers treated him with the greatest hospitality. After a meal he set out again.

The old man of the village said: "Maharaj, you have yet to cover a distance of about ten miles. There is no footpath, nor are there any villages on the way. If you venture alone, God only should be your guide. I can only show you the direction in which you have to go."

(ii) Ramdas's Chat with Ram

The old man pointed out with his forefinger the direction, and Ramdas tramped on. After walking about a mile he found himself in a dense jungle, the ground being covered with dry leaves—almost knee-deep; he waded through them. He was in fact going on at random and he was in a conversational mood.

He addressed Ram: "Divine Mother, it is yourself who has brought this child here to roam on these sacred hills. It is up to you to lead and guide him."

As he walked on, he came upon a sloping hill. Here he discovered, at the edge of a cliff, a cave—a deep hollow in a rock. He peeped into it. It was utterly dark inside. He had heard that such caves were usually lairs of wild beasts. He thought that he had now an opportunity of getting *darshan* of Ram in the form of a tiger or lion. He jumped into the cave and shouted out "Hari Om" three times and awaited the result. None came out of the cave. It was Ram's will that he should not come face to face with wild beasts. He came out.

There was yawning before him a deep precipice. This had to be climbed down.

"Now, Ram, what do you propose?" asked Ramdas.

"Fear not, child, descend," was Ram's cool reply.

Ramdas turned round and slowly lowered himself and began to crawl down. The chinks on the rough crag serving as foot-supports and hand-holds he descended. A slight slip meant a fall of over two hundred feet and certain destruction of the body. But there was Ram's assurance. Fear had taken leave of Ramdas once for all. Slowly and steadily, step by step, he got down. The body of Ramdas seemed to be like an inflated rubber doll, so light and so buoyant. Breathing had automatically stopped. The fragile foot-supports had at times been trembling, sending down bits of stone layers through the pressure of the foot, producing by their fall reverberating sounds at the depths of the valley below. What time it took him to reach the bottom of the ravine he had no idea. It all appeared to be so short. He at last alighted at the base of the rock, quite safe. Here again he cried out at a high pitch "Hari Om," making the giant hills all around resound with the echo.

Ramdas exclaimed: "Ram, how glorious you are! You have made Ramdas perform a most marvellous feat."

Ram rejoined: "This is not all, more feats are in store for you, get ahead."

Ramdas continued his journey in the cool shade of the titanic trees.

Ramdas: "O Ram, how blessed is Ramdas to be conscious of your company with him even in this lonely place!"

"My child," Ram assured Ramdas, "you shall in future be always aware of my presence with you, in you and everywhere about you. I grant you this knowledge based upon your perfect oneness with me. You and I are one."

Ramdas, hearing this, laughed through intense joy. Half-a-mile was traversed. Now he came to the brink of another precipice, steeper than the previous one, but with no footholds of any kind for climbing down. It was a smooth flat rock, running vertically down. Looking at it he giggled and said: "Ram, now you are caught. Ramdas would like to know how you will tackle the problem now."

"Soft, soft," instantly put in Ram. "No doubt you are clever but I am more clever than you can ever imagine. Look to your right. There the ground slopes down, though the incline is sharp and slippery, try that way."

Ramdas stepped towards it and dancing a caper or two, laughed and spoke: "Ram, you are a brick, but it won't do; you see the slope is not only sharp but is covered by loose earth. To put the foot on it is to slip, and Ramdas will then be rolling down like a folded mattress until he reaches the bottom; you like it, eh?"

"Ramdas, your laugh and poses are too early," observed Ram, "you don't seem to make use of the eyes which I have given you. Look well. On the incline, you will discover stumps of dried grass at some distance from one another. These are roots of thick reeds, and being dry they cannot be distinguished from the earth, but a close scrutiny will reveal them to you. They are strong enough to support your feet. Descend without any delay."

Ram was right. There were roots. Ramdas accordingly, going on all fours crept down, having the dried stumps of grass as foot-rests, one after the other, until he reached nearly the end of the incline beyond which there was again a steep chasm, the incline being no longer continuous. The situation, in which he was now placed, was supremely perilous. He had arrived at about two yards from the extreme edge of the slope, and a yard down there was only a faint mark of a stump visible which could support no more than a toe. Having stopped here, Ramdas asked: "Now, Ram, what next?"

Ram was ever ready with His cues. He piped in: "Behold, child, a twig peeping out of the depths just on the edge of the slope. It is about half-an-inch thick. Reach it by your feet, descending a yard down by the help of the small root of grass. After that you will know what to do next."

Ramdas followed Ram's instructions and had the twig clutched in between the big toe and the other toes of his left foot like a monkey. Certainly, here Ramdas remembered Hanuman, the great devotee of Sri Ramchandra. The body was felt by Ramdas as light as a feather. With one foot thus poised on the twig, he let go the other from the grass root. For a few seconds his whole body was balanced on one foot. Ramdas now shrank himself and doubling up held on to the twig with both his hands. All the time the slender twig was oscillating to and fro most ominously.

Here he looked down. The depth below was tremendous, but hurrah! Ram, you are a miracle-monger! The twig on which Ramdas was resting belonged to a tall tree, starting from the very base of the precipice. He descended slowly, and gradually came upon the stouter branches of the tree. Now the descent became easy, the tree was a veritable giant of the forest, a tree so tall that Ramdas had never seen the like of it before. He at last reached the bottom. Now Ram had his laugh at Ramdas's expense. Ramdas was silent. Every time he was beaten, and Ram would have the upper hand.

Again Ramdas lighted upon a cave into which he entered and shouted out a loud outcry of "Hari Om," but there was no response. Thenceforth, he had to pass through many a declivity, but easily. He was now running at full speed, frisking and dancing on the rocks. At last he found himself again suddenly on the banks of the Ganges. Here he had to execute a small feat on the edge of a rock projecting into the river. On the sandbank he sped on until he reached Phulchetty. In Phulchetty there was a *dharmashala* managed by Punjabi *sadhus*. When Ramdas ran towards the building, a young *sannyasi* welcomed him with open arms. He actually took Ramdas in the folds of his arms and embraced him heartily as if he had met a long lost brother or child.

He took Ramdas inside the *dharmashala*, seated him on an *asan*, massaged his legs for some time, and fed him sumptuously with infinite love. Ram, it is all Thy doing, Thou eternal love, manifest everywhere.

From Phulchetty, the same evening, Ramdas walked up to Swargashram, now only at a distance of two miles, which he reached before dark.

CHAPTER 31: SWARGASHRAM – HARDWAR

(i) Ramdas Gives It Up

When Ramdas returned to Swargashram, he directed his steps to the double *kuti* which he had occupied with the other two friends before leaving for Vasishtashram. But he found the room locked. For the night he sought refuge in a *kuti* which was in ruins. This *kuti* consisted of nothing but two walls and tin sheets covering the top. The night was cold and icy blasts were blowing into the dilapidated *kuti*. The night passed and the next day he still found the double *kuti* shut and locked.

In the same line as the fallen *kuti*, in which Ramdas stayed for a night, there was another occupied by an old *sadhu* from Maharashtra. He had known Ramdas on the last occasion. He informed Ramdas that Ramcharandas and Bhavanishankerrao had left Swargashram some days before, and Ramcharandas had locked up the double *kuti*. He expressed his keen desire to accommodate Ramdas in his *kuti*. Ramdas accepted his hospitality. The room he occupied was only ten feet by four feet. There was a slightly raised pad of earth along its width which was intended for seat and sleeping place for the single dweller. The kind *sadhu* insisted upon Ramdas's using the raised pad, and, as for himself, the *sadhu* slept and sat on the lower floor at Ramdas's feet. The *sadhu* was a short-statured man. He was given to smoking *ganja*. His *sadhana* consisted of reading twice a day the Avadhuta Gita in Sanskrit of Sri Dattatreya.

For *bhiksha* both he and Ramdas would go to the *annakshetra* at midday. One meal a day always sufficed Ramdas; such also was the case with the *sadhu*.

On account of the Kumbha Mela and also the approaching pilgrimage to Badrinath and Kedarnath, there was an unusual rush of pilgrims in advance of the set periods. They would wander in Swargashram for the *darshan* of *sadhus* residing in the *kutis*. They used to make presents to the *sadhus* of eatables, cloth, and money. The pious pilgrims, before turning away from the *kuti* after the *darshan*, would throw into the room their presents. Mostly they would fling pice. Everyday the coins collected would amount to ten to twelve annas. The *sadhu* had a *jholi* or pouch in which he stored the coins.

Armed with the money the *sadhu* would run to the small bazaar outside the ashram and procure milk, tea, sugar and eatables. He would thus prepare tea twice a day from the proceeds of the alms. Ramdas found that the *sadhu's* life became one continuous round of fetching tea materials and preparing tea from morn to eve. Even his daily readings of Avadhuta Gita had to be stopped in consequence.

As days passed, the coins commenced to pour in like a shower, sometimes silver coins also. Every day there was a surplus or balance of coins after expenditure. The *jholi* was getting heavier day by day, and the *sadhu* became madly active like a cat with a burnt tail!

Ramdas now wanted to cry halt and had a frank talk on the subject of money with *sadhu*. "Sadhuji, God has provided us with a shelter in the *kuti* and is feeding us with one meal a day. He wills that we should devote all our time to His remembrance. Now what are we doing? Tea, eatables and meal have become the sole things of our lives. You know *sadhus* have nothing to do with money. The moment you have surplus money after your creature needs are met, you think of the ways how you should spend it. You run to the bazaar for things which you can do without and get into a whirlpool of deluding activity. So, in future we shall not accept any coins from the visitors. We will pray to them not to offer any. Let us see how much we have already accumulated."

The *sadhu* at first rebelled against the suggestion, but at last yielded when Ramdas asked him to choose between him and the money. He lowered the bag from the peg on the wall and poured out its contents. The amount was about five rupees, mostly in copper coins. The *sadhu* was for the time being convinced of what Ramdas told him on the question of money.

"What shall we do with the money? Shall we give it to some other *sadhu*?" he asked.

"How can you hand over a thing to another *sadhu* when you have found it bad for yourself?" remarked Ramdas.

"Then, what is to be done?" he queried.

"The only way," said Ramdas "is to throw away the money and have done with it."

At this hint the *sadhu* opened his eyes wide at Ramdas in surprise.

"Come along, fetch the coins," saying thus Ramdas walked out. The *sadhu* blindly obeyed. Ramdas led him, both his hands full of coins, to a meshy, a thorny bush which was perfectly inaccessible.

"Now, throw the coins into the bush," Ramdas advised.

At one fling the coins flew into the thick bush and disappeared from view. Now they returned to the *kuti*. This happened in the evening. Next day, as usual, the pilgrims had again their indefatigable quest for *sadhus* and came in larger numbers than before. They were appealed to, both by Ramdas and the *sadhu*, not to make presents of money, but in spite of their pleading they threw coins on the floor of the room at its entrance, as was their wont. This time not only copper coins but also silver rupees rolled down. In the evening they found that the collection amounted to several rupees.

Ramdas gave it up—it was Ram's will—and kept quiet over the matter. The *sadhu* coolly, as if nothing had happened regarding the money matter, went about preparing tea and storing up provisions procured from the collections.

(ii) The Kumbha Mela

The main day of the Kumbha Mela approached. It was to be on the morrow. Ramdas asked the *sadhu* if he had any idea of attending the festival at Hardwar. The *sadhu* seemed to have a great desire to be present at Hardwar the next day for the great occasion. He requested Ramdas to go with him. Ramdas also wished to see the fun. That they had good fun at the fair will be clear from what follows.

They started in the afternoon. Another old *sadhu* who was a permanent resident of Swargashram also joined them. They made a halt for the night at Sat Narayan Chutty, seven miles from Swargashram. Next day, after *bhiksha*, they walked to Hardwar where they arrived at about five in the evening. Both the banks of the Ganges in Hardwar presented a seething mass of humanity. For miles all round every nook and corner was occupied by pilgrims and *sadhus*. It was a tremendous gathering. It was said that over thirteen *lakhs* of people had assembled there for the gathering.

The *sadhus*, however, wedged themselves between two groups of pilgrims on the opposite bank of the river. The *muhurta*—or auspicious hour for bathing—in the Brahma *kund* was four hours after midnight. The belief goes that those who bathe in the *kund* at this psychological hour will attain immortality. Ramdas did not appreciate nor had he any belief in that cheap method of earning immortality! God had granted him that supreme blessing already by making him pass through the necessary struggle and *sadhana*. He was there to witness the magnificent *mela* of *lakhs* of people. The very sight of the vast crowds sent him into ecstasies.

Till twelve, the mass of humanity was lying still on the banks of the river. Now commenced a movement like the huge waves rising in the ocean. Thousands of pilgrims made a rush towards the coveted Brahma *kund*. The two *sadhus* and Ramdas had to join the rabble. The *sadhus*, to prevent their being separated from each other, had their hands interlocked with one another's. The crowd had to move very slowly, sometimes they took more than five minutes to cover a yard of ground.

Hundreds of police were present to maintain order and prevent accidents. On and on they went. At certain stages the crowds halted for over half-an-hour. No further movement was possible on account of the march of a thick crowd from the opposite direction. Thousands of people at the back pressed on them. They were crushed and squeezed as sugarcane in the juice-extracting machine. The *sadhus* bellowed forth. The old *sadhu* who had newly joined them was frightened out of his wits.

"I don't want bath in the *kund* or any such blessed thing," he cried out. "I would I were out of this insufferable condition with my bones and skin whole."

But there was no escape. They had bargained for the experience and they must go through it willy-nilly. The *sadhu's* one thought was freedom from the most uncomfortable situation in which he found himself, and he counted such freedom as nothing short of immortality itself!

At last, they reached a square open place on a broad road, where a number of police, with the help of their long *lathis* used for fencing, had kept at bay two on-rushing crowds from opposite directions of the road. The *sadhus* crouched close to a sweetmeat shop on the road-side. A moment had not passed, when the *lathi* fence gave way in one direction, owing to the enormous pressure of the crowd, and what ensued was pandemonium. Cries, yells, stamping and cursing rent the air. The old *sadhu*, who was close to Ramdas, giving himself up for lost, gave out a piercing shriek.

Ramdas was leaning against the wall of the shop, and he found two men standing on his knees, two on his shoulders and one on his neck which bent down with the weight. All through this marvellous experience he was perfectly calm and collected. At that time, he remembers to have had his breathing entirely stopped, he sustained the heavy human bodies with ease. If he had fallen down he would have been trampled down to pulp, but God's protecting hand was ever on him. Ramdas now heard a piteous cry from the old *sadhu*. A stout mother had taken up a standing posture on his chest, and he was exhorting her: "O mother, you are my dearest mother. Please do come down from my chest. I cannot bear your weight. O mother, a thousand *dandavats* at your precious feet, please do!"

"I cannot do so, Sadhuji," replied the mother. "The moment I jump to the ground, I am done for; have patience for a while."

"Oh!" shouted the *sadhu*, "you are then bent upon killing me. Why did I come here at all? Cursed be the thought that guided me to this deathtrap."

The tense situation lasted only for a few minutes. The police got the crowds well in hand again and the space was cleared. Ramdas was relieved of his burdens and so also the old *sadhu*. The *sadhu* drew a long breath of inexpressible relief as the stout lady abandoned her perch upon his breast.

Till the evening of the next day they were driven hither and thither by the rushing crowds and the police, and they could not disentangle themselves from the vast and intricate human riddle. Ramdas was reminded of the perplexing fortress of the Mahabharata war. However, after the sun had gone down, they found a way out and proceeded towards Rishikesh with as much speed as they could muster.

Over a hundred casualties had occurred during the night's stampede and the violent onsets of the crowds. In the night they stopped again at Sat Narayan Chutty and next day reached Swargashram. The fright and fatigue to which the old *sadhu* was subjected in the *mela* told upon him, and he was laid up with fever and nervous debility for over a week, while Ramdas and his companion *sadhu* were sound as bells, not any the worse for the trying experience they had passed through.

CHAPTER 32: NILKANT HILL

(i) First Attempt

Ramdas continued to stay with the Maharashtrian *sadhu* in his *kuti*. Two or three days later a *sannyasi* from Nepal joined them. He felt a great attraction for Ramdas. He was a cheerful old man, stout, hale and hearty. He gave accounts of his extensive travels over the Himalayas. When he talked about hill-climbing, Ramdas got the idea of scaling the Nilkant hill at the back of the ashram and expressed his wish to the *sadhus*.

"I tried once to go up the hill, Swamiji," said the Nepali *sadhu*, "but as I could not find the way I had to give up the enterprise. Since you would be making a venture I shall be quite glad to go with you."

The other *sadhu* was also consulted and he too agreed to accompany them. Early morning, the following day, they started. They made enquiries from a *sadhu* in the ashram about the way that led up to the shrine of Nilkant, at the top of the hill. He described certain marks on the route. The party now passed through a dense jungle at the bottom of the hill. They walked up and up. They could not find out the continuation of the beaten track. Ramdas led the party. He climbed up through the thick growth of brambles and trees. The *sadhus* followed close at his heels.

"Swami, you are going on the path of the *siddhas*," cried out the Nepali *sadhu*, meaning through a trackless path.

When they covered a height of about a mile they came upon a water spring where the *sadhus* suggested a halt for rest. After refreshing themselves with a drink from the cool spring, the Nepali *sadhu* said: "Swami, we have missed the way. No good going further up. Let us retrace our steps to the ashram."

"No, Maharaj, we should not give up the attempt so soon," contended Ramdas. "Let us climb higher up and find out what there is at the top of this side of the hill."

The Nepali *sadhu* demurred, while the other was silent. He never asserted himself in anything. He had cast his lot with Ramdas's and he was willing to abide by his decision. The Nepali *sadhu* was prevailed upon to agree with Ramdas. So, again, they commenced their climb. All through, Ramdas cut almost a direct upward path. He had no patience with winding ways. The Nepali, who had a long stick which he used to good effect, was trudging behind, gasping for breath. On ascending about a mile they reached the bottom of a steep cliff, a solid, rugged and perpendicular rock over a hundred feet high. It became clear that if one could climb up the cliff, one would reach the summit of the hill.

The *sadhus* rested at the base of the cliff. The Nepali now with a breath of relief said: "Swami, now at least we can return since further progress in this direction is impossible."

Ramdas without giving him any reply stood up and gave forth a shrill and long cry of "Hari Om." The jungle and the sides of the majestic hills resounded with the thrilling utterance, but in the rolling reverberations of the sounds was also heard distinctly a corresponding call of a human voice proceeding from the top of the hill.

"Now, there is somebody at the top; Ramdas will go up," he said.

"Madness!" replied the Nepali. "There is no way to mount up. How can you go?"

"Of course, by climbing the cliff," Ramdas observed.

"Swami, do you want to commit suicide? Be advised: don't make your life so cheap and throw it away."

Ramdas heeded not. He directly bounded towards the threatening rock. He began crawling up on all fours like an ape, making the sharp, frail, slaty edges of the rough cliff as hand and footholds. They would often crumble beneath his feet, but he never lost his balance. Ramnam was being automatically repeated. The body was felt as light as a dry leaf. Higher and higher he climbed with reckless haste. Down below, the *sadhus* were watching with frightened looks his progress on the cliff. In less than fifteen minutes he scrambled over the giant rock and reached the top. He came upon a vast table-land, green with fields and vegetation. He saw also a small hut at a short distance and a hill-woman attending on a few cows grazing on the pasture. When she saw Ramdas she threw up her hands and cried in terror: "Go away, go away, don't come near me."

"Mother, which is the way to Nilkant?" Ramdas asked.

"It is far away from here. It is on the other corner of the hill," she replied in a trembling voice.

Ramdas turned in the direction pointed by her outstretched finger and faced a dense and dark forest. If Ramdas walked through this forest he could come by the shrine Nilkant at the other end of the hill. The long distance spoken of by the mother signified miles of forest. He was prepared for the task. He would get the opportunity to come face to face with wild beasts of the jungle. It presented to him a most tempting situation. He knew that it was a daring venture in which life and death had to be counted as light as straw. He had also heard that naked *siddhas* roamed over these hills. Ramdas would have their *darshan* and company. He looked down from where he was. The *sadhus* who appeared small in size from that height were awaiting Ramdas's return. At the top of his voice Ramdas shouted to them to climb up to where he was and also wildly beckoned them to do so.

"We can't do it," came the voice from the Nepali. "Come down yourself; don't lose time."

"Turn back, both of you," replied Ramdas. "He intends going to Nilkant."

"No, no, I will not return without you. For God's sake come down," and the old man—the Nepali—danced in excitement, moving his arms like a wind-mill and showing by such gestures the force and urgency of his call!

Now Ramdas was in a dilemma. A moment's thought and the Nepali conquered. Ramdas descended; slipped down by a dangerous slope by the side of the cliff. In ten minutes Ramdas was with them again. The old man embraced him through excess of joy, his eyes filled with tears. Now they rested for some time at the spring, where the Maharashtrian *sadhu* prepared tea in the *lota* belonging to the Nepali, who carried in his *jholi* some *jaggery* and a few tea leaves. The time was about four o'clock.

"Let us hurry down," suggested the Nepali with fearful concern, "you know, as the evening sets in, wild beasts saunter out of their lairs for quenching their thirst at the spring."

So the party walked on at a brisk pace. At several places, the Nepali pointed out the foot-prints of wild animals, the sight of which made them run faster. About six o'clock they came back to

Swargashram. The Nepali was by now utterly exhausted. What with the fatigue of the hill climbing, fear and anxiety, and gnawings of hunger, the old man was quite spent out.

On reaching the *kuti* they were told that there had been a *bhandara*; i.e., a special feast that afternoon at the *annakshetra*. Ramdas ran up to the *kshetra* and begged food for three *sadhus*. The *sannyasi* in charge kindly supplied the necessary quantity of food from preparations left over from the afternoon feast. Ramdas and the *sadhus* had a satisfactory meal. Thus ended the first attempt to visit the Nilkant shrine.

(ii) Second Attempt

A few days later Ramcharandas turned up. He was in Hardwar during the Kumbha Mela, but Ramdas had missed him in the vast assemblage. He insisted upon Ramdas's shifting to the double *kuti* which had been reserved during his absence.

"Ram, you had no business to lock up the room," remarked Ramdas to him. "The room is the property of all *sadhus*. During your absence so many *sadhus* were in search of *kutis*. Your reservation of the *kuti* was against the principle of *sadhuism*."

Ramdas did not wish to give up the company of the Maharashtra *sadhu* who had afforded him shelter for so many days. The *sadhu* also pleaded with Ramdas not to part with him. So for a day or two Ramdas continued to stay with him in spite of the repeated pressure of Ramcharandas who even tried to take him to his *kuti* by force. At last, finding Ramcharandas greatly upset by his unwillingness to share his *kuti*, Ramdas shifted to his room. Here Ramdas met two *sannyasi* disciples of Swami Akhandanand of Chitrakut. Ramdas again thought of going up the Nilkant hill. The Nepali *sannyasi* had left the ashram soon after his return from the disappointing trip.

Now a party consisting of Ramdas, Ramcharandas, the Maharashtra *sadhu* and the two *sannyasis* started on the adventure. But one of the *sannyasis* knew the route that led up to the Nilkant shrine as he had an occasion to visit the place before.

At this time Ramdas had come into contact with a sincere *sadhaka* from Nagpur, Ramchandra Timande, and the manager of a Marwadi *annakshetra* who were both very kind and loving to him. Ramchandra had begun to look upon him as his spiritual guide.

Before setting out on the Nilkant journey Ramcharandas had replenished his *jholi* with food-stuffs from the Marwadi *annakshetra*. He possessed already two aluminium vessels and procured from the *kshetra* a hand hatchet for cutting firewood.

Early one morning the party commenced the ascent of the hill. The *sannyasi* guide took them along the proper path which, being spiral, was easy to climb. They had to cover a distance of seven miles which they did by midday. Now they came to a small stream of water which they crossed by the help of a wooden bridge and reached a place shaded by the spreading branches of a cluster of giant forest trees, in the middle of which stood the small mandir of Nilkant and two *dharmashalas*. The party alighted at one of the *dharmashalas*.

Here a dinner was prepared for all, and by two o'clock they finished their meals. Ramdas and Ramcharandas proposed to spend some days on the hill. The *sannyasis* and the Maharashtrian *sadhu* left the hill top for the plains.

Ramdas was now for discovering the edible roots on the hill. So he and Ramcharandas began to dig for them at several places on the hill. It being summer the ground was hard and the hill-folk advised them not to try for the roots as they were deep down in the earth and that it was not the season to dig for them. So they gave up the arduous task.

Ramdas then suggested to Ramcharandas that they should give up the *dharmashala* and seek a solitary nook on the hill for spending their days. The evening was drawing near. They started inspecting the hill for a secluded and suitable spot. The sun set. They were near a tiny stream in the small valley of a sloping hill. Ramdas climbed up the slope which was covered with a thick growth of short trees. In the midst of a group of trees Ramdas sat down.

"We shall remain here tonight and, after clearing the ground, we shall have between us a small pit in which we shall make a fire to keep us warm in the night," said Ramdas.

Then they set about collecting the dry twigs and branches of trees. Soon a fire was lit; the ground was cleared of the small shrubs and thorny plants. A *lota* of water was procured from the spring for drinking purposes. The night was cold but the fire kept them warm. Ramdas acquainted Ramcharandas with what they should do on the morrow.

"Ram, tomorrow let us cut down some trees with the help of the hatchet and erect a small hut to accommodate us and spend some quiet days here."

Ramcharandas agreed. The night was passed almost in a wakeful condition. From early morning next day, they grew busy in the erection of the proposed hut. Ramdas did the digging of the ground to make it level, and Ramcharandas went about to cut down the short trees for obtaining suitable posts for the shed. They toiled till midday. Ramcharandas prepared, at the small stream, a few *rotis* and *dal* with which they satisfied their hunger and again applied themselves to the work in hand. They made marvelous progress in the construction of the needed hut. About three o'clock a shepherd of the hills came in that direction with his herd of sheep. Seeing these *sadhus* he approached and questioned them as to what they were doing. Ramdas made him understand the object of their labour.

"Maharaj," he said, "why all this unnecessary toil? There is a cave close by, most suitable for your occupation. Some time ago a *sadhu* was living in it. It is now vacant; you can reside in it instead of taking all this trouble. It is on the edge of a stream of pure crystal water.

Ramdas jumped at the idea and asked him: "Can you lead us to the cave?"

"Come along," he said, "I can take you to it instantly."

Turning to Ramcharandas, Ramdas said: "Throw up this work; let us follow him."

Ramcharandas looked amazed at the whimsical command of Ramdas, but submitted, as he had done many a time before.

(iii) In the Cave

The shepherd escorted the *sadhus* to a cave about a hundred yards from the shrine of Nilkant, on the edge of a stream that supplied water to the shrine. The place was out of the way. The cave had a wide yawning mouth at its front and, as you entered it, it narrowed until you came to a small inner cavity just sufficient for one person to sit in. They swept the floor and set up a fire. There were signs of ashes indicating its previous occupation by some *sadhu*. The sweet music of the running stream close by and the distant roars of wild beasts were heard in the nights. The cave presented a prospect at once weird and awe-inspiring, and Ramdas liked the place very much.

The victuals that Ramcharandas possessed lasted them for about five days. Meanwhile, news spread among *sadhus* and pilgrims in Rishikesh and Swargashram that two *sadhus* were living on this hill in a cave, situated in a dreadful place. Hundreds of people commenced to come for the *darshan* of the *sadhus*. They brought various presents, such as milk, grapes, sugarcandy, fried gram, almonds, etc. It was clear that God was busy in seeing that they did not feel the want of the necessities of life!

One day, Ramcharandas asked: "Swamiji, how long are we to stay here?"

"Ramdas has no idea," replied Ramdas, "It may be for months. The place has captured Ramdas's heart."

When there were no visitors they started collecting firewood. Stout, green branches were cut down and put up in the sun for drying. Ramdas was hewing down a thick stump of a dried-up tree. The axe was a small one and he had to work at it for three days, spending on it a couple of hours in the morning and evening. At last it was cut down, but the heavy log had yet to be carried to the mouth of the cave, and this task was reserved for a later occasion.

Daily the number of visitors increased. One evening a strong and well-built *sadhu* paid them a visit. He had bangles on his wrists, rings on his fingers and a *jholi* suspended on his shoulder, containing a number of things. He presented Ramdas with a big lump of charas or extract of *ganja* for smoking. Ramdas accepted the gift. The *sadhu* was a *ganja* smoker himself. After some time he left the cave. On his departure Ramdas threw the lump of *charas* into the fire and burnt it to ashes. Next day the *sadhu* turned up again. He was short of *charas*. He expected Ramdas to provide him with some from the lump given by him the previous evening.

"May I have some *charas*?" he asked.

"Ramdas destroyed in the fire the lump of *charas* you presented him with," replied Ramdas.

"Well done, Maharaj," he said with a sigh of relief. "I have become a slave to this vice and by your contact I hope to be freed from it." Thereafter, taking a great liking for Ramdas, he became a constant visitor.

Now the usual provisions for cooking *dal* and *roti* were nearly exhausted, although the gifts of other eatables were raining down every day. Ramcharandas was for the daily *dal* and *roti*.

"Swamiji," he said one night, "the provisions have run out. I intend going down to Marwadi *kshetra* in Swargashram and bringing provisions to last us for at least a fortnight. We require also earthen pots for fetching and storing water. I shall also obtain these."

"Ram," Ramdas observed, "why all this trouble? God provides us here. Let us be satisfied with the things He sends us."

"No, Swamiji, a meal of *dal* and *roti*, once a day, is essential. It is no trouble to me. I can manage to get the articles without difficulty. I have resolved upon it. I will start tomorrow morning and try to return by the evening," he said.

He was obstinate and Ramdas submitted. Early next morning, he climbed down the hill and made his way to Swargashram. That evening he was detained at the ashram. Ramdas enjoyed the perfect solitude of the cave in the night. Next day, at dusk, Ramcharandas tottered into the cave with a heavy burden on his head. He was carrying an enormous gunny bag bulging out with its contents and had also two big earthen pots hanging at his back.

He lowered the sack and released the pots and rolled on the floor of the cave through utter exhaustion. For full ten minutes he was unable to speak. He was just panting for breath. Then he slowly opened the bag and took out bundle after bundle of rice, *dal*, wheat-flour, potatoes, *jaggery*, *ghee*, sugar and what not. The provisions would have sufficed for over a month.

"What a wonderful fellow you are! Why so much?" Ramdas asked.

"So much? why, we need it all," he exclaimed. "It saves my going down frequently; for a month at least we can remain here quietly without any anxiety about food."

"Ram, you seem to trust more in these food-stuffs than in God!" Ramdas remarked.

Ramcharandas was not inclined to talk. The inner cavity in the cave was at once converted into a store-room and the bundles were nicely arranged inside it and Ramdas helped him in the work.

On the succeeding day, the fuel not being quite dry, Ramcharandas experienced great difficulty in cooking, Moreover, as the cooking had to be done in the open air, the strong breezes prevented the fire burning steadily. So that day's *rotis* were under-baked and the *dal* half-boiled. Ramdas was lacking in teeth. Somehow he managed to swallow down the raw food. Even the meals prepared on the previous days had not been well-cooked as they had told upon Ramdas's digestion. Ramcharandas was still a *sadhaka* in this line as well! The cumulative effect of the indifferently cooked food affected Ramdas and he got a severe attack of dysentery which continued for over a fortnight.

Two days later, Ramdas had a visit from half-a-dozen *sadhus*. One of them, in the course of talk, suggested: "Maharaj, why are you cooping yourself up here in this solitary place? You ought to travel in Punjab and Kashmir and enjoy the *prem* of the devotees of those parts, especially in Punjab where the people are so filled with devotion and love. You should not fail to visit that province."

Ramdas was at once impressed by his advice and believed that the hint came from God Himself for making a move from the cave. When the visitors departed Ramdas turned to Ramcharandas and said: "Ram, it is the command of God that we should depart from here and travel towards Punjab and Kashmir. Make yourself ready for starting."

The boy, hearing Ramdas's words, turned pale and then blue! He fondly glanced at the store-room.

"It is all very well," said Ramcharandas with a slow voice and a wry face. "Thank God, we are saved the terrible labour, that is, of rolling up the heavy stump of the tree from the ditch, into which it has fallen, to the mouth of the cave."

At this Ramdas could not control a laugh and the boy could not help joining him.

The stored provisions and the pots were then distributed among the hill-men and women, and by evening they found themselves in the small thatched *kuti* near the Marwadi *annakshetra* of Swargashram. The *sadhu* who had been addicted to *charas*, but who was now free from its clutches stuck on to Ramdas. He accompanied Ramdas down the hill and remained with him. He insisted upon following Ramdas wherever he went. Ramdas dissuaded him saying that he would find it very difficult to keep pace with Ramdas while walking. The weak point about the *sadhu* was that he could not walk fast on account of his bulky body. Moreover, Ramdas assured him that by keeping company with Ramdas he would not gain much, since the Truth he was in search of was within himself. Eventually, he was prevailed upon to abandon the idea of hanging on to him.

Ramchandra Timande and Brijlal Munim of Marwadi *kshetra* were overflowing in their kindness and hospitality. Ramdas proposed to travel on foot to Kashmir over the mountains. He was told that there was a path across the mountains that would lead to Kashmir; only that it was a tedious and perilous one. The undaunted spirit within Ramdas egged him on to undertake the difficult journey. Ramchandra Timande strongly opposed the idea and insisted upon Ramdas's travelling by train first to Punjab and then to Kashmir.

"Swamiji, there are two famous places worth visiting in Punjab, Chintapurni and Jwalajee. I will see that you are both provided with tickets as far as Hoshiarpur station, wherefrom you have to travel on foot to these noted shrines."

The kind-hearted friend succeeded in persuading Ramdas to leave Rishikesh with Ramcharandas by a train running towards Punjab.

CHAPTER 33: CHINTAPURNI – JWALAJEE – PATHANKOT

(i) Pain Transmuted into Joy

In the evening they reached the station of Hoshiarpur, where they spent the night on the terrace of the huge rest-house for pilgrims. Here some pilgrims provided them with a drink of undiluted warm milk and cots to sleep on. Dysentery continued to harass Ramdas's body. Early next morning they prosecuted their journey on foot to Chintapurni, which lay about forty-five miles from Hoshiarpur. They had to walk up a gradually rising tract of land. They covered fifteen miles during the day and found rest in a small village rest-house. Except stopping four or five times to answer calls of nature, Ramdas and Ramcharandas walked the distance at a rapid pace.

Ramdas eschewed solid food. He had a cup of milk while Ramcharandas procured by *bhiksha* some *dal* and *rotis* for himself. At daybreak, next day, they started again. About eight o'clock they reached a wayside hamlet. As they neared a sweetmeat shop, the eatables exhibited in the shop drew the attention of Ramcharandas. Poor boy! his mouth must have watered at the sight of the tempting sweets! There was by the side of the shop a small thatched shed for the use of customers. Ramcharandas entered it followed by Ramdas. They sat on the floor. There was none else in the shed. Ramdas thought that Ramcharandas proposed to have some rest after the three hours' walk. God's ways are wonderful! A few minutes after they entered the shed, two Punjabis came in and sat near them.

One of them saluting Ramdas enquired, "May I get for you some milk from the adjoining shop?" Ramdas gave an affirmative nod. The Punjabi then got for them two huge brass cupfuls of milk. Each cup contained about a seer of the liquid. Ramcharandas and Ramdas drank it.

Then the Punjabi asked Ramdas: "Maharaj, where are you going?"

"To Chintapurni," was Ramdas's simple reply.

"We are also on our way to the same place and I should consider it a great privilege to go in your company," he pleaded.

So the four forming a party continued their journey. Ramdas now walked at an incredibly quick pace. He suggested that they should reach Chintapurni that very night. Although he had had half-a-dozen motions due to dysentery on the way and in spite of the undulating ground, a rapid pace was maintained. They had to cover a distance of twenty seven miles. About nine o'clock in the night they arrived at Chintapurni. They spent the night outside a stable.

Chintapurni is a small town with a temple of a *Devi* after whom it was named. The belief goes that a visit to this shrine dispels entirely one's sorrows and anxieties. Hence the name of the goddess. Next day the party after bath paid a visit to the temple. The Punjabi friend, whose name was Pandit Jewandas, persuaded Ramdas to take rest for a day in that hamlet. He felt great concern about Ramdas's health on learning of the attack of dysentery.

Refreshed by a day's rest the party started again. They were bound for Jwalajee which lay about twenty five miles from Chintapurni. Again they commenced their journey at a brisk pace. At midday, they had a halt for about two hours beneath the trees on the way. By now dysentery had stopped, but, as they neared Jwalajee, Ramdas felt something wrong with his right foot. However, by evening they reached Jwalajee, where they spent the night in the ashram of Dashanami *sannyasis*, an ashram very near to the temple of Jwalajee. Here they were provided with meals and treated with great kindness and hospitality.

Next day Ramdas, wishing to find out a separate dwelling place, searched the hill for a cave and discovered a few yards above the ashram, a solid structure containing a number of vacant rooms in a line. Ramdas proposed to occupy one of these. Ramcharandas and Jewandas also became his room mates—the other friend, who accompanied Jewandas, having separated from the party on the way, as he was a college student returning to his parents who lived somewhere in the district.

Ramdas now detected a slight swelling on the sole of his right foot. However, they wished to finish the *darshan* of Jwalajee for which purpose they had come.

The temple is made of a square block, cut out of a solid mass of rock. The roofing is of plated gold having a beautiful dome with artistic designs carved on it. The dome shone with great lustre in the bright sun. It is said that the gold roof was presented by the great soldier and king, Ranjit Singh of historic fame. As Ramdas entered the temple he observed that its inside was conspicuous by the absence of any image. Within a few steps of the doorway was a small oblong pit, in which was seen a big tongue of flame waving and hissing and there were also similar smaller flames issuing out of the rock walls at other places, all round the interior of the temple. There were altogether about seven such volcanic flames. By Jwalajee is meant "flame goddess." The worship and *darshan* were of the flames.

Coming out of the temple Ramdas ascended a flight of steps to the right of the temple and came to a small shed, where he saw a circular hole bored in a rock, to the depth of about two feet, in which water was set boiling by the heat of a flame below.

Later, Ramdas heard from Jewandas that the flames in the gold-roofed temple accepted the offering of milk by licking off nearly half the quantity of the milk presented to them, leaving the rest as *prasad* to the devotee. He gave out this as his own experience.

The *darshan* over, Ramdas and the party returned to their room. The succeeding day, the swelling on the foot of Ramdas increased. It took the shape of a boil. In three days it assumed the size of a large lemon. Jewandas and Ramcharandas busied themselves applying various ointments to it so that it might ripen and burst.

All the time Ramdas, in spite of the boil, was smiling and cheerful. *Sadhus* in great numbers came to see Ramdas in that condition. The thing that surprised them most was Ramdas's smiling face, although the condition of the foot could not permit of such a merry demeanour. Ramdas hardly slept in the nights. He sat up the whole night leaning against the wall. He was experiencing unbroken ecstasy. In such a mood he would go on talking about devotion and divine vision. Jewandas, who was eager to collect Ramdas's sayings, would jot down on scraps of paper, as quickly as he could write, every bit that fell from Ramdas's lips. He used a country oil lamp made of an earthen dish. The notes covered several sheets of paper.

Seven days passed. The boil showed no signs of bursting. One early morning, a *sannyasini*, i.e., a female *sannyasi*, paid a visit to Ramdas. She saw the boil. Her heart was touched.

"Maharaj," she said, "the boil seems to be quite ripe now, it requires only opening up. I shall run down and send a barber who will open it and give relief to your foot."

So saying, the kind-hearted mother went down the hill. About half an hour later, a barber, who was also the village surgeon, turned up. Ramdas stretched out his affected leg towards him, and with a blunt instrument the barber began to operate upon the boil. The skin of the sole being naturally thick the instrument had to be used with some force. However, he made an incision, and thrusting the point of the instrument inside the boil, he pulled it out tearing up the skin. Then he squeezed out the pus. A strip of cloth was wrapped round the wound.

"Maharaj, don't do any walking for some days. If dust is allowed to enter the wound, you will get into further trouble," the barber warned.

Jewandas left Jwalajee the next day for his native place, Rawalpindi, and Ramdas also started. Some *sadhus* including Ramcharandas tried to dissuade Ramdas from travelling on foot just then, when the wound was still raw and unhealed. But Ramdas did not take their advice and came out on the road.

(ii) Ramcharandas Fails the Test

Ramdas limped as he walked. By midday they covered about ten miles and reached a small wayside hamlet. Ramcharandas undertook to fetch *bhiksha* of cooked food from the villagers. About one o'clock he returned, his cloth-sling filled with all kinds of food mixed up together. After dinner and rest they proceeded on their journey. In the evening they came to another village, where they remained for the night on a neighbouring hill top.

The following day they passed through the fertile and enchanting Kangra valley and reached at dusk a small town on an elevated plateau. Ramdas proposed that they might occupy a dilapidated rest-house for the night. But the boy was in no mood for rest, he was feeling hungry and the thought of food was revolving in his mind.

"Swamiji," he said, "I shall try to get some food by *bhiksha*. You may wait here beneath the tree."

The tree was in front of the rest-house. Ramcharandas passed into the darkness, but returned in a short time barehanded and with a wry face.

"What is the matter, Ram?" Ramdas questioned.

"I approached two houses," he replied ruefully, "I got instead of *bhiksha*, reproaches and scolding of a very virulent type, and at one place, a young man of the house mistaking me for a prowling thief pursued me with a stout stick in his hand. I raced for very life and am here."

His graphic narration made Ramdas burst into laughter. "Consider, Ram, the scoldings and the offer of blows from the stout stick are also *bhiksha*. You received the former, but why did you refuse to accept the latter, the more precious of the two?" Ramdas remarked humorously.

"Your wit is out of place, Swamiji," he said, not relishing the way in which Ramdas expressed things. "I am hungry and I must have something to eat. I shall not be baulked. I am off again."

And he disappeared once more. In half-an-hour he was back. This time his face indicated fright coupled with a sense of relief at escape from an unpleasant scrape. Ramcharandas was a simple boy, sincere and outspoken.

"Swamiji," he recounted, "two narrow shaves. Soon after I left you, some knocking about brought me to a crowded house and in the front room over a fire I saw *rotis* being prepared. I rushed into the room where a pile of *rotis* was beside the fire. The room was full of men. I stretched out my hands and requested the man at the fire to give me a few *rotis*. The man said that they were Pathans and that if I had no objection they could spare a couple of *rotis* for me and also a bit of curry.

"Now a look round presented to my sight a number of rough, burly, ferocious Pathans with shaggy and ominous beards. I lost no time; one leap from the room and I was on the road. I heard a faint rumble of laughter from the direction of the house, but I did not remain there to listen to all that. I took to my heels. I ran wildly without knowing where I was going. Now a row of huts stood before me. Here is food for me, I thought and approached one of the huts. The host welcomed me, and, coming to know the reason of my nocturnal visit, said: "Well, I have no objection to give you food. We have it ready, but I may first warn you that we are *chamars* or cobblers by caste!" "What!" I exclaimed and the next instant I shot out of the hut like a bullet from a gun and I am here! Hunger is welcome, but tasting food from the hands of Muslims and *chamars*—well, I draw the line there."

"Ah! Ram," Ramdas exclaimed, "you have failed the test. The distinction you are making is unnatural. You are out for universal vision and yet you adhere to these ignorance-born prejudices! The Muslim and the *chamar* ought to be the beloved Ram for you. Is He not dwelling in all?"

"You are right," he agreed, "but to rise above the distinction of caste is very hard. Look at the way how I was fooled by it."

"One more attempt," he said and left. In a few minutes he returned with a bland smile.

"Swamiji, come on. We have an invitation for supper in a Hindu household."

Ramdas followed him. The kind host was a touring officer. After the meal they rested on the verandah and early at day-break took their departure. By noon they arrived at Kangra. Kangra is a hilly tract of land full of shady trees and clear water springs. The climate here is cool and bracing, and so it is a health resort. Ramdas passing through the streets went outside the city and, entering the enclosure of a Mahadeva's temple, beneath two giant banyan trees, sat down on a stone pedestal in front of the temple. Ramcharandas stayed behind in the city. His first concern was to arrange for meals. A visitor to the temple seeing Ramdas came to him.

"Maharaj, I shall be so happy to offer you *bhiksha* in my house," he said. "Or if you wish to have the food here I shall bring it here."

"Ramji, Ramdas will visit your house for *bhiksha*," replied Ramdas; "but you have to feed also another who is Ramdas's companion. He will be here presently."

"All right, Maharaj, I shall come here to fetch you both at exactly twelve," he said and returned to the city.

Soon after this, Ramcharandas turned up. He informed Ramdas with great delight that after some knocking about he had at last procured an invitation for dinner for two from a pious old mother in the city.

"You need not trouble her, Ram," said Ramdas; "we have an invitation already from a merchant friend of the city. We shall go to him. He will be here to take us at twelve o'clock."

As they returned to the temple, after bathing in a neighbouring tank, the merchant came and escorted them to his house. Ramdas had requested him to feed them with a plain meal. He fed the *sadhus* with great love.

They stayed in Kangra for four or five days. One night was spent in the company of a *sannyasi* at his ashram situated in a beautiful spot. The *sannyasi* was all kindness and hospitality. The latter part of the stay was passed in the Mahadeva's temple which they had first visited. Here Ramdas met a doctor, who had newly come to Kangra for health and had taken up his lodgings in the outhouse of the temple. He was extremely kind to Ramdas. He told Ramdas the stories of his extensive travels in Europe. He had visited England, France, Germany and other countries in Europe. He was a well-read man. In the course of his talks he remembered the writings of Emanuel Swedenborg, the Swedish philosopher.

"Swedenborg, the Swede," he related, "when he saw so much misery in the world, once said with great vehemence: 'If I could only find that arch-tyrant God, who created so much misery in the world, I would strangle him to death.' What do you think of this?" he asked.

"If Ramdas were there when he said so, he would have taken the philosopher's hands up to his own throat and urged him to strangle himself, because the misery he sees in the world is of his own making."

When Ramdas's departure from Kangra approached, the doctor pressed on Ramdas a couple of rupees for expenses on the way. Ramdas declined the offer with thanks, but when it was presented to Ramcharandas he accepted the gift in spite of Ramdas's remonstrances.

Leaving Kangra behind, they continued their journey and took their position for the night on the raised platform, beneath a tree at the brink of a well on the outskirts of a village. Here Ramdas proposed to Ramcharandas a separation between them.

"Ram, you may go your own way and gather experience. Ramdas will also go alone. Remember we are both bound for Kashmir. We shall meet in that place."

At first Ramcharandas refused point-blank to accept the proposition. He grumbled, fretted and wept. But Ramdas brought home to him the absolute necessity for such a course, as it would be to his own benefit. Through independence alone does a *sadhu* learn the secrets of life and Truth. Hanging on always to an external prop in spiritual matters hampers his progress, because his vision lacks then the flexibility for expansion and universalisation. The centre of interest becomes cramped and localised, while his aim should be to comprehend and realise the infinite nature of Truth.

(iii) God in the Form of a Serpent

Early at four o'clock the next morning, Ramcharandas parted from Ramdas and proceeded on his way, while Ramdas started three hours later. At midday Ramdas came to a temple in a village and rested on a verandah. Here again, a pious householder, who visited the temple, took Ramdas to his house and fed him with rice and curds. The same evening he reached another village, where he spent the night beneath a banyan tree. There was a terrible storm in the night and a countless host of night-flies beset the place where he rested. He watched silently the whole night the ravages of the cyclonic blast and the officious attentions of innumerable flies.

At daybreak he prosecuted his journey. The foot was nearly healed. The old skin was dropping off and the new skin was getting hardened. At midday he came to the bank of a large tank surrounded by trees near a village mostly peopled by Muhammedans. He took his seat beneath one of the huge trees. A little later he went about the houses for *bhiksha*. He approached first a small thatched house, where he saw the mother of the house at the front door.

"Will you kindly feed your child with a *roti*, O mother?" Ramdas begged in Hindi.

"O sadhuji, I am a Muslim by religion while you are a Hindu *sadhu*. How can you eat food at my hands?" she asked.

"Ramdas knows no difference between a Hindu and a Muslim. You are his mother and he knows only this relation and nothing else," Ramdas answered.

She at once fetched from her house one *roti* on which was some chutney, made of green mangos. Ramdas, sitting down in the open yard, ate the food and, drinking some water from the hollow of his hands, went up to another house in the neighbourhood. Here also the same story was repeated, because the house he visited happened to be again of a Mussalman. When he told the mothers that he had no objection to eat their food, they gladly served him with a *roti* and some curry. He had his fill. Now he started to leave the place. The sun was hot. Very often he had travelled in the heat of the midday sun without caring for rest.

When he was passing out of the village a brahman spotted him, and taking him by the arm escorted him to his house and placed before him a full meal. He had no appetite, but the brahman would not let him go without accepting some *bhiksha*. So, he had to eat another *roti* at his house. He then left the village and proceeded onwards.

About five o'clock he reached Pathankot. He saw a white tower of a temple on the road-side into which he entered. The moment the *pujari* of the temple saw him, he showed great delight, as though he had been long looking for Ramdas's coming. He embraced Ramdas with great love and made him sit beside him on a cot. He offered Ramdas a sweet drink and talked to him in a most friendly manner. The night was drawing nearer.

"Maharaj, Ramdas desires to spend this night in a perfectly solitary room in your *mandir*. Kindly provide him with such a place," Ramdas pleaded.

The *pujari* at once said that there was a cave-like room underground, at the base of the main temple structure, a place free from the disturbing noises of external life. It had not been in use for a long time. Still it was fit for habitation. Ramdas agreed to occupy it for the night. Taking an old mat, the *pujari* led him down a flight of stone steps into the semi-dark room, about ten feet square, in the bowels of the earth. Dust lay heavy on the floor which was perhaps unswept for years. He spread the mat on which Ramdas sat and bade the *pujari* good-night. The *pujari* left. When night descended on the outside world, the room was merged in inky darkness. There was a single small window to the level of the outer ground.

For hours Ramdas sat on the mat in a state of complete oblivion of his body when he was brought down to the external consciousness by the sound of footsteps. He opened his eyes and saw three persons enter the cave. They had a lantern with them and also a hand harmonium and a *tabla*. They were the *pujari* and his friends. The *pujari* had also brought with him a brass *lota* full of milk for Ramdas. At his pressure Ramdas drank the milk.

"Maharaj," the *pujari* then said, "we intend to sing a few songs here. Hence we have come with the musical instruments."

"All right," Ramdas replied, "Ramdas will only be too happy to listen to your music."

The light was placed in the centre of the room and the friends stationed themselves in a line to the left of Ramdas at the base of the staircase. The music commenced. The song was in Hindi composed by a well-known saint. They sang the first verse which meant: "He is a *jivanmukta*, or a liberated soul who has discovered the joy of having Ramnam on his tongue." When they finished the first verse, there was a sudden stoppage of their song. The musical instruments also ceased to function. Ramdas turned to them to see what the matter was. All the three of them with mouths wide open and frightened eyes were looking in the direction beyond the light on the right side of Ramdas. A venomous snake was observed slowly creeping towards Ramdas. At one bound they stood up as one man and exhorted Ramdas to do the same.

"Let us leave this place, Maharaj, I can find you accommodation elsewhere," said the *pujari*. "That snake is the worst of its kind. It is full of poison from tail to head. Do get up and follow us."

Ramdas was cool and quiet, and replied: "Ram, why are you so afraid of the snake? God himself has given us *darshan* in that form. He has come with so much love to hear music. He won't do any harm. Sit down and go on with the *kirtan*."

"Impossible," cried out the *pujari*, "to sing when the messenger of Yama himself is so close at hand! We are off. We advise you to come away with us."

"Don't give way to fear. The snake will do no harm. You need not sing, but don't run away. You will know that the snake means no ill," urged Ramdas.

They would not sit down. As the serpent crept nearer and nearer to Ramdas, they turned like the hand of a clock and drew round at the tail-end of the serpent. The reptile came quite near Ramdas. He beckoned it and said "Beloved Ram, come on; don't hesitate."

He had a piece of *jaggery* tied to his cloth, which he untied and placed before the snake and said: "Beloved Ram, this is the only offering Ramdas can make you, please accept it."

The snake approached the lump of *jaggery*, and with its forked tongue licked it well for a few seconds and then came onwards. It was now only about two inches from him, but he was sitting stock-still. Somehow, it did not quite approach him, but turned its head outwards and took a circuitous path close behind him. As it emerged on the left, the friends moved round to the right side of Ramdas. They took care to see that they always maintained a distance of at least a yard from the tail-end of the snake. The snake now slowly made for the flight of steps and started creeping up from one corner of it.

"Maharaj," cried out the *pujari* in a tone of anxiety, "there are about forty steps to ascend to reach the higher ground level. The snake goes so leisurely that it might take hours to gain the top. Till then we are caught up here. Also there is no knowing when it might take it into its head to turn back into the cave. We are done for."

"Have no fear. It is going up one corner of the steps. You may safely ascend by the other," Ramdas suggested.

"Nothing of the kind," quickly put in the *pujari*; "we dare not do it. We have no such trust in it as you have."

Ramdas then proposed to stand midway on the steps, so that they might securely pass up between him and the wall, opposite to the course followed by the snake. They agreed and he took the position indicated by him. One by one, the friends went up the steps, leaping four steps at a time! Before going, they warned him again of the danger, appealing to him to follow them out of the place. They took with them, besides the musical instruments, the lantern also.

Ramdas was again immersed in pitch darkness. He regained his seat on the mat. He groped in the darkness for the lump of *jaggery* tasted by the serpent, and after some search got it. Being the *prasad* left by the serpent, he threw it into his mouth and ate it with great delight. He remained in the sitting posture the whole night, absorbed in a blissful trance.

When the first glow of the morning was filtering through the translucent panes of the small window of the cave, he found a head peering into the room from a landing step at a sharp corner of the stone staircase. It was the *pujari* peeping to make sure that Ramdas was alive! Ramdas looked at him and smiled. He then entered the cave room with his friends of the previous night close at his heels. They sat down before him and gazed at him in wonder. Then the *pujari's* attention was drawn to the spot where the lump of *jaggery* had been. Not finding it there he questioned Ramdas as to what had become of it. He replied that, being the *prasad* of the snake, he had eaten it up.

"Good God!" he exclaimed, "you are a terrible man."

"Ramdas is not a terrible man," Ramdas returned. "He is only a child and servant of God."

Then Ramdas left the cave room and temple, and proceeded on his journey.

CHAPTER 34: SUJANPUR – JAMMU

(i) A Divine Pair

Sujanpur is a large town, four miles distant from Pathankot, on the bank of a swift flowing river. Ramdas strolled up to the town in a slow and leisurely fashion. He directed his steps into the yard of a house in which lived the family of a postman of the place. The master of the house was out. His wife, as soon as she saw him, fell at his feet and begged him to be seated on a cot standing in the shade of a tree in front of the house. He complied with her request. Immediately, entering the house, she got a *lota* of water and a wooden seat. Clearing a part of ground in the yard, she sprinkled water over it and placing the wooden seat in position fetched from the kitchen a plate of a steaming meal for him.

"Maharaj, I am blest by your *darshan*. Kindly accept our humble hospitality," she appealed turning to Ramdas, her palms joined in salutation.

Ramdas washed his hands and sat down for the dinner offered so promptly and with such love by the mother. He now remembered the words of the *sadhu* at the Nilkant cave about the unique love and devotion of the Punjabis.

The meal over, the master of the house turned up. What a divine pair God had united together in the person of the poor postman and his wife! so humble, so pure and so simple. Blessed was Ramdas that he had the sight of this heavenly couple! They represented the true devotional summit to which the *bhakti* cult of Hinduism can raise its votaries. All the time, when both the husband and wife were engaged in their service of Ramdas, a four year old child of theirs was lying on a rug on a cot close by, reduced to a skeleton from a wasting disease. He approached the bed of the little patient, who was lying quite calm with looks that seemed to gaze into eternity.

The mother with some emotion said: "God gave this child to us, but it appears He wants him back."

"Mother, submit to His will in all matters," assured Ramdas. "Truly He gives and He takes away. His will is supreme and He means always well."

The words brought tears into her eyes, and she smiled in a spirit of complete resignation to God's will.

Some Punjabi friends, who came to see Ramdas, took him out to the bazaar wherefrom he was taken from house to house, and petted, fondled and fed by the love-struck mothers. During the four days that he remained at the place, over a dozen mothers went stark-mad over him. They deluged him with their pure and selfless love.

In the evenings, some friends would lead him to the river, where on its bank he used to sit with quite a crowd of visitors around him. Ramdas would then voice in an impassioned language the glory of the divine love. After the lapse of four days, he broached the subject of leaving the place for his long journey to Kashmir. He said that he would go on foot from village to village until he reached the destination.

Among these newly-acquired friends were municipal officers and rich *zamindars*. They urged him to go by rail as far as Jammu, and they would provide him with a ticket. At first he resisted their offer, as he did not wish to forego the joy of travelling on foot and coming into touch with the devotees of Punjab in the villages as he passed through them. But the friends were bent upon sending him by train and he had to yield to their loving protests against journeying on foot.

Before departing from Sujanpur, he paid a last visit to the house of the postman and spent a night with him. His wife was in ecstasy over Ramdas's infinite kindness as she termed his wish to stay with them.

Sujanpur was not a railway station. Hence they had to catch the train at Pathankot station. Three tongas full of devotees came with him as far as the railway station to give him a send-off. Most of them were mothers, whose love was boundless. The train started about six o'clock in the morning. They provided him with a drink of fresh milk and made him sit in the inter-class with a supply of sweets and fruits. When the train began to move away from the station, the mothers' hearts welled up with emotion and streams of tears poured down their eyes. He gave them a last *namaskar* and soon was out of their sight.

(ii) Depend on God and None Else

Nine o'clock that night Ramdas reached Jammu, the headquarters of the Kashmir Government during winter. Alighting from the train he made his way to the city along with the other passengers. On the way he had to cross the long bridge on the river Tawi. He was directed by one of the resident *sadhus* to seek a place of rest in the famous Raghunath temple. He passed the huge doorway that led into the precincts of the temple. The temple was situated in the centre of a vast compound. Till eleven o'clock there was a regular stream of devotees visiting the shrine for *darshan*. He took up his position on a broad open stony platform in front of the outer buildings of the compound. He selected a retired spot away from a crowd of Madrasi *sadhus* who occupied the platform.

For the first half hour there was a din and bustle of promiscuous talk among them. Then a quarrel started. Filthy abuse characterised the altercations that ensued. The party divided itself into two camps and a right royal battle ensued. And for over an hour there was confusion and noise. He looked on the play as an amused witness. He was taught by God to drink only the sweet juice of joy from every situation. Towards midnight the racket gradually died away, except for an occasional outburst of some choice epithets of abuse which the speaker had not been quick-witted enough to remember when the quarrel was in progress. About one o'clock everything was quiet but for the deep, sonorous snores that issued from their direction.

The following day he left the temple premises, when the day just like a new-born babe was still nestling on the soft and glowing bosom of the morning twilight. He wandered over the place aimlessly and saw hundreds of spires and domes of mandirs shooting up in the sky far above the habitations of Jammu. Truly Jammu is a city of temples.

As he roamed thus, his steps were unconsciously directed towards a temple of unprepossessing appearance. He entered the doorway and took his seat on the raised but dusty dias of a large tree in front of the temple. He observed a small group of devotees visiting the shrine with flowers and offerings. Ramdas's mood at the time was of perfect abandon or self-surrender. His mind was in a state of complete freedom and peace in which the thoughts of the past and plans for the future were totally absent. But his observation of the external world was keen, and he enjoyed the inner calmness as of a dispassionate witness, looking on the strange play of nature revealed before him.

He saw to his right, squatted on an elevated pedestal plastered with cement, a figure—his back turned towards Ramdas—immersed in meditation. His big turban was lying bottom upwards beside him. Ramdas watched him for a while. After a short time, the devotee having finished his prayers, started to depart, his turban properly poised on his head. He descended the pedestal and as he did so, his looks fell on Ramdas and their eyes met. He gave Ramdas a *namaskar* which he returned and the devotee walked out of the temple.

Now it might have been about ten o'clock. He discovered a rectangular open platform surrounding the temple structure. He selected a cool spot on its right, shaded by trees, and, going up to it, lay down on the hard ground, with a portion of his only cloth spread on the floor, the rest of it completely covering his body. He would always, on such occasions, assume a curled-up posture, his knees drawn up to the face. He had hardly rested there for about ten minutes when he felt somebody uncovering his cloth from off his legs. He bounded up into a sitting posture and discovered a young man beside him.

"Maharaj" he asked, "what kind of food do you usually take? I can supply you with milk and fruits if you like. The *panditji* who was erstwhile here has sent me with some money so that I may present you with whatever eatables you may desire."

"Ramdas is not particular as to what kind of food he takes," he replied; "he can eat the usual meal of rice, *dal*, etc."

"Then, will you be so good as to follow me to the house in which the *panditji* lives? He will be so happy to entertain you."

Ramdas accompanied him and arrived at the *panditji's* house. He was welcomed by the *pandit* and many others who lodged with him. They were all Kashmiri *pandits* employed in the Customs office. They were put up in the same house, their meals being cooked by a male servant. They had their families in Srinagar. It being summer, the heat of Jammu was oppressive and the *pandits*, unused to the rigours of the weather, were experiencing great discomfort from the heat. The *pandit* who invited Ramdas, Janakinath Bakshi by name, was extremely kind and hospitable. He was duly served with a meal so kindly provided by Janakinath.

Janakinath took a great liking for Ramdas and urged him to remain with him for some days. The young friend who brought him to the house, Jialal Dhar, became his constant companion. He was a student spending his time in Jammu, his school having closed for the vacation. He would take Ramdas out for long walks through the bazaar to the banks of the Tawi river. His love for Ramdas was so great that he moved with him like a shadow. He would also join Ramdas in his dances singing the names of God.

In the evenings, on Janakinath's return home from office, he would have Ramdas exclusively for himself. A few days' society of Ramdas was sufficient to make him, so to say, possessed of Ramdas. He fondled and embraced Ramdas and went into ecstasies in his presence. Thus nearly ten days passed when one night Ramdas told him, that he must be moving from Jammu to Srinagar. At this he showed signs of perturbation.

"No, Swamiji," he protested, "you should not leave us so soon. I cannot bear the very thought of it."

"Ramdas has stopped with you for a sufficiently long time," Ramdas replied. "He is on his way to Srinagar. You should not detain him any longer."

"How do you propose to go? I shall see that every obstacle is put in the way of your departure. I can prevent your getting a seat in the buses that daily run to Srinagar." The connection between Srinagar and Jammu was maintained by bus services.

"Ramdas does not depend upon your buses. He will start on foot. They say the distance is only two hundred miles. He will travel by short stages," Ramdas answered.

"Oh," he cried out, "Swamiji, don't you think of venturing on foot. The way lies through high mountains, forests and regions of extreme cold."

"Ramdas would not mind all that. Ram, who is his master and mother, will see that he passes through the perils safely, because he goes by His will."

"Well, if you are so determined to go, I shall see that you go by motor-bus. I cannot permit you to travel on foot, but my only wish is that you should give me the pleasure of your company for at least a fortnight more," he appealed.

Ramdas was obdurate. Jialal redoubled his watch. Janakinath set him on to it so that Ramdas might not give them the slip unawares. However, in two or three days, a Kashmiri *pandit*, who was to return to Srinagar on short leave with his family, volunteered of his own accord to take Ramdas with him. Ramdas agreed to accompany him. They were to start the following day. The previous evening he had left Janakinath's house when he was not at home, and gone to stay with the new friend who was to be his escort to Srinagar. In the night Janakinath put in an appearance at his friend's house. He tried his utmost to detain Ramdas for some days more, but all to no effect.

"Look here, Swamiji," he at last said, "you are going to a cool place like Srinagar leaving me in this cauldron of boiling heat. Why can you not take me also with you? If you would not do so now, at least after reaching Srinagar you can manage to draw me up to that place."

Meantime, a vacancy in the Srinagar office for which he was qualified had occurred, and Janakinath had applied for it and was awaiting the result with keen anxiety.

CHAPTER 35: KASHMIR

(i) The Kashyapa Bhumi

Next day in the company of the Kashmiri friend and his family, Ramdas left Jammu for Srinagar. The motor-bus that conveyed them traversed through a road cut on the sides of the mountain chains. When the bus trolled onward in its uphill path, it appeared as if an ant was creeping on a huge mound of earth. The landscapes and deep valleys, green with luxuriant verdure and the dense forests of pine, cedar and poplar on the heaven-kissing mountains, presented an enthralling sight of supreme beauty and grandeur. As the bus mounted higher and higher along the spiral path, new and sublime scenes of the majesty of nature unfolded themselves before his eyes and he was thrilled with joy at the enchanting vision.

At dusk the motor-bus reached the top of the Banhal mountain which was nine thousand feet above the sea level. Here the air was rarefied and the climate very cold. The party rested for the night beneath the roof of a resident *pandit*, who was all kindness and hospitality. The night was severely cold and the kind host covered Ramdas with thick blankets.

The ensuing day about eight o'clock the party continued their journey. They had a halt at midday for meals. At the approach of the evening they sighted Srinagar. The high hill of Shankaracharya with the temple on its top first became visible from a distance.

For the night Ramdas stayed at the house of a *pandit* of giant proportions, a relation of the friend under whose escort he had travelled on the bus. All the people of the house were kind and hospitable. Next day, making enquiries for the house of Janakinath, Ramdas shifted to his dwelling. Janakinath's younger brother, Amarnath Bakshi, welcomed him and provided him with a separate small room. Amarnath, Janakinath's daughters, children, wife and everyone in the house looked after him with great love and treated him as one of the family.

Amarnath Bakshi, a double M.A. of Punjab University, was a Professor of Philosophy in Sir Pratap College of Srinagar, and had achieved the distinction of first rank in the Presidency, both in Philosophy and Psychology. He is a noble, gentle and quiet-natured young man. He held Ramdas in high regard and was punctiliously attentive to his requirements.

Janakinath's three daughters were constantly in attendance on him. The elder two of them, pure and glorious souls—veritable goddesses tended and fed him with all the tenderness and care of a mother. Whenever they were with him he would feel that they always carried with them the fragrance of purity, simplicity and innocence. The younger children also had a great attraction for him. They would play, laugh and dance with him. While starting to school and on their return, some of them would straight come to him and embrace him with great fondness. The mother of the house also sought his society and felt very happy in his presence. Altogether his life in that blessed house was filled with inexpressible love and joy.

Ramdas resided in Kashmir for over three months. As on the Hardwar side, the pilgrimage to Badrinath and Kedarnath is considered to be of high importance, so also a visit to Amarnath is held in Kashmir to be of equally great consequence. There were still two months more for the pilgrimage and hence he had to wait in Srinagar for those months, as he did not want to lose the opportunity of running up and witnessing the sublimity of the charming mountains of Kashmir at their lofty heights.

Meanwhile, he had much to observe and much experience to gather in Srinagar and its suburbs. The early part of his stay was in the city of Srinagar. The houses are of old style, built of mud, and ill-ventilated and also thickly crowded. The lanes between them are narrow and full of filth and dirt. The principles of sanitation and laws of hygiene seemed to have played no part in the adjustment of life and house-building in the city. If one wanted to know what the slums were like, one had to walk through the streets of this city and dwell for some time in the houses that were huddled up pell-mell in this phenomenally unhealthy place.

The population consists of over ninety-five percent of Muhammadans, the rest being pundits of Kashmir. Kashmir came to be called by that name because of Kashyapa, the great sage, who lived there ages ago. The pundits are a very intelligent class and learned in Sanskrit. Now they have also a first-grade college, Sir Pratap College, which turns out brilliant men of first-rate university qualifications. They are a quiet and good-natured people with a strong and well-built physique. The extreme cold of winter, during which, it is said, the whole valley of Kashmir is overlaid with snow, serves to wash away the dirt and cesspools that accumulate in summer. The cold at other times of the year might tend, to some extent, to destroy the disease-breeding germs that the foul vapours, arising from the insanitary streets and surroundings, produce. But the general health of the people in the city is not up to the mark.

(ii) The Ways of Kashmiris

The dress of the people is characteristic of the rigours of the climatic conditions. Both the males and females wear a long toga or *pheran*, as they call it, reaching below the knees, made invariably of wool either of coarse *pattu* or of fine texture called *pashmina*. The sleeves of these gowns extend beyond the hands, the loose ends serving the purpose of gloves to protect the hands from cold. The old folk go about with the *pheran*, high-heeled wooden sandals having straps made of grass ropes covering their feet and an old-fashioned turban, while the young men use boots and shoes, tight pants, long coats and turbans after the Punjabi style.

The women adhere to their old mode of dress, the *pheran* with long sleeves. These have a small white veil covering only the back part of the head, and above the forehead they have a white celluloid band to signify that they are married. The unmarried and the widows are without this band. The ornaments the women wear are of the Muslim style; a number of thin wide rings are pierced through the edge of the ears. They have the custom of bearing the crimson mark on the forehead, which is conspicuously absent among the Punjabi ladies.

The Pandits are a fair-complexioned race. Some of the young Panditanis, Ramdas saw in Kashmir, possessed a beauty in feature and colour, which was quite unique and ethereal. Their gait was peculiarly their own. They would walk in all their majesty and stateliness like veritable queens.

The spoken language of both the Muslims and Pandits is a strange mixture of several tongues, Sanskrit, Urdu and Persian. It has no script. The written language, for business, legal and other purposes, is Urdu.

The fertile valley of Kashmir was in the past, before the advent of the British in India, a cynosure in the eyes of the Persian invaders, who raided and pillaged the place, converting by force most of the Hindu population to Islam. The present generation of Muslims in Srinagar are the descendants of Pandits converted during the invasions and reigns of Muslim kings. In language and mode of dress a Muslim and a Pandit have no difference. The distinction is made out from the absence of the sandal mark between the eye-brows on the face of the Muslim, while the mark is very prominent on that of the Pandit.

In regard to food, it is almost common between the two communities. Both of them are rice and meat eaters. The hubble-bubble used in smoking is in evidence in every house, and they have almost a craze for tea drinking, which they do four or five times a day. For keeping warm in winter they do not use the stoves employed by Europeans in their houses in Europe. They have small portable firepots called *kangdi* made of willow basket having a handle of the same material, with an earthen bowl-like vessel fitted into it. Charcoal is used to make fire in the bowl. These *kangdis* are kept within their *pheran* causing the heat to radiate all over the body underneath the gown.

The staple food being rice the cultivation is mainly of rice crops. The rice they produce is a big grain of reddish colour. The principal dish they are very fond of, and without which they can hardly relish their dinner, is *kadam ka saag. Ghee* and milk are seldom used by them. They take plenty of curds and cheese. Milk is abundant in Srinagar. Although the Muslim element is in the majority, there is no cow-slaughter in Kashmir, as the Maharaja's Government has prohibited it. The fruits of Kashmir are of the cold climate, and apples, peaches, pears, berries, etc. can be had in plenty and very cheap.

The religion of the Pandits is Shaivism and Shakti worship. They are opposed to the order of *sannyas* denoting external renunciation. There are *sadhus* among the Pandits and they are mostly house-holders leading a religious life. The Pandit is proud of his learning and intellectual attainments. He would say: "Where the Western philosophy ends, there the Eastern philosophy begins; where the Eastern philosophy ends, there the Kashmiri philosophy begins." The pandits are undoubtedly an intelligent and keen-witted race. Their status as brahmin prevented them from taking up avocations of manual labour, trade and handicrafts, in which fields the Muslims are widely employed. The world renowned Kashmir shawls are made by the skilled Muslim weavers. In wood carving, furniture making and papier-mache work the craftsmen of Kashmir are famous. Pandits go in only for the learned professions, but now these departments being overcrowded, they are slowly entering trade and other lines of employment.

Music is unknown among them. They sing in a droll and droning voice the Sanskrit *slokas* and *mantras* in chorus, their intonation having a distinctive touch of Persian accent.

The women in Srinagar are very backward in education, while the husbands are Bachelors and Masters of Arts. In many cases the wives are perfectly illiterate and except their Kashmiri jargon, a mixed language, through which alone they can convey their thoughts verbally, they have no other means of intercourse. But late or post-puberty marriages are very common among them. Often the girls are allowed to grow up to seventeen or eighteen years of age before they are married. The dowry system amongst them is as pernicious an incubus as in other parts of India.

Ramdas had an occasion to attend a marriage ceremony of the Pandits. When the ritual was in progress and the *purohits* were breathlessly chanting the *mantrams*, Ramdas went into the room where the celebration was held, to see the bride and bridegroom. The bridegroom could be seen whereas the bride was completely covered with a veil made of a thick white sheet of cloth. It is clear that many customs of the Pandits are borrowed from the Muslims, whose close contact with them, probably for centuries, has influenced them into adopting many of their customs and modes of living. Ramdas attended their marriage feast, but he did not partake of it as he was mostly on milk diet during his sojourn in Srinagar. The hundreds of guests assembled for the occasion were served food on the floor on which they were made to sit in three or four long rows, as is the vogue in other parts of India. But what struck Ramdas as uncommon was that the guests were served meals in big earthen bowls.

The relations between the Muslims and Pandits are very cordial. The Muslims, amongst whom illiteracy prevails to an amazing degree, are naturally undeveloped in moral culture, clean living and refined manners, although they are accomplished in arts, handicrafts, trade and agriculture. The Muslims have free access to the houses of Pandits. They can even enter the kitchen and the dining rooms of the Pandits.

Untouchability is unknown among Kashmiris, and in the Hindu-fold, caste distinction has no place, except that the Pandits make some difference in the various grades among themselves based upon the traditional superiority and prestige of ancestry. But there is free inter-dining and inter-marriage among all classes of Pandits.

Regarding the produce of the land, in addition to rice and fruit, of which latter, a large quantity is exported to other parts of India, the people cultivate saffron or *keshar* in special fields at the close of the summer. The soil of Kashmir is rich and alluvial.

(iii) Hari Parvat

For some days Ramdas did not move out of the house of Janakinath. The first outing was in the company of the lads of the house who took him to the playground, an oblong plot of plain land covered with a thick green turf, one side of which was bordered by an avenue of tall poplars. He watched the sports of the boys. Here he came in touch with some educated Muslims who surrounded him on the turf and put him various questions on religious and spiritual matters. Since his sympathies were alike for all the religions of the world, he spoke sometimes in English and again in Hindi about the greatness of the Prophet Mohammed and the value of the teachings of Koran. They eagerly listened to his expositions and evinced friendliness and love for him.

He was paying every evening a visit to the playground for some days. Then the young friends escorted him to Hari Parvat. Hari Parvat is a hill situated about a mile from the city of Srinagar. The Pandits look upon this hill with great reverence since there is also a temple of a goddess on one side at its top. They give a religious significance to a walk round the hill, for which purpose hundreds of Pandits and their women are seen every morning pouring out of their congested houses. The morning exercise and the fresh air in the open also tend to a great extent to counteract the evil effects upon their health due to the unhealthy vapours of the dirty city in which they live most of the time. The stroll and a *darshan* of the goddess on the hill they consider as nothing short of a religious duty, since on each such occasion they can withdraw their minds entirely from the cares of the world to the thought of God.

On the other side of the hill is a neatly-built fortress, once the strong-hold of the old kings of Kashmir. Ramdas visited the temple of the goddess, who is represented by a huge rock, flat on the side facing those who go to it for *darshan*. This flat surface is covered over by a thick layer of red paint and decorated with flowers and flower garlands. There are a few resident Pandits inside the temple building who are the worshippers of the goddess.

He was attracted by the cool and bracing breeze on top of the hill and spent a night alone on a stone slab lying about fifty yards in front of the *Devi*'s temple. The deep love which Amarnath bore for Ramdas made him display great anxiety about him at this time. He remained on the hill till evening on the ensuing day. Amarnath visited him in the morning and arranged for his milk. The legend goes that the hill was the trysting place of *Sapta-Rishis*—the seven ancient sages, the invisible guides and teachers of mankind.

Ramdas had frequent occasions to roam around this hill. Along the path is a small temple in charge of *sannyasis*. When he visited this temple he came in contact with a young *sannyasi*, Anand Swarup of the Gowd Saraswat Community and native of Cochin State. He had his residence in a small room in the upper storey of a rest-house near the temple. He was a sincere *sadhaka* who lived a retired life, filling his hours with a deep study of the scriptures and in spiritual discipline and contemplation. Ramdas enjoyed many blissful hours in his company. He was so kind and loving to Ramdas.

The main river of Kashmir is Jhelum, or Vitatsa as the Pandits name it, a tributary of the Indus. The river flows right through the middle of Srinagar and on both the banks of it are studded the residences of Pandits and Muslims of the place. The habitat in many cases project out into the river, supported on wooden posts. The river is held very sacred by the Pandits, but all the drains of the city empty themselves into it and render its water thick, dark, muddy and impure. The Pandits wash and bathe in the waters of this stream. Long and slim boats which they call *kisti* ply on the river. The boats are manned by Muslims. For pleasure-trips and sight-seeing these light boats are largely employed by the populace. *Kistiwalas* carry on a roaring business. A number of wooden bridges are constructed across the river to connect opposite banks.

One day a student friend, who was visiting Ramdas at Janakinath's house, proposed to take him up the Shankaracharya hill. He and Ramdas boarded a *kisti*. The skiff glided up the river until it came to a landing place at the foot of the hill. After a short walk they reached the bottom of the hill, where there was an ashram of *sannyasis*. The spot is called Durga Nag, because of a pure spring in the compound of the ashram—Nag meaning a spring.

(iv) Shankaracharya Hill

The friend and Ramdas now started ascending the Shankaracharya hill. The hill is a thousand feet above the level of the Kashmir valley. As they climbed higher and higher, Ramdas felt as if a screen was slowly being lifted to reveal the grandiose beauty of Kashmir. They reached the top, and a sweeping look all round thrilled Ramdas with a feeling of inexpressible ecstasy. The extensive and picturesque valley was now before him. The stately mountains tinted with a subtle blending of blue and heliotrope and crowned by dazzling flakes of snow were standing in all their dignity at the borders of the valley all round, like guardian angels of the land.

The vast lakes, scattered all over the valley, scintillated in the sun like huge mirrors reflecting the glory of the mountains and the groves of trees covered with green foliage. The Dal Lake, the largest of them, at the base of the hill on which he was viewing the scene, bore on her placid bosom big red lotus flowers, beside which swans gambolled and sported.

From the height, Hari Parvat was seen as a small mound of earth, the brown walls of the fortress standing out prominently on its top. Then again the river Jhelum: she was running in a zigzag course like a huge serpent creeping through the enchanting valley. The grey, dull houses in the city were visible from a long distance. What with the flashes of water, the greenery of the vegetation, the multi-hued mountain ranges and the clear blue sky above, the scenery was such that his eyes feasted on the sublimity of God's fascinating creation or manifestation.

He turned his attention to the temple. It is constructed of blocks of granite stones, oval in shape at the top and ending in a dome. It has a raised square platform on its sides. A flight of stone steps leads the visitor to the sanctum sanctorum in which the phallic emblem of Shiva, an image about three feet high, smooth and polished, stands. A *sadhu* is in constant attendance in the temple during the day-time. At the top of the temple dome and all round, at the lower ground level, are installed electric flashlights with huge reflectors. These are said to be a gift made by the Maharaja of Mysore during his visit to Srinagar. In the night, even from long distances from the valley below, these lights illumine the location and structure of the temple.

The great Vedantin, Sri Shankaracharya, when he visited Kashmir in his parivrajak or itinerant life, is said to have made his stay on this hill, and it was at his initiative that the temple of Shiva was first established on the hill. Hence to this day the hill is called after his name. The Pandits have a story in connection with Sri Shankaracharya's visit.

Sri Shankaracharya and his disciples took their abode on the top of this hill for several days, and none of the Pandits of Srinagar went up to see them and accorded them hospitality. So the sage and his disciples had to go without food and water. After some days a few Pandits paid a visit to him on the hill.

Now the sage observed: "We have been starving here for many days and you, great and learned as you are, did not think it fit to offer us the hospitality which the *shastras* enjoin on every human being as his or her *dharma*."

To this the Pandit replied: "The fault is not ours. We would certainly welcome and treat with respect and kindness those guests who would visit our city, but since you have chosen to occupy a hill, far away from the city, avoiding and renouncing the life of the world, in which also the Lord's power and glory are manifest, we are justified in our attitude towards you and your disciples. As regards your starvation, you need not have undergone it if you had possessed the yogic power by the exercise of which you could have provided yourself with all that you needed."

Sri Shankaracharya was a monist or adwaitist who looked upon the world as illusion. Probably he did not then believe in God's *Shakti* in manifestation.

He replied: "The world is an illusion. It has no existence although it seems to be existing to one whose mind is obsessed by ignorance."

"You are mistaken." retorted the Pandits, "The world does exist, it is the expression of divine *Shakti*, the supreme cause of creation, protection and destruction of all the visible forms that comprise the universe. External renunciation of the world is a folly springing from a false conception of God and His power. *Shakti* is sporting in the vast phenomena of life, change and movement in the universe. The true vision does not discard the world as non-existent but looks upon it as the manifestation of God, the *lila* of His *Shakti*."

To show Sri Shankaracharya an example of the workings of *Shakti*, it is said that a Pandit invoked the goddess with the incantation of a *mantra* and touched a spot on the ground where they sat, and instantly water as from a fountain oozed out of the ground.

The Pandits say that Sri Shankaracharya was greatly impressed by the teachings and the exhibition of God's power by the Pandits, and had to change his line of thought for the one represented by the Pandits.

In the Vision of God

CHAPTER 36: KASHMIR (*continued*)

(i) The Lake of the Mind

Another day which was a Sunday, Amarnath Bakshi took Ramdas out on an excursion to the famous gardens of Kashmir, Shalimar and Nishad Bag. In order to reach the gardens they had to slide over the glassy surface of the Dal Lake on a *kisti*. The boat passed through the river and the canals that led up to the lake, displaying as it proceeded, willows and dense vegetation along the banks of the canals. An hour's trip brought them at the landing of the Nishad Bag.

They made their way inside the garden. The scene that now spread out before the gaze of Ramdas was of exquisite charm and grace. The garden was symmetrical in its formation; a wide sheet of pure sparkling water like a band was running down, right through the middle of the garden grounds. On both sides of this shallow stream were laid out carefully designed beds of flower plants and trees of various species. The yellow and blue, crimson and white, violet and orange colours of the flowers vied with one another in lending a bewitching charm to this floral picture, painted in nature's own variegated tints. The rose, the lily, the chrysanthemum, the marigold, the carnation, the daisy, the violet and the bluebell displayed their brilliant freshness in profusion.

The evergreen cone-shaped fir trees and the giant chenar, a tree peculiar to Kashmir, cast their deep but cool shade in the garden. As they walked up the plot which is made up into several flats, he saw hundreds of fountains at work sending forth their spray twenty feet up into the air. On a higher level in the centre of the garden is situated a solid structure supported on polished stone pillars. The surrounding view of the garden is also most imposing. The garden is laid out at the foot of mountains which form its background with the extended stretch of the Dal Lake in its front.

The Shalimar garden is in several respects an exact replica of the Nishad Bag. These gardens were first put up by Shahjahan and Jehangir, the famous Moghul kings. These picturesque grounds are indeed the paradise of the Muhammadans.

While on their return journey by the same *kisti* in which they had proceeded to the gardens, Amarnath narrated a legal perplexity with which the magistrates of Kashmir were confronted. While in other places movable property, such as money and other articles are subjects of theft, here landed property is also stolen. The lakes have a thick growth of stout reeds and these areas are converted into floating fields for cultivation. Bits of these fields are often cut off by the owners of the adjoining fields with thieving propensities, and are slid over the surface of the water and tacked on to their own, which action results in law suits. By evening the party returned to the city.

Ramdas also paid visits to Vicharnag, a place shaded by giant chenar trees and with a tank famous for its sanctity, and Ram Bagh with its beautiful flower gardens and the storied *dharmashala* for travellers, both the sites being outside the city precincts.

Another day he made a trip to Harvan, a charming retreat, nine miles from Srinagar. The landscape, the lake and the running stream of dazzling water with the background of high mountains full of vegetation comprised a most fascinating sight. He felt the subtle spell of the place. The lake stood on a higher level facing the mountains. When he first saw it, a soft breeze was blowing over its bosom moving the limpid, transparent waters into ripples that suffused its surface. During the half-hour's saunter amidst the attractive scenes he directed his gaze again to the lake. The breeze had stopped and the lake shone like a huge mirror, its surface now placid, calm and still, reflecting the glorious picture of the surrounding mountains.

Pointing to the lake, Ramdas remarked to Amarnath: "The human mind can be compared to this lake. When the breeze of *maya* sweeps on the lake of the mind, waves of desire rise, disturbance ensues, but no sooner does *maya* cease to play on it than it becomes calm and peaceful as it is seen now, revealing a vision of unsurpassed splendour and joy." Before dark they got back to Srinagar.

Being of a sincere and lovable nature, Amarnath was acutely feeling the separation of Janakinath, his elder brother, who with many other pundits of his departments, by a strange act of the Kashmir Government, was ordered to remain in Jammu for all seasons of the year. About the time of Ramdas's departure from Jammu, a post in the department had become vacant in Srinagar for which Janakinath was eligible, and he had applied for it. Amarnath was in his anxiety exerting all his influence with the authorities to bring about the desired transfer. He would every day, during this time, come to Ramdas.

"Swamiji, do pray for the success of my brother," he would say, "Janakinath is so unhappy at Jammu in this hot weather and his family here is also miserable on account of his absence from their midst."

Ramdas would then simply assure him; "Trust God. Give up anxiety and all will be well."

Day after day was spent by the brother and the family on the tender-hooks of expectation. A week thus passed. One day Amarnath came to him and reported with a face bright and smiling: "Swamiji, at last my brother got the appointment. I have a wire from him to say that he will be here in a short time to join the post; this is all your kindness."

"God be praised for it," replied Ramdas. "It is all His doing."

Before the end of the next week Janakinath was in Srinagar. The first thing he did, as he entered his house, was to rush up to the room in which Ramdas lived, take him in his arms and clasp him in a fast and fond embrace lasting for several minutes. Now the whole household brightened up with cheer and happiness.

(ii) Kabir and Uddhav

During his stay in Kashmir, Ramdas had to carry on a large amount of correspondence with the friends in different parts of India. Once he received a letter from U. Sanjivarao of Bombay asking him to see a Saraswat of North Kanara who was then holding a prominent post under the State Government. Durgadas Nagarkatte was the Director of Industries for Kashmir State. The letter also spoke of his ailment, bone tuberculosis, that affected his legs as a result of which he was completely disabled from walking except on crutches. Ramdas understood that Durgadas was a busy man and so would not have thrust himself on him (Durgadas), had the thought of his physical condition not moved Ramdas. However, he took Sanjivarao's suggestion and in company with two Pandits proceeded to Durgadas's residence. The party was made to wait in his office-tent in front of his bungalow, while Ramdas had to send him a note as a visiting card. He mentioned in the note simply that he was a *sadhu* from Kanara and had directions to see him.

Even after twenty minutes' waiting there was no response to the note. Word was then sent to him to know definitely if he would like to grant Ramdas an interview. The only reply that he got was that Durgadas was far from eager to receive him!

Now Ramdas turning to the Pandits said: "God's will seems to be that he should not see Durgadas. So we shall retrace our steps to Janakinath's." While returning they saw the huge pile of building of the Industrial School. The Pandits proposed to have a look around the school. Accordingly they entered the building and passed from chamber to chamber examining the products of various industries, in which a practical course of training was given to the students by experts employed for the purpose. The experts were most affable and obliging to Ramdas. When he entered a class room where a batch of students was receiving theoretical instructions, the teacher resigned his seat to him, who converted the class for a short half-hour into one of religious instruction. He delivered a discourse on God, devotion and His Name. Both the teacher and the boys were highly elated by his presence and the talk.

Leaving this room the party finished the inspection on the ground floor and ascended upstairs. Here they entered a research laboratory where a couple of students were engaged in some experiments. One of them led the party to the office room of the professor in charge, an Indian, seated at his table. Seeing him the professor welcomed him and offered a chair. He sat down. In the course of his talk Ramdas told him how he was refused audience by Durgadas. The professor had taken a sudden liking for him.

"There must be some mistake. Durgadas does not know you, but would certainly be happy to see you," eagerly said the professor and added: "I shall send a boy to let him know about you and see that you get an interview with him. Meanwhile, please wait here."

He at once despatched a student to Durgadas's bungalow. In the meantime the kind professor showed him many pieces of intricate apparatus intended for various works of research. Ramdas looked through a microscope and saw a speck of wheat flour as big as a pea. These scientific instruments can reveal only things perceptible to the senses but in the field of spirit they are utterly useless, because the vision of the spirit can be had by the sole aid of a super-consciousness which is beyond the sphere of the senses.

Soon after this, a young man came from Durgadas's house-hold to fetch him. Ramdas met Durgadas in his office. He was an elderly man, tall and of dark complexion. He attempted to rise from the chair when Ramdas entered the room, but his complaint prevented him from doing so. He pointed to a chair in front of him and Ramdas sat down. A few words explained to him the reason of Ramdas's visit. He gave a short account of his disease and then called for some refreshments for Ramdas from which he drank a cup of milk. He was then on mere milk diet. Durgadas was evidently a busy man. He was engaged with a visitor when Ramdas went to him and many others were waiting outside for their turn. Now Ramdas stood up to depart, but Durgadas would not have it so.

"You have been so long in Srinagar," he said, "and I had no opportunity to have you with me. I will not allow you to go until you have spent some days at our house as well."

His repeated appeals induced Ramdas to remain. The Pandit-escorts who were waiting outside were told of the decision and they took leave and returned to their homes. Ramdas had stipulated two conditions for his stay: one was that he would during the time live only on milk diet and that the following day he should be permitted to go back to the city as he had shortly to leave for Amarnath on pilgrimage. Durgadas would not agree to the latter condition.

Ramdas was given a separate spacious room on the upper floor of his palatial residence and was provided with every convenience. The mothers of the house were extremely kind in their attentions. Here Ramdas had the constant society of Durgadas's two little sons, Kabir and Uddhav. Ramdas enjoyed their playful society and lisping talks. On account of his disability, Durgadas could not come up to the room in which Ramdas lived. Next day, in the afternoon, Ramdas went down and directly going to his office-room announced his desire to leave for the city. Expostulation was useless. The young man of the house had to take him back to Janakinath's where he was welcomed by all in the household with manifest delight.

About this time he received a letter from mother Elizabeth written at the instance of Raja Ram, the Thakur Saheb of Limbdi. Raja Ram offered to furnish him with a note of introduction to the Maharaja of Kashmir, Hari Singh, if he felt an inclination to see him. Ramdas replied that Ram did not prompt him from within to go in for a *darshan* of the Maharaja, but might agree in the matter, if the Maharaja himself had expressed a desire to see him. So he asked Raja Ram to correspond with the Maharaja and know his mind. He had nothing to gain by seeing anybody. He was controlled and guided by Ram in all things. As the matter was dropped, nothing further came of it.

(iii) The Mysterious Ways of God

Ramdas's stay in Srinagar by this time had extended over two months and the coveted pilgrimage to Amarnath was fast approaching. Janakinath argued with Ramdas a great deal and made an attempt to dissuade him from the proposed pilgrimage. He expatiated on the severity of the cold in that region and the difficult ascents on the hills that led up to it. But Ramdas was determined.

Ramcharandas now suddenly turned up. He was very emaciated and his feet were worn out and full of blisters. Since they separated near Pathankot in Punjab, he said that he had to undergo most dreadful trials and hardships. What with the cold, continuous tramping on foot and often starvation, he had been reduced to a terrible plight. With perfect rest, added to the tender care and nursing of the loving daughters of Janakinath, he soon became his old self.

In the company of Mother Taravati, wife of Janakinath and her small children, Ramdas and Ramcharandas went for the *darshan* of Khir Bhavani about ten miles from the city. This shrine is situated beneath the vast spreading branches of the chenar with the river Sindhu flowing on two sides of it. It is noted for the temple of the Goddess Bhavani. The temple, a small structure, is in the centre of the grounds erected at the edge of a deep rectangular pit constructed of brick and cement. This pit is intended for receiving presents of rice and milk pudding offered to the goddess. This is her favourite *prasad*; hence her name Khir Bhavani. The accumulation of pudding thrown into the pit by hundreds of devotees, who daily visit the shrine, gave out a stench that filled the atmosphere. No effort was made to keep the pit clean—maybe there was some religious significance in allowing the pudding to rot in the pit.

Mother Taravati performed her *puja* of the goddess with the help of a Pandit priest. By evening they returned to Janakinath's house at Srinagar.

"How do you like the spot Khir Bhavani?" asked Janakinath.

"The place is all right but it is a pity that the goddess should be imprisoned for all time in the midst of the most nauseating odour emanating from *khir kund*," replied Ramdas.

"True, that is also my opinion," he said laughing.

One evening, a short time before the day fixed for starting on the pilgrimage to Amarnath, Janakinath said to Ramdas: "Swamiji, I wish so much I could accompany you on the pilgrimage to Amarnath, but God's will is different. My new appointment does not admit of my taking leave just at present. However, one of my relations with his family intends going. He will have a tent of his own. I have requested him to include you and Ramcharandas in his party and he has agreed. I am also arranging for warm clothing for you both'"

The day of the departure came. It was to be on the morrow. The previous evening Janakinath met Ramdas with a downcast face, his heart sorely disturbed. The fact was, his relation had turned turtle at almost the last hour with regard to taking Ramdas with him to Amarnath, and had sent word to that effect. Hence the dejection on the face of the friend.

"Swamiji," he said, "it appears to be the will of God that you should not go to Amarnath; else my relation would not have withdrawn his promise at the last minute."

At this Ramdas drew himself up, and his body stiffened with a grim determination.

"Ramji," Ramdas replied in a firm and measured tone, looking directly into the eyes of Janakinath, "do you think that Ramdas proposed to start on the journey to Amarnath depending on your relation? God, whose servant and child he is, had put the idea into his head and it is His duty to see that it is fulfilled. There is nothing impossible for the Lord. He will yet see that Ramdas is safely led to the shrine of Amarnath."

Now Janakinath, who was observing the mood in which Ramdas was and the force with which he spoke, calmly replied: "Well, Swamiji, I am mistaken. Surely there could be no obstacle for you when you have resolved upon doing a thing." The subject was then dropped.

On the banks of the Jhelum there is a temple of Shiva, only about fifty yards from Janakinath's house. The *pujari* of the temple, Tarachand Bayu, a young man who had great love and regard for Ramdas, used to visit Janakinath's house to see and have talks with him. Some of the old type Pandits can understand Hindi and also talk in that language with a mixture of Urdu words. Ramdas mostly talked in Hindi with the ladies and Pandits who were not English educated. Tarachand Bayu would take Ramdas to his temple for bath in the river. Many an evening he had spent in the shrine listening to the reading of Yoga Vasishta in Hindi and attending the evening *puja* in the temple, when Sanskrit *slokas* and *mantras* were sung in chorus by a dozen devotees who would be present at the time of worship.

On the morning of the day when Ramdas had to start on the pilgrimage to Amarnath, Tarachand Bayu dropped in and escorted him to the temple. Ramcharandas was also with him. After bath Ramdas sat in front of the image on an *asan* provided by the *pujari*. The time might have been about eight o'clock. A young Pandit, who was a perfect stranger to Ramdas, entered the temple in haste. He had come on a bicycle and inquired for Ramdas. The *pujari* brought the Pandit into the presence of Ramdas.

"Swamiji," the young man said to Ramdas, "my father is making ready for the trip to Amarnath. He wishes to take you also with him. Kindly come with me. He is awaiting your arrival at home."

Strange are the ways of God! Here is a Pandit utterly unknown to Ramdas voluntarily proposing to have him as his companion on the trip. He followed the young guide, and told him that he would have to see Janakinath first and inform him of his intended departure. So they went to Janakinath's house and apprised the friend of the arrangement made by God for the pilgrimage. Janakinath, on hearing of it, was spell-bound. Until then it had seemed that there was not the least chance of Ramdas's leaving that day. The mysterious and sudden way in which God brought about circumstances that favoured his going struck Janakinath as purely the work of Providence. The Lord after all did not will that Ramdas should abandon the idea. Ramdas for his part was absolutely confident that he would go on the pilgrimage.

The warm dress intended for Ramdas and Ramcharandas was still with the tailor unfinished. A woollen cap and double-breast jacket were intended for Ramdas and a long cloak of the same material for Ramcharandas. Ramdas did not care for the clothes. He felt God's command had come and it was his to obey at any cost. So with two small pieces of *khaddar* cloth he started. It was decided that Ramcharandas should start on the following day with the woollen dress and meet Ramdas at Mattan or Martand, the first stage in the journey where there would be a halt for two days. Ramdas duly reached the pilgrim Pandit's house where he had his meal. The Pandit was an elderly man, tall and strongly built. By twelve o'clock they got into a motor-bus which carried them by evening to Mattan.

CHAPTER 37: THE PILGRIMAGE TO AMARNATH

(i) The Scuffle Over Ramdas

At night Ramdas and the pilgrim Pandit were lodged in a house of another Pandit, a resident of Mattan and friend of the escort. Next morning Ramdas came out of the house to have a view round. The importance of Mattan lies firstly in its clear spring of water which is collected in a small reservoir kept scrupulously clean and in which fishes sport—it is a delight to see and drink and bathe in this cool, transparent water—and secondly in the old ruins of the Marthand temple at a higher altitude. He paid a visit to the ruins; except for the outer fallen walls and a dilapidated middle arched door-way, there remains nothing of the temple. The ruins strike the observer with an idea of the majesty, hugeness and solidity of the structure when it was sound and whole. He spent an hour amidst these ruins, witnessing the surrounding landscape. The temple was of God Marthand, hence the name.

Another morning, as he was tramping along the main road towards a cave, a mile and a half from Mattan, he met at the outskirts a crowd gathered on the road. When he neared it he heard a violent altercation in progress between a Pandit and a sparsely clothed *sadhu*. From their talk Ramdas could make out that the *sadhu* had beaten a Pandit in his own house for refusing to give him some firewood for which the *sadhu* had gone a-begging to his door. There was a commotion over the affair.

Ramdas passed on and reached the wayside hill. Ascending a few yards he came up to the narrow mouth of a cave. A little away, at the front of the cave to its right, was seated a girl in *sannyasi* robes before a fire. He was drawn to the place. By her side was a shallow gap in the hill which she had made her temporary abode. She was quite happy to see him and he took a seat before her at the fire. She had some milk which she heated on the fire and presented to him, and he drank the beverage sweetened with her pure love. She was a cheerful, free and dauntless girl—such are indeed of the kingdom of happiness.

With a lighted splinter of wood provided by the *sannyasini* and which burnt like a candle, Ramdas entered the dark, narrow alley leading to the cave which was in the bosom of the elevated hill. The walls of the passage and the interior of the cave were dripping with water issuing from a hidden spring. There were two compartments in the cave, in the larger of them was the *murti* of Mahadev, and in the other, a raised slab of stone under which, it was said, lay the bones of a saint who had lived there and given up his body. After a few minutes' inspection of the cave he came out, and bidding adieu to the young mother returned to Mattan.

Ramdas marked a look of anxiety on the face of the Pandit-escort. When questioned about it he disclosed the reason with great hesitation.

"Maharaj" he said, "the thing that worries me is this. We have to start higher up tomorrow or day after. As we ascend the hills the cold will become more and more severe. I have brought blankets and clothing sufficient only for one, whereas you do not possess any for your use except the inadequate cotton sheets. I was told that some warm clothing would be sent to you through a friend of yours, but so far there is no sign of him. What shall we do?"

"Leave the matter to Ram. He will see to it, please don't worry." Ramdas replied.

Bus-load after bus-load of pilgrims was arriving at Mattan throughout the day and he was set upon by the Pandit the task of watching the arrival of Ramcharandas. Till half-past-four he sat on a low wall of a bridge where the incoming motor-buses halted.

Suddenly a young man, dressed in the latest fashion of Srinagar, and high yellow turban, came towards him and taking him by arm said: "There you are, Ramdas, I have caught you. You are to go with me to Amarnath. Although you may not remember me, I have seen you at the Nishad Bag with Amarnath Bakshi who was my teacher and is now a great friend of mine. He has asked me to take care of you; come along. I am a doctor. My name too is Amarnath. I go with the hospital camp that travels with the pilgrims as far as Amarnath with the object of looking after the health of the pilgrims. I have myself a separate tent in which you are quite welcome. You will not be wanting in warm clothes and blankets. I have plenty of them to spare for you."

Ram takes Ramdas always by surprise.

"Ramji," Ramdas spoke to the doctor, "Ramdas came here in the company of a Pandit who has been very kind to him. Ramdas must let him know of the new arrangement."

"Come with me first," he said with a mock authority which was always his way; such a kind and loving soul he was! "I do not want you to slip out of my hands. Come with me to my tent. I know the Pandit you speak of. I shall send for him and talk the matter over with him. You need not bother about it."

Catching Ramdas by the arm the doctor led him to a tent pitched on a flat plot of ground under the shade of trees. Having him seated in a chair the doctor sent a servant of his to fetch the Pandit. The Pandit came and saw Ramdas snugly lolling on a chair. Ramdas now became a quiet listener to the talk in the Kashmiri tongue between the doctor and the Pandit. His stay for months in their midst had given him so much insight into their language that he could make out the trend of their talk. There ensured a war of words between them. The Pandit did not like to part with Ramdas. He went to the length of assuring the doctor that he would provide Ramdas with clothing and blankets. The scuffle went on for about half-an-hour and the doctor in the end came off triumphant. The Pandit left the place grumbling and disappointed.

At dusk by the last motor-bus Ramcharandas also turned up. He had brought the woollen dress for himself and also for Ramdas. The same evening Ramdas met a relation of the doctor, who arranged to provide him with a long woollen cloak and an umbrella. God, when He wills to shower His favour on His children, does so unasked and in such profusion that they get dazed and bewildered.

On the following day the crowd of pilgrims moved onward and the hospital camp followed suit—so also Ramdas and Ramcharandas with two sturdy Pandits, servants of the doctor, who kept him company. The doctor rode on horseback.

By evening they reached the second stage of their journey, Phelgaon. The hospital camp was fixed on a vast plain near the bank of the river. Now Phelgaon is a most captivating place—lofty mountains on one side, a dense forest of firs and tall poplars on the other, and the smooth running river in the plateau of the valley. The vast open space with the enchanting borders lent sublimity and a unique fascination to the place. The glorious landscapes of Kashmir have been attracting tourists from various parts of the world. The charm and beauty of the landscapes, it is said, compare favourably with the world-famous sights and views of Switzerland.

In Phelgaon, in the thick crowds of pilgrims, Ramdas discovered Balak Ram Paramahams. When he so unexpectedly met Ramdas his joy knew no bounds. Ramdas found him still a slave to *ganja* smoking. He asked Ramdas for a cloth, and he parted with the spare one he had. He later learnt that Balak Ram had not been permitted to proceed further up to Amarnath by the police as he ran amok and began to assault the peaceful pilgrims, and the police drove him out of Srinagar to Rawalpindi.

When Ramdas returned to the camp he found that many new friends had joined the party, including some *vakils* and professors. Dr. Amarnath came to know that Ramdas had given away a cloth, and he took Ramdas roundly to task for what he considered a foolish act. He undertook the charge of Ramdas's spare clothes. Ramdas scarcely used the long gown, the gift of the doctor's relation. Particularly this cloak the doctor packed covertly in his kit. Whenever Ramdas put it on, a guard was kept on him so that he might not give it away.

At noon he met a white missionary who became very friendly with him. Ramdas spoke to him of God, Love and Christ. He was immensely pleased and proposed to arrange for a sermon by Ramdas in their church on his return from Amarnath.

(ii) Ramdas Rapt in the Vision

As far as Phelgaon the road was level. From Phelgaon commenced the uphill path. The winding path made the ascent easy, and Ramdas with the friends walked at a brisk pace and reached Chandanwadi long before sunset. The landscapes of Chandanwadi possessed their own unique charm. The scenes were most inspiring. Here the river rushed down-hill at a rapid speed. At Chandanwadi the pilgrims halted for a night. Ramdas was so well taken care of by the doctor that, at night, he would particularly see that Ramdas was covered with two blankets. The other friends also loved him with great zeal. But Ramcharandas did not get on amicably with the Pandits and so he kept away from the tent and threw in his lot with the *sadhus* in the open air.

Next day the party moved onwards. Ramdas was furnished by the first Pandit, with whom he had come as far as Mattan, with a pair of canvas shoes, which he put on for about thirty miles, but finding them an encumbrance threw them away. He was now going bare-footed. Except the woollen cap which he was wearing off and on, the woollen jacket and the bit of *khaddar* cloth, he had no other dress. He liked to have the body light so that he could freely run on the hills.

As Ramdas ascended higher and higher he viewed a most beautiful natural scenery that filled him with rapturous delight. The ground was now all along carpeted with short plants and grass, bearing multi-coloured blooms as though fresh blossoms were sprinkled and strewn all the way for a festive occasion.

The next stage of their halt was Vavjin. A few miles beyond Phelgaon there is a place called Nilganga where the pilgrims consider it holy to have a bath in the river. The water of the river was very cold. Ramdas, going up to the brink of the river, where a crowd of pilgrims had assembled for bath, divested himself of his clothing, and with a bare *kaupin* on jumped into the river near its bank and had three dips. When he came out of the water his body was benumbed and stiff with cold. The Pandits who accompanied him rubbed his body briskly with a woollen napkin and dressed him again, and made him drink a cup of hot tea which they were carrying in a thermos flask. Onward ran Ramdas followed by the Pandits, and by evening arrived at the high plateau of Vavjin.

Vavjin, in other words, Vayu Jin, that is Jinnee of the hurricane, is a place where furious blasts of icy cold winds are blowing at all times, often accompanied by rain. The spot is therefore wet and chilly. Pilgrims with sparse warm clothing suffered intensely from the cold here.

Here the first Pandit-escort invited Ramdas to his tent for dinner, where he met an elderly man, an Inspector of schools, in whose company Ramdas ascended a hill on the plateau. The Inspector left Ramdas half way up and climbed down, as the chill breezes were too much for him. Moreover, it began to rain. Ramdas and Ramcharandas scaled the summit of the hill and descended before dark.

Passing the night at Vavjin, the next day they prosecuted their march. About nine o'clock they reached a place called Sheshnag. The cold was now becoming increasingly rigorous. Sheshnag is a vast circular natural reservoir of water, a gigantic cavity in the mountains resembling a tub with one of its sides open. The water was of dazzling purity with a bluish grey tint. Ramdas and the party approached the margin of the spherical lake and found the water icy cold.

Turning to Ramcharandas he said: "Ramji, remove your clothing, let us have a bath in the lake." Ramcharandas shrank from the prospect.

"The water is extremely cold," he said: "do not let us bathe here."

"No, Ram, it is essential that we should have a bath in this lake. Ramdas will take his dips near the bank as he is not used to swimming, whereas you ought to take a jump into the water and have a good swim. You are young and a spirited youth. You have no cause to hesitate. Come along," urged Ramdas.

Reluctantly the lad doffed the snug and warm cloak that covered his body, while Ramdas also divested himself of his scanty garment. He first entered the water and when he came to a depth in which the water stood up to his chest, he asked Ramcharandas to take the leap, which he did, swimming for about five minutes before returning to the bank. Ramdas after three dips also gained his place. The Pandits were ready to rub and dry his body with their coarse towels.

Then the party went forward and came to Panchatarni by evening. Panchatarni is a flat valley in the midst of high mountains covered with thick layers of silvery snow. The river here was flowing at a slow pace. The pilgrims pitched their tents near the bank of the river. It must be noted that in these higher regions the sun shone dimly through a thick grey mist, and the air was surcharged with a biting cold. The haze lent a weird charm to the view of the chequered verdure and the snow-capped mountains.

About five o'clock a young man of Peshawar, Shambunath, alighted from his horse. He was dressed after the European fashion. He came to the spot where Ramdas stood gazing on the snows of the hills, rapt in the vision. Ramdas could not resist giving vent to his feelings.

"What a wonderful spectacle; how sublime is this manifestation of God! He has assumed various forms, but this particular one unfolding before our sight is simply glorious. Look all round; everywhere it is He, in the snow, the mountain, the river and the green valley "

Ramdas stopped. Thoughts melted away and words failed. For, the scene was simply indescribable! Shambunath listened with concentration to Ramdas's outburst and a change came over him. His face erstwhile pale and gloomy brightened and a smile played about it.

"Swamiji, I am blest by your *darshan*," cried out the young man, "I was sinking under dejection which I feared to be a precursor of illness. The sight of you and your exalting utterance have lifted me from depression. I now feel braced up and cheerful. I am fortunate in having met you."

Later, he introduced Ramdas to his mother, a very pious lady, and his other friends, who showered kindness and love on Ramdas.

(iii) A Woman in Distress—Amarnath Cave

Panchatarni is only four miles from the shrine of Amarnath. The pilgrims usually settle down here and go up for a few hours for the *darshan* of Amarnath and return to their tents in Pancha-tarni. Night passed and it was planned that the party in the doctor's tent should start on the short journey at about nine o'clock the next morning, return by one o'clock, and leave Panchatarni that very day and pass Vavjin the same night.

About eight o'clock an incident happened in the doctor's tent which needs to be chronicled here. The doctor and the Pandit friends occupying the tent were accustomed to massage Ramdas's legs by turns. They took great pleasure in doing this service. When Ramdas was seated in the tent at Panchatarni, the doctor and another friend divided between themselves Ramdas's legs, and were busy massaging them. At this juncture, an old female pilgrim, emaciated and weak, came to the front of the tent and cried out in distress. Her whole frame was shivering with cold as she had only a thin cotton saree covering her body. She piteously appealed for some warm clothing. Her repeated supplications fell upon deaf ears. None in the tent would condescend to part with a single piece of woollen cloth for the suffering beggar woman. The friends had brought plenty of dress and covering to stand against the cold, and so Ramdas thought that they could help the poor woman in her hour of need.

When Ramdas suggested some assistance to the woman, they declined to give it offering the excuse that they could not spare anything. Ramdas was put in mind of the woollen gown which had been presented to him and was now in the keeping of the doctor. Ramdas requested the doctor to hand over the gown to the woman. Even this the whole party opposed.

"The gown is for your use, Swamiji," said the doctor; "I cannot give it to the woman."

"Well, friends," Ramdas then asked turning to the doctor, "why are you so fond of pressing Ramdas's legs? What do you get thereby?"

"We feel happy when we do so," replied the doctor.

"Ramdas permits you to do him this service, because it grants you joy, while you would not give him happiness by yielding to his will in the matter of presenting the gown to the woman whose need of it is far greater than that of Ramdas," said Ramdas.

Then Ramdas suddenly drawing up his legs challenged the friends by the remark: "Ramdas denies you this happiness since you are not willing to give him delight by relieving the distress of the beggar woman."

This attitude of Ramdas produced the desired effect on the doctor and friends. The doctor at once fetched the woollen cloak from the hiding place and threw it on Ramdas, and he in his turn immediately transferred it to the needy old woman.

"Now here, do as much massaging as you like," and Ramdas stretched out his folded legs. And they fell to the task.

Shortly after this they started for the *darshan* of Amarnath. A four-mile walk through a narrow winding path at the edge of a hill brought them to an open, uneven and rocky vale, the river running to its right and an immense cavity gaping out of the side of the mountain to the left. Ramdas missed Ramcharandas. He was lost in the vast and confused mass of pilgrims who were reckoned to be over thirteen thousand.

After bath in the river, Ramdas made his way to the cave. The cave, a natural hollow in the mountains, is enormous in size with a wide open mouth. Already hundreds of pilgrims had assembled in it. The place where worship is offered has a *Shiva-linga* made of snow. Ramdas could not gain a view of the *murti* as it was completely hidden beneath the presents of cloths, etc. thrown over it by the pilgrims. On the right and left of the *Shiva-linga* are huge blocks of snow which represent Parvati and Ganesh. Ramdas has heard it said that Shiva's *murti* grows in size during the first fortnight of the month with the waxing of the moon and becomes smaller in dimension with the waning of it. Ramdas also saw a couple of white doves sporting on the rugged ceiling of the cave. Now hereby hangs a legend:

In the days of yore, when God Shiva and his consort Parvati resided in the cave, at the request of the latter the God narrated to her the Amarkatha, or the story relating to the secret of immortality. As God Shiva proceeded with the story, Parvati, overpowered by sleep, dozed away. At the same time a pair of doves lodged in the roof of the cave were eagerly listening to God Shiva's narration. In the place of Parvati the doves responded to the story by uttering the sound "hoo, hoo, hoo." Thereafter, it is said, the doves not only became immortal but also their species came to adopt the same cooing cry. It is said that the same two birds are still alive and are seen in the cave.

The pure and sanctified atmosphere, the glorious surroundings and sight of thousands of pilgrims, gave rise in Ramdas to waves of rapturous delight. He met at the cave, Ramcharandas. When asked about his bath he said that he had already had one.

Bath and *darshan* over, the host of pilgrims retraced their steps to their camp in Panchatarni. The doctor and his party started on their downward journey. Before nightfall they fixed their tents at a low lying hillside beyond Vavjin. Here report was brought to the doctors that a *sadhu* had given up his body at Vavjin on account of the severity of the cold. This was the only casualty that occurred among the pilgrims.

Early next day they commenced again the march down the hills. The path was now, of course, a continuous decline, and he with Ramcharandas close at his heels ran down the slopes at breakneck speed, and reached Phelgaon long before the hospital camp arrived.

The missionary either could not locate Ramdas's whereabouts, since the camp was pitched at a different place this time, or he forgot all about Ramdas and his proposal regarding the sermon in his church, as he did not turn up. God's will!

By the ensuing evening, as they now proceeded in quick marches, the party reached Srinagar. Ramcharandas, and Ramdas, of course, directed their steps straight to Janakinath's house.

A party consisting of almost all the members of Janakinath's household started on a trip to Chenar Bagh. They crossed the Dal Lake by boat and came to Chenar Bagh. The place is full of gigantic chenar trees. The view one could have from this spot when facing the lake was grand. The distant bluish mountains, the vast sheet of the still water of the lake and the clear open heavens above made up the enchanting picture. Ramdas ran, danced and skipped in the cool shade beneath the chenar trees for some time, and suddenly climbed up a slim and tall giant among them with Ramcharandas in close pursuit.

While Ramdas was going up the tree at incredible speed like a monkey, the members of the party gazed on the performance agape with amazement, not unmixed with a sense of curious delight, for they were quite unprepared for the exhibition of this aspect of his restless activity. When he reached the very summit of the tree, he shouted forth at the top of his voice, "Hari Om" three times, sending a thrill through the hearers.

Now he descended to witness the feats of *asanas* shown by Ramcharandas. During his absence from Ramdas he had learnt nearly thirty *asanas*. The presentation of the feats showed how pliable and yielding his body had become through practice. He could twist and bend it easily in so many ways. The party looked on his performance with great interest and joy. After some refreshments, the party left the spot and by evening regained Janakinath's house.

CHAPTER 38: SRINAGAR

(i) Ramdas Defies Ram

The prolonged stay of Ramdas in Kashmir was causing anxiety to the friends in India, who were deluging him with their communications urging him to leave the hills again for the plains. They were also sending wire upon wire. Janakinath and Amarnath were quite averse to his departure from Srinagar. They suggested that he should make his permanent residence in future in Kashmir and that they would arrange for his stay near Hari Parvat or Harvan. But he was becoming conscious of the pull down to the south, from the friends in Rawalpindi, United Provinces, Kathiawar, Bombay and the southern districts. When he talked of quitting Srinagar the devoted brothers would oppose the idea. With the best of motives they sometimes connived at suppressing the correspondence from the friends in other parts, but they had to abandon this subterfuge when they found that it was of no avail.

Now Gopalrao and his wife Girijabai, Saraswats of Kanara, related to Mother Rukmabai, were in Srinagar at this time. They had information about Ramdas and were very desirous of seeing him. Gopalrao communicated with Amarnath Bakshi and expressed his longing to have Ramdas as his guest for some days. Amarnath concealed the contents of this letter from him, fearing that he would leave them on hearing of it.

Meanwhile, Janakinath proposed to take him for the *darshan* of a Kashmiri *sadhu* living in a solitary spot outside Srinagar, in the suburbs. The *sadhu* was said to have been observing a vow of silence for some years. He agreed at first to go with him, but half-way, Ram wanting him to turn back, he returned to the city in spite of pressure on the part of Janakinath and other friends. The same night Amarnath, feeling that he could not any longer withhold the news of the letter from Gopalrao, delivered the epistle to him. Ramdas now decided. "Janakinath," Ramdas said, "Ram's will is that Ramdas shall respond to the call from Gopalrao instead of going out of the way to see a silent *sadhu*, who is not eager to see him. So tomorrow morning he proceeds to Gandarbal, where Gopalrao appears to be living in a house-boat, and will spend some days in his company. It is his earnest desire and the love that he bears for Ramdas that have defeated your plan of a visit to the silent *sadhu*."

Janakinath, for whom separation from Ramdas was nothing short of a painful blow, was alarmed at the prospect. Similar were the feelings of Amarnath and Janakinath's two daughters, those models of purity, simplicity and devotion. But Ramdas had to obey the command of his Lord.

The following morning Ramdas stood up to depart for Gandarbal with Ramcharandas as his companion. But Janakinath stationed himself in the doorway and said: "Swamiji, I shall see how you will leave my house. I obstruct your egress; you shall not go. I am your Ram. It is Ram's will that you shall not leave me."

Ramdas was now fired with a grim determination. He was not in a mood to brook any hindrance, however great. He spoke, and his words rang out in a measured and stern tone. "Janakinath, Ramdas must go. He cannot be foiled. Even if Ram Himself were to stand in his way he would defy Him and go."

These words and the manner of their utterance made Janakinath understand that Ramdas was not to be trifled with. He cleared out of the way and agreed to his departure. He would have Ramdas go by *tonga*, but the distance being only eleven miles Ramdas preferred to walk. After breakfasting on milk and fruits, he took leave of Janakinath and his family, accompanied by Ramcharandas.

About eleven o'clock in the morning, they arrived on the banks of the Sindhu river, where they found a number of house-boats. After a few minutes' search Ramcharandas discovered the particular house-boat occupied by Gopalrao.

Gopalrao and his wife welcomed Ramdas with excessive joy. The house-boat, a barge with a neat, beautifully furnished dwelling place, consisted of six cabins and a small terrace over the front cabin. There were the drawing room, the dining room, two bedrooms, a store-room and a bath. Artistic curtains adorned the windows, and carpets covered the floor. The boat was lit with electric lights. It was moored in a position on the river from where a charming view of the surrounding landscape could be had. The Sindhu river, noted for its blue water of crystalline purity, was meandering slowly along.

After a week's stay at this place Gopalrao arranged to have the house-boat moved to Gagribal, at the foot of Sri Shankaracharya hill, in the Dal Lake. Gopalrao and Girijabai were overflowing in their love and kindness to Ramdas. They were an ideal couple, fond of each other like a pair of doves, unsophisticated, innocent and playful like children.

When the house-boat was being moved towards the Dal Lake by the sturdy Muslim boatmen, Ramdas had an opportunity to have a quiet talk with Ramcharandas.

"Ram," Ramdas said, "you must prepare yourself to part from Ramdas. He has shortly to leave for the plains and he will not have you go down with him leaving this blessed country. You may remain in Kashmir for some years. It is a suitable place for your *sadhana*. When you are next seen by Ramdas you must present a visage illumined with the glow of Self-Realisation and eyes filled with the vision of the Infinite. Have full trust in God who is in your heart, and He will look to all your conveniences and comforts during your residence in these cold regions."

Once more the boy, who had attached himself to Ramdas, evinced signs of perturbation at the idea of separation. He grumbled and fretted over it. Ramdas used all his powers of persuasion to convince him of the necessity for carrying out his suggestion, as it would tend ultimately to his own benefit. At last he agreed to follow Ramdas's advice.

A word here for Ramcharandas would be appropriate. After Ramdas left him in Kashmir, he had one communication from him, from Rishikesh, some months later, addressed to Anandashram, Kasaragod. From that time up to date, Ramdas has had no news from him. Ramdas remembers the last advice he gave him; and this was: "You should not come to see Ramdas again, until you are radiant with the knowledge and bliss of Brahman. But it is doubtful," Ramdas added, "if you would feel the need of meeting him at all, when you have attained that supremely blessed state." Whatever it be, the sweet memory of his fellowship and of the various acts of loving service, he did for Ramdas in his wandering life, will ever remain fresh in his mind. Whatever be the so-called weaknesses he displayed, Ramdas recognised in him a *sadhaka* of a rare, dauntless spirit, at times riding on the very crest of a wave of burning renunciation, and entirely free from the ego-obsession. His main anchor of belief was that devoted service of the *guru* and of saints is the *sine qua non* of a spiritual life.

A couple of days' halt in front of a hospital in the Jhelum river, and the house-boat was finally moved into the lake and anchored at Gagribal.

(ii) Behold God's Majesty in All Things

A few days after their arrival at Gagribal, Ramcharandas departed to Anantnag. A new guest also joined them, a Sikh barrister who took his lodgings in the boat.

Gopalrao was the Vice-Principal of the Khalsa College in Amritsar. He had come to Kashmir on a pleasure-trip during the holidays. He and his wife had also visited Amarnath cave, a day or two in advance of the usual day of pilgrimage. So Ramdas had no occasion to meet them when he went up to the cave. Gopalrao was a generous-hearted and noble-minded soul. His friends were mostly Sikhs and his leanings were towards Sikhism. He held in high veneration the founder of the Sikh religion, Guru Nanak, and had studied Gurumukhi in order to be in direct touch with his teachings. He would, every night before retiring to sleep, make it a rule to go through Sukhmani, a work by Guru Arjun Singh, which is very popular among the Sikhs. Guru Nanak was a great believer in the power of God's Name. In fact, the only discipline which he prescribed for the control of mind and for spiritual meditation is the singing of God's Name and His glories.

One day Gopalrao spoke of a Sikh saint who was to visit Srinagar and whom he regarded as a *guru* or spiritual preceptor, and said that he greatly wished that Ramdas should be presented to him. A few days after they shifted to Gagribal, the saint arrived, and Ramdas had the opportunity of meeting him along with his friends in a quiet spot on a small piece of green headland in the middle of the Dal Lake. Bhai Vir Singh, popularly known as Pitaji among his disciples and admirers, was a childlike devotee. He took a great liking for Ramdas. They had a short talk on the teachings of saints, *bhakti* and the power of God's Name.

Ramdas would utilize the early mornings to climb up Sri Shankaracharya hill and lose himself in the contemplation of God. The enchanting vision of the landscape, lakes and mountains from the hill top captivated him. During one of his wanderings on the hill he came upon a cave. In one of his trips uphill, Gopalrao and his wife also accompanied him. Ramdas was given to ascending it by direct paths. So the friends, when they followed him upon the hill, had a most trying time of it as he was running up like a squirrel.

One day a young Gujarati came to the house-boat in search of Ramdas. He was the Secretary to the Yuvaraja, the eldest son of the Thakur Saheb of Limbdi. The father had wired his son to see Ramdas. The son was staying in Srinagar at the time. His motor-car carried Ramdas to the Yuvaraja's house-boat moored in the Jhelum river in front of the late Maharaja's palace. The Yuvaraja's time was fully crowded with engagements as he confessed, and so Ramdas had an interview with him for about five minutes, when they had only a formal talk about health, etc.

About this time Ramdas met K. Sadashivarao, Director of Army Audit, who had also come to Kashmir with his family on a pleasure excursion. He with his wife and two daughters came on a visit to the house-boat. Soon after this Durgadas Nagarkatte invited to his bungalow Sadashivarao with his family, Gopalrao and his wife, and Ramdas. They had a happy time of it together for a couple of days.

One morning Ramdas discovered Durgadas and Gopalrao, seated under the shade of a chenar tree in front of the bungalow, discussing the genuineness and value of some precious stones which Gopalrao had recently purchased. Ramdas approached them. Durgadas handed to Ramdas an opal and exclaimed: "What a beautiful stone!"

Ramdas at once bent down and picked up a stone from the ground and holding it up said: "Why can you not see the same beauty in this stone and majesty in the yonder mountain? Every thing is God's creation, everything is displaying beauty. Why speak only of that particular stone?" They smiled and kept silent.

Kabir and Uddhav were as loving and kind as ever.

At this time Ramdas, in the company of Gopalrao, his wife and a guide, went on a visit to the famous silk factory of Srinagar. The Muhammadan manager of the factory, who was very kind and obliging, took the party round the works. He explained to them the various processes through which the raw silk passed before the finished product, in the shape of twisted hanks of glossy yarn, could be obtained. When he was dilating upon the boiling of the silk larva by steam, in front of the contrivance intended for it, he could not help remarking with a tinge of regret: "I am sorry, but I have the ill-luck to become the means of destroying every day thousands of innocent worms." After the visit they returned to the residence of Durgadas.

Before the party broke up, Sadashivrao desired that Ramdas should pay him a visit at Rawalpindi where he was posted, if Ramdas happened to go down to the plains through that city. Ramdas, Gopalrao and Girijabai returned to the house-boat.

Ramdas's daily wanderings on the Shankaracharya hill drew him often to the cave on it. It appeared to be exerting on him a strange fascination. In the moon-lit nights Gopalrao would take him and Girijabai for boating on the lake. The glory of those nights in the midst of the bewitching charms of Kashmir does not lend itself to description. Sometimes they would also have baths in the cool waters of the lake.

Once the party visited the famous gardens of Kashmir in a special gondola engaged for the purpose. On their return trip, when the boat was midway on the lake, a storm burst and as a result the boat swayed most ominously. The inmates were frightened, but they saw with unfeigned surprise Ramdas capering with great glee. However, the storm subsided and the party regained the house-boat without any mishap.

Whenever there was a shortage of a hand in a game of bridge, Gopalrao would have Ramdas fill the vacancy. They also played a game called Bolshevik and Ramdas invariably turned out to be a rabid and reckless Bolshevik in the game.

One day Girijabai received a wire from her father at Honavar that her mother was seriously ill. The tidings upset her and she bacame wistful and gloomy. That evening when Ramdas was sitting alone on the terrace of the boat, Girijabai rushed up to where he was, and with folded hands revealed her gnawing anxiety about her mother.

"Ramdas," she pleaded, "if you would give me an assurance that my mother is all right by now, and that I would receive a wire to that effect tomorrow I should be free from a load of unbearable misery."

"Trust God, mother, and everything will be all right," Ramdas replied.

These heartening words immediately dispelled her sorrow and she became again the same lively and bright-faced girl that she was. Her pure and simple faith brought about the fruition of her wish. On the following day she got a wire from her father to say that her mother was past danger.

(iii) Illumination in the Cave

Gopalrao's vacation was now coming to a close. He proposed to take Ramdas with him to Amritsar. He engaged a special motor-car for the journey to Rawalpindi, but Ramdas's attraction for the cave on the hill did not permit him to accompany him. God willed that he should live in the cave for some days. He disclosed this fact to Gopalrao, who was greatly disappointed at the news, but had to submit to the inevitable. His deep concern for Ramdas induced him to leave word with Bhai Vir Singh, the Sikh saint, to have a watchful interest in Ramdas. He left Srinagar with his wife and the same evening Ramdas occupied the cave.

The interior of the cave was spacious although the entrance was narrow. Since the cave had been frequented by goats that grazed on the hill, the place inside was extremely dirty with their droppings and urine. There was a small chenar tree at the mouth of the cave and a flat slab of stone at its base.

Ramdas then possessed only one thin ochre-coloured, plain Kashmir shawl presented by Gopalrao, and nothing else. The floor in the cave was of two levels. As you enter you come to the lower ground, at the end of which is a raised platform reaching the back hollow wall of the cave. The ground and the pedestal were rugged and sharp bits of gravel lay thickly scattered on them. Even during the day semi-darkness prevailed in the cave. As the sun was about to set, Bhai Vir Singh came hastening up the hill to where Ramdas was and said: "I have heard that you are going to stay in this cave. You may command me to supply you with whatever you want."

"Ramdas wants nothing," was Ramdas's reply.

"No, that will not do; I will arrange to provide you with food, blankets and rugs," he exclaimed.

"Ramdas wants to remain here for some days without food and comforts. So please don't trouble yourself," Ramdas put in.

"I cannot agree with you there. You must permit me to feed and look after you. I will consider it as no small privilege. I will not allow you to starve. Tell me what you would have. Don't think that you can put me off so lightly," he said.

In fact Ramdas wished to live in that solitary spot for some days, undisturbed with the food and drink questions. But the saint was obdurate and Ramdas had to yield and stipulate: "Well, maharaj, you may provide him at midday with a small quantity of boiled rice mixed with milk; that is all."

"That is not all," he answered quickly, "what about evening? I would have you take at least some fruit and milk."

Ramdas became helpless in the hands of one who was determined to feed him. The saint left. When darkness set in Ramdas entered the cave and took up his position on the raised ground, using a part of the thin shawl for spreading on the floor, and lay down flat on the rough gravel.

About ten o'clock a stout and fair-looking boy-servant of the saint came, lantern in hand, carrying a mat of stout reeds and some blankets. Ramdas spread the mat at the place where he lay down, and having a blanket folded up for a pillow he returned the surplus blankets and bade good-night to the lad.

The cave was pitch-dark in the night. He stretched himself on the mat at full length and covered his body with his shawl. He did not feel much cold as the cave was warm within. The whole night he was awake. After midnight he heard beside him a rustling noise and squeaks as of rats which did not in any way molest him.

The night passed and the day dawned. He went out and sat on the slab of stone at the foot of the chenar tree and drank in the picturesque scenes of the lake, mountains and growth of green foliage. As noon approached he retired into the cave.

Now an old Muslim paid him a visit. He expressed his surprise at seeing Ramdas dwelling in the cave and added: "Are you aware that there are two serpents in this cave? Many goats that strayed into this cave have fallen victims to their poisonous fangs. You see a hole just a few inches from the place where you rest your head. It is their home. Did you not have any trouble from them? How long have you been in this place?"

"Ramdas has been staying here since last evening," Ramdas replied. "In the night, except that he heard the squeak of rats and a rustling noise caused by them, he had no other disturbance."

"Ah!" he exclaimed, with eyes wide open and his bearded head shaking, "they are the serpents, not rats as you suppose. They produce a cry similar to that of rats. I have not visited the cave for a long time and was under the impression that the serpents might have left the place. Now I know they are still there. Be warned. Leave this dreadful place at once. Somehow, they spared you last night; you cannot be sure of the future."

"Ramdas has no fear. He stops in this cave under the protection of God and by His command. So he would continue to reside here," Ramdas replied.

The old man nodded his head again with grave and doubtful looks. The talk turning into other channels; he spoke of a Muslim *sadhu* who had been living in the cave for thirty years and this was twenty years ago. Giving Ramdas a second warning the kind-hearted old man left.

The boy-servant of Bhai Vir Singh brought food and milk at midday and in the evening regularly. Sometimes, Ramdas would be sitting on the hill on a lower peak than that of the temple, absorbed in blissful abstraction and would forget to go down to the cave at meal time. But the faithful boy would quietly search for Ramdas with the food basket in hand and when he found Ramdas feed him wherever he might be sitting.

Bhai Vir Singh, Janakinath, Shambunath and several Sikh friends would pay him visits during the day and furnish him with pots for water and charcoal, *kangdi*, matches, etc. to keep a fire against cold, but Ramdas never used these materials. Shambunath, whom Ramdas had met at Panchatarni, desired to have him for a few days at his house on his leaving the cave.

Ramdas lived in the cave for a week, during which time he never bathed, drank or used water. Water could be had only from the lake which was at the foot of the hill, fairly three furlongs down from the cave. He never descended the hill in those days.

On the night of the seventh day he had a strange experience. It might have been past midnight. The interior of the cave was as usual utterly dark. Suddenly a brilliant bluish light lit up the entire cave. He seemed to be absorbed in that light, which lasted only for a few seconds, and then it gradually disappeared throwing the cave again into depths of darkness.

On the eighth day, early morning, i.e., the day following the vision of light, he left the cave and presented himself at the *kuti* of saint Bhai Vir Singh, who welcomed him with open arms.

CHAPTER 39: SRINAGAR – RAWALPINDI – AMRITSAR

(i) A Perilous Venture

From Bhai Vir Singh's *kuti* Ramdas was escorted by Shambunath to his house in Amirakadal, in the main bazaar of Srinagar. Shambunath's father, mother and other relations treated him with great kindness and love. He stopped with them for about a fortnight. In the course of his stay he expressed to Shambunath that God willed that he should climb up the highest mountain in the range in the front of the cave on Sri Shankaracharya hill. The idea of hill-climbing appealed to Shambunath's imagination. He also proposed to accompany Ramdas on the trip.

So one early morning, they started on the adventure. Shambunath armed himself with a thermos-flask filled with tea and also a small bag containing biscuits, bread, butter and fruits. As far as the foot of the hill they travelled by motor-car. Now they commenced the ascent. They took a path along the greatest incline and ascended higher and higher keeping in view the peak they had to reach. From the ground level the summit did not appear to be of very great height but now, as they went up, they discovered that the summit seemed to be as high up as ever. Seven hills, one after another, were passed and at last they came to the bottom of the peak they had ultimately to reach.

Up to the end of the fourth hill they walked on a rough beaten path but further on there was no track. They had to make their way through thickets and gorges and over rugged rocks. Except a couple of jackals, who took to flight at the sight of them, they met no other animals. Now the highest peak to be climbed had to be scaled either spirally, an easier method, or right up vertically. Ramdas adopted the latter course. He scrambled up using the dense growth of brown grass as hand-hold, followed by Shambunath. When they went about half-way up the slope, Ramdas came upon a small smooth rock to which he lifted himself and perching on it saw the friend behind struggling to keep pace with him, his face flushed with excitement. A look down into the valley below discovered a rare and marvellous scene. From that dizzy height a wide and terribly deep chasm was yawning at their feet. As Shambunath neared, Ramdas could not help exclaiming: "Ram, look below, what a magnificent scene!" When Shambunath turned his head to see for a moment he cried out helplessly: "Swamiji, I am gone, hold on—hold, I am slipping," and he stretched forth his arms which Ramdas immediately grasped with both hands, and with a super-human strength pulled him up bodily on to the rock on which he was sitting. Shambunath now rested with eyes closed for about five minutes before he recovered from the faintness.

"Swamiji," he then said, "please don't ask me to look down again. A glimpse of the awe-inspiring and enormous depths turned me giddy, and but for you I should have rolled down the mountain to my sure destruction."

They ascended higher still and steadily progressed through the tall grass that grew luxuriantly on the mountain, and at last arrived at the summit. The time was now about three o'clock in the afternoon. They sat down on the grass and leisurely took a view of Kashmir from that tremendous height. What Ramdas saw from there beggars description. It was the vision of the infinite expanse of space, the dim outlines of mountains looming in the distance and the extensive valley of Kashmir scintillating with its innumerable glassy lakes, relieved by vast areas of green verdure and vegetation.

Shambunath was cheerful and lively although tired. He opened the screw cap of the thermos and the bag of eatables, and they both did hearty justice to the hard-earned tiffin. They rested for about half-an-hour. Shambunath now suggested that they should make haste for their return journey since they had to reach down before dark. It was proposed that they should descend by a different way, especially by a slope which looked tempting, as it appeared to be one which could take them to the bottom easily and in a short time.

They then quickly descended the incline and came to the brink of a precipice which shut off their further progress downwards. They turned to another adjoining slope of the mountain and climbed down only to meet with a similar precipice. They turned to a third direction where they helped themselves down by holding on to the branches of trees that grew densely. Still their path was cut off by yet another vertical cliff. Here Ramdas, seeing some roots projecting out on the wall of the cliff, attempted to go down by their aid, when Shambunath intervened and said: "Swamiji, I cannot follow you that way. Do give up the path."

Ramdas had to abandon the attempt. By this time, evening was fast approaching beckoning the night, clothed in her dark mantle. Ramdas and the friend rested for some minutes beneath the trees.

"Swamiji, suppose we can't find the way down the hill, what are we to do?" questioned Shambunath.

"Why, of course, we shall stop here for the night," replied Ramdas.

"Oh!" he exclaimed, "I cannot do that in this horrible place. I am afraid of wild animals. It is time for them to come out of their lairs. Swamiji, let us try to find out the old way by which we came up."

But the way by which they had ascended was also lost. They were caught in the perplexing undulations of the vast chain of mountains. They roamed up and down in search of the old path for over half-an-hour but without success; and all the while, Shambunath was growing excited and anxious. At last they found themselves on the rough beaten path. When he saw it Shambunath's joy knew no bounds. With uncontrollable delight he leapt and danced, and burst out saying: "Swamiji, you are indeed my God. You have brought me to the path. Let us hurry up."

Now Shambunath raced down the path like a horse at full gallop. He took perilous jumps on the way. He was reckless and wild. Ramdas ran close behind him. The sun had set. Darkness was steadily encroaching upon the twilight. When they neared the base of the mountains they swerved to their left and came upon some old ruins, where they rested for five minutes and then went down to the road near a famous spring of Kashmir called Chashma Shahi. They proceeded to the spring and drank their fill. The water of this spring is reputed to possess marvellous medicinal and healing properties. Rich people and invalids arrange to have this water for drinking purposes.

Now they retraced their steps to the city. Half-way they met Shambunath's motor-car which was coming to fetch them. They jumped into it and by half-past-seven reached Shambunath's residence.

(ii) God's Will Be Done

Another day Ramdas visited Achabal, one of the most frequented beauty spots of Kashmir, noted for its small but finely cultured garden and spring. He was accompanied by Shambunath and his father. When they were about to leave the garden, Ramdas met a *sannyasi* belonging to Sri Ramakrishna Mission and had a few minutes' talk with him.

Ramdas had also a pleasure trip arranged by Shambunath by boat at the far end of the Jhelum river. Besides Ramdas and a Sikh merchant, there were in the boat a German, an Agent for light machinery, and his two young, lively daughters. The German was making a new experiment in the working of a small motor-engine fixed to the boat. The boat now raced on the water at a brisk speed. The girls were in great glee. They giggled and laughed. The German conceived an affection for Ramdas. He said that he held Indian yogis in high regard. He talked freely with Ramdas on all matters. They went through ten miles on the river and had a halt at a cool spot for an hour where they enjoyed a pleasant picnic and a bath in the river. At parting on their return, the German friend expressed a desire to see Ramdas again in Bombay where he would be going shortly, if ever Ramdas visited the city in the near future. He handed to Ramdas his card containing his Bombay address which Ramdas preserved.

From Shambunath's house Ramdas, at the request of Durgadas, shifted to his spacious residence and stayed with him again for about a week. Now Ramdas had many a talk with Durgadas. Ramdas found him a learned and well-informed man. He possessed a clear head and a vast store of knowledge. He could talk on every conceivable subject. To converse with him generally was to enjoy an intellectual feast. He spoke on philosophy and religion with as much ease as he did on other topics. He was a great admirer of Kabir and his works. One day he read out original poems of Kabir treating of the highest philosophy, and Durgadas, who was a master in Hindi, expounded them to Ramdas. He explained the meaning, entering into the spirit of the sublime teachings.

One afternoon, in the society of his son-in-law, Bhavanishankerrao who had newly come from Bombay with his daughter, Ramdas had a drive in his motor-car to Verinag, a place about fifty miles from Srinagar. Verinag, like other beauty spots in Kashmir, offered a very charming view. It was a solitary spot over the hills fully shaded with trees and watered with numerous springs. At two spots Ramdas saw natural springs oozing out of the ground like fountains. The party remained here for an hour or two and returned to Srinagar before evening.

Again another day, by motor-car, these friends took Ramdas to Mattan for visiting the narrow cave on the hills.

Bhavanishankerrao was to start for Bombay as he had come to Kashmir during his summer vacation which was coming to a close. Ramdas proposed to accompany him. But Durgadas, out of his great love, intervened. He appealed to Ramdas to remain with him for some time more. His two children, Uddhav and Kabir, also joined him. But Ramdas was determined. He was to leave on the morrow. Seats for two were arranged in a motor-bus running to Rawalpindi. In the morning on the day fixed for departure, a message came by telephone to say that the seats booked were otherwise filled up and that there were no spare seats in other buses also for the day. Now, Bhavanishanker, who had to be present in Bombay on a particular date to attend his examination, was greatly upset by the news. For, he could reach Bombay in time only if he started on the day fixed. Now Durgadas coming to Ramdas said: "Ramdas, it is Ram's will that you should not go. You must stay with me for at least a month more. So He has upset your plan of departure. We shall find a seat somehow for Bhavanishanker, but for you there would be no seat available which means that you are to stay behind."

"Ram's will be done," Ramdas simply replied.

In five minutes, another telephone message came to the effect that two seats were arranged in another bus.

"I must confess that your Ram is wonderful," Durgadas exclaimed.

"When He wills, nothing can stand in His way of fulfilling His object. His will is supreme," Ramdas said.

Ramdas therefore took leave of the loving household and seated himself by the side of Bhavanishanker, in a bus, which tore along the mountain path to Rawalpindi.

(iii) Association Makes Character

For the night they made a halt at Domel in the travellers' bungalow, and continued their journey next morning. All the way Ramdas enjoyed the lavish splendour of entrancing landscapes, the sound of the waterfalls and the pure springs of crystalline water. Long before sunset they reached Rawalpindi. Jewandas, the friend who had met Ramdas on his journey to Jwalajee and had treated him with such great kindness, was informed by wire of Ramdas's coming. But he could not, in spite of his efforts, meet Ramdas at the motor-stand. So taking leave of Bhavanishankerrao, who was to start by the evening train for Bombay, Ramdas made enquiries for the house of Jewandas, whose address he knew, and presented himself at the door of his small dwelling. Jewandas's wife, as soon as she saw Ramdas, invited him with great joy to their house and making him sit on a cot, fell to pressing his legs. Soon after this Jewandas arrived. The joy of the blessed pair to have Ramdas with them knew no bounds. Their little son was also greatly delighted.

Devout mothers of the neighbourhood poured in to see him in large numbers morning and evening and Jewandas's small house became crowded with visitors. In the evening he would be taken by the friends to a garden, away from the town precincts, where he would talk to them on devotion and the greatness of God's Name. Once when he was on his way to the garden with a dozen friends, a passerby on the road, observing Ramdas clad in ochre-coloured cloth and in the company of householders, struck a note of warning: "Beware, don't teach them (referring to the friends) that the world is an illusion or you will lead them astray". The cautious friend said as he walked off.

For Ramdas the world was no longer an illusion. He had come to look upon it as God's own expression in form and movement. For him the world stood revealed as a gigantic image of God teeming with divine life.

Ramdas spent a week in Rawalpindi during which he enjoyed a couple of days in the society of K. Sadashivarao and his family.

The next place which he travelled to was Amritsar where Gopalrao, who was given intimation beforehand, came to receive him at the station. His wife, Girijabai, was away at her mother's. He was alone with a manservant at his house in the spacious compound of the Khalsa College.

Khalsa College is an institution mainly intended for the education of Sikhs. It consists of an imposing pile of buildings. There are hostels, vast structures for accommodating a thousand students. All the professors and teachers are also provided with residential quarters within the extensive grounds of the college which can be termed a colony, having also a post office attached to it.

A special class for all boys is held every morning for imparting spiritual instruction, when they are made to sing prayers and listen to the reading and exposition of Granth Saheb, the Scripture of the Sikhs. There is a tank of pure flowing water in which the boys perform their morning ablutions.

Through the introduction of Gopalrao, Ramdas became acquainted with a few professors and teachers of the college who paid him frequent visits and invited him to dinner at their houses. All of them were Sikhs. The Sikhs are noble, industrious and kindly people. In the mornings and evenings, Gopalrao would take Ramdas on his motor-cycle to the city, to visit saint Bhai Vir Singh who had now returned to Amritsar from Kashmir. He was all kindness and love. In his house Ramdas met also an old saint, Vaddasantji who became in course of time quite enamoured of Ramdas. He would at three in the morning daily come to Gopalrao's from a long distance to see Ramdas. He would embrace Ramdas and sit beside him with his hands clasped round Ramdas's shoulders and would say: "I am coming to inhale the sweet fragrance which you radiate. To be with you fills me with a blissful intoxication." On one occasion Ramdas was sitting with the saints and a few devotees in Bhai Vir Singh's worship room upstairs where the holy book Granth Saheb was being read by turns by the devotees. Now a man at the entrance downstairs sent a request to be admitted into the *satsang*. A consultation took place between Bhai Vir Singh and Vaddasantji, and they came to the decision that the man should not be admitted since he would create a disturbance, not being a pure-hearted man. Here Ramdas intervened and pleaded on behalf of the eager devotee.

"If you consider him impure," Ramdas urged, "there is all the more reason that he should be admitted into your society. *Satsang* is the most potent power for purifying the heart of any one who comes under its influence. Do not deny the man this privilege since he seeks it of his own accord." The saints at first refused to take Ramdas's suggestion, but had to yield at last and the man was permitted to enter the room and sit beside them. The man stayed for a few minutes and then left. Saint Bhai Vir Singh then narrated a curious bit of his own experience to show how the society and influence of an evil-minded man produced disastrous results.

"Once a woman came to me," he said, "in a distressed condition. She said that she had been of late subjected to attacks of splitting headache and wanted some remedy. When asked how the complaint started, she said that she was having it since she saw a wandering *sadhu* from whom she got the *upadesh* of a *mantram*. Ever since then, whenever she repeated the *mantram*, she would feel excruciating pains in the head. When I suggested to her to give up the repetition of the *mantram* she refused to do so, as she looked upon the *sadhu* as her *guru*. I prescribed abandoning the *mantram* as the only remedy but not agreeing with my suggestion she left. In a few days she came again and her condition was much worse than before. She was finding the pains quite unbearable. When again I asked her to stop the *mantram*, she replied that she tried to do so, but could not as the *mantram* appeared to have taken possession of her. Then I suggested to her as the only course for averting its influence, to express in strong language her repugnance for the *sadhu* and a resolve not to have anything to do with his *mantram*. She refused point-blank to follow this advice as she held the *sadhu* in great reverence. She again left.

"After a week she turned up for the third time. She was quite cheerful and free from the racking ailment. She confessed that during the previous week the torments of the headache grew so unbearable that she was obliged to follow my advice and make a firm resolution not to utter the *mantram*, and this resolution she made after abusing the *sadhu* and holding him up as a loathsome creature. Immediately afterwards she added, the headache ceased and with it the influence of the *mantram*. Ever since then she was feeling her old self again. So I consider that there is no greater evil in life than association with a man whose heart is filled with bestial passions. Such a man easily communicates his nature to impressionable people who are of an emotional and weak temperament. And by the same rule, no society is so beneficial for our elevation and peace as that of a man of a noble character and pure heart."

CHAPTER 40: AMRITSAR – CHHATTARPUR

(i) The Golden Temple of the Sikhs

One evening Gopalrao took Ramdas out on a visit to the celebrated Golden Temple of the Sikhs which is their main Gurudwara. It is situated in the middle of a big tank with an overbridge on one side that leads up to the temple from the main land. The tank has all its four banks artistically covered with glazed and varied-coloured, square marble slabs. The visitors walked round the tank on this marble floor before entering the temple across the bridge. Anybody, irrespective of caste, creed or colour, has access to the temple. The only restrictions to be observed are removal of shoes by the visitor who should also have clean feet and his headgear on. At the entrance to the tank, two water taps are provided for washing the feet, and a man is appointed to be in charge of the shoes left over there.

Now the temple. It is a beautiful structure with small minarets at the corners of its roof and a dome at its centre. The entire temple except the floor is covered with gold sheets. The roof, the domes, and the walls are all of gold. When you enter the main hall through the verandah that runs along the four sides, you discover a huge book, the Granth Saheb, poised upon a stand covered with fine silk cloth and decorated with flowers and garlands. This place is the main prayer hall where the best singers congregate in front of the Sacred Book to perform *kirtan* to the accompaniment of musical instruments. There is also an upper gallery, as in a theatre, where you go up by a flight of stairs. Here the visitors sit listening to the music from the hall below. The *kirtan* goes on from three in the morning to ten or twelve o'clock in the night. Thousands of people, chiefly Sikhs, daily pay visits to this sacred shrine. During the first visit Ramdas remained in the temple only for a short time. He came again with Gopalrao at three in the morning and stayed till daybreak on the gallery upstairs. The music that wafted up to him from the hall was most charming. In front of the temple beyond the tank is the seat of one of the ten famous *gurus* of the Sikhs.

The Sikhs are proud of recounting the fierce battles their ancestors waged to preserve the temple from desecration at the hands of Muhammadan invaders. Much precious Sikh blood had freely flowed into the tank and on its borders in guarding the sanctuary. The Sikhs, even to the present day, are a martial race endowed with indomitable grit and valour. The warlike spirit was infused into them by one of their greatest *gurus*, Guru Govind, who was himself an intrepid soldier and, at the same time, their religious head. He trained his followers and formed an army for protecting their religious faith and shrines from the attacks of foreign aggressors, especially the Muhammadans. The distinctive marks of a Sikh are the beard and the uncut hair which is tied up in a knot at the crown of the head, which is invariably covered with a bulky *pheta* or turban. They have an iron wire bangle on one of their wrists and *kirpani*, or short dagger, hanging by their side. They are quiet and kind in disposition. While they look upon Guru Nanak with the highest veneration, they recognise also the greatness of saints and incarnations of other religions.

Guru Nanak, as his life shows, was a wonderful personality. He is said to have performed many miracles during his time. The oft-quoted wonder that he wrought was the turning round of Mecca. It is stated that when he was in Mecca in his itinerant life he happened to lie down with his legs turned towards the sacred shrine of the Muslims at Mecca. The Muslims holding that Guru Nanak was treating their holy temple with disrespect moved his legs round to a different posture and Mecca itself whirled round with this act. The Sikhs do not believe in caste distinctions and idol worship, prevalent among other Hindus. Their women are cultured and are free from the antiquated and borrowed customs of *purdah*, and also from the unwholesome modernism of the present day. The Sikhs have their names ending always with epithet 'Singh' which means lion. Verily, they are as noble, fearless, and powerful a people as the kings of the jungle. The splendid heroism exhibited by Akalis is recent history.

In all, Ramdas remained in Amritsar for a fortnight, and then left the city for Jhansi.

(ii) The Secret of Ramnam

As usual, at Jhansi, Ramdas stopped in the Ram Mandir into which he was welcomed with open arms by the *pandaji*. Ramkinkar, Mahadev Prasad and other friends were as loving in their attention as ever. Here, Ramchandra Gupta with a new friend, Ganesh Prasad, came down from Allahabad to see Ramdas.

An invitation from Mahoba drew Ramdas to that place. He again lived for ten days in the cave on Gohkar Parvat. Jagannath and other friends provided him with food. One afternoon a young friend came to see Ramdas. He had some wounds on his forehead and knees. He told the story relating to the injuries: "Maharaj, last evening, I was coming to see you. When I reached halfway to this place darkness overtook me. In the dim light I saw right on the path a huge leopard sitting on its haunches staring viciously at me. I was so frightened that I gave forth a shriek, and turning back fled from the place pell-mell. In the darkness I stumbled over the stones and fell down several times. However, I got clear of the grasp of the wild beast and reached home. The injuries that you behold on me were caused by my falls during that flight for very life."

From Mahoba, in response to a call, Ramdas proceeded to Chhattarpur, where he halted in the Krishna temple. Bhavani Prasad overwhelmed him with kindness and hospitality. Here Ramdas learnt that Swami Nirbhayanandji and his spouse resided at the time in Navagaon. Ramdas went to that village for their *darshan*. He arrived at their residence one evening by motor-bus. The blessed pair was overjoyed to see Ramdas, but his halt with them proved short-lived, for about seven o'clock Bhavani Prasad and his devout wife turned up suddenly in a motor-car. They urged Ramdas to return with them to Chhattarpur as the Maharaja of the State was anxious to see him. So he was back at Chhattarpur that very night.

Early next morning, Gulab Rai, son of Bhavani Prasad, secretary to the Maharaja, escorted Ramdas to the palace of the Maharaja. He was a decrepit old man, weak and emaciated. Ramdas took his seat beside him.

"I have been repeating Ramnam for over thirty years," he said, "but still my mind is as restless as ever. How then could that Name be said to possess the power of quelling the tumult of the desire-ridden mind?"

"Peace can be attained," Ramdas replied, "by the *japa* of Ramnam only when you do so in a spirit of *nishkama*; i.e., with the sole desire for liberation and peace and without longing for worldly things. God grants our prayer when we appeal to Him with an earnest fervour of the heart only for pure devotion to His holy feet and for nothing else. So the secret of Ramnam is in the taking of it for realizing the goal of life which is immortality or union with God."

"You are perfectly right. It is very hard to get *nishkama bhakti*," he observed, and changing the course of conversation said: "I have got a retainer of mine seriously ill from a gun-shot. He was one of the party who went for hunting and by oversight on the part of one of the party he was shot in the thigh. His condition is very precarious. I request you to give him the benefit of your *darshan*, and I have faith that he will be all right by your blessings."

Accordingly, Ramdas was taken to the cottage of the wounded man. Ramdas found him perfectly restless through pain, and his relations crowded round him with deep anxiety. Ramdas was made to pass his hands over the body and the affected part of the wounded man. Then he left the house and returned to Gulab Rai's. Next day he left Chhattarpur in the Maharaja's motor-car for Navagaon, where he dined in the company of the saints and proceeded by the same motor-car to Harpalpur station, and here catching a train, arrived in Jhansi. Ramdas learnt later that the Maharaja's servant had recovered from the serious hurt. God be praised!

In the Vision of God

CHAPTER 41: LIMBDI

(i) "Ramdas Wants Your Mind"

From Jhansi, Ramdas travelled towards Kathiawar and made a few days' halt at Wadhwan city. Almost the same programme as on the last occasion was gone through here. He paid visits to Bala Mandir and the *kuti* of Jivraj Baloo. He stopped with Dr. Shukla who with his pure-hearted wife, tended Ramdas with great kindness. On the termination of his stay here, he was guided by the friends of Limbdi to that state.

As on the previous occasions he made his residence at Kantilal's house, where the old story of rushing visitors was repeated. Raja Ram and Mother Elizabeth came to the house to see him. The old sugarcandy mothers daily visited him with the offerings of the sweet crystals. The wealthy brothers, Ugarchand Shet and Mohanbhai dropped in twice a day. Invitations to dinner poured in from all sides. Here Ramdas came in touch with two new friends, Popatbhai and Joshi.

Popatbhai stuck on to Ramdas for over a month. He was a pure and selfless soul. He was a Jain by birth and a staunch disciple of Mahatma Gandhi, and had the benefit of living in the Sabarmati Ashram of Ahmedabad for some years. He was clad in *khaddar* from top to toe. He observed restrictions in food. He eschewed salt and chillies. He was a simple, sincere and ever willing servant of God; i.e., of humanity. He took a great liking for Ramdas and became attached to him and so kept constant company with him.

Joshi was the Municipal Chairman of the state. He had lived for many years in South Africa and was one of those who courted jail along with thousands, in that historic passive resistance struggle led by Mahatma Gandhi. He invited Ramdas to his house where he and his modest wife and lively children showed great kindness and affection for him.

One day, at Ugarchand Shet's house, he dined with his several friends. After meals, when he was sitting in the drawing room of his palatial house, the Shet said in a mock-serious mood: "Swami, I am a business-man, a commission agent in trade and I am very wealthy. I promise you a decent commission if you would show me Ram whom I am so eager to see."

"Well," replied Ramdas, "Ramdas can show you Ram provided you present him with the kind of commission he demands. He does not want your wealth. Assure him that you would hand over the thing he wants from you and you shall see Ram in all His magnificence."

"What is it that you want?" he enquired with great eagerness.

"Do you promise before Ramdas tells you what it is?" Ramdas asked.

He thought for a while and said: "I cannot promise. Kindly tell me what is the commission you demand and I shall see if I am in a position to grant it."

Ramdas was about to drop the matter, but the Shet insisted on Ramdas's speaking out about the commission. At last Ramdas enlightened him.

"What Ramdas wants from you in exchange for the vision of God is your mind. Surrender it up to Ramdas totally and you will see God face to face."

"Oh!" he exclaimed, throwing up his hands: "I cannot do that."

"Right," Ramdas replied, "you wish to retain the mind for owning this house, your vast riches, property and relations as yours and undergo anxiety, cares and worries concerning them all. Please yourself. The truth is, unless you give over your mind entirely to the thought of God and lay everything that you cling to as belonging to you at His feet, you cannot have Him. In short, complete and unqualified surrender to God alone entitles you to His grace and *darshan*."

During his visit Raja Ram was overflowing with love, as also Mother Elizabeth, and Ramdas had several invitations to the palace and the mother's bungalow. Once a dinner was arranged by the mother to a select party at her house, "Sri Krishna Nivas." She also brought about in her garden a meeting of several saints the same morning.

A *sadhu* by name Prakashanand, famous in Kathiawar, had also been residing in Limbdi at the time. Ramdas had the privilege of coming in touch with him for the first time at this garden-party. He was over fifty years of age, short and stout in build. He used to cover himself with a soiled, torn quilt, and carry an earthen pot and two sticks. It was said that he preferred to spend his nights mostly in cremation grounds. He spoke slowly and in a low tone. He was exact, wise and simple in his ways. Besides this *mahatma* there were two or three Jain *sadhus*, one of whom came on foot from a distance of fifteen miles specially to meet Ramdas. Raja Ram, Joshi, Popatbhai and Kantilal were also present.

Raja Ram humorously remarked: "Ramdas, I am not going to present you with any more clothing. You gave away the precious things I gave you last time to some greedy brahmin."

"You may call him by any name you like, but for Ramdas he was Ram," Ramdas replied and added: "In regard to your present of clothes Ramdas never asked you for any and has no need for them. God provides him whenever he wants."

The dinner over, the party dispersed. The mother took Ramdas out on a visit to the house of Raja Ram's sister who accorded them a hearty welcome. Here Ramdas observed the remarkably meek and egoless nature of Mother Elizabeth. While Ramdas was given a cushion for a seat spread on a carpet on the floor, she was offered a chair to sit on, but she refused to take the chair as, by so doing, she would be assuming a higher position than Ramdas. She therefore squatted on the carpet beside him. At the time of leaving the house by the staircase Ramdas was jumping down the steps and the mother kindly hinted: "Beware, Ramdas, don't lose balance."

"Mother," Ramdas replied significantly, "Ramdas never loses balance."

"You are very clever, Ramdas," she remarked laughing, "you have always a ready wit."

Ramdas returned to Kantilal's house.

(ii) What Fools Them—An Explanation

One day Ramdas had an invitation from the local ashram of Jain *sadhus*. Popatbhai accompanied him to the ashram. A dozen *sadhus* including those who attended the mother's memorable garden party had a long discussion with Ramdas on the question of the moment, *ahimsa*. They put him several questions regarding the state of *dwandwatita* and *trigunatita*. Ramdas added a vein of humour to his talks and evoked frequent laughter from the *sadhus*. The leader among them asked Ramdas with a serious concern.

"Swami, don't you filter water before drinking?"

"Ramdas does not attach much importance to filtration," Ramdas replied, "unless the water is dirty. The flowing water of the river which he often used to drink with his hands needed no filtration."

"There are germs in the water which you destroy by drinking," he remarked.

"You do the same through filtration," said Ramdas. "Moreover, even the drops of water well-filtered have still germs floating in them although these are not visible to the naked eye. A look through a powerful microscope would reveal to the sight millions of live germs in them. For health it is necessary that we should drink pure water. Destruction of the germs in water either through the heat of the stomach, filtration or boiling is inevitable."

While still the talk was going on, Popatbhai pulled Ramdas's cloth from behind and hinted that the interview might be terminated and they might leave the place. But Ramdas liked to remain a little longer answering the curious questions put by the *sadhus* whom he found in quite a jovial mood. After a short time, since Popatbhai was growing impatient, Ramdas had to bid adieu to the saints.

On their way back to Kantilal's house Popatbhai observed: "Swamiji, did you not notice that the Jain *sadhus* were all the while making fun of you? So it was that I became impatient to leave the place as soon as possible."

"You are mistaken, Ram," Ramdas answered, "they were so kind. Ramdas felt quite at ease in their cheerful company."

"There you are, Swamiji," said Popatbhai, "it is this guileless nature of yours that has made a fool of me and attracted me and all others to your person."

In the evenings there would be Ramnam *dhun* in Kantilal's house and Popatbhai in his sweet voice led the *bhajan*. Dr. Shukla and other friends from Wadhwan paid frequent visits.

Ramdas's daily morning visits to Mother Elizabeth's bungalow continued, where he also met Raja Ram and Prakashanand.

Ramdas had also, in response to her wish, to visit Bama Saheb, the old Rani at her palace. The pious lady was as usual very kind and hospitable.

She asked: "How is it that we don't attain *shanti* in spite of all our efforts?"

To this Ramdas replied: "Ramdas is reminded of the popular song of Kabir in which he says: The fish is thirsty in water; at this I cannot help laughing. So although we always live, move and have our being in the infinite ocean of pure bliss, still we complain that we are miserable."

Then the learned and well-informed lady said: "True, the fish can drink water only when it turns on its side, otherwise not."

"Yes, in our case," Ramdas replied, "to completely surrender to the will of God is to turn on the side, then we are filled with the nectar of immortality."

One morning Mother Elizabeth introduced Ramdas to an American tourist, a young lady, Mrs. Pym. At the first meeting she discussed about the movement of Mahatma Gandhi and her interview with him. She held a prejudiced view about the Mahatma and his principles of public action. Ramdas told her at the close of the conversation that she was welcome to differ from the Mahatma, but to ascribe to him a deliberate aim at fame and self-importance as she did, was wrong. He added that she must admit it was but right that India should be self-sufficient and independent. India must learn to maintain herself with regard to her main needs of life, namely, food and clothing from her own produce and manufacture. Ramdas did not believe in India's isolation from the rest of the world, which would mean her decay and death. She must have free intercourse with other countries of the world, but such intercourse should be based upon equality and independence. The cult of hate was ruinous. Ramdas might not agree with Mahatmaji in all that he said and did, but he had deep regard and love for him, so be it with her and all.

In the afternoon, the same day, there was a meeting at Shet Mohanlal's residence. This time three ladies were present, each of them belonging to a different nationality. Mother Elizabeth was of course an English lady, Mrs. Pym an American and a new arrival, Miss Krouse was a German. Prince Pratap Singh, a younger son of Raja Ram, was also one of the party.

Mother Elizabeth got copies of Ramdas's second booklet, "At the Feet of God" in the publication of which she had helped and to which she had written a loving foreword, and desired that Ramdas should present them to the ladies. The ladies asked him to have his autograph on the presented copies. Accordingly, he wrote down his love and regards to them signing: "From your child Ramdas." On a previous occasion, at the wish of Mother Elizabeth Ramdas had written the same words on a copy which she had for her own use. Seeing the exact similarity of the wording in the case of the other ladies, she remarked, when they were alone together later, "Ramdas, don't you think this mother's love (referring to herself) is greater than that of others? I expected you would make some difference in your estimation of my love in comparison with that of the other mothers."

"For Ramdas all mothers are alike," replied Ramdas.

After sundry talks about the ways at Sabarmati Ashram, which was recently visited by Mrs. Pym, during which Ramdas played the role of a silent listener, he had a short conversation with Miss Krouse. This young lady had adopted Jainism and had spent many long months on Mount Abu in rigorous austerities. She was simple and childlike in her manners and talks. Dressed in plain clothes, she was frank, cheerful and unsophisticated. She glanced over the pages of "At the Feet of God".

"I do not agree with you, Ramdas, in your articles on faith," she said. "I believe that by *purushartha*, i.e., by steady and severe discipline alone, can the contaminated and imprisoned Atman be purified and liberated. I do not believe in the theory of the pristine and eternal purity and the freedom of the soul, with ignorance only as a cloud over it, and also I do not believe that the mere removal of the cloud means realisation of immortality as Vedantists hold."

"You may approach the Truth, mother, in whatever way you like. The question simply is, which is the easiest and quickest path that takes you to the goal," Ramdas observed.

After a course of milk and fruits the party broke up.

Now Ramdas received a call from Una, a far away corner of Kathiawar in Junagad State. Maganlal, the young friend who was Ramdas's companion during his former visits to this province, was now employed as a teacher in Una. It was he who was drawing him to the place. Popatbhai also started with Ramdas.

Before leaving Limbdi, Ramdas paid a last visit to Mother Elizabeth. When parting she remarked: "Ramdas, you have reached in spiritual attainment the last but one step. You have still to rise higher. You are blessed. It is all due to your *samskaras* of previous births."

Ramdas with folded palms replied: "Ramdas does not know what stage he has reached, higher or lower. Neither does he care to know. He is simply where God has placed him and he is content."

CHAPTER 42: UNA – BOMBAY

(i) The Dose of Poison

In due time, Ramdas arrived with Popatbhai at Veraval, a prominent sea-port on the Kathiawar coast. Here they stopped with a Gujarati doctor in his hospital, who took them in the evening to attend the *kirtan* and discourse of a saintly householder in the city. They also visited Prabhaspattan where, according to Bhagwat Purana, the Yadavas, members of Sri Krishna's vast family, fought among themselves bringing about the total destruction of their race. Here in an extensive plain was a small enclosure in which there stood an ancient peepal tree. The fence was of iron bars fixed on low walls. In the niche of one of the walls was seen an image of Sri Krishna in a reclining posture. It was said that this was the spot where Sri Krishna shuffled off his body as the result of his being hit by an arrow from the bow of a passing hunter.

It was arranged that Ramdas should start from Veraval by a cargo brig that was bound for Una. The brig was an open boat filled with gunny bags of merchandise. It was to leave the port in the night. So early at night Ramdas and Popatbhai boarded the vessel. The season was winter. Hence the cold was severe. The cutting sea breeze blew over the boat with full force. They possessed hardly any extra clothing. They coiled themselves in the hollows between the bags and covered themselves with the single cotton cloth they each had. The boat left the shores about ten in the night. It was believed at first that the boat would reach the port Una by the ensuing morning. But for lack of wind the boat made very slow progress; morning dawned and they were still far away from the destination. Cold in the night was now succeeded by the heat of the sun. They were well-nigh fried in the sun the whole day, the boat having reached its destination past six in the evening. They had also to observe a partial fast, for they had no food to eat except a plantain each and they had even no water to drink.

At the landing place the odour of dried fish that filled the air was too much for Popatbhai. He expressed his disgust in strong terms and did not wish to take this route for return journey.

On landing they met Maganlal and another friend who had come to receive them. A six-mile walk brought them to Una. Ramdas and Popatbhai remained with Maganlal in his rooms on the ground floor of a big building, the upper floor of which was occupied by a Parsi chemist and his family. Maganlal was living alone.

The news of Ramdas's arrival spread in the town and many people came to see him, of whom mention has to be made of a Parsi chemist, Dr. Mahadevia, a Khoja and the schoolmasters.

Ramdas had invitations to dinner from the doctor and the Parsi chemist. Their children and wives also treated Ramdas with great kindness. The Parsi chemist, a quiet, earnest and simple soul, spent most of his time in Ramdas's company. He was so much enamoured of Ramnam that he commenced repeating it ceaselessly. One day an incident happened which tended to strengthen his faith in God.

While he was sitting with Ramdas, a travelling agent of drug-stores came to interview the chemist friend. In the course of their business talk the Parsi chemist asked the agent to supply him with a certain poisonous drug. The agent expressed his surprise that the chemist's stock of that drug should have gone off so soon, as he had supplied the stuff, a good quantity only very recently. Then the question came up as to what was the maximum dose of the drug. Now the Parsi friend came to know that he had that day given to a patient a dose of the same drug by mistake twenty times the quantity of the maximum dose. The medicine was to be taken at seven o'clock in the evening and the talk here was going on at about the same time. The Parsi coming to realise the consequences of his oversight got thoroughly frightened and, losing no time, directly ran up to the patient's house. But fortunately for him the patient had not swallowed the death-dealing dose of poison. He snatched away the packet of the powder and hastened back to where Ramdas sat, and falling at his feet said with great emotion, his eyes filled with tears: "Swamiji, you have saved me today from the gallows. It is all due to your kindness." Then he narrated the whole story.

"It is the remembrance of God that saved you, friend; the saviour is always God," Ramdas replied.

For this lapse on his part he undertook a fast of three days during which he subsisted merely on water and Ramnam never left his lips. He also eschewed sleep at night. The Ram *mantram* rang on his tongue continuously.

Visits to the sugarcane fields of the Khoja friend, where he was given a cool drink of the cane juice, and to the noted shrine of Mahadev in the suburbs of the town comprised the other events of the earlier part of Ramdas's stay in Una. Latterly he was presented to the boys of the local High School, in which Maganlal was a teacher and also to the girls of two primary schools. In all of them Ramdas delivered short speeches upon "The right conduct of boys and girls."

While returning from the High School he joined in the game of cricket with the boys on the play-ground. When he stood up for bowling his very first ball knocked off the mid-wicket. Amidst the laughter of the lookers-on, Ramdas left the field.

In the hospital there was a post-mortem examination over the body of a young man who had died by an accident. With the permission of the doctor, Popatbhai was present at the examination. He carefully scrutinized all the internal organs of the human body. Directly it was over, he came to Ramdas and remarked: "Swamiji, the stomach in our body is after all such a small bag that I wonder why we stuff it with so much food. The stomach, judging from its size, needs only a small quantity of food. We must be overfilling it causing it to bulge out and produce a pot belly."

Ramdas laughed, as also the other friends who listened to his humorous but pertinent observations.

Dr. Mahadevia belonged to the Tilak school of thought. He had many a discussion with Ramdas on the question of nonviolence.

Ramdas remained in Una for over a week and his time of departure came. Popatbhai would not agree to travel by the sea route. So a bullock-cart was engaged to convey them to Veraval. They were warned that the road was very bad. The cart was half-filled with straw on the top of which was spread a thick mattress with two pillows. The sides of the carriage were fenced with loose ropes. As the cart progressed they found it impossible to assume sitting posture. The stalwart bullocks dragged the cart behind them ruthlessly over the hard, dry, rocky and uneven tract. The cart rolled on swaying from side to side, punctuated by sudden thuds and knocks. The occupants of the cart now and again bumped against each other. They had to clutch at the loose ropes of the fence for very life, lest they should be thrown out on to the road through the wide gaps on them. Sleep and rest were out of question. For all their efforts they could not retain a single position for more than a minute. They seemed to be a pair of sardines just out of the sea on the dry sands, fluttering and leaping over each other!

What with the sudden jumps of the cart and the clash of the bodies their very bones seemed to rattle in their frames. Ramdas laughed and laughed at the unique experience, and said with great amount of truth, "Out of the frying pan into the fire." Popatbhai was silent. The distance to be covered before they could reach Veraval was about forty-eight miles and would take not less than twenty-four hours. For an hour, at long intervals, there were four halts at the wayside villages. When there were only ten miles still left to reach Veraval, Ramdas jumped out of the cart and proposed to walk the distance and Popatbhai followed suit. At dusk they reached Veraval.

The cart arrived later; except for the loss of a pillow which must have dropped on the road, there was no other mishap. The night was spent in a small room on the third story of a huge business house belonging to a young merchant.

Now Popatbhai who is a man of simple habits had a deep-rooted dislike for smoking. He would go about advising every smoker, who came in contact with him to give up the habit, at the same time, expatiating upon its manifold evils. But by a strange irony of fate, he was the storekeeper of bidis for Ramdas who was given to smoking! His high regard for Ramdas would not permit of his looking upon this habit of Ramdas as condemnatory. In the small room he smoked. The windows being very high and small in size, clouds of smoke gathered in the room, thick and fast.

"Ramji, the nauseating smell of smoke must be very trying to your nostrils which are unused to it," remarked Ramdas.

"Not at all," he replied quickly; "on the contrary, the smoke you puff out has been purifying the atmosphere." Verily, true love sees no defects and this is the greatest quality of love!

(ii) God Does Everything for the Best

Popatbhai parted from Ramdas at Veraval since he had to return to Wadhwan city, his native place, while Ramdas boarded the B.I.S.N. steamer sailing for Bombay. The steamer started from Veraval in the night and reached the Bombay port in the evening next day. He made his way straight to Sanjivrao's rooms where he gave an agreeable surprise both to Sanjivrao and his wife.

This time Ramdas's stay in Bombay extended to over two weeks, and he had to go through a fully crowded programme. Hundreds of visitors from various parts of Bombay poured in to see him from early morning until late in the night, and he was kept either busy talking or entertained with sweet *kirtan* by the devotees who could sing. Of these a young friend, Ratnakar by name, arranged for two discourses by Ramdas in the hall of the Saraswat Association, Gamdevi. On each occasion there was a crowded audience mainly of Saraswats. The first discourse was in English on "The Goal of Life" and the second in Konkani on "Karmayoga." The second was largely attended by Saraswat ladies.

As Ramdas spoke extempore, which he always did, the supreme bliss he was enjoying flowed out in words. At the time he found himself in a state of perfect ecstasy. He talked freely like a child before the motherly audience, for the friends and mothers assembled heard him with all love and patience.

The substance of his discourse on the Goal of Life was: The highest gift, this human life, is granted to us by God in order to realise Him—the supreme Reality—who is eternal bliss and peace. God-realisation means universal vision; i.e., to become ever conscious of our union with an impersonal, calm, pure, changeless and all-pervading existence and look upon all form and change as the expression of that Truth. This exalted state is attained by constant attunement of the mind to the single thought of the Truth through ceaseless stream of remembrance and meditation on it. The condition of our progress towards the Truth depends upon our ardour and intensity for its attainment. When we understand the Truth as the goal of life, our approach to it becomes easy and rapid. The aim of life should not be anything short of this highest consummation of human life. Concentration of thought and effort is the first desideratum. For concentration the easiest method is the constant repetition of the divine Name. He who possesses the Name is possessed of the Truth. What has made Ramdas swim always in an ocean of bliss and peace? It is the divine Name. He is present before you, as a living example, showing the potency of the Name."

Friends invited him to Santa Cruz and Matunga where also he had to deliver two discourses. God willed that His servant and child should thus be drawn out from obscurity into the limelight of Bombay to preach about His greatness and the glory of His Name.

In the course of his discourse at Santa Cruz, when he touched upon the golden principle "God does everything for the best," he narrated a popular story in support of the deep truth underlying the motto.

Once a king with his minister followed by his retinue went into the depths of a jungle on a hunting expedition. Now the minister was well-known for his wisdom. He held the motto: 'God does everything for the best', and whenever anyone went to him for advice in his trouble, woe or misfortune, the minister would console the distressed party by inducing him to acknowledge the truth of this saying.

The king and the minister in their hunt for game separated from the followers and roamed far into the interior of the extensive forest and eventually lost their way. The sun rose to the meridian. The king was oppressed with fatigue and hunger. They rested in the shade of a tree.

"Minister" said the exhausted king, "I am sorely upset through pangs of hunger. Can you get me something to eat?"

The minister looked round and discovered fruits on the trees. Climbing up a tree he plucked a few ripe fruits and presented them to the king. The king in his haste to eat the fruit, while cutting it with a penknife, chopped off a bit of his finger. With a cry of pain he dropped the fruit and the knife, his injured finger streaming with blood.

"Oh!" he cried out. "How it pains—O minister."

"God does everything for the best," put in the minister quietly.

These words tended only to rouse the already petulant king. He flew into a rage and cried out: "Fool, truce to your philosophy! I have had enough of it. While I am suffering from excruciating agony, the only consolation you can tender is: 'God does everything for the best.' How can this be for the best when my pain is intense and real! Avaunt, I will have nothing of you in future. Get out of my sight and never show me your face again."

The king could not control himself and rising up kicked the minister furiously and commanded him to take himself off at once. While the minister was leaving the king, he calmly reiterated: "God does everything for the best."

Now the king was left alone. He tore a strip of his garment and bandaged his injured finger and was given to sad reflections, when two stalwart men were seen approaching him. They instantly fell on the king and bound him hand and foot. Struggle or resistance was utterly useless, as the men were sturdy giants in build.

The frightened king now asked: "What are you going to do with me?"

They replied: "We want you to be sacrificed at the altar of our Goddess Kali. It is the custom to offer to her a human sacrifice once a year. The time has arrived for it and we were on the look out for a human being and we are fortunate in having found you."

These words of his captors thoroughly alarmed the king. He remonstrated: "Let me go, I am the king of a province. You cannot, therefore, kill me for the sacrifice."

The men laughed and said: "Then this year's sacrifice is going to be unique, and our goddess will be highly pleased when she finds that we bring to her altar this time, an exalted personage as an offering. Come along."

They dragged the victim to the Kali shrine, not far away from the spot. He was duly placed on the sacrificial alter. Things were ready for the death-blow, when the priest observing that his left-hand forefinger was bandaged, loosened it, and discovered that a portion of it was cut off. He said to the men: "This man is not acceptable to our goddess. Set him free. The goddess wants a whole man, while the man here has a defect in his body. A bit of his finger is gone. Let him go."

Accordingly, untying the ropes with which he was bound, the men set the king free and allowed him to depart in peace.

Now the king remembered the words of the minister, uttered when his finger received the wound: "God does everything for the best"—indeed had it not been for that fortunate cut he would have by now been a dead man. He felt keenly for the ill-treatment he had meted out to his friend. He was anxious to repair the blunder by begging his forgiveness. So he rambled in the wood, called aloud the name of the minister, and at last found him.

The minister was resting beneath a tree. Going up to him the king embraced him with extreme love and said: "Friend, I seek your forgiveness for the cruelty I inflicted on you. The truth of your golden saying is brought home to me."

Then he narrated the incident of the intended sacrifice to the goddess, and how he was set free on account of the defect in his hand, caused by the knife-cut.

"Sire," replied the minister, "you have done me no harm. So there is nothing to forgive. In truth, you have saved me. While you kicked and drove me away, you may remember I repeated the same saying: 'God does everything for the best.' Now in my case as well it has come true. For, if you had not driven me away, I would have been in your company when the men of Kali captured you and, when they discovered that you were unfit for the sacrifice, they would have offered me instead, since I had no such defect in my body as the one you had so providentially acquired. So God does everything for the best."

The story produced a deep impression on the minds of the friends who assembled to hear Ramdas.

(iii) The Dance on the Head of Shiva

Durgashanker, an elder brother of Kantilal of Limbdi, resided in Bombay. He was Ramdas's fellow student during his old life at the V. J. Technical Institute of Bombay. He and his pious wife were paying frequent visits to Ramdas at Sanjivrao's. He proposed to take Ramdas on a trip to the noted Elephanta caves near Bombay.

Early one day, a party of about twenty persons including ladies started on the trip. Sanjivrao and Ratnakar also formed the party. They boarded a brig specially engaged for their use. As the brig sailed on the sea with an undulating movement, the friends entertained the party with choice devotional songs to the accompaniment of a hand harmonium, which they had taken with them. By noon they drew up at the landing jetty, leading to the hill containing the famous caves. On alighting they sought a quiet place for their dinner. They had provided themselves with various kinds of refreshments. After dinner they sauntered about to see the caves.

The first cave they entered, the largest one of the lot, was a spacious hall, cut out of a giant granite rock, supported on solid, beautifully carved pillars standing at short intervals. Inside the cave was a shrine having on its facing wall three compartments, each of which represented figures of images embossed in relief. The middle figure was the huge head of a three-faced god. The sculpture was exquisite. The faces bore a calm and peaceful appearance. On either side of this visage were life-size images exhibiting the same skill and mastery of art. To the right of the cave there was a reservoir of water fed by a perennial spring issuing from the side of the hill. To the left was a plain rock-cut temple with an open courtyard in front.

The party sat in the courtyard and again the singers entertained the party with their soul-elevating music. About three o'clock they went out looking for new places to be seen. Going round the hill, at its base were found many other small caves at various distances from each other. At one place descrying a big *Shiva-linga* in a cave-temple, Ramdas ran up in advance and mounting on the image commenced dancing on its head in ecstasy. The friends who followed later were both surprised and delighted to behold Ramdas dancing on the head of Shiva. The image was over five feet in height and three feet in diameter.

When it was nearing four o'clock they started on their homeward journey. Now the boat swayed on the waves with greater majesty, now bounded, then rose and fell. The cool evening breeze blew over them keeping them absorbed in the sweet memories of the blissful day. By evening the party reached the city.

Here Ramdas was inspired by Ram to write a letter to Anandrao of Kasaragod expressing a wish to have an Ashram in that place on the Pilikunji hill. He also suggested that it might be named "Anandashram.'

The days in Bombay passed quickly in continued rounds of bliss. The divine Name spread far and wide.

CHAPTER 43: ANGAR – SHOLAPUR ERNAKULAM – KASARAGOD

(i) The Miracles

The friends in Sholapur district were keenly longing to have Ramdas in their midst. So the next place Ramdas visited was this district. Here, as on previous occasions, he was welcomed by vast masses of people with great acclamation. He was taken from village to village in procession and honoured with the grandeur and display, peculiar to the East. In one village where he stayed for a week, there was a unique devotional ferment among its inhabitants. People of all castes and creeds mingled together. *Kirtan, bhajan, harikatha*, and feast became the order of the day.

Janardan Pant and Prem Singh were Ramdas's close companions, of whom the latter was perfectly mad with devotion. He was for days so inebriated with the divine emotion that he would be often unconscious of his body and surroundings. He spent days and nights dancing and singing God's Name.

Mothers went into ecstasies at the sight of Ramdas. Govind Joshi's wife would every evening wave round Ramdas her hands containing salt to ward off the evil eye—a custom observed by the Hindu mothers in regard to their children! Prem Singh took Ramdas to his village Diksal where, in the presence of a big gathering, he bathed him with curds and milk mixed with sugar, *ghee*, and honey which they denominate as "Panchamrit Abhishek."

A humorous incident took place during Ramdas's visit to one of the villages named Khandali. He was invited by the Kulkarni of the place. With Ramdas had come over fifty friends from the preceding villages. The meals provided by the hosts everywhere in these parts consisted of sweet cakes and *ladoos*. When all the friends assembled, sometime before dinner, Ramdas asked a boy to fetch bunches of neem leaves—neem is a tree common in that place, the leaves of which are bitter to the taste, but they have medicinal properties. The boy brought the leaves. Now Ramdas proposed to the friends to join him in eating them. At this the expression on their faces underwent a change from one of cheerfulness to its reverse. One by one they slipped away offering some lame excuse, and so Ramdas alone had to eat his share of the leaves. When the dinner time arrived, all the friends turned up without an exception!

Ramdas went round over thirty villages. It was a time of unprecedented enthusiasm, bustle and joy, both for Ramdas and the villagers. Amongst those who felt a great attraction for Ramdas and sought his constant company was the young lad Maruti, who has been mentioned in the early part of the narrative.

In Angar, Ramdas had to stay for eight days before his departure to Kame, a railway station. The eight days were characterized by incessant activities on the part of the villagers in *kirtan, bhajan*, and feasts. On the last day, Ramdas was taken round all the lanes and streets of the village in a procession consisting of thousands of people with music and the country band. The flags and other emblems of the temple were also carried in front of him. The crowds followed upto the outskirts of the village where Ramdas, taking his final leave, raced on towards the railway station which lay at a distance of nearly four miles from Angar. About fifty villagers followed him.

Word was sent in advance to the station master, a devout brahmin, who was anxious to entertain Ramdas for an hour before the arrival of the train. Ramdas and the party reached the station in the evening. They were led directly to the residence of the station master. He had expected not more than a dozen people with Ramdas and so had prepared meals only for that number. But the number actually exceeded fifty. The host and his people at home grew anxious as to how they could satisfy all the people that had come. There was no time to prepare meals again. However, the friends were asked to sit for supper and strange as it would appear, the food sufficed the whole lot and there was no deficiency in anything. An old woman of the house came out after the feeding was over, and with hands folded in salutation said: "The ways of God are simply inexplicable. He has worked a miracle in our house."

After the meals, the party sat on the platform and for about fifteen minutes Prem Singh entertained them with songs of *Brahmanand* in his melodious voice. Soon the train arrived and Ramdas got into a carriage accompanied by a few friends. Now one of the party, who came to the station for the send off, handed to Ramdas a small bag containing some groundnuts, sugarcandy, parched rice, etc. all mixed up together. Ramdas, thinking of distributing the eatables as *prasad* to the friends on the platform, who now crowded at the door of the compartment occupied by him, took them out by handfuls from the bag and commenced to distribute them freely to the friends. Seeing this, the passengers in other compartments poured down and coming to where Ramdas was, stretched forth their hands for *prasad*. He went on giving away the eatables from the bag. The amazing thing was the bag would never become empty. He must have distributed its contents to more than a hundred persons until the train moved away from the station and still the bag contained some *prasad*.

Here a few words about the nature of the villagers living in the region surrounding the Pandharpur shrine in Sholapur District may not be out of place. These simple village folk, besides being sincere and honest, have an extremely kind and hospitable disposition. No traveller or guest is allowed to go from their doors without receiving due service from the household. They are humble and unassuming in their manners. They take it that the guest is Vithoba Himself, the deity of Pandharpur and, on the side of the guest, he too considers that he is fed and kindly treated by the same deity. Their mode of living is quite plain; coarse but wholesome food and thick clothing put on in the old fashion suffice their needs. They are a hardy and industrious people. Time is of no account with them and so they are not bound by its tyranny. They are tolerant, generous, and self-sacrificing to a degree. They do not harass their minds and others' with skeptical doubts. They implicitly believe in the workings of Providence and live always in submission to Him. Their women are also of the same incorruptible nature.

(ii) A Straight Hit

For the Ekadashi, Ramdas was taken again to Pandharpur where he came across troops of devotees whom he had met on his visit to the villages. From Pandharpur on his way to Akalkot, wherefrom he had an invitation, he made a halt for a day in Sholapur.

Prem Singh, who was in his company, desired that he should stop with a relation of his who was a great devotee. Ramdas agreeing, the party consisting of Janardan Pant, Prem Singh, Maruti and Madhavrao proceeded to the devotee's house. Here already a noted saint was a guest of the householder and a *puja* of a photo of the saint's *guru* was in full progress when Ramdas entered. Ramdas directly went up to the verandah where the worship was held. A seat of cushions was by the side of the photo, the *asan* of the saint. Prem Singh, who carried a deerskin for Ramdas, spread it on the cushion and beckoned him to take his seat on it. Ramdas unconsciously obeyed and sat down whilst all the congregated people were standing and the saint was performing the *puja* in all eclat.

The *puja* over, the saint without caring even to look at Ramdas, retired to an inner room of the house as a mark of displeasure at the apparently insulting behaviour of Ramdas. In fact, Prem Singh had unwittingly made him sit on the *gadi* or *asan* of the saint who must have surely boiled and fumed at Ramdas's gross insolence.

But Ramdas was unconcerned and indifferent. Next, to make reparation for the lapse and scenting unpleasantness, Prem Singh, preparing another seat by the side of Ramdas, requested the saint to come out and grace it, which he however did with manifest reluctance. Then garlanding both, he saluted them. The saint was not yet pacified.

The saint asked Ramdas who his *guru* was to which Ramdas replied, "Ramdas's *guru* is residing in his own heart and in the hearts of all." At this the saint sniffed contemptuously and left his seat.

In the evening, as usual, in the programme of the saint there was reading of Dasbodh, the well-known work of Saint Samarth Ramdas, the eminent *guru* of Shivaji of historic fame. In the course of his discourse the saint levelled at first veiled sarcasms at Ramdas and at last broke out into the peroration: "Nowadays, it is common for any man in the street to don the *sannyasi* robe, pose himself as *guru* and travel from place to place for collecting disciples. Of this type you have one in the person of the *sadhu* sitting here," and he pointed his finger directly at Ramdas. Ramdas could only smile at the invective. After his *pravachan* was over, Maruti, the lad, was called upon to speak on the oft-quoted and sublime *sloka* of the Gita: "Sarvadharman parityajya…" etc.; "Abandoning all *dharmas* come to Me alone for shelter, grieve not, I shall liberate thee from all sins." The boy delivered himself in a breathless outflow for about half-an-hour. Lastly the saint asked Ramdas to speak a few words in Hindi.

At first Ramdas started on the universal *darshan* which he emphasized as the goal of all spiritual endeavour. Then he came to the means of its attainment. He held out service of saints and Ramnam as the only *sadhana* for the purification of the mind and heart, which was the essential condition for achieving that supreme vision. He congratulated the assembled devotees on their good fortune in having an opportunity for serving a saint. Pointing to the saint by Ramdas's side, he added that there was a saint for them to serve and be benefited. He exhorted them not to allow such a God-given occasion to slip by.

For the night Ramdas was escorted to the house of a merchant devotee who once had an occasion to entertain him at Angar. He was away from home, but his pure-hearted wife welcomed him and the party into her house. The saint whom Ramdas met at Prem Singh's relation's house had asked him to be present next morning when he would expound Yoga Vasishtha. But Prem Singh stood resolutely against Ramdas's attending it. The friends who were with him made adverse comments on the saint's behaviour towards him. But he stopped them saying: "Why do you forget that it is Ram Himself playing that part? He assumes various characters."

Early on the following day, the party left Sholapur by motorbus for Akalkot. By midday they reached the town and were put up in the house of a friend named Taksade. He was all kindness and hospitality. This friend arranged for a discourse in English by Ramdas at the *Samadhi* temple of the late renowned saint of the place, Akalkot Baba. A few hours before the engagement, an elderly *vakil* who was stricken with grief over the demise of his near relation came to see Ramdas. In his talk he roundly attacked faith in the existence of a God. Ramdas had a few words with him and a marvellous change came over him. He took Ramdas to his dwelling and was all humility and kindness.

In the evening, among a large number of friends who attended the discourse at the temple, the *vakil* friend was one who sat straight in front of Ramdas. The latter spoke for about forty-five minutes. He observed the *vakil* shedding streams of tears. It was evident that he was touched by Ramdas's repeated exhortations to believe in God and develop devotion to Him.

That very night Ramdas had to start from Akalkot to Bangalore. The railway station lay at a distance of six miles from the city. A horse *tonga* was hired to take him to the station. The *vakil* friend was there to take final leave of him. When the *tonga* was about to start, the friend was overpowered by strong emotion and wept on account of separation. Then, again, as the *tonga* was nearing the railway station, Maruti cried like an inconsolable child at the thought of his approaching severance from Ramdas. Janardan Pant took him to task for his exhibition of feelings in that manner, reminding him of the high philosophy he used to propound while dilating on the Gita *slokas*.

They reached the station and, when the train arrived, Prem Singh and Madhavrao also started weeping. So in the midst of their wails Ramdas and Janardan Pant, who proposed to accompany him as far as Bangalore, got into the train and left Sholapur District.

(iii) A Mother Sees a Vision

In due time the train slowed down at the Bangalore station and halted. Alighting they made their way straight to Malleswaram in the company of Bhavanishankerrao who had come to the station to receive them. In Bangalore, Ramdas, this time, spent only a few days. Janardan Pant gave the devoted household the delight of listening to his *harikatha* performance. The day of departure having come Janardan Pant left for his district by an earlier train. At the time of bidding farewell to Ramdas, Janardan Pant also wept, when Ramdas reminded him: 'Ramji, what is this you are doing? What about your words to Maruti when he manifested similar feelings?'

Ramdas also started at the appointed time and it was night. His next destination was Ernakulam in Cochin State. The railway carriage in which he travelled was crowded. He secured a seat at the corner of a short bench. A passenger on the bench was sleeping at full length and Ramdas sat in such a manner as to cause the least disturbance to the sleeping man. The seat in front of him was occupied by three men, two of whom were Musalmans. From their gilt turbans and the showy badges, they appeared to be *sepoys* of some eminent personage. A steady look at the oval brass plates on the red badges revealed the fact that they belonged to the Cochin State. Both the *sepoys*, as night advanced, began to doze in their seats. The elder of the two, fearing that his neat gilt turban might tumble down while nodding through sleep, placed it near Ramdas on his seat and commanded him in a gruff voice: "Hey, take care of my turban; see that it does not fall down. Watch and guard it well!" Ramdas signified by a 'hum' that he would do as bidden.

The *sepoys* now entered deep into the land of sleep, and Ramdas fell to watching the precious turban given in his charge. A little later, the sleeping man on his bench stretched his legs straight, and Ramdas had to move on to the very extremity of the bench and so was obliged to take up the turban and place the valuable charge tenderly on his lap. Still further the passenger lengthened himself. Ramdas thought that he was not an ordinary human being but an India-rubber man, for he seemed to stretch himself to any extent! Ramdas now, seeing the floor below the opposite seat vacant and free from luggage, slipped down to the place with the turban. Placing the turban near his head on a portion of his cloth, Ramdas took a reclining posture since the low place did not permit of sitting upright.

The train ran on unmindful of the fantastic positions assumed by the passengers who were huddled up within its compartments. Ramdas also dozed away. As the morning light was streaking in through the windows, he was startled by a soul-racking, sharp and strange cry above him. It was the gruff voice of the *sepoy*, owner of the turban, who was heaping curses on the rogue who disappeared with his head gear. Now Ramdas slowly slid out of the nook with the turban in his hand. At the sight of the turban, the *sepoy* leapt through joy and wresting it from Ramdas's hands cried: "So you were below the seat! Ha! how could I know? Thank Allah, I have my turban back." And he stroked his long grey beard with evident self-complacence.

Ramdas now came to Shoranur Junction where he met Sanjivrao in whose escort he caught the train to Ernakulam and, by midday, reached the destination.

As usual, Ramdas stopped with Sanjivrao at whose house in the mornings and evenings a number of friends who had been visiting Ramdas on the previous occasions came to have talks with him. After dark there would be *kirtan* every day in Sanjivrao's house by his wife and children who sang in a melodious voice the abhangas of Tukaram and other saints and also God's Names. A few friends including Veeraraghava Iyer would attend the function. All the friends would be absorbed in the blissful contemplation of God for about two hours when the music was going on.

In regard to the recent illness of Veeraraghava Iyer, an extraordinary incident which took place has to be described here in some detail. Sometime ago this friend fell seriously ill and his life was despaired of. He dropped into a state of coma having lost all external consciousness. In this state he remained for a whole night. His devoted wife was in close attendance on him. She was keeping watch on this critical night. Past midnight, an irresistible wave of sleep overpowering her, she fell into a short nap. When she woke up with usual anxiety she beheld a strange vision. She discovered a *sannyasi* sitting on her husband's bed by his side. She was surprised how the *sadhu* could have come at that time of the night. But her heart was elated with hope that her husband would recover after such an assuring sight. The vision lasted for a few moments. The figure of the *sannyasi* disappeared, but her heart fluttered with faith and hope. Next morning Veeraraghava Iyer came down to normal consciousness with a decided turn in his illness towards recovery. In a few days he came round and was entirely free from the illness. Now his wife had no occasion to see Ramdas although her husband was seeing him at Sanjivrao's every time he visited Ernakulam.

On his complete recovery his wife spoke to her husband of the vision she had on that particular night and gave a clear description of the *sannyasi* she had beheld. Strange as it seemed to Veeraraghava Iyer, he found that her description exactly tallied with Ramdas and he expressed it to his wife, who thereafter felt a great desire to see Ramdas. He narrated this incident to several of his friends. This time when Ramdas was in Ernakulam, Veeraraghava Iyer's wife specially came to Sanjivrao's house with presents to see him and convinced herself and others that she had seen that memorable night of her husband's illness the form of the very *sannyasi* whom she was seeing in Ramdas. Strange indeed are the ways of God! Ramdas's stay in Ernakulam coming to a close he departed from thence for Kasaragod which he reached in due time.

(iv) Anandashram

Ramdas reached Kasaragod. After *darshan* of Gurudev and others, he remained at Anandrao's, occupying the small room of his private office. Anandrao was contemplating the erection of an ashram for him and was awaiting his return. He with Ramdas and some others went one morning to the Pilikunji hill in search of a suitable site for the ashram and at last discovered a beautiful spot belonging to Chandavar Sanjivrao. On negotiating for the plot with Sanjivrao, he agreed to hand over the small piece of land entirely for the ashram as a gift on condition that, if at any time the activities of the ashram as a religious institution should cease, the property should go back to him.

The work of constructing the building was taken up by Anandrao in right earnest, and it was hurried on as the monsoon was fast approaching. The ashram consisted of a tiny room with a raised pedestal against one of its walls to serve the purpose of a cot, and a square open verandah for receiving visitors and holding small *kirtan* parties. All round the four sides of the ashram, a belt of tulsi plants was planted. The site had a charm of its own. On its southern side was the beautiful view of the Payashwini river and green fields, and on the other side were hills covered with a dense jungle of tall trees. Soft, cool breezes always played about the ashram coming from the river. In the morning and evening the air was filled with the sweet music of birds. Before the ashram was occupied Ramdas paid hurried visits to Mangalore and Puttur. Kuber Anandrao escorted him to Puttur where he was put up at the Police Inspector Sundarrao's house. Hearing of his arrival many residents of Puttur, both friends and mothers, came to see him. An enterprising young man, full of zeal for the uplift of the school boys, had started a trial institution called Shanti Shibir where boys were trained in the discipline of the body and mind. A diet free from salt and chillies was prescribed. The chief principle on which the institution worked was the observance of *brahmacharya*. Life was systematized, and rules and regulations controlled the activities of the students, so that they might grow up into pure, noble and fearless sons of India.

Ramdas was invited to this institution by Raman Nambiyar, the headmaster of the High School—an earnest, simple and pure soul. Thus he was brought into contact with the young aspirants and their patriotic leader. He was asked to speak a few words on *brahmacharya* to the boys which he did in a short speech.

The next item of interest during his stay in Puttur was the visit to the noted Sri Krishna Mandir of Sri Krishna Rao, the veteran saint of the place. Kuttanmam, as he was known to all, was all kindness and love. He possessed a glorious record of religious service and led a life of purity, simplicity and devotion. Always *kirtan*, *bhajan*, and readings from religious texts were going on in the *mandir* presided over by the venerable saint.

Ramdas gave some discourses on devotion and allied subjects in Sundarrao's house which were attended mainly by mothers. He was taken to several houses for dinner and *kirtan*. Ramdas's brother by old birth, Narsingrao, also had him for a night's *kirtan* and dinner at his house. Here Ramdas noted the power of Ram *mantram* on a devotee, Gopal Pai, who had the repetition of the Name going on audibly even in his sleep, his very snoring was continuous, sonorous chanting of the *mantram*!

Soon after Ramdas arrived at Kasaragod he paid a flying visit to Mangalore. He stopped with Sitaramrao in Mangalore and also paid a visit to Mother Rukmabai at her father's. At Sitaramrao's he met an itinerant, educated *sadhu* who started a conversation with him on the proof of the existence of God. Ramdas had a few words with him but, as he seemed to be a skeptic and not open to discussion, Ramdas refused to be dragged into further discussion with him.

One afternoon, when Ramdas was sitting in the portico of the house with some mothers, a young man was seen standing at the gate of the compound with a bunch of plantains in hand. He stood for nearly an hour looking in the direction of the portico. When the mothers departed he came up and offering the plantains to Ramdas fell prostrate at his feet. Making him seated by his side, Ramdas went on talking about the power of God's Name and the blissful nature of true devotion of God. As he spoke on, the young man's eyes were filled with tears which coursed down his cheeks in streams. When Ramdas finished he again prostrated at Ramdas's feet and begged: "Be gracious to give me the *upadesh* of Ram *mantram*."

Ramdas immediately initiated him with the *mantram* and he left. Ramdas was to leave Mangalore for Kasaragod the next day. An hour before departure this young man suddenly turned up, an utterly changed man! He wore the ochre or orange-coloured robes of a *sannyasi* and his head was clean-shaven and he had a *lota* in his hand.

He was a bright and healthy-looking lad having the light of meditation in his eyes. He was the youngest of four brothers who ran a coffee hotel in Mangalore. The eldest was a devout soul and was spending his time mostly in *kirtan* and *bhajan*. Ramdas heard the story of the youngest brother's conversion from him. It appeared, immediately on leaving Ramdas, the youngest brother whose name was Rayu got his head shaved and had his clothes dyed in red ochre. For his initial *bhiksha* Rayu presented himself before the door of his brothers and called out for alms in the Name of God. His brothers were both pained and surprised at the transformation in Rayu. They tried to persuade him to give up the *diksha* and return to live with them to which he replied: "I am not related to any of you and am no longer yours. I belong to God in future and my life is for His devotion and service." On receiving *bhiksha* he walked away from the place and came straight to Ramdas at Sitaramrao's house. He accompanied Ramdas to Kasaragod. After a week's stay at Anandrao's house, Rayu left for Northern India.

The ashram work was getting on apace. When all things were ready, with a few select friends including Kuber Anandrao and Savoor Shankarrao who had come down specially for the occasion, Ramdas proceeded with the singing of God's Name to the ashram. Gurudev, though weak with old age, having desired to attend the opening of the ashram, also came. For over an hour *bhajan* went on and choice songs were sung by some pious mothers. At the close of the function Ramdas spoke on universal vision for about half-anhour. After distribution of *prasad* the friends dispersed.

CHAPTER 44: KASARAGOD

The foregoing chapters of this narrative were written some years ago. To bring the narration up-to-date, the account that follows is now appended to it. It is also intended to make this supplement as brief as possible by going over only the most outstanding features of Ramdas's later experiences.

Life at Anandashram, Kasaragod, was also filled with events which are worthy of chronicle. The earlier part of it ran on smoothly except for the crowds of visitors who assembled in the ashram either for performing *bhajan* or listening to the talks of Ramdas. Then commenced a period marked by celebrations during which the singing of the Lord's Name and glories went on continuously for twenty-four hours attended by hundreds of the devotees of Kasaragod.

Spiritual aspirants, young and old, had recourse to the ashram. Of these, mention may be made of a few who were, as it were, whole-time *sadhakas*, because they remained in the ashram during night as well. Ramanath Kini, Kanda, Purnanand and Krishnappa were the principal aspirants. Ramanath Kini was a young man who possessed not only a steadfast devotion to God but also a spirit of dispassion towards the pleasures of the world. Krishnappa was also a remarkably earnest and enthusiastic devotee. Kanda and Purnanand were of advanced age. They devoted their time mostly in taking part in the *bhajan* and repetition of God's Name. They were one and all exceedingly kind and loving to Ramdas.

Ramdas's daily food which consisted of a small quantity of boiled rice, milk and curry in the afternoon and fruit and milk in the night, was provided by Anandrao. Although he lived in a quiet and out-of-the-way retreat, he was kept engaged in talks, correspondence and other activities till late in the night.

Now a few main incidents during his stay in the ashram will be recounted here.

Krishna Bai, whose life in some detail has already been written and published in a booklet, visited the ashram in the company of some other ladies. From that time, her attraction for the ashram and Ramdas grew in intensity until at last she dedicated her life to the service of God and became a prominent co-worker with him. Her radiant personality, the selfless and silent service she rendered in the ashram, her pure overflow of love towards all alike, shone out of her and revealed her inherent greatness.

She underwent innumerable persecutions when she was thus walking heart and soul along the divine path, but all through it, she maintained her cheerful and patient nature untouched and unruffled. Those aspiring souls who came under the influence of her dazzling purity were redeemed.

Rama Bai (Ramdas's daughter by the old birth) with her husband was one of the constant visitors of the ashram. As she imbibed the discourses of Ramdas on devotion, during which he spoke also impressively on *vairagya*, the girl's mind turned away from the world, awakening in her heart a deep love and longing for God. Thenceforth she appeared to have been caught in the grip of a severe mental struggle. She lost all taste for the things of the world. She curtailed her domestic activities, reduced her food and finally gave up all interest and attachment to her house and became absorbed in God-thought. This state of things naturally frightened her husband and others in the house. Her one cry to Ramdas was: "Make me love God." This state continued for some months. However, after a great deal of persuasion by him, she came round and lived a normal life, of course without detriment to her love and devotion to God.

About this time, Mother Rukmabai, although she was ailing due to the chronic attack of asthma, came to stay with him at the ashram. The aspirants and devotees and principally Krishna Bai served and attended on her with great love and reverence. She bore bravely the discomforts of the ashram life. However, at the pressure of Ramdas, she went back to live with her daughter, coming to stay in the ashram off and on.

Soon after the ashram was started, two young women, schoolmistresses from Kasaragod, became regular visitors to the ashram. Both of them were unmarried but they were real spiritual aspirants. Purity and nobility of character shone on their faces. They got instructions from Ramdas regarding the methods for repetition of the Name and meditation. With earnestness and zeal they acted up to these instructions. One day both of them questioned him whether a woman can maintain *brahmacharya* all her life. Ramdas replied, "Certainly." At this they were highly pleased. They put themselves under strict discipline, started evening *bhajan* at home, regulated their diet and thus led an austere and chaste life. Blessed mothers! May the light of God ever illumine your hearts and all the ways of your lives!

Through correspondence, Ramdas was in touch with innumerable devotees in various parts of India. A year passed away in the ashram and these distant friends longed to see Ramdas again. Letters commenced to pour in from all parts appealing to him to leave the ashram and start on another tour. Since he had no command from Ram to go from the ashram he stuck on to it. Efforts through correspondence having failed, the friends of Maharashtra deputed Janardan Pant to visit the ashram in person to persuade Ramdas to go over to them under his escort. Janardan Pant and Sri Krishna Deshpande arrived. Their advent yielded immense joy to devotees of Kasaragod. Janardan Pant performed a *kirtan* at which hundreds of them assembled. But in spite of Janardan Pant's assiduous attempts to induce Ramdas to start with him on a tour, he had to turn down his proposal. He had not at the time, the least inclination to respond to his loving invitation. It was all so willed by God. Janardan Pant's disappointment was indeed great, and at the time of his departure he was moved to tears and exclaimed: "What message can I carry to the devotees of Sholapur who are so eager to have your *darshan*?" Ramdas had nothing to say in reply except to request him to convey to the devotees his appeal namely, that they should not cease repeating the Lord's Name and feeling that Ramdas was ever with them. Janardan Pant and Sri Krishna Deshpande left.

Among the saints who visited the ashram and gave Ramdas the joy of their *satsang* were: Swami Pranavanand, Swami Anandashram and Dwarakadas.

Swami Pranavanand, an elderly *sannyasi*, was a great and noble soul. At the very sight of Ramdas he conceived a love for him which can only be compared to the love of a mother for her child. His stay was very short being only for a day. In the night he would join Ramdas when he danced in ecstasy taking the Lord's Name. The swami, at the request of the devotees of Kasaragod, delivered a discourse on the tennis ground near the *munsif's* court. At the swami's pressure, Ramdas was made to fill the president's chair. After his discourse Ramdas spoke a few words on the unity of religions.

Shortly after, Swami Anandashram, the spiritual head of the Saraswat community, arrived at Kasaragod and took his residence in the precincts of the Sri Pandurang temple. Of course, the members of the Saraswat community went in large numbers for his *darshan*. At the repeated pressure of a friend among them, Ramdas was also taken over to him for *darshan*. Ramdas was made to take his seat opposite to him in an arm-chair in a small room on the first-floor of a house. The elite of the community had also assembled at the place. Ramdas duly honouring the *swamiji* with salutation took his seat. At the first glance he discovered the *swamiji* to be a pure and great soul. His handsome features radiated the glow of spiritual light. Ramdas felt perfectly free and blissful in his company. Without ceremony Ramdas started recounting to him the incidents of his trip to Kashmir and Amarnath. In a few words he discoursed upon the *siddhanta* of Kashmiris, that is, of Shiva and Shakti. Soon after, Ramdas, taking leave of the *swamiji*, returned to the ashram. A few days later, the *swamiji* in company with his disciples paid a visit to Anandashram. The occasion was characteristic of his broad-mindedness and kind and affable nature. After spending an hour or thereabouts in Ramdas's company, during which Ramdas alone spoke a few words on the value of solitude and *satsang*, the *swamiji* left the ashram and went back to the temple.

Dwarkadas's stay in the ashram extended over two months. While he was a devout and pure soul by nature, he was given to smoking *ganja*. The intoxication of this drug would unsettle his mind and turn him into a violent and irritable man. He carried with him a few small brass images of God for his daily worship. He was performing the daily worship after bath on the front verandah of the ashram. About this time Mark Sanjivrao was coming to the ashram for the nights.

One day Ramdas was called away to Rama Bai's house for attending their *bhajan*. In the ashram there were Ramnath Kini, Mark Sanjivrao, Dwarkadas and two other devotees. After the *bhajan* was over Ramdas returned to the ashram at about nine o'clock in the night. Meanwhile something had happened in the ashram. Dwarkadas was found to be sitting in a corner with a wry face nursing his knee-joint. The tale came out. When Ramdas was away there was a friendly scuffle between Dwarkadas and Ramanath Kini in the course of which Dwarkadas tumbled down from the verandah, his knee striking hard on the floor of the yard. He was fretting and grumbling over the accident. Ramdas consoled him. It must be related in this connection that Mark Sanjivrao was an early sleeper. He would therefore insist that all the members in the ashram go to bed early. So by ten o'clock all retired to sleep. It might have been about eleven o'clock when a loud grunting noise proceeded from the direction of Dwarkadas which awakened the sleepers. Mark Sanjivrao was the first to cry out. Rubbing his eyes he lifted up his head from the pillow and inquired what the row was about. Ramanath Kini from outside enlightened him with the information that Dwarkadas was the cause of the disturbance. Now Ramdas drawing the attention of Dwarkadas asked him what the matter was. He replied: "I just now remembered my dead father and as a result of it could not help weeping over his separation." Sanjivrao assured him that he would meet him some day and everything would be all right and that he might for the present sleep the matter off. For a time there was a lull and Sanjivrao and others entered again into the depths of sleep. Not many minutes had passed before a piercing yell startled Sanjivrao and others. This time Sanjivrao shot out of bed and going up to the dimly burning lantern, turned up its light, and, arming himself with it, directly made for the place where Dwarkadas was sleeping. All the time he was muttering: "Let us lay the ghost once for all. The devil is at its tricks again. We shall find out what the matter with him is." He held the lantern before Dwarkadas's face, allowing its full glare to fall upon him; "What is wrong with you?" he bellowed. The reply came: "I want to attend the first call of nature."

"Why don't you?" anxiously asked Sanjivrao.

By this time Ramdas was also standing beside Sanjivrao.

"Look here, have you no eyes to see? My knee-joint has swollen and I cannot walk," he replied pointing to his knee, on which there had appeared a protrusion as big as a tennis ball.

Mark Sanjivrao was a man of tact and resource. He called Kanda and Ramanath Kini for help. Dwarkadas, on account of his incessant smoking of *ganja*, had a lean and emaciated body. Under instructions from Mark Sanjivrao, Kanda and Kini raised Dwarkadas by the armpit, one on each side. He was easily lifted up. Mark Sanjivrao with lantern in hand became the leader. With his usual swinging gait and long strides he walked in front, lantern in hand, and the two friends at the back carried the bent frail figure of Dwarkadas, lifting him right above the ground. Ramdas watched the procession. He was taken near a pond and the business over, in the same style, pomp and circumstance he was carried back to bed. Mark Sanjivrao, after a parting word of advice coupled with a warning and a threat not to make any more horrible noises, retired along with the others to rest.

Purnanand used always to have discussions over religious beliefs and practices with Kanda who was his chum and of the same age. The outer verandah of the ashram had a screen on one side made of palm leaves. The screen was fixed about a foot from the edge of the verandah, leaving a dark gap in between. One day Purnanand sitting on this edge of the verandah was with great enthusiasm exhibiting to Kanda the various modes of *asana*. In the process, his back being turned towards the enclosure, he slipped backwards and tumbled down the dark gap. His two legs and hands alone were seen shooting outwards. There was a hue and cry. None could resist roaring with laughter at the ludicrous situation into which our yogic aspirant had fallen. Kanda who was a stout and strong man stepped forward, and pulling him out both by the legs and hands put him the question: "What do you call this *asana*?"

One afternoon Purnanand and Ramdas were alone in the ashram and they were sitting on the verandah. Now Purnanand's son, a young man, dropped in. Coming straight to Ramdas he squatted facing him. He said: "I have come to teach you, if you would condescend to become my disciple." Ramdas replied: "Ramdas is your humblest disciple and would be highly grateful to you if you would teach him." Ramdas awaited his reply in an attitude of perfect humility. All the time Purnanand was fuming with rage at the behaviour of his son, but Ramdas signed to him to keep quiet. The son proceeded: "You have to know that the world is the manifestation of Ram. He dwells in all beings, creatures and things. This vision you have to attain if you aspire for absolute liberation. Do you understand?"

"Yes, by your grace," Ramdas replied.

Purnanand was restraining himself from dancing with fury, and curbing his tongue from hurling curses on his son. No more questions were asked. There was silence for some time. Then the son spoke again. "Swamiji, I have a question to ask you."

"What is it, Ramji?" Ramdas said.

"You see, in the nights when I sit up for meditation, my mind wanders. Can you prescribe a method by which I can have steady concentration and meditation?"

Ramdas said: "Ram, you are simply wonderful. Have you forgotten that you are the *guru* of Ramdas who has come to teach him what he does not know; viz., about God-realisation? Whence is this question about the restless mind and all that? You are veritably Ram Himself."

"No, no," he impatiently cried out, "I am not Ram, I am Ravana. Hit me so that I may behave better." Saying this he laid his head at the feet of Ramdas, and when Ramdas raised him, he found that the friend's face was wet with tears. Soon after he left, Ramdas learnt from Purnanand that his son had a bet with his friends in the bazaar that they should stand him a treat in a tiffin shop if he succeeded in making Ramdas angry; and if he failed he would stand them a treat instead. Poor friend, he lost the bet!

Dwarkadas's worship of the images went on regularly day after day. The time of his departure came. The day previous to it he was as usual engaged in his worship having the *murtis* spread out on a cloth in front of him. Ramdas was at the time sitting on his *asan* outside. Kanda who was a so-called untouchable, which fact Dwarkadas could know only the day before, came to the ashram as usual but this time with a bunch of ripe plantains as a farewell offering to Dwarkadas. He directly came up and was about to place the gift at the feet of Dwarkadas when the latter suddenly flared up and shouted forth: "How dare you come near me? Don't you see that I have put on the sacred cloth and am doing *puja*? Get away from my presence." At these sharp words Kanda shrank back and quietly going into a corner took his seat. Ramdas observed the whole game. Getting up from his place Ramdas quietly proceeded towards Dwarkadas, and before he could know why Ramdas was coming to him, collected the images and the *puja* materials by folding up the cloth on which they were placed and making the whole thing into a sling, with all the force at his command flung them into the ditch at the right side of the ashram.

Dwarkadas was stunned, and gazed at Ramdas with looks filled with awe. Ramdas then told him: "Look here, Ramji, your devotions have been taking decidedly a wrong turn. That devotee before you," pointing to Kanda, "came to you with a heart full of love and reverence and was about to offer you a precious gift of fruits. Now you chose to discard him. That means you have discarded the very love of God. For you in future the living human image should be God. Therefore, get up and prostrate at the feet of Kanda whom you have wantonly insulted. He is your Ram, God and all. This is the vision that you need. Worshipping brass images and conceiving hatred for man is not devotion. Be quick to repair your gross blunder." Instantly Dwarkadas got up and going to Kanda fell at his feet. Thereafter, until he left the ashram he was engaged in repeating God's Name and prostrating before everyone, to whatever caste or creed he or she belonged, who visited the ashram.

The call from the devotees from Maharashtra and Northern India for Ramdas became insistent. At last he could not resist it. Ram gave him the command to go out and fulfil their wishes. Accordingly he wrote to Janardan Pant asking him to come over and fetch him.

The news of Ramdas's intended departure created quite a sensation amongst the adherents of the ashram. Of them Krishna Bai was affected most. Till then she was spending her nights with her children in the house in which she resided. Now she insisted that he should permit her to stay in the ashram for the nights. Mother Rukmabai in spite of her ill-health remained in the ashram but as regards Krishna Bai, he was not willing that she should keep away from her children in the nights.

One evening as usual he had to remind her to return to her house. In fact she used to be so much absorbed in the service of the ashram that she would entirely forget to mark the passage of time and to leave the ashram even when the darkness of night was closing upon the world. On this occasion she was most reluctant to leave for her house. In so many ways she appealed to him to allow her to remain in the ashram. But in view of her children he could not agree to that. She left.

The following day, about eight o'clock, a cultivator turned up bringing the news that Krishna Bai was found lying down in a jungle at the top of the hill near the *bhutasthana*, one of her legs swollen and herself partly unconscious. At once Ramdas with some others in the ashram ran up to the place. They found her sitting beneath a tree, her clothes all soiled with mud and earth and one of her legs swollen up to the knee. Ramdas with the help of the friends conveyed her to the ashram. He learnt from her lips that she had spent the night partly in the outer yard of the ashram and partly in the jungle where she was found. The refusal on the part of Ramdas to let her stay in the ashram had deeply affected her. She said she could not return to her home. The swelling was due to a snake bite, but Krishna Bai was perfectly calm and her face was as radiant as ever, not a shadow of pain marring it. However, by God's grace, she recovered.

Among the earnest aspirants who visited the ashram was one named Gunda, a native of Puttur. He came on leave from Bombay where he was employed. At the closing period of his leave he came to see Ramdas. A brief talk with Ramdas brought about a far-reaching transformation in him. He at once abandoned the idea of rejoining his post in Bombay and made up his mind to stick to Ramdas. At his request Ramdas initiated him with the Ram *mantram*. No sooner did he repeat the *mantram* for half-an-hour than he was so far carried away by the spiritual emotion caused by it that he began to dance in a wild ecstasy. Thereafter he turned his mind and life entirely to the thought of God and service of the ashram. He was a silent man, humble, unobtrusive and assiduous. He was a simple, pure and great soul.

The day for departure arrived. Ramdas left Kasaragod in Janardan Pant's company and the railway platform was fully crowded with the devotees of Kasaragod including Krishna Bai, Mother Rukmabai, and others.

CHAPTER 45: BANGALORE – SHOLAPUR

In due course Ramdas and Janardan Pant reached Bangalore and were put up at Bhavanishankerrao's house in Malleswaram. Their stay here was only for a couple of days. At the wish of the devotees in the house, Janardan Pant performed a *kirtan* which was also attended by the people of the neighbourhood. At the time, there was in the house a *purohit* who was called in for some religious ceremony. When Ramdas retired to the room, which he occupied for rest, the *purohit* came to him and read him a severe lesson. He took him roundly to task for abandoning the householder's life. Ramdas silently swallowed the 'bitter' pill and dismissed the matter with a smile, for explanation and argument with him were found to be of no avail.

Their stay in Bangalore coming to a close they left for Sholapur. At Sholapur station a batch of friends was awaiting their arrival. Govind Ramakrishna Joshi and his son-in-law were among the party. At this time, the annual celebration at Madhavrao Kulkarni's house in Anjangaum was in progress, and it was proposed that Ramdas should first attend this function and then proceed to Uple-Dumala. They were also joined at this place by Prem Singh. The party in due time reached Anjangaum. The celebration at Madhavrao's was then in full swing. Ramdas felt great elation in the company of Madhavrao and other devotees.

Anant Buwa, son-in-law of Govind Ramakrishna Joshi, entertained the assembly with his *kirtan*, and Ramdas had also to deliver a discourse on *bhakti*.

From Anjangaum the party consisting of Ramdas, Janardan Pant, Prem Singh and two devotees from Uple-Dumala, who had specially come to invite and escort Ramdas, started in bullock-carts. They reached in the evening a small wayside village called Yavli. Remaining here for the night the party, early the following morning, prosecuted their journey towards Uple-Dumala. The reception which the people of Uple-Dumala accorded to him was simply beyond description. Men, women and children of all castes, creeds and races had with one mind joined hands in making the reception a grand success. He was led through the streets of the village in the midst of a huge procession to the accompaniment of fire-works, *bhajan* and the Indian band. The devout mothers, the front yard of whose huts along the path were swept and besmeared with cow-dung and ornamented with *rangoli*, stood on their door-step with light and offerings. The scenes all around manifested the signs of a gala day. Festoons decorated the houses and the roadways. The procession after passing through all the streets of the village at last halted in front of Babarao Kulkarni's house, and Ramdas was taken inside the house where preparations had been made for his stay. The house was filled with the enthusiastic crowd to overflow. The continuous refrain of the divine Ram *mantram* rang forth from every one in the assembly. Soon it was followed by dancing. The Muslims of the place also took whole-hearted part in the reception. To the surprise and delight of the Hindu devotees a pious Muslim joined the dancers singing aloud the Ram *mantram*. Singing and dancing continued the whole night. The devotees appeared to have forgotten themselves in the ecstasy produced by the melody of the divine Name.

His stay in this village prolonged for about eighteen days. People from the neighbouring villages also came in hundreds to swell the concourse. The divine Name "Ram" issuing from the lips of every one in the village surcharged the atmosphere with intense spiritual fervour.

The programme of *bhajan*, *kirtan*, feasts and discourses by Ramdas was worked out in a regular rotation. The devotees poured on him their pure and glorious love in every possible manner.

To give a detailed account of the events, during his residence at this place, would be a laborious task. So he puts down here one or two important items.

Among the devotees of the village was a young widow belonging to the *shudra* caste. From a month previous to his visit to this village, this devout soul had been observing a rigorous fast avowing that she would taste food only after Ramdas had taken a meal prepared by her at her house. The young mother whose name is Anjani Mata came to him and invited him for dinner. Meanwhile, the other devotees of the place had already divided up the days of his stay among themselves for the offering of food to him. He now placed the problem before them and pleaded on behalf of the mother. One of the devotees volunteered to forgo his turn in favour of Anjani Mata. So he had the unique privilege of enjoying the nectarine food prepared by that divine mother.

One day he had an invitation from a Muslim. Ramdas went to his house followed by many brahmin devotees. The strangest part of it all was that the faithful Muslim condescended to perform Ramdas's *pada puja* in the proper style. When the *puja* was over, the Muslim going inside his small hut brought his long suffering wife out on the verandah where Ramdas sat and making her sit beside him prayed to him to pass his hands over her body. It was evident from the condition of the woman that she was sinking under a slow and continuous fever. She had been reduced almost to a skeleton. As requested by the Muslim, Ramdas passed his hands on her head and back and also gave her a part of the milk given to him by her husband. Then he left the place. Some days later when he was away in another village, he came to know that this ailing mother having been cured of her fever in about a week's time was able to help her husband in the fields. All glory be to the great Lord whose will is so powerful and whose ways are so mysterious!

In the evenings Ramdas would run to the bank of the local river and dance in circles in which hundreds of the village devotees joined, singing the divine Ram *mantram*. Altogether his stay in Uple-Dumala was marked by the supreme triumph of love in the light of which people of every denomination mingled together in a spirit of perfect equality and brotherhood. Where the love of God manifests there the darkness of conventional distinctions that breed strife and misery disappear. O Lord! Victory ever attends Thy Name.

The account of Uple-Dumala cannot be complete without the mention of a few prominent devotees of the place. Raghunath Maharaj, Krishnaji Pandharinath, Bappa Saheb, Babarao Kulkarni and a Gujarati merchant were the outstanding figures who contributed their wholehearted services towards not only the success of the programme but also in planting the seed of the divine Name in the hearts of all the villagers.

At the pressing invitations from the neighbouring villages, Ramdas visited, on leaving Uple-Dumala, Bhatambare, Kaudgaum, Ambe-Jawalajee and many other villages. Everywhere thousands of people came to meet him. The so-called untouchable classes freely came forward to touch his feet. Devotion and love rose in floods. The Name of God spread far and wide and the hearts of the people bathed in an ocean of joy. The reception he got in every one of these villages was exactly similar to the one he had while entering Uple-Dumala.

About this time the annual Kartik festival at Pandharpur was approaching. So, on the suggestion of Janardan Pant and other devotees, Ramdas went with them to Pandharpur for this festival. This time he and the party stayed in a *dharmashala*. He was made to visit the temples for *darshan* of Vithoba. On the last day of his stay he spent a few hours beneath a cluster of tall trees near the banks of the Chandrabhaga river. Here he met all the devotees who had come for the occasion from the various villages he had visited. He received also an invitation from Digambar Kulkarni, a *vakil*, to his place, Usmanabad. Ramdas promised to fulfil his wish after completing his tour in the Sholapur District.

From Pandharpur Ramdas and party went to Angar via Anjangaum. They had to halt at Anjangaum for a day. There were now a dozen devotees in his company. As usual they were guests of Madhavrao. Here an incident took place which is worthy of note. Madhavrao and the members of his family were overjoyed at his visit and set about making preparations for a fine feast. Meantime an old relation of Madhavrao in a neighbouring house, was seriously ill. Madhvrao had, of course, his fears because he had intimation early that morning that the condition of the old man was precarious. About nine o'clock news reached the ears of Madhavrao and his household that the old man had passed away. Now Madhavrao was of orthodox belief and practice. According to the orthodox rules, when a near relation died, the entire family is considered to be polluted by the death, and under such pollution religious functions of any kind are tabooed. Even to touch them or to eat food at their hands is held to be irreligious. The sad news at this happy juncture greatly upset Madhavrao. All the work of their preparations suddenly stopped. Madhavrao with a face cast down with regret and disappointment came to Ramdas and apprised him of the unpleasant tidings. In reply he assured him that there was nothing wrong. "God would not have your function spoiled. The old man may not have died. Let us wait for further news." Strange as it would appear, a quarter of an hour had not passed after this talk, when a messenger came running to tell Madhavrao that the old man still breathed and the supposition that he had died was wrong. Hearing this, Madhavrao's joy can be better imagined than described. Cheer again lit up the faces of the members of his house on whom for a time a shadow had fallen. The preparations went on apace. After dinner Ramdas was taken to see the old man. Although alive he had not clear consciousness of this side of life. After a few minutes Ramdas returned to Madhavrao's. When he was leaving Anjangaum, about four o'clock, by which time the last person in the house had partaken of the feast, news came again that the old man died, and this time once for all.

At Angar Ramdas was received by the devotees of the place with as much love and devotion as on previous occasions. *Kirtan, bhajan,* and feasts were the order of the day. After a short stay here, Ramdas and the party proceeded to Uppalai where again he was welcomed into the modest and sacred hut of Govind Ramakrishna Joshi. Oh! what words can adequately express the overflowing love, simple faith and exalted devotion of this glorious couple, Govind Ramakrishna Joshi and his wife Radhabai. Here again a full programme of *bhajan, kirtan,* and dinner was gone through.

From Uppalai, at the invitation of the Jahagirdar, Raghunath Maharaj Yeshwant, he proceeded to a village called Ashti. It so happened that when Ramdas came to the Jahagirdar's house his wife was in her menses, and it is the custom with the brahmins, during such periods, a lady should observe segregation and should not be touched, as such touch is considered to be pollution. The Jahagirdar was in a fix as to the management of the kitchen. With the help of a neighbouring lady he got meals ready for the guests. All the time the Jahagirdar's wife was feeling greatly disappointed that she could not take part in the festivities. Most of all she took to heart that she was losing the opportunity of even touching the feet of Ramdas.

He had, as prearranged, to stay with the Jahagirdar only for a day. The anxious mother appealed to Ramdas through her husband that he should prolong his stay at their place until she passed the period of pollution which is generally three days, but Ramdas could not accede to her wish. So about four o'clock the same day he started. When he came out of the house he saw the mother in a corner of the front yard. On a sudden prompting from Ram within, Ramdas went up to her and asked her to touch his feet. She hesitated but he assured her there was nothing wrong if she touched him as he was not only her child but the Lord had freed him from all conventional restrictions. The mother responded with a face suffused with delight and laid her head at his feet. The *darshan* over, he turned towards the friends who were waiting for him. They must have been not a little astonished at this strange act of Ramdas, but they were calm and indulgent.

Mention has to be made that at this place also he came in contact with two Muslim friends who were extremely kind to him.

Passing through various other villages Ramdas with the party came to Khandali. Wamanrao Balwant Kulkarni was as kind as ever in the loving service of his guests. Soon Digambar Kulkarni came here to take Ramdas with him to Usmanabad. They took a train to Usmanabad where he remained Digambar Kulkarni's guest. The visit to this town is memorable in many respects. Some of the prominent events relating to this visit are chronicled here.

On the second day of his arrival he had invitations from two merchants. He was first taken to the house of one of them in a motor-car followed by a procession and with an English band playing in front. The reception Ramdas received at his house was right royal. Evidently the merchant was a rich man. Ramdas was made to sit on a raised dais, decked and decorated like a throne. As soon as he took his seat the merchant induced him to discard for the time being his plain *khaddar* cloth and put on instead laced and silk clothes. He besmeared Ramdas's body and face with sandal paste, heaping on him at the same time various costly presents. After partaking of the *prasad* they had him photographed. When it was time to depart, Ramdas divested himself of the rich robes and redonned his plain *khaddar* piece. The merchant insisted upon Ramdas's accepting his costly gifts of clothes, etc. Declining the offer with thanks Ramdas said: "These glittering things are not meant for a wandering *fakir* like Ramdas; so you have to excuse him for not accepting them."

Ramdas left the merchant's house in company with another merchant who took him to his house where he was treated with similar hospitality.

The house of Digambar Kulkarni became a veritable *bhajan mandir*. The Name of God resounded within its walls throughout the day and till late in the night. He would sit in a spacious hall in the upper storey of the building whilst all the devotees who assembled there would stand in rows against the walls and sing the Lord's Name in chorus. Digambar Kulkarni took the lead in *bhajan*. On the day following Ramdas's arrival, a Hindu *vakil* from the neighbourhood came in and took his seat beside him, and latterly stood up and joining the chorus danced with the others. When *bhajan* stopped and lull was restored, this *vakil* approaching Ramdas sat down facing him.

"Swamiji," he began, "I greatly wish that you should hear the tale of my conversion. It came about in a wonderful way. In the first place I must tell you that until an hour ago I was a rank skeptic. My house is situated adjoining this. I could hear from there the loud singing going on here. When I heard it and also the thumping on the floor of this storey, I made enquiries as to what the noise was about. I was told that a *sadhu* had arrived at the house and that the singing and dancing was on account of him. I thought that the people in the house were extremely foolish that they should behave so boisterously simply because some wandering mendicant was present with them. I did not stop merely thinking of their folly but felt a curiosity to see the *sadhu* who was the cause of so much commotion in the house. I decided to have only a peep at him from the staircase and then turn back. Accordingly I slowly entered the house and went up the staircase to a height from which I could have a good view of the *sadhu*. I saw, but my mind refused my turning back. I felt an irresistible desire to climb further up and enter the room and I did. I thought there was no harm in witnessing the fun. I sat and watched with a queer state of mind the progress of the *bhajan*. I was tickled to behold stout-bodied educated men jumping and dancing. I could not stop at that. I came to think: "What does it matter if I repeat the *mantram sotto voce*? Nothing wrong I suppose if I do so, and I commenced muttering the *mantram* to myself, my hand automatically clapped in a slow key. 'What if I stand in a corner just as the others do? I would not bellow forth like them. Repeating merely with the lips will not be detected.' Suiting action to the thought I got up and stood in a far corner in line with the others and my lips moved and I uttered the *mantram* inaudibly. My hands continued clapping. 'If I sing a little louder the sound will be drowned in the chorus, and nobody the wiser and no harm done.' I went on taking the *mantram* a little louder. All the time my feet were feeling restless. 'What does it matter if I slightly move the feet up and down?' and I did move the feet. So far I was aware of the course of my conduct. What followed next, I confess, is beyond me to say."

The fact was he had danced more wildly than the others, sung more loudly than the others and clapped hands more furiously than done by others.

At the close of his narration a friend in the party whispered into his ears advising him to receive initiation of the *mantram* from Ramdas. He replied to the friend: "There is no need for it. I know what I am about. The initiation is meant for people like you."

Soon after, the photographer came with a dozen copies of Ramdas's photo taken on the previous day. The assembled devotees eagerly secured a copy each, of whom our *vakil* friend was one. On getting his copy, this friend, going near Ramdas, took out of his pocket his fountain-pen and handing the photo and the pen to Ramdas requested him to write down on the top of the photo the Ram *mantram*. Observing this, the friend who advised him to get initiated roared with laughter and exclaimed: "There you are. What is this if not initiation?"

"No, no," returned the *vakil* friend. "I am simply asking him to write down the *mantram*. That is all."

Another day Ramdas was invited to the local High School where he had not only to speak a few words to the students but also distribute prizes to them.

Two more events that occurred, one following closely on the other, are of utmost significance. One afternoon, about forty persons belonging to the cobbler caste came to pay a visit to Ramdas, passing through the streets in procession singing the Lord's Name to the accompaniment of cymbals, *veena*, and *mridang*. He received them at the gate of the *vakil's* house. They considered it no small privilege that they could approach him and touch his feet. Before leaving they expressed a desire that he should attend their congregation to be held in his honour in their locality, at nine o'clock in the night. The same day he had another invitation from the prominent brahmins of the place for a *harikatha* performance at the Sri Panduranga temple of the town. It was decided that he should proceed to the temple directly after his visit to the locality of the cobblers had terminated.

About eight in the night a big group of the cobbler devotees came to take him to their place. He passed through the streets in procession joined also by many brahmins of the town and the devotees who had accompanied him, and reached the spot fixed as the trysting place for the people of the cobbler community. Here the gathering that he met was unimaginably vast. He was given a seat in an open shed where the chiefs of the community performed his *pada puja*. Then commenced the programme of *darshan*. The process may be compared to the tale of the locusts and the granary. Each man, woman or child of the community was individually presented to Ramdas and, since there were many thousands of them assembled, the function of presentation slowly and regularly continued indefinitely. The brahmin friends who had come with him freely mingled in the crowd of the so-called untouchables rubbing shoulders with them. They even accepted the *prasad* of parched rice distributed by the cobblers. Time flew. The period allotted for the function which was one hour exceeded. The crowd around him for a furlong was so thick that exit through it was well-nigh impossible. He consulted some of the friends as to the hour of the night and learnt it was eleven o'clock. He was due as arranged at the temple at ten o'clock. Where was escape from the crowd when it was increasing in proportion minute after minute? He came to the edge of the verandah which he occupied and saw before him the huge mass of humanity clamouring more and more for *darshan*.

Suddenly he took a leap into their midst, as one from the deck of a boat takes a jump into the ocean, and passed through the crowds like a live wire. He wriggled, jumped, rolled and almost swam through them. At last he reached the road and then flew like wind, but he was not going in the direction of the temple. He visited, at the request of a *vakil*, his house and remaining there for a quarter of an hour again raced towards the temple. As he went forward the whole mass of the cobbler community followed him. He reached the temple. A big gas-light was at its entrance and in a vast *pandal* in front of the temple were collected over a thousand people of the higher castes. He directly entered and passed through the crowd. He found them all inside, expecting his arrival. He took his seat on a raised and decorated dais prepared for him. It was indeed a mammoth gathering. As he entered the place the people of the cobbler caste also freely made their way inside and mingled with the brahmins by taking their seat in between them. He was watching from his seat the wonderful work of God which brought a people who were despised as untouchables in close touch with the intolerant brahmins, and that too within a temple. The brahmins turned their faces to each other, stared, winked and whispered. The situation was extremely tense. Ramdas simply smiled witnessing the strange phenomenon before him. Suddenly stillness and silence pervaded the place. As the saying goes, you could hear a pin drop. Such was the stillness that came upon the assembled people. On one side was standing the *haridas* who was none other than the headmaster of the local High School. His opening words were: "My tongue refuses its function at the sight of this unusually crowded audience. I must declare that I am having vishwarupa *darshan*. It is practically proved that distinctions of caste, creed and colour are the offspring of utter ignorance. It is the supreme Lord Himself who is manifest as all beings. I am blessed by the sight."

This was all he said and closed his *kirtan*. These two incidents that took place, close upon one another, really baffle description. What peace and bliss, what freedom can man enjoy when he attains the vision of God in all creatures and things! But as it is, he is a slave to false traditions that breed hatred and strife between man and man.

Ramdas's stay coming to a close, he and the friends started to depart. A motor-car was engaged to take them to the railway station. The party took their seats in the motor-car which stood at the entrance of Digamabar Kulkarni's house. The devotees of the place crowded round the car to bid him farewell. Just when the car was about to start, the *vakil* friend, the new convert to the path of devotion, hurried through the crowd and opening the door of the car placed his head on Ramdas's feet. After a while Ramdas raised him to find him sobbing like a forlorn child. Gazing on Ramdas he questioned between sobs: "O! Swamiji, when shall I see you again?" The motor-car moved and gathering speed ran on.

Catching the train for Bombay, Ramdas with Janardan Pant travelled towards that great city.

CHAPTER 46: BOMBAY – SOJAT ROAD – KASARAGOD

As usual Ramdas halted at Sanjivrao's house. On this occasion as well he went through a programme set by the friends of the place, almost similar to the one at the time of his last visit to Bombay.

He delivered a discourse in the Saraswat Association Hall before a crowded audience on God-realisation. Then again he was invited to Santa Cruz where he spoke for a short time on the principles of devotion, after an exposition by Janardan Pant on some portion of the Dasbodh of Samarth Ramdas. At Sanjivrao's, evening *bhajan* and *pravachan* on Dasbodh by Janardhan Pant became a daily programme.

Suddenly Anant Buwa also turned up. At Sanjivrao's request he performed a *kirtan* in his rooms. He was a fine musician and was assisted in his performance by his two sons who were experts in playing upon the harmonium and the *tabla* in the course of the *harikatha*. Anant Buwa gave an apt illustration of the incorrigible human nature which does not allow a person to keep up a steady and unruffled longing and aspiration for God. He said: "A mother in the house rocks her child in the cradle and, lulling it to sleep, goes on her task of fetching water from the well. She returns with the pitcher filled and, passing by the way of the cradle, peeps in to see what the child is doing. Finding that it is sound asleep she goes in and empties the pitcher and, when coming out again for another turn, she hears a low cry from the child. Going up to the cradle she gives it a swing and the child sleeps again. Once more she fetches another pitcher of water and finds that the child is a little more restless than before and is crying louder. She goes to the cradle and gives it one more swing and the child sleeps. Thus swing after swing, the child is lulled to sleep." He concluded: "Similar is the case of people in the world. They cry for the Lord for a time and then forget everything about Him and one birth is gone; another birth, the child cries again and forgets all about it the next instant. Another birth passes away, so on and so forth *ad infinitum*. Unless and until we cry aloud, fully awake from the sleep of ignorance, we can never dream of freeing ourselves from the cycle of births and deaths and finding eternal union with God."

Of the visitors, mention has to be made of one whose name is G. Balasubramaniam. At the very first sight of Ramdas he felt a strange fascination for him. He was then holding a good position as a shorthand typist in a well-known bank of Bombay. He might have sat with Ramdas for not more than five minutes when he said to him in a spontaneous outburst as it were: "Swamiji, I will go with you. I am determined to follow you on your tours. I shall be your stenographer and will see that your speeches and talks are correctly put down in writing. I am prepared even to go with you to foreign countries."

Saying thus he awaited Ramdas's reply. Ramdas looking at him said: "Ram, are you not married? Haven't you any family at home? What is this you are saying? Do you mean to leave them and follow Ramdas?"

He replied: "I have nothing to do with all that. My one concern is to cast my lot with you." Then Ramdas asked him to consider well over the matter and then come to a decision. The subject was dropped. But he did not forget Ramdas. When dictating these lines to him, Ramdas finds that he has been coming more and more intimately in touch with the great mission which God has started through the Anandashram of Ramnagar. Verily, God has not been lacking in providing able instruments to further the work of His service for which alone He has enabled him to dedicate his entire life. Ramdas cannot ignore the fact that the Lord Himself in the form of these instruments is fulfilling His own purpose.

During this visit, among the devotees who came into intimate touch with Ramdas besides Sanjivrao and Ratnakar, were also Karnad Gopalrao, Durgashankar Upadhyaya as also Haldipur Narayanarao. Here, Janardan Pant separated from Ramdas as he had to return to Narkhed in Sholapur district.

Hearing of Ramdas's arrival at Bombay, Bhuderbhai and Chhotabhai of Wadhwan came down to take him over to their place.

In Wadhwan, as on the previous occasion, he stayed with Dr. Shukla. The latter and his wife Shantiben bathed him in the streams of their pure love. *Bhajan*, devotional music by Chhotabhai and talks with the visitors who assembled day after day to listen to the words of Ramdas, comprised the routine. At the request of the headmaster of the place, he delivered a speech in their school hall on universal love before the students who had assembled for the occasion, and also paid visits to the Bala mandirs.

Ramdas visited Zoravar Nagar where he spent a night in the house of Chunibhai and also paid a visit to the prominent Congress leader of Kathiawar, Manilal Kothari, who was at the time ill and bed-ridden. He was delighted to see Ramdas. In the course of conversation, he asked Ramdas whether he should continue to take part in politics after recovery. He was much dispirited because Mahatmaji was at the time in jail. He opened the talk with the remark that he wished he had the same free and blissful life which Ramdas was leading. Ramdas replied that the work he was doing was great and noble. Worry comes in when any work, political or otherwise, is done with a selfish motive. The secret of liberation in action lies in doing all works without the ego-sense. Here what is demanded of us is perfect self-surrender through dedication of all our actions to the Master power that controls the universe.

"Oh! how hard it is to be free from the ego and then act. I feel I am simply caught up. I cannot imagine that I could perform action bereft of the ego-sense. It is so hard," he said.

"Nothing is hard provided you strive whole-heartedly to attain the end in view. It is quite possible to live and act as a free instrument in the hands of the Almighty," Ramdas rejoined.

"You may be right—nay, you are right, but for myself such a state is not within the realm of possibility. However, I shall not forget you. Some day I shall make you come to me again; if not I shall go to you. Now a link is formed between us which nothing can snap," he spoke with vehemence.

"The link is there always. We are eternally united. We are eternally one. Realise this." Saying thus Ramdas took leave of him after partaking of some refreshments.

In Wadhwan Ramdasanudas came all the way from Northern India to meet Ramdas. On account of some malady his sight was very weak. However, he stuck on to Ramdas for over a month during his tour in Kathiawar.

From Wadhwan Ramdas proceeded to Limbdi. In Limbdi he met the old friends Raja Ram and Mother Elizabeth and a host of others. The same programme as on the last occasion was gone through.

At the instance of Mother Elizabeth, Ramdas was called upon to deliver a discourse in the State High School on universal love. In the hall, besides a large gathering of students, were also seated near Ramdas, Mother Elizabeth, a European missionary and Pratap Singh. He spoke for about three quarters of an hour on the universal nature of love, a subject which was so dear to him. He said in the course of the speech that human life attains its highest perfection only when it is gifted with the vision that sees the one eternal Life Principle, pervading throughout the universe and dwelling in the hearts of all creatures and things. The animation and activity inherent in all the objects of creation, have their inception in the basic Truth underlying the entire manifested universe. At the conclusion of the discourse, he cited instances from the teachings of the great incarnations of the world in support of his statement: "Buddha, Krishna, Mahaveer and Muhammad, all stood for universal love and their messages insistently proclaimed that the supreme nature of the ultimate reality or God is love. To realise love and make it an active power in us, it is essential that our heart should dazzle with purity and intellect enlightened with wisdom. Unless these conditions are fulfilled none can enter that kingdom of immortality which would bring him face to face with the supreme Deity who is eternal splendour and all-inclusive Love."

When the speech ended, the Christian missionary congratulated Ramdas on his speech, but reminded him that he had made a grievous omission in not mentioning Jesus Christ in the same breath as the other incarnations. Ramdas assured the missionary that although he had failed to refer to Christ, he held Christ in the highest reverence and understood him as an exalted example in whom is revealed the highest glory of universal love.

A little later he again had an opportunity to meet the kind missionary at his bungalow. It was evident that the missionary was a great lover of Christ. He asked Ramdas: "Why don't you follow Christ?"

Ramdas replied: "Ramdas has enthroned Christ in his own heart and ever feels his union with the great Teacher whereas you seem to believe that Christ is an outside ideal to hold communion with, as a person apart from you. Christ is truly the Lord of our life, soul and body. Does he not say 'The Kingdom of God is within you'? Verily God or Christ is ever with us."

The day of his departure from Limbdi was fixed, but Raja Ram and Mother Elizabeth pressed him to postpone it for a day later, for the next day Raja Ram would start Bhagavat Saptaha at his palace in memory of his late Rani Saheb. Ramdas agreed to be present at this religious function only for the first day. The Saptaha continues for seven days. So on the opening day of the Saptaha he sat for a few hours in the midst of the devotees who assembled to listen to the reading of Srimad Bhagavat by an aged Pandit of the State. The succeeding day he departed from the place.

In company with Dr. Shukla and Popatbhai, Ramdas visited a distant village called Dhanduka. Mother Rewaben, the headmistress of the school, had invited him to her place. She had paid a visit to him with this purpose at Wadhwan. He spent a day under her hospitable roof.

From Dhanduka he and the party made directly for Rajkot via Wadhwan. He had only two companions with him during this visit, Popatbhai and Ramdasanudas. At Rajkot he met Madhavram Raval, a pure and devout soul. This young man had spent the early period of his life in the ashram of a famous saint, Sri Nathuram Sharma, undergoing strict spiritual discipline. He was now in Rajkot in the employ of the State. Ramdas and the friends with him occupied the travellers' bungalow. The devotional temperament of Madhavram would reveal itself whenever he sang *bhajan* and got into moods of ecstasy. On the following day the party left Rajkot and as planned, reached Veraval in due time. From Veraval they travelled by taxi to Una where Maganlal was living.

During his visit, he and the friends resided in a newly built hospital ward near the quarters of Dr. Mahadevia. The friends of the place treated him, as on the last occasion, with great love and hospitality. A few days after their stay, there took place a riot between Hindus and Muhammadans in which many, on both sides, received severe injuries. The friction between these communities, breaking off and on in several parts of India, has been creating a perplexing and grievous problem for the leaders of both the communities to tackle with. What is needed on the part of both is an attitude of respect for each other's faith. Both the Muslims and the Hindus have, at their back, equally brilliant traditions, and that they should fight each other exhibits their ignorance or wilful forgetfulness of their glorious past.

After a week's stay Ramdas and Popatbhai took leave of the friends and travelled towards Wadhwan again. As Dr. Mahadevia desired that Ramdasanudas should continue to remain with him for the treatment of his eye-disease, he decided to stay behind.

Duly reaching Wadhwan, Ramdas with Dr. Shukla, came to Ahmedabad.

On the way to Ahmedabad they alighted at a wayside station where they went for the *darshan* of a Jain saint in an ashram which was said to have been occupied, at one time, by a famous saint, known as Mastram. It appears that the saint originally belonged to the European community.

In due course they reached Ahmedabad where they stayed with Dr. Shukla's brother. Here many friends of the place came to see Ramdas. Except that he reprimanded in strong terms an educated man, holding an academic degree, for his gratuitous attack on saints in general, there was nothing worthy of note.

From Ahmedabad Ramdas travelled towards Sojat Road where Dr. Raval lived. On his way by train at the Abu Road station, a Gujarati devotee pressed him to break his journey. He spent a blissful night in the company of this friend and the pious members of his household. It has been very often expressed by the householders that it is next to impossible to live a life of utter devotion to God in the midst of the world. This statement was falsified so far as the household of this Gujarati friend was concerned. All members of the family lived, moved and had their being in absolute remembrance of God. Calmness and patience ever prevailed in the house. The friend was a pure man eking out his bare subsistence from the income derived from a petty job. Even kings and potentates might well envy his contentment. He was so pure, simple and loving. Life is indeed blessed when it is lived in the spirit in which this young man lived.

The following day Ramdas prosecuted his journey and the Gujarati friend travelled with him for some stations and then returned. Ramdas reached Sojat Road where Dr. Raval was eagerly waiting for him. Here he spent a few quiet days. One evening Raval took him out for a stroll to a distant railway bridge. They sat down on a selected spot. In the course of the talk that ensued Ramdas expounded three main principles that should guide the conduct of a human being, (1) Right food; (2) Right action; and (3) Right society.

"Right food consists of such food as is free from the ingredients that cause irritation in the body and the mind. *Satwic* diet comes under this head. What is to be avoided in regard to food is the food that would set the mind in a whirl of desires and cause disease in the body. This comes under the name of *rajasic*, i.e., fiery, and *tamasic*, i.e., stale food."

"Right action is that action in which the idea of the self is totally absent. Here the consideration of *ahimsa* or *himsa* does not apply. Any action performed with the object of attaining a selfish aim should be avoided, be it of the nature of *himsa* or *ahimsa*. Therefore, selfless action is right action and selfish action is wrong action."

Right Society: "That society in which you feel that you are elevated, in which the mind is purified or even drawn inwards and you come by the peace of the Eternal, is right society; be the person, with whom you associate, of a lower or higher caste, of a western or eastern nationality. Avoid the company of those people by whose contact your mind is defiled and your senses go out of control, even though they happen to belong to the highest caste or race. Associate with the pure and eschew the company of the impure. This should be held as the standard which is ever true without regard to any other considerations."

After a brief stay with Raval he caught the train for Agra.

He travelled, of course, by third class. After passing some stations Raja Ram, i.e., Thakore Saheb of Limbdi, who was also travelling by the same train in his special saloon, came to know that he was in the train. He approached Ramdas and persuaded him to occupy his car, at least as far as a certain junction where the trains were changed. Raja Ram was on his way to Delhi. There was a small compartment in the saloon-car fully equipped, which was used by Mother Elizabeth when she also travelled with Raja Ram. Ramdas occupied this compartment. Before doing so he talked for some time with Raja Ram on the greatness of universal vision. The unexpected meeting proved to be highly blissful. At the junction Ramdas separated from Raja Ram and returned to the third class carriage.

Having been informed of his coming, Ramchandra Gupta was waiting at the station to receive him. He took Ramdas to the city and made him occupy a small newly built *dharmashala* in the precincts of a temple. Here he met many devotees and friends of the place.

It is common knowledge that the Taj Mahal of Agra is a world-famous building. Ramdas, in the company of Ramchandra Gupta, went to see this fascinating structure. Many a poet and writer of imagination has lavished his genius in describing the charming beauty of Taj Mahal. It is rightly said by one of them that the Taj Mahal is 'a dream in marble' It is erected in memory of Mumtaz, wife of Shah Jahan. The mausoleum exhibits the exquisite art of Moghul architecture. To fully describe it here would cover pages. He entered the Taj Mahal and witnessed the designs and carvings on the walls and the dome in the centre of the building. Next coming out he ascended one of the four minarets and remained at the top, a spectator of the vast scenery all around and the Jamuna river flowing close at the back of the mausoleum. Beautiful gardens with rectangular water reservoirs, facing the building, were laid out to heighten the enchantment of the place.

The next place he visited was the huge fort of Agra. His sight was charmed with the innumerable Mahals on which also the sculptor had exhausted his rare skill and unremitting labour. They are also of the Moghul type. When they were returning from the fort they met outside, a huge crowd of locusts settling down on the plain, in front of the fort. These creatures, as everybody knows, are the most dangerous pests that feed upon the crops and devastate the land upon which they choose to alight.

Having received a call from Jhansi, Ramdas went down to the place. The friends of Jhansi, especially Mahadev Prasad, were keenly looking for his arrival and on seeing him went into ecstasies through sheer joy. This time he resided in a *kuti*, far away from the city, lying on the way to the railway station. He had the unexpected delight of meeting again Swami Ramanand from whose kind surveillance he had slipped away at Pilikoti Ashram. He also evinced unfeigned delight on seeing Ramdas. On the following day Swami Ramanand left the place and Ramdas became the sole occupant of the *kuti*. All the old friends of Jhansi gave him the joy of their company. Mahadev Prasad remained with him day and night.

Then for about two or three days he was taken out of Jhansi by Triveni Prasad on a visit to Lalitpur and Trikamghar, an Indian State. Later he also visited Mahoba, Konch and Jalgaon in the course of which he met Jagannath, Bankeylal Gupta and Ganesh Bajpai.

Not a week had passed in Jhansi, when a letter from Ramabai at Kasaragod was received by him intimating that Gurudev had expressed a desire to see him, and Ramabai proposed that he should not delay in fulfilling Gurudev's wish. He did not know what to do. He felt that he could not go back to Kasaragod before he had completed his all-India tour. However, when Triveni Prasad, who was looking after Ramdas in every way, was consulted in the matter, he emphatically suggested that he should respond to the call. He stated that there was no time to lose and Ramdas ought to start that very day. He agreed. Triveni Prasad took him to the Jhansi station and, procuring for him a through ticket to Kasaragod, saw him seated in the night train bound for Madras. Ramdas found himself tearing along towards the south for the *Darshan* of Gurudev. Duly he reached Madras where he stayed with Dr. G.S. Katre, in Mylapore. Next day he caught the Mangalore mail and reached Kasaragod. Alighting he directly went up to Anandrao's house for the *Darshan* of Gurudev. Gurudev was highly pleased to see him. He was at the time almost bed-ridden. Soon after, Ramdas proceeded to Anandashram. Krishna Bai was looking forward to his coming like the proverbial *chatak*. As in the past she commenced visiting the ashram and rendered him her loving service.

The question arose as to whether he would again travel to the north for completing the original programme. He himself was not certain of the future plans. About ten days later Janardan Pant, hearing of Ramdas's return to Anandashram, suddenly turned up. He had now availed himself of a sufficiently long leave to go with Ramdas on his visit to various North Indian cities in response to the invitation of friends of those places. He was eager to see Punjab and Kashmir. So he suggested that Ramdas should start again for the North and that he would keep him company. Ramdas agreed with him. Once more there was a flutter amongst Kasaragod devotees. They laid all the responsibility for this tour on the shoulders of Janardan Pant and roundly took him to task for it. This attack on him was the first of its kind, as he had to face worse music in the course of his travels with Ramdas.

CHAPTER 47: RAWALPINDI – KASARAGOD

Ramdas on the day fixed, departed from Kasaragod again for Northern India with Janardan Pant. Reaching Madras and again staying with Dr. G. S. Katre for a day, they entrained for Nagpur. At Nagpur they remained for two days with Kalle Sadashivrao. Then travelling further north they arrived once more at Jhansi. This time he stayed here for about ten days. Here he met also Swami Nirbhayanand and Purnanand.

On the due date Ramdas departed with Janardan Pant straight for Rawalpindi. In Rawalpindi he was as usual put up at Pandit Jewandas's residence. His halt was short. He was eager to finish off the Kashmir trip and then, on return, spend a few days in Rawalpindi. So in three or four days he and Janardan Pant found themselves under the hospitable roof of Pandit Janakinath. Janakinath and his family were as before all love and kindness. Pandit Amarnath was also there at the time. His stay in Srinagar this time was only for ten days. Here a word about Janardan Pant would not be out of place. He expected that by keeping company with Ramdas he would have a happy time of it, but his experience was quite the reverse. His ignorance of the English language was for him a great handicap. Ramdas conversed with the friends, at every place he visited, in English. Besides, being nurtured and bred in the orthodox atmosphere, Janardan Pant found the ways of the people, in the midst of whom he was forced to live, strangely unpalatable. He had come to Srinagar expecting to see in that land of Pandits an ideal state of things. But his disillusionment must have been shocking. The stinking air of the city and the ill-ventilated mud houses of the Pandits, and the meat eating and untidy habits of the people were things he had not bargained for. When visiting the Shalimar and Nishad gardens the party had to pass through a canal on a canoe manned by Muhammadans. The nauseating stench of the canal was too much for Pant. Ramdas could very well make out when he noticed the facial contortions of Pant, while he was sniffing at the trying odour of the canal that he must have been deeply repenting the false step he took in coming to Srinagar. To top it all, when Ramdas proposed to the Pandits after a week's stay that he must be permitted to leave Srinagar shortly, they all but tore Pant to pieces, presuming that he was at the bottom of Ramdas's early departure from their midst.

Before leaving the place, Ramdas and Pant remained with Shambhunath for a few days. One night Janakinath came here to see Ramdas. He took him out for a walk to a *maidan* close by. As they walked, Janakinath had a long talk with him. The gist of it was that Ramdas by a mere wish should bring him face to face with God. If self-surrender was the goal he should see that Janakinath attained it by a mere blessing from him. In reply Ramdas made him understand: "Self-surrender is a task mainly resting upon the efforts of the *sadhaka* or the devotee. God wants us to be conscious instruments in His hands. God's grace alights on the devotee when he has acquired the necessary qualifications for it."

Janakinath would not agree. He stated that he was perfectly weak and powerless and could not do the necessary *sadhana* for bringing about the needed surrender. Everything must be done for him by God Himself. If there was to be surrender, God alone should see that He provided him with the conditions for such a surrender. In short, he looked to God to shower on him all that was best that lay in His power to grant. To this Ramdas said: "Since you know the truth that God alone is the real power and the only power that should mould your life, bringing about a divine transformation, then where is the question of attaining self-surrender? You have already realised the Truth. Your worry and fretfulness have no significance. In so far as you are manifesting these feelings, Ramdas takes it that you do so for mere play."

He would not be convinced. The talk went on till late in the night. It appeared, after all, that Janakinath meant by his talk nothing more than a loving pastime.

When the appointed day arrived Ramdas left the hills of Srinagar for the plains. Of course he came down to Rawalpindi again. Here again he met Swami Anand Swarup who dwelt in a solitary house removed from the city. Ramdas was paying him visits every evening, and at his rooms devotees of all sects would assemble to listen to his talks.

One day a Sikh devotee who was greatly taken up with Ramdas—a daily visitor—read out a few verses from Guru Arjun Singh's Sukhmani, and explained the meaning to the assembled party. Guru Arjun Singh has propounded that man comes by the highest beatitude of life, viz., spiritual illumination, only through the grace of saints. He held that no *sadhana* or *tapasya*, even of the most severe type, could entitle the *sadhaka* to the attainment of this supreme state. The saint chooses to throw the light of his grace on any man who comes in touch with him and that instant the fortunate soul attains *moksha*. There is no such condition as fitness or otherwise of the aspirant to receive or not to receive the saint's grace. He rightly contends that if divine grace depended upon the condition of the aspirant, it cannot be all-powerful. Since it is all-powerful, no qualification of any kind for an aspirant is necessary for the reception of the divine grace. He concluded that the absolute power of grace rests entirely with the saint. Whomsoever he chooses, he elevates, blesses and liberates. This is the incontrovertible law of grace.

Another time, at the request of some friends, he went for the *darshan* of a *sannyasi*, residing in the house of one of them. A party consisting of Swami Anand Swarup, Jewandas and two or three others, visited the house. The *sannyasi* was all humility and treated Ramdas with great kindness and love. Ramdas seated himself beside him and the other friends also did the same. In the course of conversation the saint, who appeared to have a large number of disciples in Rawalpindi and other places, and whose practice of yoga was the Raja Yoga of Patanjali, put to Ramdas the question: "What do you prescribe as the best method for control of mind?"

Ramdas replied: "So far as his experience goes he can assert that the continuous repetition of the divine Name can easily produce concentration of mind."

"Before I proceed to express my opinion on the solution you have offered, I will lay before you a bit of my own experience," the *sannyasi* continued, "I have been for many years struggling hard to bring under subjection the restless activity of the mind. I have adopted the method of Ashtanga Yoga. I regulated my food according to the strict rules of *satwic* diet. For some months I lived all alone on the banks of Ganges far beyond Rishikesh. I worked on at the practice systematically throughout the period of my stay there. Even with all my strenuous endeavours I found I could not attain any measure of concentration. I then felt so depressed, despaired of success and disgusted with life, that I thought of committing suicide by jumping into the river. Somehow I resisted this impulse and I am here with this question which sorely troubles me day and night. But I fail to see that the method prescribed by you can be of any avail. I do not believe in it. This is my candid and considered opinion."

To this Ramdas said: "Swamiji, you seem to be quite arbitrary in rejecting a method which Ramdas holds forth as most conducive to attaining concentration without your giving a fair trial to it.

Ramdas spoke to you about the power of the divine Name not from mere hearsay or taking the hint from books. You may depend upon it he speaks upon this subject on the authority of his own experience. Since you desired to know, Ramdas gave his solution to your problem."

"I have no faith in the path of *bhakti*," he replied. "I do not believe in sentimental religion. I have no patience with those who say that devotion and taking of the Lord's Name leads one to God-realisation. I have not found the path for myself, but I know *bhakti* is not the way."

When the *sannyasi* came to this definite and final conclusion, Swami Anand Swarup, who was so long calmly listening to the dialogue, was roused at the closing words of the *sadhu*. In an indignant tone he rated the *sannyasi* as follows: "Then what business had you to raise the question at all? Having raised it in the spirit of a learner you ought to have accepted the advice couched in the reply. You are combating it without possessing the least knowledge of the matter. Swamiji has conclusively solved your problem. It is of course for you to take it or not, but you should not have peremptorily condemned it. You are asked to give a trial to the method placed before you. However that be, it is clear from your own confession that you have woefully failed in the path chosen by you. Still the wonder is that you pose yourself as a *guru* and canvass a number of disciples. What are you going to teach them? Evidently to drown themselves in the Ganges river! Why do you impose yourself upon harmless people and, living in their houses, feed upon them? You are strong enough to work for your food. Divest yourself of the misleading ochre-robes that you have donned to fool the world. Be honest and remain true to yourself and save thereby many a gullible soul from being led on a path which will take them nowhere. This is my advice to you. Follow it and be wise."

The *sannyasi*, whom Ramdas was watching when Swami Anand Swarup was taking him to task, had all the time his face lit up with a self-complacent smile. He was unruffled and cool as a cucumber. Turning towards Swami Anand Swarup, in a low, gentle and modulated voice, he spoke: "Swamiji, the irritable nature that you have exhibited does not become your garb. You have unnecessarily wasted a good deal of your precious energy in the ebullition of anger. I am a humble soul and you are a great *mahatma*. I am not sorry for myself, but I regret that I became an unintentional cause of the violence you did to yourself."

After this there was a lull and, the meeting having terminated, Ramdas stepped out of the house with the other friends. The *sannyasi* came out on the road to bid the party farewell and Ramdas could not resist clasping him in a fond embrace, at which Swami Anand Swarup must have been not a little surprised.

Another day, at the combined wish of the devout mothers of the city, he delivered a discourse on Krishna Prem in a religious institution. There were over two hundred ladies present on the occasion and it was purely a ladies' gathering. He spoke in Hindi for about one hour. He poured himself out in a stream of ecstasy on the sublime nature of Love. He brought out many telling incidents in the life of Lord Krishna wherein the Lord's love for his devotees was revealed in all its magnificent glory. He concluded with the peroration that Lord Krishna was the very personification of infinite love, light and joy.

The mothers, who listened to his discourse with rapt attention, were supremely happy. They were the votaries of Lord Krishna who was their life, soul and everything. Blessed mothers, may you ever be inebriated with the magic spell of Lord Krishna's Name and Love!

The discourse over, he returned to Jewandas's house. He was seated on the terrace of the building. He heard from there a spirited talk going on at the entrance of the house below. It ceased, and a friend apprised him about the persons engaged in the talk at the entrance. It appeared two members of the detective police attended Ramdas's discourse that day and followed him up to Jewandas's house. The fact was, Ramdas was wearing a *khadi* cloth and Janardan Pant, besides being dressed in *khadi*, was also wearing a *khadi* white cap. The detectives thought that Ramdas was a politician in the garb of a *sannyasi*. Since they found nothing incriminatory in his discourse they came as far as the house to inquire after his antecedents, mission, etc. They went away after receiving satisfactory information from Jewandas's wife.

In the course of his stay in the Punjab he was taken by Jewandas on a short trip to his native village Hazro, where Ramdas came in contact with many devotees of the place, including a Muslim holding broad views. Here he cannot fail to mention that he received kindness and hospitality from many devotees in Rawalpindi at their houses, of whom Gurudas Ram and a Sikh Sardar were two.

Soon after he returned to Rawalpindi, he departed for Agra. In due time he reached Agra where again he and Janardan Pant were lodged in the outhouse of the temple. During this stay Ramdas gave a discourse in the *vaishya* boarding house. The young men of the house put him various questions and he elucidated their difficulties, drawing upon his own life and experience. They were all of good cheer and treated him with great love.

Among the friends who paid him visits in the temple were two from Etawah, Suraj Narayan and Hridaya Narayan. They took him with them on a visit to Etawah where they accommodated him in the local Theosophical Lodge. Many friends of this place, here as well, crowded at the lodge in the evenings to listen to his discourses. He had, as in other places, a blissful time of it.

From here he was escorted by Hridaya Narayan to Mainpuri where his parents lived. He was welcomed with great joy by all the members of the household and he spent a delightful night in their pure and loving company. Dharm Narayan, father of Hridaya Narayan, was a great and noble soul, and his talented sons had inherited the sterling qualities of the father. Again returning to Etawah, he and Janardan Pant left the city straight for Dhanbad, passing on the way Benares and Allahabad.

At Dhanbad the Gujarati friend, Ratilal, was awaiting his arrival at the station. Ratilal lived far in the interior in Katrasgarh, a noted coal mine district in Bengal. The party with Ratilal motored from the station to Katrasgarh. Ramdas remained here for about a week. At this time he availed himself of the opportunity of visiting the coal mines. A small occurrence at this place deserves notice. The time was when picketing was the rage. Young school-boys were taking keen interest and active part in this movement. A lad of the house proved to be an intrepid picket. It appeared he was arrested by the police for picketing a liquor shop. As is customary the policeman questioned him: "Who is your father?"

"Mahatma Gandhi."

"Where is your home?" was the policeman's next question.

"Jail," was the prompt reply of the boy.

At this, the boy was set free and sent home.

After a week's stay in Katrasgarh he and Janardan Pant proceeded to Calcutta where they stopped with Parab and B.S. Rao. These two friends divided between them the earlier part of his stay in Calcutta, since they lived in the same building. At nights on Saturdays these friends with some others of their society would repair to the terrace of the building and spend the whole night awake in their own mode of meditation and spiritual discourses in which Ramdas once joined them. Both the friends were overflowing in their kindness to these itinerant guests.

Then he with Janardan Pant spent a few days with P. Shivshankerrao at whose house Janardan Pant performed a *harikatha*, largely attended by the interested public of the place. Another *harikatha* performance was also arranged in a *bhajan mandir* belonging to the resident Maharashtra community of the city. Here Janardan Pant had for his subject Sri Samarth Ramdas and Shivaji. In the course of his discourse his fiery nationalist spirit, which had been from a long time suppressed after coming into close contact with Ramdas, was roused. He spoke with great vehemence about the fallen condition of India and passed a scathing judgement upon those whom he held responsible for it. For some time past, after he severed his connection with political activities in which he was engaged when Ramdas first met him he was mainly a religious preacher. The people assembled for his *kirtan* were not prepared for this digression on his part at which they must have been not a little perturbed. Realizing the situation Janardan Pant returned at once to the main theme of the performance. Ramdas's stay in Calcutta continued for about ten days during which he received nothing but kindness and love from all friends of the place.

The next move was directly for Madras, and after a couple of days' journey by railway they reached the city for the third time. On this occasion the stay with Dr. G.S. Katre extended over a week. Here also Janardan Pant had an opportunity to perform a *kirtan* at the request of the friends of that city.

From Madras they travelled to Kumbakonam. Savoor Shanker Rao, the friend who has so kindly written an introduction to this book, had come to Madras to take him over to his place. Savoor Shanker Rao is a vastly learned man. In his spacious bungalow, of which the big drawing room was his library, where he had a very fine collection of books dealing with philosophy, religion and general literature, Ramdas spent a week most blissfully. His wife, a simple, child-like and noble soul, joined heartily with her husband in the *bhajan* that was held in the evenings. Ramdas hardly moved out of the house. Some professors of the college, of which Savoor Shanker Rao was the then principal, came to see Ramdas and had talks with him. Here Janardan Pant, whose leave had by now expired, separated from him and returned to join his duties at Narkhed.

Ramdas's next place of visit was Ernakulam. Here he spent a few days, in the company of P.Sanjivrao and many other friends of the place and then left for Kasaragod again. Of course, he occupied once more Anandashram, situated in that calm retreat beyond the hills.

The usual routine of ashram life restarted. Krishna Bai paid her daily visits and did her selfless service in the ashram. A week after his arrival, Krishna Bai's brother-in-law, having returned from Europe, came to Kasaragod to take over his family and Krishna Bai and her children to Dharwad. Really, it was a wrench for Krishna Bai so suddenly to tear herself off from her association with Ramdas and the ashram. At his request, she however departed with her brother-in-law and others.

Before proceeding to narrate the events that followed, it is necessary that a word should be said relating to the intense life of self-sacrifice Krishna Bai led during his all-India tour. Gurudev was bed-ridden and Rukmabai, owing to her severe attacks of asthma, was also in a similar condition. In those days Krishna Bai's life was mainly spent in attending on the patients. As a nurse at the bedside of a sick person she can be said to be rarely equalled. She would give herself away to such service heart and soul. She tended both the patients a thousand times more tenderly and carefully than their own mothers would have. For that matter, her entire life is an oblation to selfless service of all, irrespective of condition, person, time or place.

With regard to the service rendered to the above mentioned patients, Ramdas heard from their own lips their deeply grateful and loving words of thanks to her and praise of Krishna Bai's divine nature.

Another fact which cannot go unnoticed is that Gunda, a great selfless devotee, true to Ramdas's request, remained in the ashram mostly alone, all the time that Ramdas was away from it. He now became Ramdas's whole time attendant. After returning from the tour Ramdas scarcely left the ashram for the town, and gradually the number of visitors also dwindled away, until for the last few months of his stay, he was singularly alone in the ashram except for this loving and faithful friend.

About two months having thus passed, under peculiar conditions which are not worthwhile narrating here in detail, as bid by Ram, Ramdas went on a month's fast and a vow of silence. Of course, he was living on a moderate diet of milk. About this time he also got an anonymous letter threatening his life, if he did not abandon the ashram at once. A fortnight after the beginning of the fast, Vidyacharya, a friend from Sholapur, came down to see him. Vidyacharya was naturally disappointed that he could not freely discourse with Ramdas. Also he was much pained at the scanty diet on which Ramdas was then living. One night, it might have been between eight and nine o'clock, Ramdas, Vidyacharya and Gunda were sitting on the outer verandah with lantern burning in their midst. Vidyacharya and Gunda were deeply absorbed in singing devotional songs. Suddenly, without any notice, Krishna Bai made her appearance. Ramdas wrote on a slip of paper and showed it to her: "After all, you have come," and also enquired in it if she came alone. He also wrote in the note: "Mother, you have come to your own home. The ashram shall in future be your permanent place of residence."

Most of the way from Bombay, where she had gone from Dharwad, she had travelled alone with a single cloth and nothing besides. Thereafter, she stayed in the ashram day and night. Vidyacharya left and Gunda also went to Puttur, his native village, for a change.

Under instructions from Ramdas, Krishna Bai now started on a course of steady and continuous discipline in meditation and *asana*. On his advice she also visited every day four or five houses of devotees in the town where she gave the benefit of her presence and service to the devout ladies of the household. Meanwhile his fast for one month came to a close, but as he was not satisfied with it, he went on a further fast for three days, taking only water. Then again, he proposed to go even without water. This last absolute fast was observed only for one day and he had to break it due to the most pathetic appeal from Chandrasekharrao, Ramabai's spouse. Thenceforth he came to his old diet of one meal a day. Now Ramdas and Krishna Bai used to be alone in the ashram in the nights.

A fortnight after the breaking of the fast, when Ramdas was busy taking a fair copy of the earlier chapters of this book, and Krishna Bai sitting as usual in her posture of meditation on the verandah where she slept for the night, a man of a coarse appearance but of strong build, belonging to the working class turned up, with a lantern in hand. The time must have been about 10 p.m. Ramdas came out leaving his work and enquired of the visitor what he wanted. He replied: "Some friends possibly from a distant place have arrived at the bungalow on the top of the hill and have sent word through me to ask you to go there to meet them."

Ramdas's heart, when he heard this, overflowed with love and he said within himself: "At what a great sacrifice these friends must have come from a long distance out of their pure longing and love for Ramdas." At once he made up his mind to go up to them. The messenger said that he would remain in the ashram until Ramdas returned. Taking the lantern of the ashram he started asking Krishna Bai to wait until he returned with the friends, but she said she would also like to go with him. The sturdy messenger also falling in with Krishna Bai's idea said that she might also accompany him. So both walked quickly up the hill and reached the traveller's bungalow, but to their surprise and discomposure they found that there was nobody waiting for them in the bungalow. Ramdas at once scented some mischief, for, the messenger had deliberately remained behind in the ashram during their absence.

Now both quickly retraced their steps to the ashram. On reaching the place they found that the messenger with his lantern had disappeared. On going up the verandah they further saw a quantity of nightsoil splashed at the entrance of the room and a number of pieces of a broken earthen pot. This was the work of the nocturnal visitor for discharging which alone he must have come. Without feeling the least repugnance or disgust Krishna Bai at once fell to the task of cleaning the floor. She cleaned the floor actually with her hands while collecting the rubbish from which was issuing a most revolting stench. Within half-an-hour the place was swept and washed. The beauty of the whole thing was that all the while, when she was engaged in this work, she was patient, cheerful and smiling. Ramdas, on entering the room, found a brass spittoon which was daily used by him had alone been taken away, and a few drops of the nightsoil had disfigured the manuscript of this narrative. The night passed without anything further happening.

Again after a week or thereabouts, at almost the same hour of the night, two men came to the ashram of whom one was the previous visitor. It was a dark night. The ashram was so situated in a dense jungle that within two furlongs around it, there was no other habitation. This time the visitors appeared to have come with a sterner mission. For the first few minutes they demanded of Ramdas many articles that were in the ashram including a framed board containing the name 'Anandashram' artistically formed in glass beads. He handed over these things to the visitors without any hesitation, and asked them if they wanted anything more. When this business was going on, he was standing just at the entrance of the room on the verandah and Krishna Bai was beside him. The lamp was on the raised pedestal on which he usually sat, to the right side of the entrance. As soon as the visitors thought that the time for carrying out their intention had arrived, one of them took the lantern and with a sweep sent it flying into the courtyard, by which act the lantern broke and was suddenly extinguished. Now they found themselves in utter darkness. The man, who threw away the lantern, rushing up towards Krishna Bai fell upon her. Beside her was a copper pot filled with water. Ramdas was at the time a little away from the front door. Realizing the situation he closed his arms upon the body of the man who was attacking Krishna Bai, with the object of preventing him from doing harm to her, but the other man who was watching the situation pulled Ramdas from behind with all his strength, making him give up the hold on the other man, and held him tight within his arms. Ramdas's whole body thrilled and he in a loud voice uttered the Name "Ram" three times. Simultaneously as it were, the Name "Ram" issued twice from Krishna Bai's lips. At the sound of this Name, the man who had well-nigh clutched Krishna Bai's throat to strangle her, let go his hands and started like a scared creature to run away from the place. Beholding him taking to his heels, the other man, who was holding Ramdas in a tight embrace, set him free and jumping down the verandah followed suit. When leaving Krishna Bai the man who attacked her pushed her down, causing the small of her back to strike with great force upon the hard rim of the copper vessel, and the next instant she rolled down the verandah to the surrounding yard of the ashram. In the dark, by taking her name aloud, Ramdas located the place where she fell. He ran up to her and they stood together, Ramdas exclaiming: "Oh! Ram, what is this you are doing?" Then Krishna Bai said: "Nothing is the matter. Don't accuse Ram, everything is all right."

Beyond the fields, on the right side of the ashram, there was the house of a cultivator who must have been observing from his front-yard the strange happenings at the ashram. When he heard the sound "Ram" "Ram" in a loud key from Ramdas and the sudden darkness that enveloped the ashram, he suspected some mischief and came running. It took him about five minutes to pass through the fields in the dark and reach the ashram. But the grim visitors of the night had fled away. With the help of a match they lit a torch made of palm leaves. On his enquiry Ramdas related to him all that had happened. He said: "I shall sleep here tonight and see how those blackguards will dare to molest you again."

For the night it was all right. What about the future nights? Turning to Krishna Bai Ramdas appealed to her not to remain in the ashram in the nights from next day onwards. He would prefer to be alone in it. But she would not agree, "Whatever happens to me I will not stay away for the nights." Seeing that she was determined and persuasion was futile, Ramdas at once made up his mind to leave the ashram for good and get out of the place. Instantly he started with Krishna Bai for the town, and the cultivator friend, who was also joined by another, accompanied them as far as Chandrashekarrao's house, situated in the heart of the town. When Ramdas was walking fast towards the town closely followed by Krishna Bai, she appealed to him in a piteous tone: "Papa, what are your future plans?" He replied that he did not know.

"It is Ram's command to leave Kasaragod at the earliest opportunity. He will go wherever Ram leads him." He said.

To this she said: "Please do not abandon me. I have no place and no refuge except you. Permit me to follow you wherever you go."

"No, no. Do not think of doing so," Ramdas replied.

In a rising emotion she waylaid him, appealed again and insisted upon his giving the word. He yielded and agreed. They reached Chandrashekarrao's house. Thus ended the memorable events of this night.

As was natural, the household was shocked to hear of the dreadful situation through which Ramdas and Krishna Bai had passed at the ashram. The fall on the water pot had caused permanent injury to the lower end of Krishna Bai's spinal cord. In spite of the excruciating pain, she was patient and cheerful as if nothing had happened to her. His resolution was made that he should leave Kasaragod the very next day. The night passed. By the earliest train on the following day he and Krishna Bai with Chandrashekarrao came to Hosdurg. In Hosdurg there were some mothers who were keenly anxious to have him at their house for some days. To fulfil their long cherished desire, on alighting at the Kanhangad station he directed his steps straight to their house. The party was received by the kind mothers with great joy. His future plans were unsettled.

CHAPTER 48: RAMNAGAR – ANANDASHRAM

After a few days' stay, Ramdas and Krishna Bai, at the invitation of T. Bhavanishankerrao, came to Manjapati, now known as Ramnagar, for the opening ceremony of his newly built house at this place. T. Bhavanishankerrao and others pressed Ramdas to have an ashram built near the Manjapati hill, which place was discovered to be not only solitary but also possessing all the scenic grandeur of the country-side.

The selection of the spot for the construction of Anandashram has indeed a deep significance. Without knowing the antecedents of the place, Ramdas was prompted to choose it intuitively. He later discovered that the place, which is known as Manjapati, was at one time covered with a thick forest and that *sadhus* and *sannyasis* were doing *tapasya* in it. It was also said that the hill is sacred because in olden days there was on it a temple and a tank, faint traces of which are still to be seen. Tradition has it too, that Hanuman, when he was returning to Lanka, carrying the hill of Dronachala, dropped a portion of it, at this spot, and that portion forms the present hill. In this connection Ramdas can say definitely that God must have had strong reasons for directing his servant Ramdas to this place. Both Hanuman and he were the votaries of the same Name, Ram, and both were born on the same day in the Hindu calendar year. This cannot be a matter of mere coincidence: it must be part of a plan, divinely ordained. That probably accounts also for the visions that some devotees occasionally get of Sri Hanuman visiting the *bhajan mandir* of the ashram. One such was vouchsafed in the early years of the ashram to Srimati Devibai alias Appibai. She related to us one day a wonderful vision she had when she slept in the ashram *bhajan mandir*. She saw a huge figure of a monkey entering the Bhajan Hall, walking up to the *asan*, prostrating before it, and then leaving by the back door. The vision had made such a deep impression on her mind, that when she was relating it, she felt highly elated, for she thought, it was Hanuman himself who had given her his *darshan*.

Agreeing to the suggestion of the friends he decided to have an ashram erected on a small hillock by the side of a towering hill—the highest in the range. At once God, who gave the idea, set him to work for accomplishing it. He wrote appeals for funds to the innumerable friends all over India, with whom he had come in contact during his itinerant life, for making up the cost of the new ashram. The encouragement and help he received on all sides was simply marvellous. Within a month of his arrival at Ramnagar the work of erecting the ashram building was started. The friends who offered the suggestion heartily joined in it. The ashram was begun only three months before the breaking of the monsoon; so the work had to be hurried on. In three months the main ashram building and an outhouse behind it were completed.

The Scenery

While to the right side of the ashram there is a chain of undulating hills, in front there lie extensive grounds formed by groves of trees and corn-fields. To the left the vision can sweep over about four miles a vast plateau covered with thick vegetation, plains and scattered houses, having at the far end the Arabian sea with its blue expanse of water. Behind the ashram are rows of hills covered over with verdant growth, having on both sides beautiful coconut topes, whose crests wave majestically in the strong breeze that blows over them from the sea. To stand out on the ashram hill and cast a look around means to present to the sight a most fascinating picture of nature dressed in her variegated colours. When the sun is midway in the heavens and its rays are reflected on the waters of the sea, it looks as though a vast sheet of silver is shining at a distance. After a few monsoon rains, when the green grass like a mantle spreads over the hills and plains, the surroundings offer a bewitching sight to the onlooker. The atmosphere prevailing at the ashram and over the surrounding land is surcharged with perfect calmness and peace.

The Opening Celebration

The opening ceremony of the new ashram, which is also named Anandashram, was held on the 15th May 1931. In response to the invitations, hundreds of people from different parts of India assembled for the occasion. *Bhajan, kirtan,* feast, and distribution of food, etc., to the poor went on for ten days. The hills of Ramnagar resounded with the thrilling music of the Lord's glorious Names. From Maharashrta about half-a-dozen devotees attended the function. Janardan Pant, Raghunath Maharaj, Govind Ramkrishna Joshi, Krishnaji Pandharinath and Madhavrao Kulkarni were amongst them. These devotees took whole-hearted part in the *bhajan* and *kirtan.*

At the opening ceremony, as requested by the assembled devotees and friends, Ramdas delivered a short speech. Briefly put, it ran as follows: "Ramdas has the supreme delight to speak to you today a few words at the inauguration of this holy ashram. The ideal which the ashram holds before it, is universal love and service, based upon a vision of divinity in all beings and creatures of the world. Here every man, woman or child, to whatever denomination, creed, or caste the person may belong, shall have free access. This is a place where every effort will be made to cultivate the spirit of mutual love and service, so that what is realised within its walls may prove as an example for the right conduct of human life in the outside world. The Lord is our help and guide in all matters. May He with all His bounty shower His blessings on the great service which this home of love and bliss has undertaken to discharge!"

Krishna Bai, although greatly weakened by the injury she had sustained at the Kasaragod ashram, brought all her rare skill and indefatigable energy to bear upon the management of the function. Every programme was gone through with exactness and regularity. It must be admitted that Krishna Bai is a born organizer, and exhibits in all things her wonderful capacity for handling difficult situations, for soon after the opening of the buildings, torrential rains accompanied by thunder, lightning and storm swept over the ashram building. But the radiant and ever calm figure of Krishna Bai was moving about in the assemblage like an angel ministering to the minutest wants of all. None of the visitors went without her special care and service. In short she had her maternal eye upon all alike.

At the time of the opening of the ashram, we had the most illuminating sayings of the great religious teachers of the world, neatly written out in block letters, on thick sheets of paper, in English, Sanskrit and Marathi; and these were framed and hung up on the walls of the Bhajan Hall. Also the Ram *mantrum* was painted on the walls in different languages. The sayings were:

1. To those men who worship Me alone, thinking of no other, to those ever harmonious, I bring full security. (IX, 22—The Gita)

2. God is love: he who dwells in love dwells in God and God in him. (Jesus Christ)

3. God resides in that heart in which there is compassion, forgiveness and peace. (Sant Tukaram)

4. He who wears out his body in God's service, who has Ram Nam always on his tongue, who walks always on the path of righteousness, such a servant of the Lord is blessed on this earth. (Samarth Ramdas)

5. Dedication of wife, son, house and life to God is the perfect path of devotion. This is truly called worship. (Ekhath Maharaj)

6. Abandoning all duties, come to Me alone for shelter: sorrow not, I will liberate thee from all sins. (XVIII, 66—The Gita)

After the lapse of a few years, many of these were replaced by the pictures of these Teachers, which are still adorning the walls of the ashram. They are those of Sri Ramakrishna, Sri Saradamani Devi, Sai Baba, Jesus Christ, Sri Aurobindo, Sri Ramana Maharshi, Buddha, Zoroaster, Swami Vivekananda, Guru Nanak Dev, and Gurudev.

Ramdas had realised the unity of all religions, and his love and admiration go out to all the spiritual teachers equally. He is at once the servant of the Almighty, and a child of saints. How blissful it is to feel and be conscious of this truth!

Mother Rukmabai

A few days after Ramdas left Kasaragod, Mother Rukmabai who was still staying at her daughter's house, came to Ramnagar and after a short stay proceeded to Madras to spend a few days with her nephew. She had a great mind to live permanently with Ramdas in the new ashram. But God willed otherwise. Soon after her arrival in Madras her asthmatic complaint took a serious turn. Her condition became critical. At this time her nephew questioned her as to whom she wanted to see and she at once replied: "I want to see Krishna Bai." She also added: "If I should at all recover, it is possible only under her tender and careful nursing. For, during my last illness at Kasaragod, when I was at the very doors of death, she alone could save me from its jaws." But it was not possible for Krishna Bai to go to her. A few days later came the news that she passed away. May her soul ever rest in peace!

A word about her in this connection will not be out of place. She was a true, noble and faithful partner in his old life. It was but natural that when God took Ramdas away from her company and made him dedicate his life entirely to His service, she felt no small amount of pain, but latterly when she came to stay with him in Kasaragod ashram she thoroughly understood the intention of God in bringing about the transformation in his life. Naturally of a religious temperament, thereafter her devotion became so intense that she burnt with the aspiration to attain the vision of God. The Lord's great Name continuously dwelt on her lips and even to the last moment she maintained the remembrance of God and dropped off the body in that exalted consciousness.

Gurudev

More than five months after the opening celebration of the ashram, Ramdas received the tidings that Gurudev, who was living with his son in Kasaragod, renounced his body, on the 8th November 1931, at 5:30 p.m. On the 13th day, i.e., on 20th November, his first *punyatithi* was observed in the ashram, during which we held *bhajan* throughout the day and night, and the next morning we fed four hundred poor people in his blessed memory. Many devotees from Mangalore and Kasaragod attended this function. In the last period of his life, for some months, he had reached a stage in which he remained perfectly unattached to the world, retaining all the time not only his consciousness of the external life, but also his jovial and cheerful nature. It was the wave of grace, compassion and love that rose from his magnanimous heart that turned Ramdas's life towards its fountainhead—God—ultimately granting him the highest vision of immortality, bliss and peace through perfect union and oneness with the immanent and transcendent Godhead.

Commemoration of Gandhiji's Fast

Mahatma Gandhi's fast of twenty-one days ended on the 7th May 1933. In commemoration of this event, a bodhi tree was planted in front of the ashram.

The Vision

In October 1933, the first issue of the English monthly magazine, "The Vision," was released from the ashram. The object was to present to the spiritually inclined people in India and abroad, the lives and teaching of saints of all religions, to publish their pictures whenever possible and to lay before them, Ramdas's own spiritual experiences. Ramdas was its first editor. The Marathi and Malayalam editions ceased publication after running for a few years.

The *Fakir* Becomes an *Amir*

After some years at the suggestion of friends, due to rheumatism and the weakened state of his body brought on by long and repeated tours, Ramdas had to use a chair for sitting, and a cot for sleeping. Krishna Bai also got for him a raised, artistically-made, wooden dais, on which he sat during *bhajan* time. He was made to wear stockings, a woollen coat, and a muffler round his neck, and looked like a *bada sahib*. When he sat leaning on the cushioned chair, the *fakir* looked like an *amir*. How wonderful is the *lila* of the Lord! Ramdas dances to His tune and is happy.

A Scottish friend, who contributed articles to "The Vision," and was carrying on correspondence with Ramdas, once wrote to him, taking objection to the title of "His Holiness," which some writers in "The Vision" had used before his name. He strongly urged that Ramdas should not accept this title. Ramdas wrote in reply that it was immaterial to him whether people gave him honour or its opposite. If he took notice of one, he had to take notice of the other also. But his actual position, by the grace of the Supreme, is that he is beyond both. So Ramdas is prepared cheerfully to accept praise or blame, whichever it pleases people to give him.

Patrons and Donors

It must be understood that God alone, who is the one benevolent ruler of the worlds, made possible the establishment of this ashram. The activities of the ashram are day by day extending owing to the generous donations it is receiving from innumerable, selfless, pure and noble souls from different parts of India and abroad. All credit for any work or service rendered by it is due to them. Many of these are friends, whose self-effacement is so complete that they have enjoined on him not to reveal their names in connection with the lavish help in money and other ways offered by them for the furtherance of the ashram mission. So without mentioning their names Ramdas acknowledges their loving cooperation with infinite gratitude.

Relief to the Poor

Periodically, and also particularly during celebrations, distribution of foodstuffs to the poor is one of the important items of ashram service. On such occasions relief is rendered to thousands of people. The ashram is open to all people irrespective of caste, creed, colour or nationality. Willing and cheerful service on equal basis is offered to all of them.

Ashram Buildings

The main ashram consists of a *bhajan mandir* in front enclosed by arched walls, the upper part of which is ornamented with cornice work which gives the hall not only an artistic view but also a distinctly imposing and charming appearance. At the back of the *bhajan mandir* is a small room for Ramdas's occupation. The out-house which is situated directly at the back of the main building is made up of four rooms, two on each side, having a pathway between, one side of which was used as a kitchen and the other for the residence of casual guests.

Later, another small building was erected in the ashram compound for purposes of conducting the editorial and official business of the two magazines and correspondence. The cost of this building was met by the generosity of the Thakur Saheb of Limbdi, Sri Daulat Singh, to whom Ramdas expresses his feelings of gratitude.

It was with great sorrow that Ramdas heard of the passing away of Sri Daulatsinghji, whom Ramdas mentioned at several places in this book. Whenever Ramdas went to Limbdi, the Thakur Saheb would take him to his palace and treat him with all love and hospitality. He was a devotee of Sri Krishna and had also a great regard for saints. He was also charitable by his nature and had donated large sums to various philanthropic institutions. He had a noble and devout partner in life, who departed this life earlier than he.

During Ramdas's absence on tour in 1938, Krishna Bai built two houses for poor Harijan families, and three for ashram workers. She herself supervised their construction. She also made new roads and other improvements in the ashram compound, besides getting the Bhajan Hall and other buildings painted.

As the old cow-shed was inadequate for the increasing number of cows, a bigger one has been constructed. For want of funds we could build only a thatched house. But the building is very spacious. This was also planned by Krishna Bai and the work was carried on under her direct supervision.

From the very beginning of the ashram, *sadhus* started coming daily to the ashram. In course of time their number increased to such an extent that it became a problem to find accomodation for them. So we constructed a separate building for their use, which goes by the name Sadhu Dharmashala. During the first year of his itinerant life, after renouncing the world, Ramdas was travelling in the company of the *sadhus* and *sannyasis*, as related in his earlier books. It was really they who looked after him with great care and affection. It was in their company that Ramdas had gone through rigorous austerities, in which they also had participated, whether they liked it or not—

being strongly attached to him. Accordingly, when these wandering mendicants come to the ashram, they are given food and lodging. As soon as Ramdas sees them, he is reminded of those memorable days, of wild freedom and joy spent in their company.

In the pious memory of Heble Annappayya, a great devotee, who spent his last days in the ashram, his sons, principally Ganesh Heblekar, who is deeply attached to the ashram, have raised a *samadhi* on the *asthi* of Annappayya. It can be seen in the ashram compound, facing the *dharmashala* for *sadhus*. There is a marble tablet on it, with the inscription of his name, and the dates of his birth and death.

Gatherings

Principal N.B. Butani proposed that a gathering be held in the ashram during the Christmas holidays of 1938. He sent invitations to ashram friends living in different parts of India. Preparations were made on a large scale for this gathering. Special *pandals* were erected and these were beautifully decorated. As the days of celebration approached, devotees and friends started pouring in, and on the principal days of the celebration, there was a large number of people. The ashram was humming with activity. The ashram had had no such gathering till then. One ought to have seen Krishna Bai in those days—how her radiant personality was moving about, like a flash of light, inspiring all workers to carry on the duties entrusted to them with energy and enthusiasm. There was no scarcity of anything. The important item of the programme was feeding. Thousands after thousands were fed from morning till late in the night. It was all a most blissful experience, never to be forgotten. Ramdas was witnessing the whole *lila* with no small joy, and he found people belonging to various castes, creeds and places mingling with one another as friends and brothers, on the basis of spiritual kinship. Truly, real happiness can be attained by humanity only when it is aware of the indwelling spirit that unites all members of the human race into one world union or family. Here, in the total absence of the ego-self, manifests a cosmic consciousness, in which all distinctions are lost, and every one experiences the bliss eternal. Although Ramdas's health at this time was weak, he could take part in all the functions, without feeling the least strain, as he was, all throughout, conscious only of joy and nothing else. It was surely a memorable event in the life of the ashram.

The December gathering of 1940 was also noteworthy in many respects. Principally it was so, because of the large number of devotees who had gathered together, without any expectation that it was going to be a gathering at all; each came, without knowing that any others were coming.

Electric Lighting

There is a saying of a saint, often quoted in Maharashtra, "God is the fulfiller of a *satya sankalpa* (pure wish) of His devotee. The devotee makes a plan and God works it out." In the nights, specially the dark ones, it was found difficult for the ashramites and the visitors to move about in the ashram grounds. Moreover, snakes of all kinds crawled about within the compound. Ramdas felt that it would be well if we had an electric installation, so that the buildings and the various roads and paths could be well-lit. This wish he expressed in the presence of some friends. God did not take long to see that an electric installation was set up in the ashram. During nights the ashram now looks from a distance like a fairy-land with its powerful dome-light visible for miles around. Ramdas remembers in this connection the Biblical words: God said: Let there be light! And there was light! So it was here.

A *gerrua* flag is also attached to the tall post on which the dome-light is put up. It is the emblem of the ashram signifying renunciation, love and service.

Sri Krishna Vidyalaya

God fulfilled Ramdas's wish, to start an elementary school in Ramnagar, for imparting education to children living in it and in the surrounding villages. The foundation for the building was laid by Krishna Bai in the year 1940 on her birthday, with the singing of Ramnam, a large number of devotees attending the function. At the time when this function took place, we clearly felt that God blessed this enterprise, as there was a thrill in the air, of blissful anticipation, as all joined with implicit faith and perfect confidence.

B. Krishnaswamy Iyengar, retired Principal of the Engineering College, Bangalore, and V. V. Patankar, retired Executive Engineer, Mysore Government, Bangalore, prepared the necessary plans for the building.

A cement image of Goddess Saraswati, in a standing posture, with a *veena* in her hands, beautifully painted, is installed in a niche in the front wall of the Vidyalaya building. Goddess Saraswati is the symbol of *Vidya*; i.e., learning. She presides over our educational institution, and surely Her grace is abundantly pouring on it. The school is named Sri Krishna Vidyalaya. The opening ceremony took place in the year 1942 on Ramdas's birthday. It was the inauguration of the beginning of a new life for the poor, destitute and neglected children, often seen roaming aimlessly about the ashram. Ramdas's long cherished desire was now fulfilled. God's grace is really bounteous.

Besides teaching the three R's to the pupils, we introduced handicrafts such as hand-spinning, basket-weaving, clay modelling and coir work. The children are trained also in gardening and vegetable growing. They have the usual outdoor games and the indoor play of *kollattam* and *lezim*. We admit into the Vidyalaya children of all classes and castes, including Harijans and Muslims.

In the Boarding Home, the children are given a bath and a washed set of clothes every morning, before breakfast, which they take after a prayer. Then, again, when the classes begin, all the pupils assemble in the central hall of the school and hold prayers. Visitors have observed that the children look clean, smart and intelligent, and that the children of the higher castes cannot be distinguished from those of the Harijans, in regard either to cleanliness or the expression on the face. The light of God dwells, alike in all beings, to whatever category they belong. Only conditions have to be provided for this light to shine out. The man-made division, on the score of birth, race and other considerations, are wholly unnatural and meaningless.

The central room of the Vidyalaya is used as a prayer hall by the school children and teachers, at the beginning and at the end of the school work. In this room, we have, on the walls, pictures of Sri Ramakrishna Paramahamsa, Swami Vivekananda, and Sri Ramana Maharshi, presented by the devotees of the ashram. In one of the bigger halls of the school, the children hold *bhajan* every Thursday, before the school closes for the day. Friends have presented to the institution benches, maps, pictures, slates, library books, equipment for games, and other articles of school use. The school observes, annually, its Opening Day and also other days of religious and national importance.

Sri Krishna Udyogashala

In addition to the educational work undertaken by the ashram, it was proposed to start an industrial school so that the children, after finishing the elementary course, may be trained in some handicrafts. To start with, for this purpose, we used the house on the property presented to the ashram by Dr. S. R. U. Savoor. We also built a thatched shed in front of it for locating handlooms. In the verandah of the house, we held training classes in leather and horn work. We were feeling that the space in this temporary arrangement was not sufficient. Naturally the idea of constructing a new, pukka building came into being and an appeal was made for funds. Shankar Mallapur, who had taken a leading part in the collection of the Shashtiabda Poorthi Fund, requested his boss Sri Bhogilal Patel to bear the entire cost of the building which came to about Rs. 28,453 which he graciously did in the name of his wife Srimati Ichhabai Bhogilal H. Patel as her contribution to the above Fund. He has stipulated that the building should never be used except for industrial purposes. The plan of the building was prepared by Sri D. G. Karanjgaokar, a well-known architect of Bombay, who then, happily, had come on a visit to the ashram. It is a beautiful, spacious and well-ventilated structure in the school compound. It is named Sri Krishna Udyogashala. Its opening ceremony was performed on the 44th birthday of Krishna Bai on 25th September 1946. Friends contributed towards its equipment and maintenance. The four old looms destroyed by fire in the temporary thatched shed were substituted by ten new ones bought from the donation of Ramprasad M. Dave of Ahmedabad. There is a show-room in the building in which the manufactured articles are kept for sale. In course of time, we had to abolish the leather and horn section. Instead we have started hand-spinning, tailoring and handweaving.

The Shashtiabda Poorthi Fund

Here a few words must be said about the Shashtiabda Poorthi Fund, a reference to which has been made above. The idea of collecting a fund for a purse to be presented to Ramdas on the completion of his 60th year first orginated with U. Sanjiv Rao of Bombay and afterwards took the shape of a resolution moved by R. N. Haldipur and adopted at a special meeting of the Bombay branch of the Anandashram held on 26th December 1943 with S.R. Hattiangadi in the chair. When the proposal was conveyed to Ramdas for acceptance he only thought that God was arranging for the clearance of debts incurred by the ashram in His service, the outstandings at the time having accumulated to the tune of about Rs. 48,000. He accordingly agreed readily to what he felt to be a divinely inspired move started by the Lord Himself in furtherance of His own cause. The Fund was closed early in 1947 when it reached a total of about Rs. 104,775, exceeding the target of one *lakh* fixed. A statement regarding the disbursements made out of the collections was published in October 1946 in "The Vision." The nature of the financial crisis that was thus tided over will be realised from the fact that about Rs. 55,500 had to be paid to clear off the debts and deficits incurred by the ashram during its 16-year life of ever-expanding service. It is also noteworthy that whatever money was received from time to time were spent away then and there, under the heads stated, so that no balance was left out of the Fund when it was closed.

The Dispensary

In the early days of the ashram we had been giving only homoeopathic treatment to the ailing persons who resorted to us for medical relief. We had opened also a section for dressing of wounds and for the rendering of first aid to the injured. Both these activities were conducted in a part of "The Vision" office building. As the number of patients increased, we felt the need of having a separate building for the dispensary outside the ashram compound. It was proposed also to open an allopathic section in the dispensary. An appeal was made for funds through "The Vision". As the amount collected for constructing a dispensary building was inadequate, it was decided to use the Pushpa House, which was built by Principal N. B. Butani in memory of his youngest daughter Pushpa, for the purpose of the dispensary. The necessary permission for such use was most heartily given by Butani and his wife when they were approached for the same. We shifted to this place all the dispensary equipment from the room in "The Vision" office; and from that time onwards we have been carrying on here the medical relief on a wider scale.

Visitors

The ashram has the happy privilege of being blessed occasionally by the visits of noted saints and devotees of God. By their presence in it they infuse into the inmates enthusiasm in the discharge of their humble duties. The following is a brief account of a few of such saintly visitors:

Swami Nityanand, a great *yogi*, was residing in Hosdurg. He made several improvements in the old, neglected Hosdurg fort. He was attracting people from all parts of the South Kanara District, and even from far off places. His *darshan* was rightly considered by devotees to be of immense spiritual benefit. Ramdas had the opportunity of meeting him once, when he was dwelling in the Panch-Pandav caves. He had no cloth on his body except a *kaupin*. He was dark in complexion, but possessed a tall, fully-developed, well-proportioned body. One of his characteristic features was that his face was always suffused with most bewitching smiles. As he was seen always sunk in divine bliss, his devotees gave him the name Nityanand—meaning everlasting bliss. One day towards the end of the second year of the ashram, one of the ashramites, Krishnappa, brought him to us. We gave him due honour and made him drink the cool water of a tender coconut. He did not speak a word. After remaining with us for about ten minutes, he went away.

Mahant Sri Rampratapdasji Guru Hanumandasji, a saint of Ahmedabad came to the Ashram with a party of devotees. At one time he was a very orthodox *sadhu*, observing strictly the rules of caste distinctions. After coming to the ashram, he gradually shook them off, and mingled freely with the ashramites. Every year, for several years, he was undertaking the *yatra*, as he called it, to South India, when he would pay visits to Sri Ramanashram and Anandashram. He used to find great joy in feeding and clothing the poor, for which he would spend lavishly.

Yogi Ramaiah one of the prominent disciples of Sri Ramana Maharshi, came with two other friends. Ramdas felt very happy to see him. His eyes have a light which is perfectly other-worldly, and you feel that he is imbued with the spirit of dispassion. When he sat silent at any place Ramdas could clearly see that he was conscious of only one existence. This is the attitude of those whose mind is ever in tune with the Eternal. Their look shows that their heart is elsewhere. Ramdas remembers the instance of the hen that sits on its eggs for hatching. If you observe a hen thus occupied, you find a peculiar vacant look in its eyes, as its internal gaze is fixed on its eggs. The eyes then appear blank, devoid of every kind of expression. Such are the eyes that see and see not. For, they look into the Infinite and not at the relative world. Yogi Ramaiah knew only Telugu; Ramdas could, therefore, communicate with him only by signs. Ramaiah attempted to express himself, but his language was a jumble of Telugu and Tamil with a sprinkling of English words. We used to have good laugh at this, in which he also used to join. Ramdas cannot forget the delicious mangos he brought for him. They were as sweet as he himself.

Swami Siddheshwaranand turned up suddenly one day. He was President of the Ramakrishna Ashram, Bangalore. Ramdas was really delighted to see him. He was full of light, love and devotion. He spent with us only a few hours.

Swami Gurudevanand, whose original name was Sridhar Kamat, belonging to Goa, paid a visit to the ashram. After a few days' stay he took *sannyas* and assumed the new name. For some days he was engaged in meditation, in the cave on the Manjapati hill, where a serpent seems to have been freely moving about. He was an earnest *sadhaka* imbued with a spirit of renunciation.

Sadhu Sadananda, a German, who had joined the Gowdiya Math, came with his *sannyasi gurubhai* Krishnakant. He had *sannyasi* clothes, a tuft on his head, and a *mala* round his neck signifying that he was a Vaishnava *Bhakta*. The *gurubhai* was an Assamese. Sadhu Sadananda had been, it appears, a Professor in a German University and was a man of great learning and attainments. But he was found to be very simple in his nature and ways. In fact, we loved him at first sight. His *gurubhai* was active and took part in the service of the ashram. Sadhu Sadanand was so charmed with the ashram and its surroundings that he wished to return again and settle down in a small cottage, which, he said, he would build for himself, near the ashram. At the time he came there was a proposal to stop the publication of "The Vision". Hearing this, Sadhu Sadanand persuaded us to keep the magazine going.

Just after the completion of the fifty-seventh birthday festivities of Ramdas, Swami Hariharanand of Sri Ananthaswami Math came to the ashram, with a party of his devotees. By reason of his coming, the birthday celebrations were extended by four days, during which period he performed three *harikathas* in the *pandal* erected on the plinth of the proposed dining hall and kitchen. Swami Hariharanand is a saint full of devotion. He is also a gifted singer. He attracts a large number of people to his *kirtan* and keeps them absorbed in listening to the inspiring words that flow out of his mouth, dealing with *bhakti*, *jnana*, and *vairagya*. The three *harikathas* related to (1) Sakhubai, (2) Damaji Panth, and (3) Shabari.

Throughout the description of the lives of these three saints, he brought out clearly how the Lord's Name was their light and refuge, and how by its power alone they were able to attain God-vision. He laid stress upon sincerity, purity of heart and faith as the essential qualities required for the realisation of God. The Swami is well-read in religious literature and has studied the lives of the saints of all parts of India. He was, therefore, able to quote freely from the teachings and songs of Kabir, Eknath, Tukaram, Jnanadev, Samarth Ramdas, Tulsidas, Purandaradas and others. We had a most blissful time throughout his stay with us.

Swami Advaitanand and Ratilal Lakhia visited the ashram. Ramdas had met Swami Advaitanand at Vishnubhai Thakur's place at Patna. Ramdas felt very happy to have him. After a stay of three days with us they left.

K. Krishna Bhagat is a well-known banker of Tellicherry. He came to the ashram with his wife, Rama Devi. He is a devout soul. Ramdas here is concerned with his wife, who, at the time, had reached an advanced stage on the spiritual path. She was developing a childlike nature and her heart was constantly in tune with God. This was apparent in all her ways and doings, which were free and spontaneous. She has, thereafter, visited our ashram several times. Latterly we found that she was rapidly blossoming into a radiant being. The last time she came, she had evolved to such a state that she could spiritually awaken people who came into contact with her. She had many devotees and admirers. She used to sing *bhajan* and go into trances, and Ramdas also heard that she danced in ecstasy, when her heart was filled with divine emotions. She teaches that love is the one thing that an aspirant should develop, in order to realise God. She emphasises the value of congregational *bhajan* as the way to keep our minds absorbed in the thought of God.

Sri Prem Bhikshu of Gujarat, whom Ramdas had met at Ahmedabad, came one day to the ashram unexpectedly. He is full of love and devotion. Ramdas remembers his fair face, with a full black beard on it. Whenever Ramdas sees him, he is reminded of our Sikh friends of Punjab. His love for Ramdas is indeed great. His talks with Ramdas are sweet.

Swami Srivasanand, a *sannyasi* belonging to the Ramakrishna Mission of Bangalore, came to the ashram with some devotees of Mangalore. Ramdas had a delighful time with him. He was about seventy years old at the time. His face was bright with spiritual lustre. He was a learned Swami, well-versed in Sanskrit and had started a Vedanta College at Bangalore. He worked hard for the spiritual uplift of the younger generation. He passed away a few years ago.

Sri Dilip Kumar Roy, one of the prominent disciples of Sri Aurobindo, came to the ashram on a fine morning. We were very happy to have him with us for a few days. His child-like nature endeared him to us all. There is always light and cheer on his face. He is a gifted singer. His musical concerts are very popular all over India as they thrill the hearts of the listeners. He sang with great devotional fervour in the ashram hall during the evening *bhajan*. He is also a reputed poet and essayist. He occasionailly contributes his inspiring poems to "The Vision."

Srimad Anandashram Swamiji of Sri Chitrapur Math, Shirali is, as Ramdas has described him in the earlier parts of this book, a spiritually illuminated personality. It was indeed a gala day for all ashramites when they welcomed him. Krishna Bai had made special arrangements in Sri Narasimha Iyer's house to accommodate him there. The days that he spent with us were memorable, in that we were all merged in a sea of rare bliss. In the evenings, His Holiness graced the ashram *bhajan mandir* at the time of the *bhajan*. On the last day, at the close of the *bhajan*, he delivered an inspiring discourse on *dharma*, which besides being eloquent and impressive, was marked by sparkling wit and humour. His radiant figure comes before our mental vision.

Sri Punit Maharaj, a saint of Ahmedabad, paid us a visit accompanied by eighty followers. He gave us the joy of listening to his *bhajans* and discourses in Gujarati. He has the power of holding the audience under his spell by his remarkable devotion. It is evident that by his contact, hundreds of aspirants have immensely benefited. He has a large following in Bombay and Ahmedabad. He is most unassuming and simple in his nature. He is a votary of Ramnam. He makes his disciples sing the Name in chorus and it is a blissful treat to those who sit by his side on such occasions.

Sri Mangesh Ramachandra Taki Maharaj, alias Sri Dada, is a famous saint of Jogeshwari, near Bombay. He came to the ashram with a few disciples. He is the very embodiment of divine love. He is purely *satwic* in his temparament and his talks are the outflow of his heart which is saturated with devotion. He is familiar with the songs of the saints of Maharashtra and other provinces of India. His father was also a great saint. He resides in Sadbhakti Mandir in Jogeshwari. He stayed with us for five days and gave us all great joy. Really, the most important landmarks in the life of the ashram are the visits of saints and *mahatmas*.

Cultivation of Paddy

From about four years, the ashram has taken up the cultivation of paddy crops on the lands extending to about 15 acres belonging to the ashram. In this work Krishna Bai is deeply interested and so it is carried out under her direct supervision. The ashram has engaged the services of about 50 workers, men and women, living in the vicinity. All the activities of the ashram including the paddy cultivation are performed by these workers. As the whole system is being worked on a community basis, every worker enjoys the full benefit of his work, in the shape of both wages and share in the produce. The co-operative spirit and whole-hearted enthusiasm of the workers are mainly responsible for the yield of rich harvests every year. The ashram has also fruit gardens yielding mangos, sapotas, jack fruits and coconuts besides vegetables.

Conclusion

The first edition of this book was published in 1935. Since then many changes have taken place in the ashram. Although an attempt has been made in this chapter to bring the main story of the activities of the ashram up to date, it must be admitted that it has not been possible to record here all the changes in detail. The original routine of ashram life has altered. Many old workers have given place to new ones, as is but natural in the life of a growing institution. Additional houses and buildings have been put up on the ashram lands, some of them by friends and devotees who have willingly placed them at the disposal of the ashram for the accommodation of the perennial stream of visitors and other uses. The ashram has also secured hundreds of new friends, while many devoted souls have departed, whose loss is almost irreparable.

Since the starting of Anandashram in 1931 till 1938, Ramdas went once on an all-India tour and twice to many places in South India and Saurashtra. He did not again move out of the ashram till 1949, from which year he has been going for a few months every year to various places all over India, mainly Bombay and Saurashtra. In 1954, he went on a world tour, a detailed description of which is given in the book <u>World Is God</u>, written by him on his return to India.

A small temple has been constructed in the colony of Madigas (Harijans) about a mile from the ashram. A beautiful bronze plaque of Sri Hanumanji, the great devotee of Sri Ramachandra, presented by Messrs. Wagh and Sons, sculptors of Bombay, is installed in the temple. Ramdas performed the installation ceremony. The Madigas gather in the temple once in a week and do *bhajan*. The temple is kept neat and holy.

Sri Gunvantrai T. Kamdar, a merchant-prince of Saurashtra, has constructed an ashram in Bhavnagar. In the course of his tours of Saurashtra, Ramdas laid the foundation stone for this ashram building, and again in the following year, went there for its opening celebrations. The ashram is named Ramdas Ashram. Since its inception, Ramdas had been spending a month or two in it every year, during winter. A large number of devotees attended *bhajan* in the ashram and also came to listen to Ramdas's talks. In the other months of the year, renowned saints are invited to the ashram and treated with great hospitality by the management. The saints give unique joy of their holy company and the benefit of their spiritual discourses to the devotees of the place.

The Silver Jubilee of Krishna Bai's renunciation was celebrated in Anandashram on a very grand scale. A phenomenally large number of devotees came for the function from all parts of India and also a few from abroad. As arranged, the occasion was marked by the conclusion of the two-year Nam-Likhita Japa, in which devotees from all over India took part, with a total of 33 *crores* while the target aimed was only 25 *crores*.

By the indefatigable efforts of Mahant Sri Sudamdasji of Rokhadia Hanuman Temple, Porbandar, a new, beautiful and prominent *mandir* of Hanuman has been constructed in the same compound as the old temple. At the pressing invitation of the Mahant, Ramdas paid a visit to Porbandar for performing the *pratishta* (installation) of the images in the *mandir*. The celebration took place with a great *yajna* performed by Sri G.T. Kamdar, who co-operated whole-heartedly in the functions and contributed towards the complete success of the great event.

Ramdas here concludes this long story of his experiences with the fervent prayer that the work of the ashram may gain, by the grace of God, greater strength, as years go by, enabling it to be a centre from which love and service may radiate to all parts of the world and thus fulfil the great purpose of God.

HARI OM TAT SAT

Footnote

The Sri Krishna Vidyalaya is run by the Harijan Welfare Department of the Government of Kerala, from 1955. The Sri Krishna Udyogshala was handed over as free gift to the Nileshwar Handloom Weavers' Co-operative Society. The dispensary has also been handed over to the Government. The paddy fields have been distributed among the ashram workers as free gift.

In the Vision of God

GLOSSARY

Accouchement	The process of giving birth
Ahimsa	Non-violence
Akhada	Abode of *sadhus*
Amir	A ruler
Anna	A coin worth 1/16 of a rupee that is no longer in use
Annakshetra	Free feeding house
Asan, asana	A yogic seat or posture
Ashram	Abode of a saint, monastry
Ashtanga Yoga	A spiritual practice governed by eight rules
Asthi	Bone; skeleton
Atmaghata	Self-destruction
Bada Sahib	Affectionately, "grand sir"
Bania	Merchant
Barfi	An Indian sweet
Bhajan	Sharing of devotional songs
Bhakta	Devotee
Bhakti	Devotion
Bhandara	Food prepared as an offering to God
Bhiksha	Alms
Bhutasthana	A temple structure
Bidi	Country leaf cigarette
Brahmacharya	A spiritual discipline involving strict continence
Brahman	The ultimate reality, or a member of the brahman caste
Brahmanand	Supreme joy
Buwa	A term of respect given to saints in Maharashtra
Chamar	The caste of the untouchables
Charas	An extract of *ganja*
Chatak	An Indian bird which depends only on rain water for drinking
Chawl	Block of buildings
Chela	Disciple
Chenar	A huge tree unique to Kashmir
Chesta	Pranks
Chilam	A clay pipe for smoking
Chintapurni	"Dispeller of woes"
Chutney	An East-Indian condiment
Crore	Ten million
Dal	Preparation of pulse
Dandavat	Prostration with the entire body lying flat on the ground
Darshan	Visit or vision
Devi	Goddess
Dharma	The spiritual principle of cosmic order and purpose
Dharmashala	Rest house
Dhed	Pariah
Dhun	Chorus
Dhyan	Meditation
Dilruba	A stringed instrument played with a bow
Diksha	Initiation
Durbar	A public reception

Dwandwatita	State of being free from pairs of opposites such as pleasure and pain etc.
Ekadashi	A spiritual day that occurs twice in the lunar month
Fakir	A spiritual ascetic
Gadi	A seat of honor
Ganja	Cannabis
Gerrua	Red ochre
Ghee	Clarified butter
Ghotala	Maze
Goshala	Cow-shed
Guru	Spiritual preceptor
Haridas	A religious preacher, servant of God
Harikatha	Religious discourse and storytelling, often attended with music
Himsa	Violence
Hookah	Water pipe
Jiggery	Coarse dark palm sugar
Japam, Japa	Repetition of God's Name
Japa-Mala	Prayer beads for repeating God's Name
Jilabi	An Indian sweet
Jiva	Individual soul
Jivanmukta	A liberated soul
Jnana	Divine knowledge
Jholi	Sling or shoulder bag made of cloth
Kadam ka saag	A Kashmiri vegetable dish of roots and greens
Kamandal	Water vessel carried by *sadhus*
Kambal	Blanket
Kandamool, Kand	Edible jungle roots
Kangdi	A fire pot used in Kashmir
Kaupin	Loin cloth
Khaddar, Khadi	Hand-spun and hand-woven cloth
Khichdi	A special Indian rice dish
Khir	A sweet rice pudding dish
Kirpani	A short Sikh knife
Kirtan	Devotional music
Kisti	A small boat
Kollattam	A southern India folk dance accompanied by the striking together of sticks
Kripa	Grace
Kshetra	Free feeding house
Kula Devi	Family Goddess
Kumbha Mela	A Hindu religious festival celebrated four times in 12 years; also *Kumbh Mela*
Kund	A tank or small reservoir
Kuti	A small hut occupied by *sadhus*
Ladoo	Sweet ball
Langoti	Loin cloth
Lakh	A hundred thousand
Lathi	Bamboo stick
Lezim	A folk dance where dancers carry a small musical instrument with cymbals
Lila	Divine Play
Linga	An image denoting Lord Shiva
Lota	A small handy water vessel
Madhukari	Collecting doles of cooked food from four or more houses
Mahatma	Great soul
Maidan	Plain or vacant strech of land; empty grounds
Mala	Prayer beads

Mandapam	Decorated structure
Mandir	A Hindu temple
Mantram	Incantation
Math	Hindu monastery; abode of religious or spiritual head of a section of society
Maya	Illusion
Mela	Fair
Moksha	Liberation
Mouni	A silent one
Mofussil	A rural location
Mridang	Indian drum
Munsif	A judge
Murti	Image
Nagar bhajan	A procession of devotees singing hymns
Namaskar	Salutation
Namaz	Muslim prayer
Nam-sankirtan	Singing God's Name
Nirguna	Impersonal aspect of God
Nishkama	Desireless
Pada Puja	Washing and worshipping the feet of saints and deities
Panchikarana	The Vedantic theory of how everything came into being
Pandaji	Pilgrim guide
Pandal	Temporary shelter made of mats
Parabhakti	Higher *bhakti*, or *bhakti* that comes after *jnana*
Parikrama	Circumambulation, or the path around a hill
Pashmina	A fine woolen fabric similar to cashmere
Patel	Village headman
Pathshala	A village school offering basic education
Pativrata	A true and chaste wife
Pattu	A homespun woolen fabric resembling tweed
Pheran	A cloak
Pheta	Indian headgear
Prasad	Food offered to God
Pranayam	Breath control
Prem	Love
Pravachan	Discourse on a religious text or spiritual subjects
Puja	Worship
Pujari	Worshipper, priest
Poori	Fried wheat bread
Punyatithi	Death anniversary
Puranic	Expounder of scriptures
Purdah	Seclusion
Purohit	A family priest
Purushartha	The four aims of human life
Raja	King or prince
Raja Vidya	"Royal Science;" the knowledge of Raja Yoga
Raja Yoga	"Royal Yoga;" the path of self-discipline
Raja Yogi	A devotee of Raja Yoga
Rajasic	A fiery nature
Rajo-Guna	The quality of passionate nature
Ram mantram	An incantation containing the word Ram
Ramsmaran	Remembrance of God
Rangoli	Artistic designs on the floor drawn with a white powder
Rani	Queen or princess

Riddhi-Siddhi	Supernatural powers
Rishi	Sage
Roti	A piece of home-made bread
Rs.	Abbreviation for an amount in rupees
Rudraksha	A large-sized bead dear to the devotees of Shiva
Sadhaka	Aspirant
Sadhana	Spiritual practice
Sadhu	Saint, mendicant
Saguna	An aspect of God with qualities
Saheb	Honored one; a title of respect
Samadhi	A trance condition or a saint's tomb
Samskara	A mental impression, recollection, or psychological imprint
Sannyas	Renunciation
Sannyasi	A religious mendicant
Sannyasini	A female religious mendicant
Sapta-Rishis	The legendary seven ancient sages who guide humanity
Saptaha	A seven days' celebration during which Divine Names are sung continuously
Satsang	Society of saints
Satua, Sattu	Roasted Bengal gram flour
Satwic	A harmonious nature
Seer	An unit of measure equaling 1.25 kg (1.792 lb)
Sepoy	Derived from the Persian word *sepāhī* (ﯼﺳﭘﺎﮦ) meaning "infantry soldier"
Shakti	Primordial cosmic energy, the Goddess Shakti
Shamiana	A kind of canopy
Shanti	Tranquility
Sharan	Surrender
Shaivism	The worship of Shiva
Shiva-linga	Image of Shiva
Shudra	The lowest caste, that of workers
Siddha	A person who has achieved spiritual realization
Sloka	A couplet of Sanskrit verse
Syce	Groom or stable attendant
Tabla	A pair of Indian drums
Tamasic	An inactive nature
Tapas, Tapasya	Austerity
Tapaswi	An ascetic
Tapobhumi	A place sanctified by austerities
Tiffin	Light lunch or snack
Tonga	A light horse-drawn two-wheeled vehicle
Trigunatita	A state beyond the three qualities
Upadesh	Initiation, advice, teaching
Vairagya	Dispassion
Vaishya	The Hindu caste of merchants and farmers
Vakil	A lawyer
Veena	A stringed instrument of music
Vidya	Knowledge; learning
Yajna	Sacrifice
Yajna kund	Sacrificial altar
Yatra	A procession of pilgrims
Yoga-danda	Arm-rest used in yoga practice
Yogi	A practitioner of yoga
Zamindar	A landowner who leases to farmers
Zenana	The part of a household reserved for women

Made in the USA
San Bernardino, CA
18 February 2020